# LARGE-SCALE MACRO-ECONOMETRIC MODELS
## THEORY AND PRACTICE

# CONTRIBUTIONS
# TO
# ECONOMIC ANALYSIS

141

*Honorary Editor*
J. TINBERGEN

*Editors*
D.W. JORGENSON
J. WAELBROECK

NORTH-HOLLAND PUBLISHING COMPANY
AMSTERDAM · NEW YORK · OXFORD

# LARGE-SCALE MACRO-ECONOMETRIC MODELS

## Theory and Practice

*Edited by*

**J. KMENTA**
*University of Michigan*

and

**J. B. RAMSEY**
*New York University*

NORTH-HOLLAND PUBLISHING COMPANY
AMSTERDAM · NEW YORK · OXFORD

ISBN: 0 444 86295 1

*Publishers*
NORTH-HOLLAND PUBLISHING COMPANY
AMSTERDAM • NEW YORK • OXFORD

*Sole distributors for the U.S.A. and Canada*
ELSEVIER NORTH-HOLLAND, INC.
52 VANDERBILT AVENUE,
NEW YORK, N.Y. 10017

Library of Congress Cataloging in Publication Data
Main entry under title:

Large-scale macro-econometric models.

(Contributions to economic analysis ; 141)
1. Economics--Mathematical models--Addresses,
essays, lectures. 2. Econometrics--Addresses,
essays, lectures. 3. Economics forecasting--
Mathematical models--Addresses, essays, lectures.
I. Kmenta, Jan. II. Ramsey, James Bernard.
III. Series.
HB141.L36     339'.0724     81-14126
ISBN 0-444-86295-1 (Elsvevier North-Holland)
                                        AACR2

PRINTED IN THE NETHERLANDS

# Introduction to the series

This series consists of a number of hitherto unpublished studies, which are introduced by the editors in the belief that they represent fresh contributions to economic science.

The term 'economic analysis' as used in the title of the series has been adopted because it covers both the activities of the theoretical economist and the research worker.

Although the analytical methods used by the various contributors are not the same, they are nevertheless conditioned by the common origin of their studies, namely theoretical problems encountered in practical research. Since for this reason, business cycle research and national accounting, research work on behalf of economic policy, and problems of planning are the main sources of the subjects dealt with, they necessarily determine the manner of approach adopted by the authors. Their methods tend to be 'practical' in the sense of not being too far remote from application to actual economic conditions. In addition they are quantitative rather than qualitative.

It is the hope of the editors that the publication of these studies will help to stimulate the exchange of scientific information and to reinforce international cooperation in the field of economics.

*The Editors*

# Preface

The rapid development of large-scale econometric models in the last two decades has been accompanied by the development of the skills needed to construct, estimate, and manipulate such models for forecasting and policy analysis. The procedures adopted to achieve this purpose have been to a considerable extent pragmatic, involving ad hoc adjustments and personal judgements. As a result, there has been a growing gap between the precepts of econometrics expounded in the textbooks and taught in the classrooms and the practice of econometrics by the producers of macro-econometric models. This gap has led to a considerable amount of academic criticism of the macro-econometric model building activity, particularly since this activity has been consuming a large and growing amount of resources. Non-academic criticism has also been growing in its intensity and in its diversity.

It was thus considered desirable to organize a conference at which the major proponents and the academic critics of the large-scale econometric models could meet, discuss their differences, and consider constructive suggestions for narrowing the existing gap between theory and practice.

The conference was sponsored by the National Science Foundation and the National Bureau of Economic Research and took place in Ann Arbor, Michigan on October 26-27, 1978. The conference was organized into four sessions, each session consisted of a presentation of papers, a formal discussion of the papers, and a general discussion from the floor. In the preparation of this volume, each of the papers was anonymously refereed and subjected to editorial comments. The papers have been extended to include contributions by Alan Powell, whose extensive experience with model building in Australia was thought to be of special interest, and by Clive Granger, whose expertise in time series analysis is of particular relevance to one of the hotly debated issues at the conference. Each contributor and discussant was asked to be responsible for the final production of his manuscript in a camera-ready form for this volume. The final chapter, which contains a summary of the general discussion, is based on the taped recording of the proceedings of the conference.

The comments have been substantially abbreviated, paraphrazed, and re-organized according to subject matter. Since the tape recording was in many places of very poor quality because of noise and other disturbances, some contributions to the discussion had to be omitted and others may have been reported less accurately than we would prefer. We apologize for these shortcomings.

In the preparation for this volume we have incurred debts to a number of people. A special commendation is due to Daniel Kohler for serving as a very able rapporteur for the conference, to Pat Barkey and Jeffrey Pliskin for skillful and patient transcription of the tapes, and to Mary Braun and Kris Maki for very able assistance in managing the conference. The financial support of the conference by the National Science Foundation and the provision of conference facilities by the University of Michigan is greatly appreciated. One of the editors, Jan Kmenta, would also like to acknowledge the support of the Humboldt Foundation of Germany and of the Institute of Econometrics at the University of Bonn in the final stages of the preparation of the manuscript.

# List of Participants

F. Gerard ADAMS, University of Pennsylvania
T.W. ANDERSON, Stanford University
Albert ANDO, University of Pennsylvania
James H. BLACKMAN, National Science Foundation
Karl BRUNNER, University of Rochester
Gregory C. CHOW, Princeton University
Carl F. CHRIST, John Hopkins University
Michael R. DARBY, University of California, Los Angeles
M. DUTTA, Rutgers University
Otto ECKSTEIN, Data Resources, Inc.
Ray C. FAIR, Yale University
Stanley FISCHER, Massachusetts Institute of Technology
Gary FROMM, Stanford Research Institute International
Stephen M. GOLDFELD, Princeton University
Clive W.J. GRANGER, University of California at San Diego
George R. GREEN, Bureau of Economic Analysis
Zvi GRILICHES, Harvard University
Laszlo HALABUK, Hungarian Central Statistical Office
Bert G. HICKMAN, Stanford University
Albert A. HIRSCH, Bureau of Economic Analysis, U.S. Dept. of Commerce
E. Philip HOWREY, University of Michigan
Saul H. HYMANS, University of Michigan
Peter D. JONSON, Reserve Bank of Australia, Sydney
Lawrence R. KLEIN, University of Pennsylvania
Jan KMENTA, University of Michigan
William S. KRASKER, Harvard Business School
Edwin KUH, Massachusetts Institute of Technology
David LAIDLER, University of Western Ontario

G.S. MADDALA, University of Florida

Michael D. McCARTHY, Wharton E.F.A., Inc.

Stephen K. McNEES, Federal Reserve Bank of Boston

Allan H. MELTZER, Carnegie-Mellon University

Franco MODIGLIANI, Massachusetts Institute of Technology

Daniel H. NEWLON, National Science Foundation

Alan A. POWELL, University of Melbourne, Australia

Edward C. PRESCOTT, University of Chicago

James B. RAMSEY, New York University

Robert H. RASCHE, Michigan State University

Kurt SCHILDKNECHT, Swiss National Bank, Zurich

George R. SCHINK, Wharton E.F.A., Inc.

Peter J. SCHMIDT, Michigan State University

Harold T. SHAPIRO, University of Michigan

Christopher A. SIMS, University of Minnesota

W. Allen SPIVEY, University of Michigan

John B. TAYLOR, Columbia University

James TOBIN, Yale University

Bruce VAVRICHEK, University of Maryland

William J. WROBLESKI, University of Michigan

Tzong-shian YU, Academia Sinica, Taiwan

Arnold ZELLNER, University of Chicago

# Contents

# I.   INTRODUCTION

LARGE-SCALE MACRO-ECONOMETRIC MODELS
J. Kmenta, J.B. Ramsey (editors)
© North-Holland Publishing Company, 1981

MODEL SIZE, QUALITY OF FORECAST ACCURACY,
AND ECONOMIC THEORY

Jan Kmenta

Department of Economics
University of Michigan
Ann Arbor, Michigan
U.S.A.

James B. Ramsey

Department of Economics
New York University
New York City, New York
U.S.A.

In recent years the ongoing debate about the accuracy and usefulness of macroeconomic models has intensified and acquired some new dimensions. Three main issues are at the forefront of the contemporary debate, namely size of model, purpose and assessment of forecasting accuracy, and evaluation and comparison of models. The debate is heated since professional reputations, income, and markedly different policy implications hinge on the outcome, and the discussion is protracted because no one yet has a position that is acceptable to everyone.

Some observers, both in and out of the profession, claim that conventional macroeconomic modelling is virtually useless for forecasting or for policy analysis, and that it would fail in any attempt at cost-benefit analysis. Others, especially those whose careers are involved, naturally see the matter somewhat differently. These researchers see a constant if not continuous improvement in the role and use of macro-models by the private and the public sector. They also claim, the current difficulties notwithstanding, that macro-models provide the best of the currently available alternatives for obtaining forecasts and engaging in policy analysis.

While it is too much to expect to achieve a widespread agreement on any of these issues much less on all of them in one symposium, one would hope at least for a clarification of the arguments and for a settlement of some confusions and disagreements. To this modest end the Conference on Macroeconometric Models was held in Ann Arbor in the Fall of 1978.

The following few comments will outline in more detail some of
the macro-modelling difficulties being discussed at this time
and indicate the main area of contribution of each of the
invited papers.

I   MACRO-ECONOMETRIC MODEL SIZE AND PERFORMANCE

The first difficulty with an examination of model size and
performance involves deciding how one should and could measure
"size."  First, researchers have a highly pragmetic concern
about size because size effects the properties and computability of simultaneous equation estimators when the number of
explanatory variables in a hypothesized system of equations
exceeds the number of observations.  (For a review of the
literature on this point see the Maddala paper in this book.)
But the notion of size, in the sense of "number of structural
relationships in the system," can be related to the objectives
of macro-modelling.  The question then immediately arises as to
whether an increase in model size is related to the effectiveness of a macro-model; for example, do larger models predict
better than smaller ones, assuming one has managed to choose an
appropriate measure of size?

The question, if not the answer, becomes more transparent when
we recognize that the intuitive notion of size which scholars
are trying to define actually refers to the level of aggregation.  Hence, a simpler but basically equivalent version of the
above question is:  How does the model's level of aggregation
affect the model's effectiveness for forecasting or for policy
evaluation?

The first aspect of the answer can be easily formulated; the
greater the degree of detailed information one wants about an
economy, the lower the level of useful aggregation  and, in
general, the bigger the model size.  Thus if one merely wishes
to forecast levels of aggregate investment, a quite small,
highly aggregated model might suffice; but if one wants to
forecast levels of investment by industry, then a much larger

and considerably more disaggregated model is required.

The second aspect concerns the validity of the empirical assumption that the composition of the aggregates used over the estimation period did and will remain constant. In short, if the relative shares by industry do not change and are not expected to change in the near future, forecasts and policy analysis using an economy-wide aggregate called investment would be appropriate. But if it is known that the relative shares of industries have changed or will change significantly, then one must disaggregate to the industry level and use a large size of model, at least by all current definitions of size.

This point can be illustrated by the following simple analogy. Suppose the manufacturing sector consists of only two industries for which the reduced form investment equations are as follows:

$$y_1 = X_1 \beta_1 + \varepsilon_1$$
$$y_2 = X_2 \beta_2 + \varepsilon_2$$

where $y_j \to Tx1$, $X_j \to TxK$, $\beta_j \to Kx1$, and $\varepsilon_j \to Tx1$ $(j = 1, 2)$. Let the aggregation rule be $y = (y_1 + y_2)$, $X = (X_1 + X_2)$, and $\varepsilon - (\varepsilon_1 + \varepsilon_2)$. Then the aggregate investment equation can be represented as:

$$y = X\beta + \varepsilon$$

if and only if either $\beta_1 = \beta_2$ or $X_2 = kX_1$ where $k$ is a positive constant for all observations. Note that the latter gives:

$$y_1 + y_2 = X_1 \beta_1 + X_2 \beta_2 + \varepsilon_1 + \varepsilon_2$$
$$= X_1 (\beta_1 + k\beta_2) + \varepsilon_1 + \varepsilon_2$$
$$= (\frac{\beta_1 + k\beta_2}{1 + k}) (X_1 + X_2) + \varepsilon_1 + \varepsilon_2$$

Thus $\beta = (\beta_1 + k\beta_2)/(1 + k)$, and constant shares of the explanatory variables for each industry to ensure the stability of the aggregate coefficient $\beta$.

A final question is as follows.  If forecast or policy information is needed only at some given level of aggregation and
if it is known that the composition of the aggregates will remain constant, then one may wonder whether there are any gains
in forecast accuracy from using a more disaggregated and
larger size of model.  This question can be examined with the
help of the preceding example.  Suppose we wish to forecast
some future value of y, say $y_o$, equal to $(y_{o1} + y_{o2})$, for
some specific values of X, say $X_o = X_{o1} + X_{o2}$ of dimension
1 x k.  Let us assume that $\varepsilon_1$ and $\varepsilon_2$ satisfy all assumptions
of the classical regression model, and that X is a non-
stochastic matrix.  Two forecasts of $y_o$ are readily available,
one obtained by adding the forecasts of $y_{o1}$ and $y_{o2}$, the other
obtained directly from the aggregate equation.  Under the
specified assumptions the method of least squares is quite
appropriate.  Then we have:

Disaggregate forecast

$$\tilde{y}_o = X_{o1}\hat{\beta}_1 + X_{o2}\hat{\beta}_2$$
$$= X_{o1}(X_1'X_1)^{-1}X_1'y_1 + X_{o2}(X_2'X_2)^{-1}X_2'y_2$$

The mean and the variance of the forecast error are

$$E(y_o - \tilde{y}_o) = 0$$
$$Var(y_o - \tilde{y}_o) = \sigma_{11}[1 + X_{o1}(X_1'X_1)^{-1}X_{o1}'] + \sigma_{22}[1 + X_{o2}(X_2'X_2)^{-1}X_{o2}']$$
$$+ 2\sigma_{12}[1 + X_{o1}(X_1'X_1)^{-1}X_{o1}'X_{o2}(X_2'X_2)^{-1}X_{o2}']$$

Aggregate forecast

$$\hat{y}_o = X_o\hat{\beta}$$
$$= X_o(X'X)^{-1}X'y$$

The mean and the variance of the forecast error are

$$E(y_o - \hat{y}_o) = 0$$
$$Var(y_o - \hat{y}_o) = (\sigma_{11} + \sigma_{22} + 2\sigma_{12})[1 + X_o(X'X)^{-1}X_o']$$

If, as assumed, $X_2 = KX_1$ and $X_{o2} = KX_{o1}$, then it immediately
follows that the variance of the disaggregate forecast
error is exactly the same as the variance of the aggregate

forecast error. But it is also clear that the conditions needed for this result to follow are most stringent.

## II  PURPOSE AND PERFORMANCE

A second item for debate is the claimed dichotomy between the objective of forecasting versus the objectives of understanding the system or of "detailed policy analysis". The dichotomy is false. Some researchers claim that if all one wishes to do is merely to obtain good forecasts, then the elaborate structural specification and detailed identification analysis of macro models is of little use and the results obtained are certainly not worth the extra cost over that for relatively simple multivariate time series models. This claim seems to the editors a naive one; what distinguishes forecasts based on models utilizing the full panoply of economic theory and correct statistical methodology from those which do not is the <u>confidence</u> one has in the estimates and in the evaluation of the accuracy of the estimates. To cite a crude example, one may, over some historical period of time, get close agreements between actual levels of the nominal gross national product (GNP) and the level of sun spot activity. But until someone has developed a plausible theory relating the two phenomena, one must regard the result as serendipitous; unfortunately serendipity is not an unusual event in forecasting!

In short, the statistical happenstance of high correlations between time series, especially after empirically selecting a prediction maximizing lag structure, cannot by itself be regarded with much confidence; what happened in the past need not be true for the future. Unless we have some theoretical structure in which we place considerable confidence and which "explains" the observed relationships, we can place little if any faith in the longevity of the empirically observed correlation.

Thus structurally based models are preferred not simply on the
criterion of estimated forecast accuracy over some necessarily
limited time horizon, but because the theoretical underpinnings lend credence to the empirically observed results.
When we attain an "understanding" of the reasons behind the
relationship, we have some faith that we have estimated the
parameters of a model approximating reality and therefore that
we can expect with some confidence that the estimated relationships will apply to the forecast period.  The mere statistical
search for correlations that are useful for forecasting does
not benefit from this attempted understanding of economic relationships.  Further, all the profession's experience to-date
strongly suggests that the complexity of economic relationships
make it highly unlikely that relatively simple systems of
historically determined correlations will prevail for more than
a few quarters at most.  Specifying a dichotomy of purpose
"forecasting" versus "understanding," is in short an irrelevant
criterion in choosing the type of model.

But there is a dichotomy of purpose which is important and
which has been the source of much bitter confusion -- the distinction between scientific and business-oriented macro-models.
Members of the academic profession, when acting only as
academics, are most interested in scientifically oriented
models; professional model-builders, even when they also happen
to be academics, are engaged in an essentially different pursuit even though both parties talk about policy analysis and
forecast accuracy.  The distinction is pure only in abstract
discussion, for in practice all models in use encompass
elements of both the scientific and business approaches.

The development of scientific macro-models needs no elaboration to academic economists since purportedly at least we are
all committed to the principles of scientific inference and to
the correct use of statistical methodology, no matter what our
degree of Bayesian proclivities.

Scientific macro-models are basically designed for testing economic hypotheses, for learning about and further understanding the operation of economic systems. Forecasts are important, but mainly as statistics for the testing of the hypotheses forming the model's structure. In this role, the use of judgemental manipulation of the estimates by the model maker is completely destructive. Scientific inference, which relies on a full specification of the model that can then be duplicated by others, is destroyed by the incorporation of modeller idiosyncracies in the "estimation" of the models.

The business use of macro-models is quite different. At the most trivial level, professional macro-modellers have time constraints not faced by academic scientists; forecasts and policy evaluation statements are due at certain specific dates which the modellers must meet, and numbers have to be cited, no matter how dubious one may be about them. The scientific modeller does not usually face this constraint; if his hypotheses are rejected he can persevere in model reconstruction no matter how long it takes.

More fundamentally, the business use of macro-models really involves an approach to modelling closer to the concept of "response surface methodology"; that is, the underlying theory used is assumed to hold, at least in broad outline, and the objective is to get as good a fit as possible in order to make a quick, but reasonably accurate, forecast for the near term. In such uses the judgemental manipulation of results by an experienced modeller can be of immense importance in generating a historical record of successful forecasts. In fact this is all important, since what the modellers are selling to their clients is not scientific theory but a proven track record of reasonably accurate forecasts, no matter how they were obtained. If a modeller were to be most successful at generating "accurate" near-term forecasts with no model at all, then, given the nature of the game being played, he would also be financially successful and would dominate the field of forecasting. There is nothing inappropriate about the modeller's idiosyncratic

procedure in a business venture; but it is not science, does
not provide us with any more information about how the economy
functions, and does not enable the rest of us to learn how to
better our own forecasts.

Academic scientific models should be judged on their inferential merits and in terms of the correct use of statistical
methodology and development of economic theory.  Macro-models
oriented to business use should be judged by different criteria
-- mainly on whether they provide the desired product to the
clients at a competitive price.  The confusion over the distinct purposes and methodologies of these two approaches to
modelling has led to a needlessly acrimonious debate which is
largely irrelevant.  As long as models for business use that
involve judgemental manipulation and continuous refitting are
consistent with their response surface methodology, and as
long as short cuts induced by time constraints are recognized
as such and evaluated according to the appropriate criteria
(which are quite definitely not the standard criteria for
statistical inference), then much confusion and needless debate will be avoided.

III MODEL EVALUATION

After the final comments in the last section it is now clear
that the business and scientific models need to be distinguished.  The discussion in the remainder of this chapter will be
restricted to scientific models.

Model evaluation in the macro sphere has really involved a
special case of model comparison and discrimination.  The forecast performance of most macro-models is compared to that of
some relatively simple, standard time-series with little
economic theory behind it.

Model evaluation per se involves specification error tests,
examination of the small-sample distributions of the various

estimators and statistics, and a detailed examination of the applicability of the maintained hypothesis. Little evaluation of macro-models has been carried out due to technical difficulties, not the least of which are very small degrees of freedom for such analyses.

Let us concentrate, therefore, on the naive time-series model comparisons. Even in this context there has been some lack of clear-cut purpose. We have already made the distinction between obtaining a short-term forecast on the faith that the naive time-series model will continue to be a useful approximation in the future and the confidence one has in a structural model which attempts to approximate reality. Of course, the level of confidence one has in the structural model compared to time series extrapolation is directly dependent on the confidence one has in the underlying theory. A large structural macro-model based on a theory in which one places little confidence will not yield much confidence in its estimates, no matter how big and complex it may be. Such a model can be no better than naive forecasting models and, owing to computational complexities and losses of degrees of freedom, could be considerably worse when compared to short-term forecasts of macro-aggregates.

The second aspect of weighing the performance of macro-models against naive time-series models is that the comparisons need to be confined to time periods in which discrimination is feasible. Thus if an economy can be characterized by the simple rule of "last year's level plus 5% plus white noise error," then no macro-model, no matter how big, no matter whether it is even a true model, can do better in forecast accuracy than a model based on that simple rule. Indeed, a macro-model is likely to do worse by comparison under such circumstances due to its vastly greater information requirements. But in economic systems, as opposed to engineering systems under carefully prescribed side-conditions, it is unlikely that any simple historical set of time-series

correlations will provide reasonably accurate forecasts for
very long.  Worse, one has no theoretical structure to understand whether, when, and how the simple observed relationship
will change -- and possibly in dramatic fashion.  In consequence, the only useful comparisons are over time periods in
which simple model structures shift in ways that the larger
macro-model has been designed to explain.  No useful comparison
can be made if structural shifts occur which are unincorporated
in either model.  Further, if one is examining alternative
policy issues, then the very nature of the situation is one
in which the structure of simple models is expected to shift
by design.  In such circumstances there is no substitute for
the macro-model.

An alternative device for comparing models is that of comparing
the number of "turning points" correctly forecast (and sometimes that number minus the number incorrectly forecast).
While this idea sounds like a plausible criterion, it is somewhat simplistic in that one must first learn in a stochastic
environment how to distinguish a turning-point from the simple
effects of white noise in the series.  Thus, a better model
predicts turning points in the conditional mean and ignores
purely random fluctuations.  Once again comparisons can be
made only when there is evidence that in fact a "turning point
in conditional mean" has occurred.  Unfortunately, turning
points in conditional mean seem to be relatively infrequent
for most time series in macro-models.  With other series such
as net investment or changes in inventory stock, the difficulty
is to separate the turning points from the inevitable white
noise with large variance.  Since definition of the former is a
function of the model itself, the identification of turning
points is not a trivial issue.

One means of comparing theories is to state that the better
theory will "explain" a wider class of phenomena.  Consequently,
the modelling of "better theories" in this sense will tend to
involve more relationships, more endogenous variables and often

relatively fewer exogenous variables so that by most conventional measures of size, better theories will require larger
models for their testing and are harder to identify.

A final issue which is a source of great debate is whether
models should be compared on the basis of their <u>ex ante</u> forecasts, i.e., those forecasts which require predictions of the
exogenous variables, or on the basis of their <u>ex post</u> forecasts, i.e., those forecasts which require the historically
observed values of the exogenous variables. All of the
statistical analysis of macro-models is conditional on the
values of the exogenous regressors in any event, so that the
issue involved is not one of whether to condition on the exogenous variables. The statistically valid statement to which
the standard assigned probabilities of error can be made must
be in terms of the <u>ex post</u> forecasts. <u>Ex ante</u> forecasts involve the prior prediction of the exogenous variables for
which there is little, if any, theoretical justification; one
merely hopes that the past observed time-series characteristics
of these variables will hold in the future. The confidence
one has in <u>ex ante</u> forecasts cannot be greater and usually is
less than the confidence one has in the predictions of the
exogenous variable values.

While <u>ex ante</u> forecasts must inevitably be used in policy making situations, the statistically valid comparisons between
simple forecasts and model forecast performance should logically
be on the basis of <u>ex post</u> statements.

However, there is a difficulty when comparing the forecast performance of alternative models which differ in their set of
exogenous variables, even when using <u>ex post</u> forecasts. If
one model is bigger than another in that it treats some variables as endogenous that the other regards as exogenous, then
the bigger model will on average tend to have larger conditional
forecast variances in those equations in which the disputed
endogenous variables appear as regressors. In short, there is
often a complicated trade-off between the number of relation-

ships which can be "explained" or forecast and the accuracy of
each forecast.  Some researchers have tried to find a way to
keep the two models on an "equal footing" in terms of forecast
comparisons.  However, in multiequation systems a single and
simple criterion such as forecast accuracy is insufficient to
capture all the relevant differences between models.  This is
true even if forecast comparisons are made in terms of the reduced form equations.

IV AN OUTLINE OF THE CONFERENCE PROCEEDINGS

The conference was organized into four sessions.  The first
session entitled "Forecasting Economic Variables" included
three papers.  The first, by Klein et alia, performed the most
useful service of surveying a number of the major personalities
in the macro-modelling sphere and queried actual behavior and
methodologies used.  The following paper by Shapiro contained
general comments on the relative accuracy of macro-models.
The Kelejian and Vavrichek paper was concerned with the general
topic of size in macro models and its relationship with forecast accuracy and policy analysis.  Kelejian and Vavrichek's
main result is that the forecasting performance with respect
to a particular endogenous variable using the reduced form
equations relates to size only through the number of predetermined variables involved.

In Session II Maddala discussed the all-important question of
the definition of size with particular reference to the technical difficulties in obtaining system estimators with desirable properties.  Taylor's paper was concerned with the question of the role of economic theory in determining the appropriate size of a macro-model, where size is defined as the
number of stochastic equations in the model.  The role of
economic theory in determining the required degree of disaggregation (conversely in determining size) is important only
in the context of a set of clearly specified policy questions
for which the model is to be used to obtain answers.  One im-

portant question which is explicitly addressed is that of quantitatively measuring the effects of eliminating parts of a model which do not relate directly to the specific variable whose forecast is sought. The paper by Eckstein dealt with the extent to which the practical realities of large scale macro-model building enable a researcher to incorporate micro-economic theory.

In the third session Ando addressed a theme similar to Eckstein's. The author's major complaint was that the bulk of economic theory refers to steady state systems whereas the majority of macro applications must handle systems in disequilibrium.

The Fromm and Klein paper points out that recent empirical experience with macro-models demonstrates clearly the pressure on the growth in model size. Basically the issue refers back to the discussion in the previous subsection in that a greater degree of disaggregation is needed if one has reason to believe that the composition of the macro aggregates is going to change. Fromm and Klein point out that this is exactly what has taken place in the last few years on the supply side of macro-models.

The paper by Sims is completely different in its orientation and provides the main counterpoint to the more traditional and structurally oriented macro-models. Some of the criticisms of macro models, especially the business-oriented ones, is that they are often implicitly "estimated" on the basis of "let the data tell the story." The Sims approach is explicitly of this type and can be viewed as a procedure for selecting and estimating the appropriate coefficients of a reduced-form model driven by a multivariate stationary stochastic series.

The last two papers were presented in the final session on the evaluation of macro-models. The McNees paper is most useful because its objective is to evaluate the alternative procedures for the evaluation of the models themselves. The Chow paper

concentrates on model evaluation with special reference to
size, where size is defined as the number of functionally independent parameters in the model.  The block decomposition of
a simultaneous equation system into a series of subsystems is
smaller than one which cannot be so decomposed.  The key idea
is that because usable models must be approximations to actual
demand equations (since, for example, not all prices can be
included in a regression) the essential approach must be one
of determining an appropriate degree of approximation.

The formal conference papers have been extended to include an
extensive "position" statement by Alan Powell, some pertinent
remarks on the time-series approach to modelling by Clive
Granger, and the comments of the discussants.

V IN CONCLUSION

The editors are sure that a careful reading of the papers contained in this volume will help to clarify a number of issues
involved in the evaluation of and understanding of the role
played by the size of a macro-model.  Further, the understanding of that role will be highlighted by the contrasts in
approach and methodology provided by the Granger-Sims time-
series view of modelling.  A greater sense of the relative
strengths and weaknesses of such models, a clearer evaluation
of the practical limits of the models posed by data scarcity,
and a more precise insight into the special and perhaps
peculiar inferential problems involved in the estimation and
use of macro-models must benefit the profession and will significantly modify and perhaps improve the policy use of such
models.

## II.  FORECASTING ECONOMIC VARIABLES

LARGE-SCALE MACRO-ECONOMETRIC MODELS
J. Kmenta, J.B. Ramsey (editors)
© North-Holland Publishing Company, 1981

THE PRACTICE OF MACROECONOMETRIC MODEL BUILDING

AND ITS RATIONALE

E. Philip Howrey
The University of Michigan

Lawrence R. Klein
University of Pennsylvania

Michael D. McCarthy
Wharton Econometric Forecasting Associates, Incorporated

George R. Schink
Wharton Econometric Forecasting Associates, Incorporated

I.  Introduction

The purpose of this paper is to provide an accurate description of the current state of macroeconometric model building and the use of these models for forecasting and policy
analysis.  This task is complicated by the fact that there are
several areas in which there is no consensus on a best-practice
methodology.  There are, for example, debates on the appropriate level of aggregation (Orcutt (1961), Laffer-Ranson (1971),
and Fromm-Schink (1973)).  Generally, the more realism that is
built into the model, the larger and more disaggregated the
model becomes and the more complicated and difficult it is to
estimate the parameters of the model.  There are also difficult and unresolved issues concerning the appropriate estimation procedure.  At an even more fundamental level, complications may arise because the data base available for model
construction may not conform satisfactorily to the needs of
the model builder.  Some data series may not exist and others
may be measured with considerable error.

Model builders have sought ways to cope with these problems, but their responses have not been uniform.  In view of
the absence of a consensus on several important issues, it was
decided that it would be useful to conduct a modest survey of
existing practices.  The survey, which was distributed to a
selected set of "established" model builders, focussed on a
variety of model-construction issues.[1]

The questions that were included in the survey are as

19

follows.

A.  General Theoretical Specification

A-1.  Why model?

A-2.  How is model size determined?

A-3.  What is the role of economic theory?

A-4.  What is the role of institutional information?

A-5.  What is the role of social accounts in model design?

A-6.  What is the influence of data availability?

A-7.  What is the influence of the users of models?

        a) Policy makers.

        b) Private sector users.

A-8.  How are models designed in hierarchical structure?

B.  Estimation and Validation

B-1.  How is statistical inference used in model construction?

B-2.  How are hypotheses tested?

        a) Complete system dynamics.

        b) Partial theory (theories of the firm
          and household).

B-3.  How are models validated?

C.  Forecasting and Policy Analysis

C-1.  How are forecast prepared from the models?

C-2.  How are models adjusted in the forecasting procedure?

C-3.  Do the models contain important but hard-to-predict
      (exogenous) variables?

These three groups of questions reflect a particular and we believe useful conceptualization of the various stages of econometric model building and forecasting.  The first group of questions is concerned with the decisions that must be made at an initial stage of the study.  The second group of questions are relevant to the next step in model-building: confrontation of the model with the data.  The final set of questions is concerned with the use of econometric models in forecasting and policy analysis.  There are, of course, interrelationships between these groups of questions.  For example, the level of aggregation chosen for the model may depend on the way in which the model is to be used in policy analysis or forecasting.  The remainder of this paper summarizes the responses that were obtained from the model builders and elaborates on them where appropriate.

## II.  The General Theoretical Specification of a Model
### A-1.  Why Model?

There are some who believe that it is not sensible to build macroeconometric models.  Underlying such a belief is the conviction that the conditions for valid aggregation of well-defined micro-economic relationships are not met and hence that stable relationships among economic aggregates will not exist, especially in the face of policy changes.  Lucas (1976), for example, has on these grounds been critical of the use of macro-econometric models for policy analysis.  Others have observed that potential measurement errors in aggregate data may be sufficiently large as to defeat the purposes of econometric modelling.  Morgenstern's (1963) comments are particularly apropos in this regard.  Still others (Cooper (1972), for example) have argued that macroeconometric models do not perform as well in forecasting as simpler univariate time-series models or judgmental procedures, so that as far as forecasting is concerned an econometric model is more complicated than necessary or at least not cost effective.

The respondents did not address any of these issues directly.  It is clear from the responses, however, that an important motivating factor in macro-econometric modelling has been a desire to address policy issues; thus, simple time series models are not viewed as a viable alternative to econometric models.  Selected responses to the "Why Model?" question are presented below.[2]

### Adams

I define a model as a useful simplified representation of the real world.  I view the model as being useful for prediction and for testing the impact of exogenous events, and simplified, because the real world is beyond our current capacity to articulate fully.  The degree of simplification, of course, also depends greatly on the purpose for which the model is to be used.  A relatively complex model is necessary if detailed policy alternatives need to be considered or detailed output is required.  To forecast a few major aggregates, however, we may be able to get along with a highly aggregated model. Modern multi-purpose models are highly disaggregated.

### Keith Carlson

The St. Louis model was developed as an empirical estimate of a model based on the modern quantity theory of money. The underlying purpose was to assess the impact of alternative monetary and fiscal policies within such a framework.

### Gregory Chow

To test economic hypotheses and estimate parameters pertaining to individual structural relations and to study properties of the entire economic system; to provide economic forecasts and to study policy questions.

### Otto Eckstein

The DRI model was developed for forecasting the economy and for policy simulation.

### Gary Fromm

To understand the structural processes underlying observed phenomena; for prediction purposes to conduct policy simulation; to examine possible effects of structural change; to gain theoretical insights.

### Albert Hirsch

A model provides a systematic and disciplined approach to analysis of the dynamic behavior of the macro-economy. When "estimated," it measures the (hopefully stable) parametric behavioral relationships that determine the macro-economic variables and their major components. Econometric forecasting models, unlike judgmental approaches, are subject to various validation tests. Hence over time models evolve and, we think, improve through adaptive learning and innovation.

One advantage of the econometric modelling approach is that the procedure can be fully documented, and alternative models and procedures can be more fully tested against one another in the hope of finding better models. Judgmental forecasting procedures do not lend themselves to such a process. Only one of the respondents made note of this consideration. Over the years, purely judgmental policy descriptions have often been received with understandable doubt on the part of those who seek justification for the particular policy prescription. As imperfect as current models may be, the econometric model approach offers the possibility of complete documentation and hence replication.

Two of the respondents, Chow and Fromm, placed emphasis on a need to know the structure of the underlying system.

Fromm correctly notes that this information is needed if the implications of structural change are to be examined.

In summary, a model provides a reproducible framework for systematic thought about economic phenomena. To the extent that the parameters of the model correctly reflect the structure of the economy, the model is a natural vehicle for comparative economic studies -- comparing the economy at different times or at the same time under different impacts, and comparing different analyses of the working of the economy. A-2. How Is the Model Size Determined?

The respondents generally indicated that the uses to which the model was to be put would dictate the model size. Accordingly, the St. Louis model, which was intended for examining the implications of monetary and fiscal policy for a very few aggregates, is relatively small. Eckstein noted that the desire to be able to account for a wide range of policy instruments resulted in a relatively large DRI model. There was a general recognition that there was a balancing between cost, benefits, and model size. Larger models typically contain larger lists of exogenous variables and permit a wider range of policy experiments, but they cost more than small models. Large staffs are required for data maintenance, model management, and simulation.

Surprisingly, none of the respondents suggested that one of the benefits from disaggregation would be increased forecast accuracy. This question has been addressed from time to time. Fromm and Schink (1973), for instance, addressed this issue in connection with the Brookings Model and concluded that there was a positive correlation between model size and predictive accuracy. Additional evidence, though not of an entirely conclusive sort, is implicit in the work of McNees (1978). The problem with using the results compiled by McNees is that while the models surveyed by McNees differ in size, there are also important differences in forecasting methodology that complicate comparisons of forecast accuracy across models. There does seem to be something of a consensus (at least among macro-model builders) that the large structural

macro models do perform better than the simplest of small
models such as univariate ARIMA time series models (McNees
(1978), Prothero and Wallis (1976), and Hirsch, Grimm, and
Narasimham (1976)).

The evidence on the relationship between model accuracy
and size is somewaht thin and inconclusive at this point, and
while it may be true for present day U.S. macro models that
a positive correlation exists between accuracy and size, it
is hardly clear that such a result will hold for all classes
of models.  In fact, we can easily imagine the construction
of a model that is so large and complex that mistakes in
model management could lead to very serious errors.  While
none of the model builders explicitly addressed this issue,
there is a general consensus that the current technology of
data bank management and model building is such that an
adequately large equation system (400 + equations) can be
maintained without undue risk of model management errors.

The respondents' comments to "How is Model Size Determined?" follow.

### Keith Carlson

Model size was determined by the purpose of the model: assessment of the impact of alternative policies on the key aggregates of the economy such as GNP, prices, unemployment, and
interest rates.

### Gregory Chow

By the need to include the essential relationship governing
the important variables whose behavior we wish to study,
balancing the costs of having too large a model (in terms of
specification errors, difficulties in statistical analysis,
and costs of obtaining additional information on an extended
list of exogenous variables) and the costs of omitting essential relationships.

### Otto Eckstein

Today, model size is determined according to the goals of
forecast optimality and simulation capability.  Because of
the important role of raw material prices, including such
items as food and world oil, as well as the importance of
financial behavior by businesses, governments, and financial
institutions in government, optimal forecasting model size
has increased greatly.  This is the principal reason why
the DRI model is so large.

The spectrum of exogenous variables is determined by the desire for simulation capabilities both by the model managers for the sake of exploring alternative policy solutions and for use by policy agencies. Some exogenous variables can be endogenized for simulation purposes to achieve better simulation properties -- e.g., foreign activity variables.

At an earlier stage, the DRI model also included numerous variables, many of them recursive, because they were of value to forecast users. However, after a few years, we decided that the need for highly detailed forecasts of variables that do not add to overall forecast performance can better be met through separate model efforts.

Gary Fromm

Model size is a function of data availability, the process being modeled, the uses to which the model is to be applied, the richness of the theory, and the resources available for model construction.

Albert Hirsch

Model size is determined essentially by three factors:
(a) What is believed to be an adequate degree of disaggregation to derive meaningful and stable relationships.
(b) The degree of endogeneity. Each new variable to be explained requires a new equation. Also, equations are substituted for exogenous variables when it is believed that the model can yield a superior forecast to a forecaster's pure judgment.
(c) The detail of information demanded by users.

It is apparent from these responses that model use, data availability, the available theory, and cost of implementation are important determinants of model size. It is not clear from these responses the extent to which cost is a limiting factor in determining the size of macro-econometric models.

A-3. What is the Role of Economic Theory?

The respondents' answers to this question were terse. The St. Louis Federal Reserve proprietors (Andersen and Carlson) described their model as being founded on "the modern quantity theory of money", and note that an attempt was made to develop estimates of the short- and long-run effects of monetary expansion on the endogenous variables of the model. That model does not focus directly on the structure of the economy but takes a reduced-form approach. Thus, the first-order equilibrium conditions (and hence decision rules) for the household sector are not explicitly included in the model. On the other hand,

the properties of the model have been found to be consistent
with propositions suggested by the theories of the Chicago
School.  For example, some of the Andersen-Carlson (1976) conclusions based on the properties of their model are:

    1) Monetary actions are the dominant factor contributing
       to short-run economic fluctuations.

    2) Monetary actions have little if any lasting effect on
       real variables, i.e., money is a veil.

    3) Fiscal actions, holding monetary policy fixed, have
       only a transitory affect on economic activity
       (presumably real).

    4) The private economy is inherently stable.

The other respondents, most of whom are large-scale macro-
model proprietors, offered little more than the observation
that economic theory has been an aid in specifying behavioral
relationships.  Eckstein did indicate that economic theory
provides "the requisite simulation properties (including
multipliers) that the model must pass in the validation process."  All of the large-scale U.S. models that are popularly
used (BEA, DRI, Chase, and Wharton) are known to have properties similar to the simple IS-LM model (McCarthy (1972) and
Christ (1976)).  That is, monetary expansion is expected to
increase output and lower interest rates; an expansionary
fiscal policy increases output and raises interest rates.
Presumably, Eckstein is suggesting that an acceptable model
must have multiplier properties that are not at odds with the
IS-LM orthodoxy.  But it is likely that he was suggesting more
than this; namely, that there are a series of "generally
accepted" propositions regarding economic response patterns,
provided by or predicted by economic theory, that all model
structures should satisfy.

Micro-theorists sometimes complain that macro-econometric
models are not consistent with established micro-economic
principles.  Macro-modelers, on the other hand, are typically
anxious to include in their models as much micro-theoretic
detail as is feasible.  Indeed, although the aggregation problem may not be treated formally, the well established theories
of individual household and firm behavior are plainly visible
in the macroeconometric specification of investment, production,

and consumption functions of large-scale models currently in use (Klein (1980)). A comparison of the structure of modern large-scale macro-models with the structures used for the earliest macro-models (for example, Klein (1950)) reveals that the models of today use much more micro-economic theory -- and institutional information -- than was the case thirty years ago or even ten years ago. No one argues that macro-econometric models can not be improved and if history is any guide, we can expect to see even more micro-economic theory in the next generation of econometric models.

If micro-economic theory is to have an even more important impact on macro-economic model formulation, it is essential that more thought be given to how the hypothesized micro-relationships can be expected to manifest themselves in macro-economic aggregates. It is also important to recognize that micro-economic formulations can not always be applied uncritically on the macro level. Systematic changes in the composition of some aggregate may not be included in the model. This by itself does not necessarily rule out the existence of a stable relationship among economic aggregates, but it may not be sensible to impose the restrictions implicit in a neat mathematical solution to a micro-economic problem on the macro-economic relationship. For example, the requirement that homotheticity properties be imposed on macro-economic production relationships may be inappropriate if the homotheticity restriction is really only a simplification to help the theorist obtain a well-defined and elegant mathematical relationship.

Turning to some specifics we note that the typical consumption demand curve found in econometric models is very much in the spirit of

$$C_{it} = a_0 + a_1\, YD_t + a_2\, C_{i,t-1} + a_3\, P_{it}/P_{ct}$$

where

$C_{it}$ = real consumption expenditures on good i in period t

$YD_t$ = real disposable income in period t

$P_{it}$ = implicit price deflator of $C_{it}$

$P_{ct}$ = implicit price deflator of aggregate consumption
      expenditures.

Fromm has argued that this is much in the spirit of the demand
function that one would expect to get from a linear expenditure system model with habit persistence.  Expenditure systems
are simplified systems of demand equations that deal directly
with multicollinearity and a paucity of degrees of freedom.
However, the theorist would probably argue that expenditure
systems lead to much more complicated forms (see, for instance,
Pollak (1970)).  Among other things, the theorist would point
out that lags in the other consumption components (and savings)
should also appear on the right-hand side of the equation for
$C_{it}$, and that more than one relative price should be present.
Macro-model builders would at this point protest that collinearity and degrees of freedom would pose serious problems
if they were to estimate such a relationship, and ask the
theorist if he could suggest any guidelines for imposing
restrictions on the unmanageable equation.  It is this
interplay between theory and estimation that has produced the
macro-econometric models that are in use today.

The theory of the firm equations in many of the macro
structural models are roughly in the spirit of the simple
structure shown in McCarthy (1972).  McCarthy began considering a simple single period equilibrium model without lags in
which a monopolist chooses output, labor, capital inputs, and
hence price in a manner that maximized profits.  The production function and the demand curve chosen for the McCarthy
example are

(1)        $q = Ae^{\lambda t}L^{\alpha}K^{1-\alpha}$                    $(0 < \alpha < 1, A > 0)$

(2)        $p = Bq^{\delta}$                          $(-1 < \delta < 0, B > 0)$

where
            p = output price
            q = quantity of output
            L = labor input
            K = capital input.

Letting

   $p_L$ = the price of labor
   $p_K$ = the price of capital,

it is easy to verify that the first-order conditions for a
maximum are

$$L = A^{-1/\alpha} e^{-\lambda t/\alpha} K^{(\alpha-1)/\alpha} q^{1/\alpha}$$

$$q = B^{-1/\delta} p^{1/\delta}$$

$$p = [\alpha(1 + \delta)]^{-1}(Lp_L/q)$$

$$K = (1 - \alpha)(1 - \delta)(pq/p_K).$$

The first of these marginal conditions is obviously analogous
to the "labor requirements" function found in many of the
models, the Brookings Model (1965), for instance, and the
Wharton Models as well as the BEA Model to name a few.  The
equation for p will be recognized as the common "mark-up" on
unit labor cost rule; many variants of this equation can be
found in the various structural models.  The last equation
with $p_K$ interpreted as a user cost of capital is nothing more
than a steady state version of a Jorgenson (1965) type investment equation.  Finally, McCarthy chose to interpret the
equation for q as the monopolist's perceived demand curve or
his output decision function, conditional on p.  Given this
interpretation, the possibility that the actual quantity of
output demanded would differ from the monopolist's output
decision becomes open, in which case inventory changes would
be computed as the difference between actual sales and output.

   Economic theory does suggest that due, among other things,
to costs associated with changing the values of p, q, L, and
K, adjustments to equilibrium will not be instantaneous; distributed lags will be involved.  Theory, of course, does not
suggest the precise nature of the lags; accordingly, the
specification of the lag structure is left open.  Casual observation of the economy, however, does indicate that firms can
adjust their labor input faster than the capital input, suggesting that the lag structure for the labor input be of a
somewhat simpler and faster sort than that for capital.

In practice, real sectoral value added is taken as a
proxy for q. A purist might object to this on the grounds
that for it to be valid the production function would have to
be separable in labor, capital and intermediate inputs. The
alternative to not making such an assumption could involve
serious collinearity problems during estimation. The assumption seems plausible enough in any event.

In early versions of macro-models, labor supply (labor
force participation) was generally treated in a relatively ad
hoc manner or treated exogenously. (See for example, Fair
(1976), Duesenberry et al., (1965), or McCarthy (1972)). Such
formulations failed to take into account shifts in the demographic composition of the population, which are known to have
had important implications for the measured unemployment rate
(especially in the 1970's), and failed to recognize that consumption, savings, and labor supply are jointly determined
variables at the household level. This last point suggests
that among the variables entering the labor force participation
equations should be those variables which were found to be
important in the consumption equations. We have begun to see
these factors being considered in the labor force participation
equations in the more recent versions of macro-models. For
example, the most recent version of the Wharton model includes
an equation in which real aggregate compensation of employees
enters the labor force participation rate equation with a
strong positive influence. A variable measuring the age
composition of the workforce is also included. It is curious
that this variable does not enter the consumption functions
also. Nevertheless, innovations of this sort are steps in the
right direction. It would not be unreasonable, however, to
suggest that in the next round of estimation further steps
should be taken towards a more integrated treatment of the
household sector (and the business sector). We would also
like to suggest that the merging of the flow of funds data
with the National Income Accounts in model construction would
provide an opportunity for developing a more integrated treatment of the financial, household, government and other sectors

of the economy. In the case of the household sector, for instance, we might begin by considering models in which consumption, labor supply and portfolios are jointly determined.

One can identify other areas in which economic theory has influenced model structure. The supply and demand structure for money found in the MPS model (Ando (1980)), for instance, and in the Wharton models (McCarthy (1972)), and the Coen-Hickman Model (1976) are examples. Still there are areas in which relatively excess ad hoc procedures appear to rule. In spite of Phelps' work (1970) it is far from clear that we understand the structure underlying the Phillips curve, or that some version of the Phillips curve can be expected to be stable. One of the problems here is that wage rate determination is not in many cases governed by the competitive model. Unfortunately, economic theory has not shed a great deal of light on the operation of imperfect markets. Things are further complicated by the fact that the data-base is weak in this area because the degree of labor-market imperfection varies across regions and industries. It is not possible at this time to categorize neatly producers who face relatively competitive conditions and those who face varying degrees of monopsony.

Thus economic theory can be seen to play a very important guiding role in the specification and validation of macroeconometric models. Inadequate theories, deficient data, and difficult computation and estimation problems, however, make the relationship an evolutionary and creative rather than a rigid one.

A-4. What is the Role of Institutional Information?

Institutions influence, at least to some extent, the way in which economic activity is organized. Eckstein correctly noted that there is institutional information in every relationship in the model. Some of this information is directly related to monetary and fiscal policy. For example, personal taxes enter the calculation of disposable income which in turn enters the consumption functions. Excise taxes (should) enter various final demand and sector price deflator equations; useful lives for tax purposes, investment tax credit rates, and

corporate profit tax rates enter the calculation of user cost
of capital, an important variable in the investment equations.
In addition, the federal personal and corporate tax equations
often include information on the tax rate structure.  Key
Federal Reserve policy parameters, the discount rate, the required reserve ratio and sometimes the level of non-borrowed
reserves commonly enter the money supply curves of the larger
structural models.  The government expenditure data - usually
treated exogenously - enter the models in a plausible manner,
and the federal government budget information is particularly
important at forecast time.

Another type of institutional information not usually recognized as such are the procedures actually used by the
Federal government in constructing the National Income Accounts
and other data series used by the models.  This information is
invaluable in understanding the nature of the data series being
used and their limitations.  Knowledge of how the numbers are
constructed often suggests a convenient equation specification.
The equations for inventory valuation adjustment and capital
consumption allowances are examples of the use of such knowledge.  Other examples are the time that it takes to place an
order, construct a house, negotiate capital financing, and
produce goods that govern the time shift and length of distributed lags in the system.  Finally, returning to Eckstein's
point we note that even the parameter estimates themselves
should reflect institutional information about the household
sector, the business sector and the other sectors of the
economy.

A-5.  What is the Role of Social Accounts in Model Design?
Here we begin by presenting some typical answers.

Eckstein:

Even today, the National Income and Product accounts provide
the basic framework for the macro-model.  They represent the
flow of income and expenditure, and also provide a framework
for various capital stocks.  However, the flow of funds data
framework is simultaneous with the National Income Accounts in
the DRI model today, and represents about 200 out of the 800
relationships.  The input-output framework plays a somewhat
more subsidiary role.  While detailed production indexes are
calculated through the flexible input-output coefficient

technique and the results enter the simultaneous block through utilization rates and other variables that affect prices and profits, the degree of simultaneity is much smaller than the simultaneity for the flow of funds and the National Income Accounts.

Hirsch:

The national income and product accounts (NIPA's) determine the structural design of the core of the model (GNP, its major components, national income, income distribution, and price determination). Many non-NIPA series are used, of course, but all are directly or indirectly related to NIPA data in the model. In our new stage-of-process price sector, information from interindustry (input-output) accounts is used to derive some extraneous parameter estimates.

The model proprietors among the respondents gave a fairly clear idea of the role of the social accounts in their respective models. The DRI model utilizes both National Income Accounts and flow-of-funds information. The same is true of the Wharton Quarterly Model. The BEA, DRI and Wharton Quarterly and Annual Models all make use of input-output accounts in one form or another. The Wharton Annual Model links the input-output accounts with the national income accounts in a detailed, formal way. This model probably has the highest degree of feedback between the supply and demand sides of the economic system. All the structural models use national data other than those available from the social accounts; for example, employment, hours, and earnings data from BLS, and interest rate data from the Federal Reserve System.

We close this section by noting that our previous remarks concerning the construction of the national data base apply here as well. Knowledge about the procedures used in constructing the data base actually plays an important role in the specification of an econometric model.

A-6. What is the Influence of Data Availability?

Generally the respondents recognize that their model's size is restricted by the degree of disaggregation in the national data-base. The responses of Eckstein and Hirsch are representative.

Eckstein

In designing the DRI model, we emphasize the information

quality of series.  We do not place major emphasis on early
availability.  We use other econometric techniques to gain the
benefit of quick information.  This approach is possible because in the United States the National Income Accounts are
available with rather little delay.  In the case of flow of
funds data, there is no practical choice; they are all available with delay, and if elaborate financial modelling is to be
included in the model, this body of data cannot be avoided despite its slowness.

Hirsch

Model construction is constrained by the framework of the
NIPA's, which provide the "core" data of the model.  Thus in
many cases, equations are not estimated using the best available data (in terms of the theoretical requirements of the
equation), as they would be if only single equation models
were being built.

Second, in other instances, non-availability of ideal data
requires use of proxy variables; e.g., despite much research
to find more direct labor market variables for wage rate
functions, one invariably ends up using some kind of unemployment rate.

Third, we are fortunate at BEA to have access to some unpublished series and in some instances to the agency's statistical
personnel for constructing new, not otherwise available, series.

    One of the respondents did note that the unavailability
of good data often required the use of proxy variables.  The
unemployment rate was cited as a common proxy and the difficulties with this variable illustrate the problems that arise
in this connection.  It is used in the Phillips "type" curves
for wage rate determination, as an indicator of "tightness"
in the labor market.  Unfortunately the unemployment rate is a
unidimensional labor market measure and it can't possibly capture all the relevant information about labor markets.  Does a
tight labor market as measured by a relatively low unemployment
rate necessarily signal an increase in wage-rate inflation?
Because skill requirements differ across industries, labor
market conditions can also be expected to differ.  The present
labor data base is seriously deficient.  In early versions of
the Wharton Model the demographic composition of the unemploy-
ed was introduced in the wage determination equation.  At the
present time, there is more extensive consideration of
demographic factors in the labor market equations.

Problems of missing data were only indirectly addressed. The problems of capital stock data -- needed as inputs to production functions -- are well known. However, most macro-model builders would probably prefer to have the best estimates that BEA could produce rather than resort to the use of various proxy measures. Structural model builders have also had to cope with shifting productivity. Again a time trend is often used in the production functions, but technical progress simply does not take place at a smooth pace. There is no model in which technological advance is largely endogenous, and it is doubtful that there will be until a growth accounting system is maintained on a continuous basis. We are thinking of something considerably more extensive than the system maintained by Denison (1970). Such a system would report detailed information relevant to technological change by industry. Detailed R & D information would be required as well as information on skills, age and experience, and detail on plant and equipment. Lack of this information is one of the primary reasons why we have yet to obtain a satisfactory explanation of the U.S. productivity slowdown in the 1970's. If the models are to address economic growth policies in a satisfactory manner, we shall need a better database in the entire area of technological change.

None of the macro-models has as yet a satisfactory spatial dimension. While systems of regional models have been developed, these systems do not feed back to the macro-model. In principle, much of the macro-model output could be generated by adding outputs from regional models. Part of the problem here is data availability; employment, earnings and personal income are the only areas where a reasonably complete set of regional data are found.

Adams' response to the questionnaire makes an important point.

It would be good to consider what the social accounts should be from the point of the model builders. What do we need? Would it pay to organize a stand on this and to present it to the appropriate organizations?

There is a need for better communications between the commu-
nity of model builders and the managers of the data system.
A-7.  What is the Influence of Users on the Models?

To summarize in a single sentence:  Modellers are influenced in designing models by their perceived clients.  The
St. Louis Federal Reserve modellers are relatively isolated
from outside pressure.  The BEA model structure is influenced
primarily by the public-sector clients.  Much the same is the
case for the Federal Reserve Board Model.  Finally, the models
which are generally available and used in both private and
public sectors are influenced by both.  The pressure in the
public sector is in the direction of expanding the number of
policy levers in order to make the models more useful for
bureaucrats and legislators.  There is pressure from the
private sector to expand the models in order to study closely
particular industries and key problem areas such as energy,
transportation, and balance of payments issues.  Pressure
comes from the private sector to expand the models to make
them more useful for micro forecasting and analysis, while
giving, simultaneously, a picture of the economy as a whole.
Some of the comments are informative.

### Adams

The influence of the policy makers is considerable.  We have
continually had to adapt and at times expand the Wharton model
in order to address issues posed by policymakers.  This can be
seen in the refinements introduced to the tax revenue equations
over the years.  Another recent example is the change in the
Wharton Annual Model structure designed to allow it to address
better the energy issues.  In general, the influences of policy
makers is seen in the expansion of the number of policy levers
in the models.  The influence of the private sector has been
less but still significant.  Certainly the increase in the
model's size reflects our desire to provide more relevant
private sector forecasting information, as well as a desire to
obtain more accurate over-all forecasts.  The private sector
forecasting needs have also been a factor in directing our
efforts to improve the forecasting accuracy of various parts
of the models.

### Chow

a.  The influence of policy makers is seen in the choice
    of policy instruments in the model, the choice of the
    important endogenous variables, and the choice of re-
    lationships to stress, including possibly some disag-
    gregate relationships.

    b.   The influence of private sector users?

       Same as (a) above. Private sector users may also be concerned with the appropriate government instruments.

## Eckstein

There is no direct influence of policy makers on the design of our models. As a service enterprise in a market economy, DRI must be alert to the needs of our clients, including policy makers. As a result, the models are designed to be useable. This mainly is felt through the inclusion of additional policy levers for simulation studies, certainly not in the selection of hypotheses in the construction of the model or of add factors in the forecasting process, or in the selection of add factors in policy simulation.

## Fromm

    a.   Policy makers force an emphasis on achieving improved accuracy of policy simulation results.

    b.   The private sector generates pressure for more detail relevant for micro purposes.

## Hirsch

The BEA model is designed primarily for the use of policy-makers, though outputs are also sent to Government agencies that use them to help anticipate operational needs. Accordingly, the model is structured with an emphasis on policy -- mainly, fiscal policy -- variables. Occassionally we have designed parts of the model specifically in response to suggestions made by the Council of Economic Advisers.

A-8. How are the Models Designed in Hierarchial Structure?

    The St. Louis Federal Reserve model is an example of a purely recursive system, the simplest of hierarchial structures. The hierarchical structure of Keynesian type macromodels is relatively easy to describe. There is usually a group of variables which are not influenced by current endogenous variables or exogenous variables. Plant and equipment expenditures - for the regulated sector for instance - could fall into this category. Capital consumption allowances are treated in this manner also for model solution purposes in the Brookings Model and in the Wharton Model. The number of variables which fall into this category is typically small, approximately 5% of the endogenous variables in the Wharton Model. The equations just described -- the recursive block -- provide input into a relatively large simultaneous block typically consisting of a hundred or more equations. Finally,

in the case of the models managed in the private sector, the
solutions for the recursive and simultaneous blocks provide
inputs to a host of satellite models which do not feed back
to the simultaneous and recursive parts.  Some examples of
common satellite models known to be maintained by the private
sector macro-models are:

1.  Systems of regional econometric models for states,
    SMSA's, and counties;

2.  World commodity market models for lead, zinc, copper,
    etc.;

3.  Automobile, transportation, truck and aviation models;

4.  Models of regional energy demand -- electricity in
    particular.

Most of these satellite sectors are so small relative to
the economy that the feedback effects can be expected to be
small.  We are approaching a point, however, where the feedback from regional models cannot be ignored.  The time will
come when a comprehensive system of regional labor market
models with relative price links to each other and with employment, population, and wage rates determined at the local level
will be constructed.  Such a model could be merged with a macro
model of the U.S. with wage rate, manhours, and employment
equations in the macro-model replaced by the regional system.
In such a model wages and employment at the macro-level could
be determined by aggregating the regional totals.

Only a few of the respondents answered this question.

Eckstein

In earlier DRI models, only the circular flow of income and
expenditure, some elements of the price-wage block and much
of the financial sector were simultaneous.  However, the
advances in computer and software technology have made it
possible to include most of the variables in the model in the
simultaneous block.  There is a small block of preliminary
variables, and another small block of recursive variables that
are of intrinsic value but not needed for the representation
of the economic process.  But the bulk of the model, including
all of the income-expenditure block, wages and prices, the
detailed production and utilization equations and most of the
financial sector, is simultaneous.  We feel strongly that this
is a characteristic of the actual world.

Hirsch

An a-priori methodology translates farm futures prices into

farm wholesale prices. This methodology, combined with judgmental projections of real farm output, also yields farm GNP (current prices) and nonfarm proprietors' income. These variables feed into the main GNP model (e.g., farm prices help determine PCE food prices). Single equations using main model outputs predict (1) the consumer price index, (2) the wholesale price index, and (3) the Federal Reserve industrial production index -- variables with virtually no feedback into the main model.

## III. Estimation and Validation

It is really not practical to handle the group B questions separately. The use of statistical inference and hypothesis testing are really part of the entire model validation process. For orientation purposes it seems best to start by reviewing the respondents' answers.

### Carlson

Each of the equations originally underwent extensive testing regarding its specification. Since its original development, validation has been based on dynamic simulations of the model. Also, simulations have been conducted outside the sample period to check the model's performance as new data become available.

The model, as currently constructed, does not really provide a vehicle for hypothesis testing. It could be argued that the original development of the model consisted of hypothesis testing, but once the specifications were set, it served as a test only to the extent that it "explained" evolving experience tolerably well.

    a. As a check on how the model is doing, dynamic simulations are conducted. As of yet, this procedure has not formed the basis for a rigorous hypothesis test. There is some work underway along these lines, however.

    b. Ultimately, the behavior of the aggregates should be traceable to microeconomic behavior. However, up to this point we have not done any work with testing microeconomic hypotheses.

### Chow

#### Validation

By examining properties of individual equations, such as the standard errors of the individual parameters and the sizes and behavior of the residuals, studying goodness of fit of the entire system using (ex-post and ex-ante) forecasting errors, properties of the reduced form and the final form including various multipliers and stochastic properties (in the time or frequency domain) and the checking of properties of subsystems imbedded in the model.

Hypothesis Testing

a. Complete System Dynamics

By studying goodness of fit of the entire system using (ex-post and ex-ante) forecasting errors, properties of the reduced form and the final form including various multipliers and stochastic properties (in the time or frequency domain).

b. Partial Theory

By examining properties of individual equations, such as the standard errors of the individual parameters and the sizes and behaviors of the residuals.

Statistical Inference

Since there is a great deal of fishing for the correct specification, the usual tests of hypotheses concerning the properties of the resulting fitted equations no longer have the correct "text book" probability interpretations. However, the "standard errors" still serve as a useful guide on the goodness of fit.

Eckstein

Validation

This is a very big question. In summary, the DRI procedure includes the following tests:

1. Individual equation testing through the standard test statistics and dynamic single-equation simulation;

2. Full dynamic historical simulation, 1966 to present;

3. Tests for simulation properties, including the standard multipliers, as well as a variety of other properties suggested by economic theory and general economic understanding;

4. Destructive testing by assuming extreme values for policy and other variables;

5. Ex ante solution, and particularly long-run solutions, to assure that the model has sound, balanced growth and simulation properties in the forecast intervals.

Hypothesis Testing:

Each equation of any importance is embodied in an experimental version of the model and the validation tests sketched above are performed. We apply a set of standard valuation criteria to evaluate one equation against another: for example, we calculate the root mean square error in a full dynamic historical simulation, for a short list of variables, and other things equal, would pick the equation that performs better. All our equations are examined to be consistent with traditional microeconomic theory. But there are many equations that are consistent with the theory, and the more difficult question is to select one out of that subset.

## Statistical Inference

All the equations have to pass the standard statistical tests, including the corrected R-squared, the Durbin-Watson ratio, etc. Occasionally an equation will be used despite an inferior Durbin-Watson ratio if the only means to eliminate that flaw is to go through a transformation into autoregressive form. We generally avoid that form because of its poor simulation properties. We occasionally also include variables of marginal statistical significance if there is a strong case for them in general economic understanding and theory.

# Fromm

## Validation

Models are generally validated by predictive tests (conditional and unconditional) and by checking correspondence with received theory and institutional characteristics. More work needs to be done on validation criteria and procedures.

## Hypothesis Testing

Complete system properties are studied by solution and simulation under varying conditions including stochastic shocks; comparisons are also made of the model's spectral properties with those of the actual data.

## Statistical Inference

Statistical inference is generally poorly used. The procedure of stating the hypothesis to be tested prior to estimation should be followed.

# Hirsch

## Validation

Models are validated by the following procedures:

a. single-equation criteria (statistical, theoretical, judgmental)

b. sector simulations

c. full model simulations

d. analysis of multipliers

Some or all of these are used depending on the degree of respecification being done.

## Hypothesis Testing

Relatively little new theoretical development is done. Consistency with established theory is tested principally at the single-equation level (including long-run or steady-state criteria). Competing specifications are tested by comparisons of simulations (see validation procedure outlined above).

Statistical Inference

Classical goodness-of-fit and significance tests are
used at the single-equation level. Tests of prediction
outside of sample periods are made wherever possible by
truncation of the regression period and prediction over
the post-sample period. Sometimes tests for structural
stability are made.

In reviewing the respondents answers we shall begin with
statistical inference and hypothesis testing. Surprisingly
none of the respondents said anything about the choice of
estimators, i.e., the method of inferring the numerical structure of the model. It appears, however, on the basis of conversations with the respondents, that ordinary least squares
(OLS) is still a very popular estimator. This may be surprising
to some, given the work that has gone into devising consistent
simultaneous equation estimators. There are, however, some
good reasons for the continued popularity of ordinary least
squares. Among them are the following.

1. OLS is relatively inexpensive and the computations involved are easy to explain.

2. Many of the structural models are so large that none of
   the consistent structural estimators can be used without
   modification. Typically the number of behavioral equations exceeds the number of observations; thus, even if
   the system is linear in the parameters and in the variables, the use of three stage least squares (3SLS) and
   full information maximum likelihood (FIML) is virtually
   precluded, unless the form of the covariance matrix of
   errors is somewhat arbitrarily restricted. Generally
   the number of exogenous and pre-determined variables
   exceeds the number of observations. Accordingly, if
   k-class procedures are to be used, some rule must be
   found for excluding a subset of the exogenous variables
   for the first stage regressions. One popular procedure
   has been to use as first stage regressors the first n
   principal components of the exogenous variable matrix,
   where n is less than the number of observations.[3] One
   problem with excluding a subset of the regressors from
   the first stage regressions is that the proper set of
   first stage regressors will differ from equation to
   equation. (Fisher (1965) first suggested a criterion
   for choosing a proper set of first-stage regressors).
   If the first-stage regressors are to be tailor-made for
   each behavioral equation, k-class estimation becomes
   expensive.

3. It is generally recognized that the case for the use of
   k-class estimators, or modified k-class estimators, is
   based on their potential for bias reduction. When one

considers higher order moments such as the variance or mean squared error, this argument cannot be made.[4] Thus the case for using a k-class estimator cannot be considered to be a strong one. These estimators are cumbersome to use for large models, and while they may reduce bias, they often do so at the expense of increased variance.

All the authors noted that they use the standard test statistics including "t" and "F" tests and Durbin-Watson statistics for testing hypothesis about coefficient signs and magnitudes and autocorrelated error structures. Tests of a judgmental sort are also made at this stage to ascertain that the parameter signs and magnitudes conform to the dictates of economic theory such as propensities to consume should be positive and bounded by zero and one, own price elasticities should be negative, and single-equation dynamic responses should be stable. At this stage it is also common to check how well the structural equations track turning points.

One respondent noted that "there is a great deal of fishing for the correct specification," and that the usual hypothesis-testing procedures no longer have the textbook probability interpretation. Indeed, if there is a great deal of experimentation, the power of "t" tests may be quite weak. On the other hand, "exploration of the likelihood surface" may be unavoidable if prior knowledge is absent and there is no way to specify the explanatory variables in advance. With the advent of inexpensive and easily accessible computer programs and data-banks, fishing for statistical significance has become increasingly prevalent. Thirty years ago the facilities for such intensive exploratory work were simply not available. This is clearly a potential problem for which there is as yet no generally accepted solution.

The testing procedures discussed thus far are all concerned with single-equation validation. Two types of tests are common in connection with system validation:

1. Tests of the systems predictive accuracy ex post and ex ante.

2. Tests of the model's multiplier properties, and of the stability properties.

In testing for predictive accuracy a common procedure is to produce a series of one-period ahead simulations two-period ahead simulations, and so on. Root mean squared errors, mean absolute errors, Theil coefficients, and other measures are commonly computed. There is a wide literature today which documents the performance of various models in such tests (Klein and Burmeister (1976), McNees (1978) and Haitovsky et. al. (1974)). What the modeller is looking for here is, among other things,

1. Information on how fast errors build up as the forecast horizon lengthens.
2. Information on how the model performs relative to "naive" alternatives.
3. Information on how the model tracks turning points in the business cycle.

A very common procedure is to test individual equations or blocks of equations against competing equations or blocks by replacing one subset of equations with another and to compare various measures of complete system error performance.

Univariate time-series (ARIMA) models are sometimes used as "naive" alternatives against which structural econometric models are compared. It is now generally recognized that each of the endogenous variables in a structural econometric model has a univariate ARIMA representation, provided the exogenous variables can be characterized by a stationary stochastic process (Zellner and Palm (1974)). Moreover, if the econometric model provides a correct characterization of the process, the ex ante as well as ex post forecasts of the structural model will have a smaller error variance than the ARIMA model predictions. Thus from a model validation point of view, comparisons of forecast accuracy of time-series and structural econometric models provide consistency checks on the econometric model. As with many of the other validation "tests" described above, no formal tests of significance are as yet available.

Multiplier studies are another important tool for complete system validation. The objective here is to determine that the

model responses to shocks are in conformity with the dictates
of economic theory, and to examine the stability properties
of the system. Again, there is a wide literature which documents such validation studies (Klein and Burmeister (1976)).
In the case of a Keynesian-type system the sort of things that
the modeller is looking for are the following.

1. Expansionary government expenditure and tax measures
   should ten to increase interest rates, employment and
   income.

2. Expansionary monetary policy should increase income and
   lower interest rates.

3. An increase in government expenditures devoted solely to
   the purchase of goods should have a lower GNP multiplier
   than purchases devoted to the purchase of services, at
   least in the short run. In the case of a pure goods
   purchase, inventories are drawn down, and production to
   replace them takes place only with a lag. In the case
   of one week, for instance, the government goods purchase
   multiplier should be close to zero. In the case of
   government purchases of services the multiplier should
   be greater than 1 even in the first quarter. Not only
   does GNP increase due to the increase in government
   purchases and the role of that variable in the GNP
   identity, but also consumer incomes are raised and this
   should result in increased purchases of all types of
   consumer items (goods and services).

4. Because of lags in the response of employment to increased output, expansionary measures should result in
   initial profit increases which are large relative to
   wage bill increases. This lag in the employment response will also appear as a short term increase in
   productivity, which in turn could be reflected in a
   slight downward pressure on prices in the very short
   run.

5. Accelerator considerations would probably lead the
   modeller to look for indications that the process of
   adjustment to equilibrium is not monotonic.

6. The balanced-budget multiplier should be positive.

   While the main reason for doing extensive multiplier
experiments is to identify weak spots in the model, the
modeller is also seeking to learn about feedback properties
possessed by the model that could not easily by identified on
the basis of a review of the individual equations. Sometimes
hypothesized feedbacks don't materialize; sometimes unsuspected
feedbacks are found.

   By way of concluding this discussion of validation, we

note the absence of an objective, generally accepted approach
to model validation.  The static and dynamic properties that
an investigator expects to find may depend on the theory that
is adopted at the outset and may not therefore be the same for
all investigators.  In addition, formal tests of significance
are, for the most part, not available.

IV.  Producing a Forecast and Policy Simulations

C-1.  How are the Forecasts Prepared from Models?

C-2.  How are the Models Adjusted in the Forecasting Procedure?

     The respondents suggest a fairly consistent sequence of
procedures although some would omit or limit their use of
some of them.  The sequence is as follows.

   a.  Update the model data-base with the most recent
       historical information.

   b.  Develop forecast period projections for the exogenous
       variables.  The specific list of variables differs
       from model to model but generally includes government
       spending and tax policy variables, federal reserve
       monetary policy variables, and international activity
       (world trade volume) and import price variables.  The
       respondents fall into two groups concerning the speci-
       fic procedures employed at this stage.  The first
       group, which produces "best estimate" ex ante fore-
       cases, devotes substantial effort to developing
       estimates of the "most likely" values for these
       variables utilizing a combination of official govern-
       ment budget estimates, judgements by knowledgeable
       "insiders", stated policy objectives, and their own
       experience.  The second group, which produces "con-
       ditional" ex ante forecasts, specifies plausible
       forecast period paths for the exogenous variables and
       typically studies the impacts of altering the pro-
       jected path of one or more of the exogenous assump-
       tions.

   c.  Estimate an initial set of constant adjustments (also
       referred to as error adjustments, add factors, inter-
       cept parameter changes, or constant term parameter
       changes) based on (1) historical single equation
       errors or (2) ex ante judgment concerning the impact
       of recent or anticipated future events which will
       not be captured by the estimated structural equations.
       The specific procedures followed by the respondents
       for making type (1) adjustments include not making
       any such adjustments, making the adjustments based
       on the estimated serial correlation properties of
       the single-equation residuals in the sample period,
       making adjustments based on ad hoc mechanical proce-
       dures such as average error over several pre-forecast
       periods, and making adjustments based on a judgmental
       analysis of the recent historical single-equation

and expected future errors.  The choice of the
procedure for type (1) adjustments involves a crude
form of hypothesis testing.  If the null hypothesis
that single-equation disturbances in the forecast
period are drawn from the same distribution as the
sample-period disturbances is rejected, some type
of plausible intercept-drift model is chosen for
adjusting the equation.  Examples of type (2) adjustments include anticipated strikes and wage and price
controls.  The forecaster typically has information
on the order of magnitude of these effects and
attempts to adjust the corresponding equations appropriately.

d.  Modification of the single equation coefficients
    other than the constant terms (intercept) coefficients.
    This is suggested by a few of the respondents.  In
    practice, this procedure is used sparingly and usually
    only to incorporate things like tax law changes where
    the model parameters are functions of the specific
    provisions of the tax law.  At the research level,
    variable-parameter models have been considered exten-
    sively, but are not used very much in working models.

e.  Modification of forecast results based on partial
    first forecast period data or survey data on antici-
    pations or intentions.  Mechanically, this involves
    modifying the constant adjustments in the forecast
    period to produce results which are "consistent"
    with external information.  Examples include using
    data on auto sales for the first month or two of a
    quarter as a control for quarterly projections of
    auto sales, using monthly sales data as an indicator
    of quarterly consumer expenditures, and using invest-
    ment anticipations data as a "guideline" for predicted
    business fixed investment expenditures.  This proce-
    dure is generally employed only by the group of fore-
    casters preparing "best estimate" forecasts, and
    generally no hard and fast rule is available as to
    how much a forecast will be modified in light of
    such information.

f.  Modification of the initial set of constant adjust-
    ments and/or exogenous assumptions on the basis of
    the "reasonableness" of the resulting forecast.
    Criteria for "reasonableness" include: the implied
    values for summary measures not directly produced
    via behavioral equations such as the unemployment
    rate, the personal savings rate, factor productivity,
    and the wage and profit shares of income.  Unprece-
    dented results, which are clearly implausible, typi-
    cally lead the forecaster to introduce a modification
    to the forecast.  Growth, unemployment, or inflation
    rates resulting from an initial set of policy assump-
    tions which are sufficiently adverse to suggest that
    policy makers would alter the policy will lead to
    changes in the initial policy assumptions (i.e.,
    policy is in part an endogenous variable).  Finally,

> forecast results which are radically different from
> other forecasts may lead to modification of the
> forecasts.  These procedures are utilized only by
> "best estimate" forecasters, and no fixed set of
> rules are employed.

The specific responses are as follows.

### F. Gerard Adams

Forecast preparation with a model involves updating of the
historical database to include all the most recent information,
developing forecast horizon projections for important exogenous
variables, examining single equation errors over the most
recent historical period to determine appropriate error adjustment values, and reviewing information on forecast period behavior such as monthly data for the first forecast quarter or
anticipations (survey) data.  The important exogenous variables
include measures of government fiscal policy, federal reserve
policy, world trade (activity) levels, and import prices.
Error adjustment, as we do it, is essential to keep the model
on track.  An alternate approach is not to adjust or to minimize adjustment, but the problem with that is that one looses
credibility with the user if the take off point of the forecast is way out of line with reality.  These error adjustments,
or constant adjustments, also are used to enter the estimated
impacts of anticipated future events such as strikes.

### Otto Eckstein

The actual forecasting process is an elaborate exercise in
information processing.  This exercise includes null solutions
to analyze the recent record of error, econometric filters
applied to various surveys, and a variety of other analyses.

The models themselves are not adjusted in the forecasting
procedures.  However, add factors are developed which are
estimates of the most probable path of future error terms for
the equations.

The forecasting process also requires the determination of
values for the exogenous variables.  To some extent, this is
done by analysis of the theories by which policy makers are
operating, also from the public pronouncements, and finally
from the implications of those assumptions as seen through
the model.  If the initially assumed policies produce politically unacceptable answers, the policy assumptions have to be
re-examined because policymakers are behavioral, and therefore
are likely to change the values of those policy parameters.

### Ray C. Fair

Generally forecasts are produced once a quarter for about 16
quarters ahead.  Monetary policy is endogenous in the model.
Exogenous fiscal policy variables are forecasted using proposed budget numbers whenever possible.  Simple extrapolations
are generally used for exogenous foreign-sector variables.  No
subjective adjustments are applied to the forecasts.  The
model is re-estimated up to two quarters before the beginning
of the forecast period.

Albert Hirsch

How forecasts are prepared

a. Major exogenous variables

Government expenditures, monetary policy variables, housing starts over the early forecast quarters, foreign economic conditions, import prices, energy materials prices, and exogenous elements in Government receipts, imports, and exports -- are gotten by analysis of developments and discussions with experts in relevant areas. In the case of Government expenditures and receipts, exogenous elements are largely supplied by the Government Division of BEA, which translates budgetary data into NIPA terms. Exogenous components of imports and exports are obtained from the Balance of Payments Division of BEA which makes detailed projections of the international transactions accounts.

b. Constant adjustments are applied where necessary to stochastic equations. An initial set of adjustments is derived on the basis of recent single equation residual behavior, taking into account serial correlation characteristics of the equation. Special factors affecting past data or current or future expected events (strikes, etc.) are also used in setting the initial adjustments.

c. Further adjustments may be made after initial trial runs on the basis of partial current-quarter information pertaining to outputs and "judgmental" factors. Judgmental factors include (i) "reasonable" behavior of summary measures not directly determined by examination of individual behavioral equations (e.g., unemployment rate, personal saving rate, productivity, factor shares), (ii) unprecedented behavior (not necessarily disallowed); (iii) inexplicably large differences compared with other available projections, including survey-based projections.

These remarks reflect a recognition that models have significant limitations given the high probability of misspecification, their generally over-simplified representations of reality, the poor estimation of parameters, and their inability to anticipate and reflect structural changes. Accordingly, the intelligent application of a model, especially to forecasting, requires that the user be a good "current analyst" of the economy. The model constitutes only a component of the modeller's total knowledge about the economy and the modeller should be aware of deficiencies in the model, particularly in relation to recent and future events. In short, a mixed econometric and judgmental approach is superior to either approach by itself.

The issue of whether or not to use constant adjustments centers in part around whether one is attempting not only to provide a forecast but also a reproducible procedure for making forecasts.  Those who advocate using no constant adjustments, or only constant adjustments which are determined on the basis of estimated serial correlation properties of the single equation residuals or some other statistical procedure, typically argue from a point of view that one should separate the art and science of forecasting.  Those who advocate the use of constant adjustments based, at least in part, on judgmental inputs argue from the point of view that their own and others' intimate knowledge of recent and expected economic events which are not accounted for in the structure of the model should be incorporated to produce the "best possible" forecast.  Judgmental inputs make a forecast irreproducible, in the sense that no two individuals would produce identical forecasts with the same model, and raises the issue of whether an accurate forecast is due primarily to the forecasters' ability or the model's quality.  Since it is possible to produce a preliminary forecast using only mechanical adjustments and a second forecast by adding the judgmental adjustments, it would be possible to resolve this issue with a sufficient forecast history.

A slightly different issue is that these constant adjustments in general improve forecast accuracy.  While the truth of this remark must in large part depend on the accuracy of the outside information available to the individual making the judgments, the limited information available suggests that even constant adjustments generated by ad hoc mechanistic procedures produce better short-term (up to four quarters head) forecasts than no adjustments and that judgmental adjustments are slightly better than mechanically generated adjustments (see, for example, Haitovsky, Treyz, and Su (1974)).

The modification of constant adjustments and/or exogenous assumptions based on preliminary model results either due to partial quarterly data, survey data, or on the basis of a priori reasonableness criteria is the most controversial aspect of the forecast procedure.  Almost all "best estimate" forecasters employ these procedures to some extent.  Clearly, the more stringent the a priori constraints that are placed on a forecast the less relevant the model becomes to the forecasting process.  At the extreme, the model becomes nothing more than an accounting constraint.  While none of the respondents advocate such an extreme position, it is difficult if not impossible for an outsider to determine whether the forecast reflects primarily a forecast based on the structure of the model or primarily the a priori information of the forecaster.

C-3.  Do Models Include Important But Hard-to-Predict Variables?

The specific variables listed by the respondents as hard to predict are not precisely the same for each forecaster but many variables are common.  The responses can be grouped into hard-to-predict endogenous variables and hard to predict exogenous variables.  The hard to predict endogenous variables can be grouped as follows.

    a. Variables determined via an identity as a difference between two other endogenous variables (or the sums of endogenous variables) such as unemployment, corporate profits, and net exports.

    b. Items which have high variability such as manufacturing new orders, inventory change, inventory valuation adjustment, housing starts, and capacity utilization rates (primary and advance processing industries in particular).

The hard-to-predict exogenous variables enumerated include:

    a. International trade volume and international prices

    b. Monetary policy variables -- nonborrowed reserves, the re-discount rate, and the prime rate

    c. Stock market prices

    d. Basic commodity prices

    e. State and local expenditures and surpluses.

The hard-to-predict endogenous variables which are determined via an identity as the difference between two other endogenous variables, to the extent that economic theory dictates that these variables should logically be predicted in this fashion, can only be better predicted by improving the equation specifications underlying the two other endogenous variables.  While improving these specifications will improve the prediction of these "residual item" endogenous variables,

one should still expect relatively larger prediction errors
for these variables.

V.   Some Summary Observations

The preceding discussion has tried to describe the current
practice of macro-econometric model-building and forecasting.
The details of current practice include the following:

(i)     specification of large scale models, with the
        exception of the model of the St. Louis Federal
        Reserve Bank;

(ii)    the use of (sometimes "stylized") economic theory
        in model specification;

(iii)   reliance, to a large extent, on single-equation,
        least-squares regression methods of estimation;

(iv)    the use of seasonally adjusted data series; and

(v)     the use of equation adjustments in extrapolation,
        particularly in forecasting.

Each of these points will now be discussed in some detail to
indicate the rationale for the approaches that have been
pursued in connection with macro-econometric modelling.

(i) The paper by Fromm and Klein (1981) on model size
spells out in more detail why mainstream models are relatively
large. (A model of five-hundred or more equations is not
uncommon.) The increasing size of macro-econometric models
over the past nineteen years (since the inception of the
Brookings Model Project) is in part a response to user demands
for more detail, an attempt to approximate the "general
equilibrium" economic system more closely, and to deal with
special events such as food and oil crises, international
trade and exchange-rate changes, and environmental concerns.
The advances in computational facilities has, of course,
facilitated these developments.

The econometric models currently in use are vastly more
complicated and more informative than the models of twenty or
thirty years ago. These large-scale models are not unmanageable black boxes, but the sheer size of the models precludes
the use of some methods of statistical inference. It is
generally felt that the increased detail included in these
models has enhanced our understanding of the economy.

(ii) Economic theory is used in a fairly general way in

equation specification, but dynamics of adjustment, imperfections in markets, legal practices, and periodic political intervention have made it necessary to go beyond strict textbook-type reasoning. There is little evidence that more intensive use of current "Keynesian" theory would give better performance or understanding than is now achieved, although perhaps some new theory would be helpful. The following theoretical restrictions are generally found in most models:

> homogeneity conditions are met, usually in steady state form;

> strict accounting rules prevail;

> market clearing (possibly with time lags) is imposed; and

> parameter values are restricted wherever possible in accord with economic theory to achieve a parsimonious parameterization and stability of the dynamic system.

These restrictions are typically applied to individual equations or small groups of equations.

(iii) There has been extensive experimentation with various alternative estimation procedures for simultaneous equations models. The experience with alternatives to OLS indicates that only modest improvements in model performance have been achieved through the use of more sophisticated estimation procedures. Greater emphasis has been placed on the importance of flexibility to deal with data refinement and revision, and incorporation of new blocks of equations. At the current time, most operating macro-models are in a state of flux in which re-estimation and system "enhancement" are proceeding simultaneously. It will probably be a long time before macro-model building settles down to a "steady state". It is therefore not surprising that there is too little time available to devote much attention to sophisticated estimation procedures.

(iv) The major type of data adjustment is for seasonality. Most user groups rely on official series and interpret model results in this way. The use of seasonally unadjusted data would confuse interpretations of model results. Most model builders feel that seasonal adjustment is not a high-priority problem in connection with forecasting and policy analysis.

(v) One of the most controversial issues is the use of
constant adjustments (add factors, subjective adjustments, etc.)
in forecasting.  This procedure had its start some 25 years
ago in connection with the use of the Klein-Goldberger model.
It was only experimental at that time, but became firmly
established after it was used in the first generation of
Wharton Models.  The idea is simple.  A better dynamic forecast is obtained when the model is started on track.  Moreover,
if the adjustments are made to constant terms alone, the
system reaction pattern is essentially left intact.

Instead of looking at the procedure as an adjustment
of a parameter estimate, the constant term, we can look at it
as the attempt to assign a non-zero value to the additive
error term.  The zero value is the mean, but extraneous information, not used or not available in the sample period estimation process, may lead to the assignment of non-zero values
to the error term in the extrapolation period.  The experience
of the past several decades indicates that some adjustment
technique is essential for the attainment of relatively accurate forecasts.  However, it is generally felt that model
adjustments should be based on firm outside information not
contained in the model.

With the relatively small samples that are available,
it would be surprising if all the diverse situations that are
likely to confront the economy in the future or even, on an
ex post basis, outside the sample had been covered.  With
small-sample estimates it is no wonder that large major events
require a reconsideration of parts of a system.  This is
generally done in a minimal way by adjusting the constant terms
in the equation, leaving the other coefficients, and hence the
system dynamics, intact.

FOOTNOTES

[1]A questionnaire was distributed to all of the partici-
pants in the Model Comparison Seminar of the Conference on
Econometrics and Mathematical Economics sponsored jointly by
the National Bureau of Economic Research and the National
Science Foundation.  Responses were received from F. Gerard
Adams (Wharton Econometric Forecasting Associates), Keith
Carlson (Federal Reserve Bank of St. Louis), Gregory Chow
(Princeton University), Otto Eckstein (Data Resources, Inc.),
Ray C. Fair (Yale University), Gary Fromm (the Brookings
Model), and Albert Hirsch (Bureau of Economic Analysis, U.S.
Department of Commerce).

[2]These responses are either direct quotations or a very
close paraphrase of the survey response.  Not surprisingly,
the responses are fairly terse but they do reflect differing
points of view and emphasis.  The purpose of the text is to
organize and amplify the responses.

[3]For a discussion of the principal components approach
see Dhrymes (1970), or McCarthy (1972).

[4]On this point, see McCarthy (1972), Chapter 4.

REFERENCES

Anderson, L., and Carlson, K. M., The Saint Louis Model Revisited, in: Klein, L. R., and Burmeister, E. (eds.), Econometric Model Performance, (University of Pennsylvania Press, Philadelphia, 1976).

Ando, A., The MPS Model: Its Theoretical Foundations, Mimeograph, Department of Economics, University of Pennsylvania, (1980).

Christ, C. F., Judging the Performance of Econometric Models of the U.S. Economy, in: Klein, L. R., and Burmeister, E. (eds.), Econometric Model Performance, (University of Pennsylvania Press, Philadelphia, 1976).

Cooper, R. L., The Predictive Performance of Quarterly Econometric Models of the United States, in: Hickman, B. G. (ed.), Econometric Models of Cyclical Behavior (Columbia University Press, New York, 1972).

Dennison, E. F., Why Growth Rates Differ (The Brookings Institution, Washington, 1970).

Dhrymes, P. J., Econometrics: Statistical Foundations and Applications (Harper and Row, New York, 1970).

Duesenberry, J. S., Fromm, G., Klein, L. R., and Kuh, E. (eds.), The Brookings Quarterly Econometric Model of the United States (Rand McNally-North Holland, Chicago, 1965).

Fair, R. C., An Evaluation of a Short-Run Forecasting Model, in: Klein, L. R., and Burmeister, E. (eds.), Econometric Model Performance (University of Pennsylvania Press, Philadelphia, 1976).

Fisher, F. M., Dynamic Structure and Estimation in Economy Wide Econometric Models, in: Duesenberry, et. al. (eds.), The Brookings Quarterly Econometric Model of the United States (Rand McNally-North Holland, Chicago, 1965).

Fromm, G., Implications to and from Economic Theory in Models of Complex Systems, American Journal of Agricultural Economics, 55 (1973) 259-271.

Fromm, G., and Klein, L. R., Scale of Macro-Econometric Models and Accuracy of Forecasting, this volume.

Fromm, G. and Schink, G., Aggregation and Econometric Models, International Economic Review, 14 (1973) 1-32.

Haitovsky, Y., Treyz, G., and Su, V., Forecasts with Quarterly Macroeconometric Models, (National Bureau of Economic Research, New York, 1974).

Hickman, B. G., and Coen, R. M., An Annual Growth Model of the U.S. Economy, (North-Holland, Amsterdam, 1976).

Hirsch, A. A., Grimm, B. T., and Narasimham, G. V. L., Some Multiplier and Error Characteristics of the BEA Quarterly Model, in: Klein, L. R., and Burmeister, E. (eds.), Econometric Model Performance (University of Pennsylvania, Philadelphia, 1976).

Howrey, E. P., Klein, L. R., and McCarthy, M. D., Notes on Testing the Predictive Performance of Econometric Models, in: Klein, L. R., and Burmeister, E. (eds.), Econometric Model Performance (University of Pennsylvania, Philadelphia, 1976).

Jorgensen, D. W., Anticipations and Investment Behavior, in Duesenberry, J. S., et. al. (eds.), The Brookings Quarterly Econometric Model of the United States (Rand McNally-North Holland, Chicago, 1965).

Klein, L. R., and Burmeister, E., (eds.), Econometric Model Performance (University of Pennsylvania Press, Philadelphia, 1976).

Klein, L. R., Economic Fluctuations in the United States (University of Chicago Press, Chicago, 1950).

Klein, L. R., Economic Theoretic Restrictions in Econometrics, in: Symposium on the Criteria for Evaluating the Reliability of Macro-Econometric Models (IBM Scientific Center, Pisa, Italy, 1980).

Laffer, A. B., and Ranson, R. D., A Formal Model of the Economy for the Office of Management and Budget (unpublished, 1971).

Lucas, R. E., Econometric Policy Evaluation: A Critique, in: Brunner, K., and Miltzer, A. (eds.), The Phillips Curve and Labor Markets (North-Holland, Amsterdam, 1976).

McCarthy, M. D., The Wharton Quarterly Econometric Model of the United States (Economic Research Unit, University of Pennsylvania, Philadelphia, 1972).

McNees, S. K., An Accuracy Analysis of Macroeconometric Models (Mimeograph, Federal Reserve Bank of Boston, 1978).

Morganstern, O., On the Accuracy of Economic Observations (Princeton University Press, Princeton, 1963).

Orcutt, G. H., Greenberger, M., and Rivlin, A., Micro Analysis of Socioeconomic Systems: A Simulation Study (Harper and Row, New York, 1961).

Phelps, E. S., et. al., Money Wage Dynamics and Labor Market Equilibrium, in: Phelps, E. S. (ed.), Microeconomic Foundations of Employment and Inflation Theory (Norton, New York, 1970).

Pollak, R. A., Habit Formation and Dynamic Demand Functions, Journal of Political Economy, 78 (1970) 745-763.

Prothero, D. L., and Wallis, K. F., Modelling Macro-economic Time Series, Journal of the Royal Statistical Society, 139A (1976) 486-468.

Zellner, A., and Palm, F., Time Series Analysis and Simultaneous Equation Econometric Models, Journal of Economics, 2 (1974) 17-53.

LARGE-SCALE MACRO-ECONOMETRIC MODELS
J. Kmenta, J.B. Ramsey (editors)
© North-Holland Publishing Company, 1981

## PERSPECTIVES ON THE ACCURACY OF
## MACRO-ECONOMETRIC FORECASTING MODELS

Harold T. Shapiro*
David M. Garman**

*Professor of Economics and Public Policy, The University of
    Michigan, Ann Arbor
**Research Assistant, Research Seminar in Quantitative
    Economics, The University of Michigan, Ann Arbor

## I.  Introduction

Times of economic crisis have always (since Joseph in Egypt)
generated considerable - though often transient - interest in
the potential value of business cycle theories (metaphysical
and otherwise) as guides to the short-run evolution of the
economy.  The modern (20th Century) evolution of economic
forecasting has, in fact, a symbiotic relationship both to the
development of theories designed to explain fluctuations in
macroeconomic activity and to the generation of an ever-broader
spectrum of high-quality data on economic activity.  It is,
therefore, useful to consider forecasts from large-scale
structural macroeconometric models, as part of a longer term
and continuing effort to perceive the future course of the
economy.  Other techniques preceded them, coexist with them,
interact with them, and will perhaps survive them.  On the eve
of the systematic application of modern statistical analysis
to macroeconomic forecasting, Marshall seems to have anticipated
both the "romance" and frustration of macroeconomic forecasting.

> It is conceivable that a body of able disinterested
> men, with a wide range of business knowledge, may
> ultimately be able to issue predictions of trade storm
> and trade weather generally, that might have an
> appreciable effect in rendering the employment of
> industry more steady and continuous.[1]

The potential value of "accurate" macroeconomic forecasts in
helping to stabilize macroeconomic activity has continued to

attract many new disciples for macroeconomic forecasting, while
its failure to realize adequately this potential has always
permitted the survival of skeptics.  Marshall himself seems to
have remained rather skeptical.  One half century later, the
following comments by Moore (1969) reflect the continuing
skepticism and hope on these matters.

> Economic statisticians do not enjoy an untarnished
> reputation for accurate forecasting - (yet) we have
> also had our share of successes - (we must) try to
> arrive at a balanced appraisal.

The intervening period, however, witnessed an unusual
amount of effort devoted explicitly to improving the ability
to anticipate the short-run evolution of an economy.  There
have been substantial investments in generation of economic
data, in development of economic theory and formulation of
appropriate statistical procedures.  As a result of these
efforts, it is widely perceived that much more is now understood about economic environments.  As economists, we believe
that the capacity to understand (rationalize?) developments in
the economy is vastly improved, but we remain much more skeptical about the ability to anticipate future developments -
even in the short-run.  This skepticism is, moreover, supported
by a well-documented contemporary record of faulty predictions
that may have led, at times, to the selection of ill-advised
policies in both the public and private sectors.  Two of the
more "celebrated" errors were the prediction of a post World
War II recession and the failure to anticipate the more recent
concurrence of accelerating inflation with slowing real growth
rates.[2]  In the interim, less dramatic errors and some major
successes mark the economic forecaster's record.  Interest in
economic forecasting, however, has remained intense as the
capacity to anticipate economic developments is critical to
improving economic decision making.  Further, in a market
economy, wide-spread interest in regular business forecasting
is a natural development, as implicit in many market transactions are forecasts of future possibilities - possibilities
which do not seem dominated by one or two individuals or
institutions.  Indeed, as long as public and private agents

must make decisions that require judgement as to the future of economic events, forecasts will not only continue to be made, but acted upon.

Considered as a branch of econometrics, the broad purpose of macroeconometric models is to improve decision making in the context of an uncertain environment. Economic forecasts, whether generated by these models or otherwise, are never perfect. There is always either some error or some relevant aspect of reality they do not address, or both. It should be understood that econometric models, even structural econometric models, are simplified images of the "true" economy that highlight certain aggregate relationships for generating useful insights into the possible evolution of the economy. In constructing such macroeconometric models, we are always choosing among alternative approximations. The exact nature of these approximations will depend principally on the overall structure of the economy, the intended use of the model, the availability of data and the stability of particular relationships. Further, it is important to note that the available data sample is small relative to the variety of events that would have important impacts on the economy. It will remain true that these models will normally be in a stage of transition as they are adapted to changing circumstances and interests. Their worth to decision makers hinges on whether the "core of stability" that characterizes macroeconometric models is sufficient to provide useful information through the ever-changing circumstances that characterize any economy.

Quite aside from these general considerations, existing structural macroeconometric models have certain well-documented shortcomings (McNees (1976A, (1976B), Zarnowitz (1978)). The failure of existing models, for example, to properly articulate the role of wealth or the impact of the government's budget constraint has been widely noted (e.g., Christ (1975)) and obviously places limits on the uses of such models. Similarly, the continuing difficulty of explaining, within the context of these models, changes in labor force participation leaves considerable margin for improvement in the specification of their structures and  the quality of their forecasts.  It is, therefore, quite clear that in their current form, the output from these models is inadequate for certain highly important economic policy decisions.  It is equally clear, however, that their increasingly wide-spread acceptance and use in certain important contexts may be considered prima facie evidence of their current value.[3]

The critical question is whether these models, as forecasting tools, can play a significant or increasingly significant role in improving decision making on relevant matters of economic policy.  That is, we would like to know not only whether they have had an impact (i.e., affected decisions) but whether higher quality decisions resulted from this interaction.  These questions are difficult to answer since the available evidence consists of a series of forecasts, decisions, and associated outcomes that are connected in a complex and often uncertain fashion and are themselves the result of a wide spectrum of important factors which are difficult to disentangle properly.  Furthermore, the environment within which forecasts have been generated has changed significantly over time (e.g., ability to employ gradually improving data bases and statistical procedures) making inter-temporal comparisons somewhat hazardous.  Despite these difficulties, this paper will attempt to provide some perspectives on these matters.

It should also be borne in mind throughout that the appropriate criteria for measuring the "success" of a macroeconometric model and/or the forecasts that it helps generate will depend on the particular use that is anticipated for the output.  Simply put, evaluation is problem-dependent.  Further, the impact of a particular model or procedure may not be related solely to its accuracy but, for example, to its accessability and comprehensability to decision makers.  Undoubtedly, however, accuracy remains the key measure.

Given current forecasting technologies in the area of economic policy, we must still accept the probability of being seriously wrong a good deal (20 percent?) of the time. Required accuracy, however, is a relative matter.  In order to

establish a useful standard of accuracy in any given circum-
stance the impact of a forecast error must be clearly articulated. The implication of a $10 billion error in forecasting
GNP may be quite different for the decision makers in an individual firm vis a vis those charged with formulating aggregate
economic policy. The idea of accuracy is given meaning only
by placing it in the context of some decision. For those that
must take action, forecasts are a means of decreasing uncertainty which is their real value. For economists, forecasts
also help us choose between alternative theories and statistical procedures, but this is a distinctly different benefit.
Evaluations of forecasts may be quite different for decision
makers vis a vis those interested in "hypothesis testing"
(searching?). A good example is the discussion of the comparative forecasting performance of macroeconometric models in
ex ante and ex post modes. Ex post forecasting is of little
direct interest to the decision maker, but is a critical component of model evaluation for economists and econometric model
builders.

Although it is clear that use of structural macroeconometric models and their forecasts has steadily increased in
the last three decades, they remain only one of the important
techniques used by forecasters in industry and government. Informal GNP models, Input/Output models, leading indicators,
autoregressive models, and anticipation surveys, remain important alternative procedures for generating ex ante forecasts.
It is, difficult to assess to what extent the relative importance of structural macroeconometric models has changed in the
last decade since most forecasters either directly or indirectly
now use a number of different techniques in combination. The
existing evidence seems to indicate that each of these techniques does, at times, yield some additional independent information. Given the nature of the available record, the failures
and successes in anticipating the future evolution of the
economy cannot always be easily attributed to one particular
technique.[4]

In assessing the contribution of large-scale structural

econometric models, the search for a standard of measurement
normally focuses on alternative, possibly less costly, techniques.  We should recognize at the outset, however, that
adequate time series data on well-defined consistent ex ante
forecasts simply do not yet exist.  The evidence available
consists of small samples characterized by rather complex correlation structures which limit the useful application of
available formal statistical inference procedures.  Appraisals,
therefore, rely on descriptive measures and, while judgements
from this evidence may be instructive, they are limited.  In
particular, as noted below, evaluation of contemporary ex ante
macroeconometric forecasts from large scale models relative to
other alternatives is quite sensitive to the nature of the
forecast period (initial conditions).  Given these problems,
the existing record is not sufficient to support strong conclusions.  Nevertheless some key issues can certainly be clarified and this is the aim of our paper.

    In order to provide an appropriate perspective for evalu-
ating the "successes" of these models, we begin with some observations on the "successes" of alternative techniques.  Our
attention focuses on efforts in the United States and on ex
ante forecasts of the indicators of national economic activity.[5,6]  In concentrating on ex ante forecasts we must,
given the procedures employed by "practitioners", often deal
with the output of "models" that are not completely and objectively specified.[7]  Even the ex ante forecasts generated from
structural econometric models involve the use of judgement and
intuition, often in a critical role.  These elements, however,
are not often as carefully and completely specified as other
inputs.  Despite these reservations it is the ex ante forecasts
that are critical for decision making and these forecasts do
yield insights into how effectively particular sets of procedures are using available information.

    In the post World War II era, the continuing work of
Victor Zarnowitz and his colleagues at the NBER have provided
a continuing summary record of the ex ante forecasting "success"
of a wide variety of techniques.[8]  This work serves to provide

a convenient metric to any assessment of the forecasting performance of large-scale structural macroeconometric models.
There are, however, some even earlier less well-known efforts
at systematic economic forecasting that deserve consideration
in the current context. We turn briefly to this record.

II. The Early Record

In addition to his pioneering work in the development of
economic theory, W. S. Jevons had a strong interest in the
collection and analysis of economic data. Moreover, he seems
to have had an active interest in marketing information about
the state of the economy. The last page of his 1863 pamphlet
on the value of gold advertises The Merchants' Atlas and Handbook of Commercial Fluctuations, which he said was in progress.
Apparently, Jevon's proposed handbook did not receive an over-
whelming response as it never got off the ground.

A contemporary of Jevon's, an Ohio farmer by the name of
Samuel Benner, may have been the first of regular forecasters
in the U.S. From 1876 to 1907, he published sixteen editions
of Benner's Prophecies of Future Ups and Downs in Prices which
was revealingly subtitled, "What years to make money on pig-
iron, hogs, corn and provisions." Benner plotted the mentioned
series and noticed regularities in their fluctuations. The
generation of these regular fluctuations he thought to be due
to some regular, but unexplained, meterological cycles. From
his analysis, Benner formulated the "Cast Iron Rule" that "one
extreme invariably follows another." His predictions were
based on a simple univariate analysis of the past regularities
in a particular economic time series.

The twenty years following Benner's last edition was a
boom period for forecasting. In 1907 there was only one
commercial agency doing business forecasting but it was just
beginning and not well known. By 1927, there were more than
a half dozen forecasters with a national clientel and a large
number of businesses had established internal groups to assess
the business outlook. It can be noted that in 1927 five of
the large commercial forecasting services had combined

subscription lists of around 35,000.  Many others during this
period received forecasts through various business journals or
as an offshoot of various stock market forecasting services.
Moreover, scholarly associations were not immune to the forecasting fever of the 20's.  Both the American Statistical
Association and the American Economic Association held annual
sessions on the economic outlook and on improving the collection and analysis of economic data.

The first of these early forecasting services, the Babson
Statistical Organization, was begun by Roger Babson in 1904
and began forecasting in 1907.  Babson began by analyzing
Benner's series in order to develop an index of economic activity.  When one of his former professors at M.I.T. drew a
normal line through the index and suggested to him that Newton's
Law of Action and Reaction might apply to economics, Babson
adopted and marketed the idea.  A more general index was formed
by scaling and weighting twelve series[9] and a line of "normal"
business activity superimposed.  The summary plot of this was
called the Babsonchart, and served both as an index of economic conditions and as a forecasting device.  Forecasts were
based on the notion that over the cycle, the areas above and
below the normal line must be equal.  The length and intensity
of a depression was said to be equal to the length and intensity of the preceding "over-expansion."

The next of these forecasting services, the Brookmire
Economic Chart Company, began in ]911.  Brookmire believed
that early indication of changes in business activity could be
gained from certain business and financial series.  By looking
at correlations over various time lags of a number of series,
he formed three indicators that tended to move in a particular
sequence:  1) an index of bank credit, 2) a speculative index
(equity prices), 3) an index of general business activity.
The expected relationship was that the index of bank credit led
the speculative index by several months and that a turn in the
speculative index correctly anticipated changes in the direction of the general business activity index.  These three indexes were marketed as the U.S. Barometer Chart and were used

to make forecasts of general business conditions. To our
knowledge, Brookmire was the first forecaster to study correlations across economic time series in order to isolate systematic lead/lag relationships between various aspects of economic
activity. Although there was some initial work done using
spectral methods of analysis for business cycle forecasting
(Moore (1914)), no regular forecasts were developed from these
studies.

Another notable forecasting service, the Harvard Economic
Service, began after the Harvard University Committee on
Economic Research commissioned Professor Warren M. Persons to
do research on forecasting. In 1918 and 1919, Professor
Persons investigated the possibility that there was a regular
sequence of economic events that could be used as the basis
for short-term forecasting. The resulting Harvard ABC index,
in most essential respects, was the same as the first Brook-
more index. Forecasts of general business conditions were
based on "leading" movements in certain indices of banking
and stock market activity, although forecasts were modified in
light of special factors or a close resemblance of the current
to a particular historical situation. To disseminate the
forecasts, as well as other statistics and current research,
the Review of Economic Statistics and the Weekly Letter were
begun. Although changes were constantly being made and the
forecasts were considered an expression of the research,
Harvard's poor performance in late 1929 and the early 1930's
caused it to be one of the first of the large services to
cease forecasting.

These groups were the early leaders in developing more
systematic methods for generating economic forecasts. Their
initial methods were adopted and, in time, supplemented and
expanded upon by other forecasting services such as Moody's
Investor Services, Standard Statistics Company and the National
City Bank of New York, as well as important research groups -
especially the National Bureau for Economic Research (NBER).

Another famous forecaster of this period was Irving
Fisher. From 1911-1920, he published an annual forecast in

the American Economic Review based on his equation of exchange.
In these articles  he analyzed the course of the money supply
(M) and velocity (V), charted their paths, and gave his views
of the implied outlook for business.  Fisher, however, was
"surprised" by the great depression.  He failed to forecast
the downturn or recognize the severity of the depression after
the downturn had occurred.  He then ceased to publish any
further forecasts.  During the 1930 ASA meetings, Fisher went
to some length to explain that his forecasts were, of course,
conditional on the assumption of no drastic changes in M and/or
V!  Perhaps we could consider the Fisher model to be the first
macroeconometric forecasting model.  Although no estimated
parameters were involved the issue of "stability" of relationships has continued as a dominant theme in assessing the forecasting potential of macroeconometric models.

    The year 1929 represented a cyclical peak in the activity
and influence of these forecasters.  Their widespread failure
to anticipate the Depression drove many out of the forecasting
business - among them both Fisher and Harvard Economic Service.
As might be expected, the survival rate was highest among those
services who did not depend solely on revenue from forecasting.
Thus, while the Harvard Economic Service folded quickly because of its poor 1929-30 record, National City Bank could
continue in spite of an equally poor performance.  In fact,
during the decade of the Great Depression, banks were the
leading source of business forecasts and their efforts provide the longest uninterrupted forecast records.  Moody's and
Standard (eventually continuing as Standard and Poors) also
provided services other than forecasting and were able to
shift emphasis away from the forecasting service itself.
Babson provided other services, but was also able to claim,
unlike the others, that their forecast had given advanced
warning of the downturn.  Babson's penchant for predicting a
downturn as soon as business seemed to have recovered from the
last drop caused him to become pessimistic well ahead of this
downturn - and others, both realized and not realized.

    Efforts to evaluate the forecasting performance of these

early forecasters are limited by the qualitative nature of
many of their forecasts. Consequently, utilization of many of
the current "standard" evaluation techniques is not always
possible. Proceeding with evaluation at all requires that, to
some extent, subjective judgments be made. The first major
evaluation of these forecasts was conducted by Garfield Cox
(1930). Cox selected six forecasters that made predictions on
a regular basis for most of the period from November, 1818
until December, 1929. Representative excerpts were taken from
the forecasts of each service for each month. Two methods of
evaluation were used; first, to test for the general adequacy
of the forecast and second, to test the adequacy of turning point forecasts.

For the first test each month's forecast from each forecaster was scored for "definiteness" on a 1/4, 1/2, 3/4, 1
scale and for "correctness" on a -1, -3/4, ... 3/4, 1 scale.
Forecast adequacy was taken to be the product of these two
scores. Monthly adequacy scores were averaged both across and
within services so that comparisons could be made for particular periods of time or by forecasting service. The main results are summarized in Tables 1 and 2.

Table 1

Forecast Accuracy Scores by Forecast Service
(Maximum Score = 1.0)

| Forecast Service | Adequacy Score |
|------------------|----------------|
| Standard | .54 |
| Babson | .45 |
| Brookmire | .31 |
| Harvard | .31 |
| National City Bank | .23 |
| Moody | .21 |
| Average (1918-1929) | .34 |

Table 2

Forecast Accuracy Scores by Year of Forecast
(Average of Six Services, Maximum Score = 1.0)

| Year | Score |
|------|-------|
| 1919 | .27 |
| 1920 | .37 |
| 1921 | .48 |
| 1922 | .53 |
| 1923 | .10 |
| 1924 | .30 |
| 1925 | .55 |
| 1926 | .29 |
| 1927 | .18 |
| 1928 | .43 |
| 1929 | .11 |

In order to provide both a benchmark and metric with
which to interpret these results, we constructed a number of
naive models (based on the Federal Reserve index of industrial
production) that generated forecasts over a six month forecast
horizon.  These forecasts were then scored in a manner similar
to that described above.  The results strongly suggest that a
great deal of the implied forecasting ability of these early
services was due to their ability to extrapolate recent trends
and even then in a rather naive way.  More than two-thirds of
the "adequacy" scores achieved above are due to the continua-
tion of very simple recent trends.  Further, given that business cycle peaks occurred in early 1920, 1923, 1927, and 1929,
it is immediately clear that these services seemed to have done
poorest at the upper turning points.

Another evaluation of the forecasts of this period was
done by Andrew and Flinn (1930) at the invitation of the
editors of the Journal of the American Statistical Association
for the 1930 meeting of the Association.  The authors considered
yearly forecasts by eleven forecasters made during November
and December of 1924 to 1929.  Brief quotations representing
the forecast of the level and movement of wholesale prices,
short-term money rates, auto production, stock prices, and

building construction were scored on a 1, 1/2, 0, -1/2, -1
scale. Results were similar to those of Cox with an average
score over all forecasters of 0.39. It was found that the
most successful forecasts were for money rates, commodity
prices and auto production. The poorest results were for
equity prices.

Cox (1930) also specifically tested the capacity of these
forecasting techniques to predict turning points. The major
turning points were selected for the 1918-1929 period and the
forecasting services were scored from the point in time when
the first of the services correctly anticipated the turn until
just after the turn.[10] Each month each service was scored for
timing and amplitude and recognition. Scores were averaged
and compared between services over business cycle turning
points. Cox interpreted his results as showing some modest
ability to generate forecasts better than those from "no
change" or "naive extrapolation" methods. Similarly, Andrew
and Flinn's (1930) ratings for specific turning points revealed a very modest amount of forecasting success at these
crucial moments.

To develop a more useful perspective on the ability of
these forecasters to recognize turning points, the Cox scores
can be translated into the type of turning point scores used
by Zarnowitz (1967) and Moore (1969) in analyzing forecasts
generated in the 1950's through the mid-1960's.[11] Zarnowitz
and Moore applied their turning point analysis to one-year-
ahead annual forecasts. Generally these were made in the
fourth quarter for the year ahead. Exact comparison with the
Cox results is not possible because early forecasters used no
set time horizon. As an approximation, two assumptions were
tried. First, the forecast of each January was assumed to
apply to the next twelve months and scored for turning points.
Second, the forecasts of each January and July were assumed to
apply to the next six months and scored for turning points.
Further, the index of economic activity being predicted differed from the Industrial Production index (IP) and GNP figures
that occupied Zarnowitz and Moore's attention. Nevertheless,

the comparison is interesting

|  | Early Forecasters (1918-1929) | | Zarnowitz-Moore Groups (1947-1965) | |
|---|---|---|---|---|
|  | 6 mo. horizon | 12 mo. horizon | 12 mo. horizon | |
|  | Index of "Business" Activity | | $GNP^{12}$ | IP |
| Percent Observed Turning Points Missed | 55.6 | 55.3 | 25.0 | 17.6 |
| Percent of Predicted Turns that were False | 39.4 | 10.5 | 7.0 | 33.3 |

On the basis of these statistics, the Zarnowitz/Moore group certainly demonstrates some considerable improvement over earlier efforts. However, considering the lack of information of comparable quality, the framework now provided by various macro theories and the level of statistical analysis, the performance of the "Early Forecasters" is, perhaps, better than might be expected. The greatest problem for both groups of forecasters was predicting downturns, but the average decline in industrial production from the peak to the trough was 19% in the early period and only 9% in the latter. Thus, the "target" was much smaller in the later years. In addition, the relative frequency of turning points also declined somewhat in the later period. Finally, quite different secular movements in prices in the earlier period makes relative accuracy of predicting current dollar GNP a rather poor standard of comparison.

The year 1929 was the global peak in the influence of the then existing methods of business forecasting. During the 30's, skepticism about the old methods was prevalent and by the 1940's new types of alternatives appeared - among them the large-scale structural econometric model.

An exception to this declining trend in the generation of short-term macroeconomic forecasts was the founding of the Institute of Applied Econometrics by Charles F. Roos in 1938 (Roos [1957]). The formation of this institute was encouraged by Mr. Roos' successful prediction of the 1937 recession. The initial intent of the new institute was to produce short-term

(three to nine months) forecasts of aggregate economic activity
with emphasis on isolating, in advance, business cycle turning
points.  A leading indicator approach was used which centered
on an analysis of new orders, growth in the money supply and
business spending.  In 1943 the name of the institute was
changed to the Econometric Institute and their interests shifted to longer term forecasting.  The institute's most influen-
tial long-term forecast was published in 1949 as The General
Outlook for the American Economy 1949-1960, a forecast which
ran counter to a good deal of business pessimism at the time.

With the post World War II economic expansion, interest
in economic forecasting quickly revived, but the structural
econometric model and other procedures that could take fuller
advantage of the rapid new developments in statistical analysis, the availability of better economic data and new more
advanced computational facilities, were now effective competitors for the attention of decision makers.  Throughout the
1930's and 1940's, the United States Department of Agriculture
continued to issue forecasts for selected macroeconomic aggregates.  These were largely judmental forecasts appropriately
constrained by the National Income Account identities, to be
used as an aid in farm planning.  The forecast horizon was
generally one year or less.  Baker and Paarlberg (1952A, 1952B)
and Cavin (1952), have provided an evaluation of these efforts
with respect to their forecast accuracy.  These forecasts did
marginally better than single trend line extrapolations, but
displayed no capacity to anticipate turning points in industrial production or total demand.  Interestingly the weakest
forecasts were in the area of farm prices.

III.  The Contemporary Record

As more high-quality information on the economy became
available, and as the structure of macroeconometric theory took
greater root, researchers began to take a greater interest in
structural models.  An initial model was formulated by Frisch
(1933), followed by the famous efforts of Tinbergen (1937,
1939) and Klein (1950).  Regular forecasts from these structural models began with forecasts for the Netherlands from

Tinbergen's model in the 1940's with <u>regular</u> U.S. forecasts
not appearing until the early 1950's.  Controversy over the
use of macroeconometric forecasts, however, began sooner.
In the United States it began with one of the first forecasts
issued, the so-called Hagen-Kirkpatrick forecast for the
immediate post-World War II period.

For the post-World War II era, there has been a continuous series of studies considering the record of economic
forecasters (e.g., Zarnowitz (1962, 1976, 1978)).  Interest
has centered not only on the overall performance of economic
forecasters, but on relative performance of various techniques.
The record of macroeconometric model forecasts has been given
special attention as these represented a new entry in the
"field."  As noted above, the controversy started immediately.
From the beginning the controversy centered on the issue of
the stability of the estimated relationships forming the
foundation of the structural models.  This issue motivated the
early exchange between Klein (1946) and Woytinsky (1947) in
the immediate post World War II years and has yet to be fully
resolved.  That exchange centered on the stability of the
consumption function and the implication of its inherent
stability or volatility for the potential of econometric model
forecasts.  While the particular focus has certainly shifted
somewhat, the issue of stability remains at the heart of
discussions.  Despite interest in the relative performance of
various techniques, a limiting difficulty in assessing this
issue is that most forecasters, directly or indirectly, use a
combination of techniques.  "Judgmental" forecasters may use
outputs of econometric forecasts as inputs to their own considerations, and vise versa.  Thus improvement in the performance of economic forecasters must be attributed to the whole
spectrum of improved forecasting and data generation techniques
that have characterized the last three decades.

Perhaps the earliest evaluation of the forecasting
capacity of an econometric model was Christ's (1951) study of
predictions generated by the Klein model for the year 1948.
Christ (1956) also produced a similar evaluation of the fore-

casts generated by the Klein-Goldberger model for the years
1951 and 1952. These initial studies ought to have been quite
discouraging to model builders as they showed that very simple
naive models outperformed these two early econometric models
in most cases. A series of more contemporary studies (e.g.,
Cooper (1972), Cooper and Nelson (1975)) also seemed to find
that simple ARIMA models outperformed structural econometric
models for most variables. These studies, however, were based
on very small samples and often focussed on a single period
(one-quarter) forecast horizon. More recent studies, (e.g.,
Hirsch et al (1974)) covering a longer period of time reach
opposite conclusions and indicate that the superiority of
structural econometric model forecasts increases with the
length of the forecast horizon. Indeed, the most recent study
by Christ (1975) also finds that the ex post forecasts of the
well-known U.S. econometric forecasting models clearly outperform ARIMA models in the period studied (1956-1970). Although
we believe the weight of the evidence now supports this latter
conclusion, the time series available for testing such comparisons is, once again, not rich enough to reach final judgments.
All these studies do reveal that most structural econometric
models do not yet capture all the relevant time-series information on many of the endogenous variables. The structural
econometric models, of course, would seem to have an advantage
in dealing with non-linearities.

The most comprehensive record and evaluation of ex ante
economic forecasts in the post World War II period has been
created by Zarnowitz (1967, 1972, 1978) whose work covers both
econometric and non-econometric forecasts and provides a very
useful starting point for our considerations. With respect to
annual one-year ahead forecasts of current dollar GNP Zarnowitz
finds that:

a) forecast errors are now less than one percent of GNP
   and declining slowly (in percentage terms) over time

b) forecast errors are considerably smaller than those
   generated by simple naive models

   c) there is little systematic difference between the
      forecasting performance of econometric models and other
      <u>operational</u> procedures

   d) the record demonstrates very limited capacity of any
      of the techniques to detect reversals in the economy
      well in advance.  There is, however, a capacity to
      quickly recognize turns once they have begun.  The
      forecasts are generally late in recognizing periods
      of unusually rapid growth and even later in recogniz-
      ing slowdowns.[13]

   With respect to constant dollar GNP, a more modest record
exists in two respects.  First, there were few <u>ex</u> <u>ante</u> forecasts issued prior to the mid-1960's.  Second, as a percent of
the target, the forecast errors are somewhat larger.  In fact,
the forecasts of current dollar GNP have often "benefitted"
from the strong negative correlation observed between forecast
errors in predicting prices and constant dollar GNP.  Again,
the major errors occur at turning points, and there seems to
be little systematic difference in the performance of the
various operational techniques in this respect.

   The record that Zarnowitz studies with respect to quarterly
forecasts reveals very similar qualitative judgments.  Remark-
ably, the record available is derived almost exclusively from
the output of econometric models.  Forecasts of current dollar
GNP are superior to those for real GNP, but in both cases,
forecast errors rise steadily as the forecast horizons increase.
The correlation between predicted and actual changes is higher
for real GNP, but relative to size of actual changes, real GNP
errors are larger than current-dollar GNP errors.  Over the
first four quarters, forecast errors are, on average, about
the same as for annual forecasts.  Again, these forecasts,
outperform simple naive models.  In general, the worst forecasts are those generated by ARIMA models and naive models -
especially when the forecast horizon is more than on quarter.[14]
Interestingly, while the relative superiority of the econometric forecasts decreased beyond a one-year time horizon
during the 1960's, the reverse is true through most of the

1970's. The forecast record with respect to price inflation,
however, is not reassuring. In fact, the ex ante forecasts
tend to be little better than a projection of the most recently
observed rate of inflation.

In summary, Zarnowitz's results seem to indicate that
although steady progress is being made in capacity to predict
both current and constant dollar GNP, current ability to predict reversals in economic activity and to adequately anticipate new movements in the rate of inflation remains limited.[15]

For the period of the 1970's, the most careful record of
the ex ante forecasting performance of quarterly econometric
models has been presented by McNees (1976) who compares their
performance with the "forecast" produced by the ASA/NBER group.
McNees finds, as did Zarnowitz and Moore, that the timing of
the forecast release is quite important, with later forecasts
(later in the quarter and/or year) being somewhat more accurate. Also, consistent with the Zarnowitz results are findings
that forecast accuracy declines with lengthening horizon
(although not always dramatically, especially with respect to
forecast changes) and that, in general, forecasts of current
dollar GNP are relatively more accurate (as a percent of
actual) than real GNP. Again, this latter result is explained
by observed negative covariances in forecast errors for constant dollar GNP on the one hand and inflation rates on the
other. In the earlier post-war period, forecasters tended
to over-predict rates of inflation and underpredict growth
rates. In the 1970's the record is marked by the reverse
tendency. In addition, the available record does not enable
one to choose a "best" econometric model. Assessment of
relative performance of models depends on the variables of
interest, length of horizon, etc., and no model dominates
others in all respects. Finally, McNees finds that the
forecast of the ASA/NBER group is generally at the median of
the econometric model forecasts. This latter result is similar to Christ's (1975) finding in assessing the ex post
forecasts of these two groups.

The key question is on standards to be used in inter-

preting results achieved and displayed by McNees (1976).
Klein (1973) and Fromm and Klein (1976) and more recently
Fair (1978) have offered suggestions in this respect which
provide a useful starting point.  At the Twentieth Anniversary
Conference on the Economic Outlook at the University of
Michigan, Klein suggested the following as standards of accu-
racy:

   a) for GNP, less than one percent error in the level, and
      5 to 10 percent in the change

   b) for unemployment rates, less than one-half percentage
      point

   c) for aggregate price indices, less than one index point

   d) for short-term treasury bill rates, less than 100
      basis points.

Somewhat later an "ultimate" standard was suggested by Fromm
and Klein (1976) for contemporary econometric forecasts.  In
summarizing error statistics generated by ex post within
sample simulations of a set of the best known U.S. econometric
models they note:

> The error statistics for this group of simulations
> are about as low as we could expect to realize with
> "noisy" economic data.[16]

These standards for a forecast horizon of one year involve
errors of only 50 basis points in short-term interest rates,
one-half an index point on aggregate price deflators, and
somewhat less than one-half a percentage point on unemployment
rates.  The standards for GNP, however, remain at about one
percent of the level.  At the current time, the evidence
strongly suggests that these more stringent standards remain
aspirations only.  Ex post simulations of the same models
outside the sample period yield errors two to three times those
particular standards and as the authors note are "... just on
the borderline of being usable for policy application."[17]  In
fact, on the basis of the errors generated in the "out-of-
sample" simulations, all the models fail the earlier unemployment rate standard.  Over half fail the lower interest rate

standard, and most fail Klein's initial proposed standard for
inflation rates.  With respect to GNP, virtually all models
fail the one-percent benchmark beyond the first quarter.

In a more recent study Fair (1978) has proposed a method
both for deriving estimates of the overall uncertainty attached to an econometric model forecast and for decomposing
the expected error into its basic sources.[18]  Using successive
re-estimation and stochastic simulation of the model and a
number of important assumptions, Fair derives estimated standard errors of forecasts for his model (see Fair (1976)),
for the period 1978 to 1981.  The standard errors of forecast
for the key macroeconomic indicators 4 and 8 quarters out can
be summarized as follows:

|  | Forecast Horizon (1978.1) | |
|---|---|---|
|  | 4 Quarters | 8 Quarters[19] |
| Real GNP (percent of forecast mean) | 1.96 | 2.27 |
| GNP Deflator (percent of forecast mean) | 1.87 | 3.45 |
| Unemployment Rate (percentage points) | .82 | .71 |
| Bill Rate (percentage points) | 1.17 | 1.72 |

Although these estimates are derived from a particular model
at a given point in time, they do provide some useful overall
perspective.  Of the three sets of standards noted here, these
are the most forgiving (realistic?).

As has been documented elsewhere (e.g., Evans, Haitovsky
and Treyz (1972), Haitovsky, Treyz and Su (1974)), the ex post
forecasts of econometric models are inferior to the models'
(and their proprietors') ex ante forecasts.  It is useful,
therefore, to compare the McNees results with either of the
above standards.  In summary, such a comparison leads to the
following conclusions:

1) With respect to prices, unemployment rates and short-
   term interest rates, ex ante forecast errors fail all
   the proposed standards at forecast horizons of three
   and six quarters.

2) With respect to the level of current and constant dollar GNP, the standards are met at a time horizon of three quarters, but not at the six-quarter mark.[20]

3) As in the Zarnowitz results, current dollar GNP forecasts do better than their constant dollar counterparts.

4) If forecasts are evaluated in terms of predicted changes, GNP, unemployment rate, and interest rate forecasts all satisfy the first (more lenient) set of "level" standards proposed by Klein (1973), and, therefore, the "Fair" standards. However, the forecast errors for both current and constant dollar GNP fail - beyond the first quarter - to be between five and ten percent of actual changes.

5) Generally speaking, errors in predicting growth rates in GNP rise quite slowly over a six-quarter forecast horizon. This is especially true with respect to current dollar GNP predictions which benefit from negative correlations between forecast errors in real growth and inflation rates.

6) Forecasts of federal budget deficits are politically sensitive and easily may affect government policy. Unfortunately, the data presented by McNees (1976) indicates that the ex ante forecast errors in this "balancing item" were too large ($25 billion six quarters out) to be very useful.

Although ex ante forecasts of structural econometric models do not yet meet standards suggested by Klein, recent studies (e.g., Hirsch, et al (1974), Prothero and Wallis (1976), Christ (1975), Howrey et al (1974), Zarnowitz (1978)), indicate that these models, even in their ex post mode out-perform ARIMA models, at times by quite substantial margins. This is especially noticeable when the forecast horizon extends beyond one quarter. For one quarter horizon there is little difference between these alternative techniques.

The ability of econometric model forecasts to out-perform
"naive" alternatives represents a change from the early post
World War II days and must be attributed to a combination of
improved model-building techniques, improved data, and improved understanding of the economic system itself.  In this
latter respect econometric models have played a significant
role especially regarding our understanding of the dynamics
of the system.

On the other hand, it is important to note that forecasters who do not use econometric models - at least directly -
achieve ex ante forecasting records very similar to those
generated by the models.  These forecasters, however, generally
provide much less useful information on the nature of the
anticipated evolution of the economy with respect to components
of GNP and national income and their detailed quarterly movements.[21]  With the bias of model builders, we would also
state that these forecasts are in most cases conditional on
the readily available output of the econometric models.  There
is, of course, also some feedback in the other direction.

The finding that ex ante forecasts of econometric models
out-perform their ex post forecasts remains a concern to both
model builders and their "clients" (i.e., decision makers).
Possible explanations are many and no satisfactory resolution
of this issue has yet been achieved.  It is quite clear that
confidence of decision makers in predictions from econometric
models is a function of both ex ante and ex post forecasting
performance.  In either the ex ante or ex post modes, evaluation of relative performance of these models over the last
two or three decades is limited by the small sample of outcomes.  It is clear from the evidence that such evaluations
are dependent, in part, on the cyclical status of the economy.
At this juncture available evidence, therefore, permits only
partial judgments.  A similar observation holds regarding the
demonstrated advisability of combining various forecasting
techniques.  The optimal combination undoubtedly shifts over
time and seems to be, at least in part, a function of initial
conditions.

Finally, we should consider Leading Indicators and their capacity to assist forecasters (see Moore and Shiskin (1967), Hymans (1973), Vaccara and Zarnowitz (1978), Moore (1969, 1974), and Alexander and Stekler (1959)). This, after all, was the "first" technique, tracing back to the early years of the current century. How does it compare to forecasts generated by econometric models? Despite continued work leading indicators, even after careful filtering (to eliminate their chronic tendency to yield many false signals), have an effective forecast horizon that is very short. Although they outperform simple autoregressive schemes in predicting real GNP one quarter ahead and can provide, at times, useful additional information to econometric model forecasts, on the whole the evidence supports the superiority of econometric model forecasts.

The record of successes and failures of forecasts from large-scale structural econometric models has been widely noted and is largely understook at least by most practitioners. At this moment in time only provisional judgments are possible, not only with respect to the forecasting record but with respect to such issues as size, aggregation and identification. The "acceptance" of the output of econometric models by decision makers is heavily influenced by their demonstrated performance at certain crucial sensitive times. Standard error statistics do little to reveal this type of information. For example, the perceived quality of the advice generated from these models at times of changes in Presidential administrations may have long-ranging impacts not only on economic policy, but the willingness of decisions makers to rely on these models in the future. Despite some successes, therefore, humility once again suits us all and will serve us well.

Footnotes

[1] Marshall, A. (1923), p. 262.

[2] For an analysis of the forecast errors in the immediate post World War II period see Sapir (1949).

[3] The proportion of forecasts in the ASA/NBER survey that rely primarily on econometric models has risen from one-eighth to one-third in the last decade and almost two-thirds of this group now rely on such models in important respects.

[4] Provocative support on the desirability of combining different types of forecast techniques is provided by Granger and Newbold (1974, 1975).

[5] We have not located any systematic record with respect to the accuracy of economic forecasts in foreign countries in the post World War II era. Theil (1961, 1966) reported on the ex ante forecasting performance of an annual econometric model of the Dutch economy and compared this to the ex ante forecasts being generated in other Scandinavian countries using a variety of forecasting procedures. Sims (1967) has also reported on the ex ante forecasting performance of the Dutch Central Planning Bureau model in the period 1953-1963. The period covered was the decade of the 1950's and the early 1960's in the Dutch case, but only the early 1950's for the other countries. The forecast errors were considerably larger (in percentage terms) than those achieved by U.S. forecasters. However, even in the case of the Netherlands, forecasts from econometric models proved superior to simple extrapolation techniques by a considerable margin. In the case of turning point predictions, somewhat over 25 percent of economic re-versals were missed and about 40 percent of forecasted rever-sals were false signals. These latter results are not quite as good as the records of U.S. forecasters compiled by Zarnowitz (1967), but are based on a much smaller sample. In Britain the debate over the accuracy of econometric forecasts has been more acrimonious than informative. (See Kennedy (1969), Worswick (1975), Polyani (1973), Ash and Smythe (1973) and Ash (1975)).

[6]Although it is difficult to address the issue of forecast accuracy without simultaneously dealing with the size of models, the role of economic theory and the role of statistical inference, we leave all these matters to other conference papers and participants.  We merely note here that the number of estimated parameters relative to the number of observations is often high enough to eliminate the use of some statistical procedures and that the connection between parameters and behavior remains unresolved.  (See Koopmans (1950), Liu (1960) and Fisher (1965)).

[7]Howrey et al. (1978).

[8]Other important studies have been those of Christ (1956, 1975), Stekler (1970), Theil (1961, 1966), Fromm and Klein (1976), McNees (1976).

[9]Immigration, value of building permits, liabilities of business failures, FRB check transactions, a WPI, dollar value of exports and imports, foreign money rates, 4-6 month prime commercial paper rate value of crops, rail earnings, and an index of stock prices.

[10]Peaks:  March 1920, May 1923, March 1927, July 1929. Troughs:  March 1919, March 1921, July 1924, December 1927.

[11]Forecasts made by government, business and academic economists, with or without a macroeconometric model.

[12]In evaluating the forecasts of the Dutch Central Planning Bureau over the period 1953-1962, Theil (1966) reports that with respect to the volume of private production that 25 percent of the turning points were missed and 40 percent of the predicted turning points were false signals.

[13]Fels and Hinshaw (1968) found similar evidence in their study of the forecasts of eight "analyses" and the Federal Reserve Open Market Committee.

[14]Howrey, et al (1974) have demonstrated, in part, why ARIMA forecasts do relatively better with only a one-quarter forecast horizon.

[15]Zarnowitz also finds that a significant percent (1/3) of the forecast errors are what he terms "base errors", or errors due to inadequate preliminary data. Cole (1969) has provided a more detailed analysis of this phenomenon. An interesting article by Howrey (1978) outlines a general approach to the more efficient use of preliminary data in econometric forecasting that should decrease variance of forecast errors.

[16]Fromm and Klein (1976).

[17]Fromm and Klein (1976).

[18]The error terms in the model, the error from using estimated coefficients, the error in projecting exogenous variables, and the error for using a mis-specified model.

[19]Analogous results for a simple autoregressive model are 4.74 for real GNP, 6.20 for the GNP deflator, 2.19 for the unemployment rate, and 1.83 for the Bill rate.

[20]The capacity to meet these standards, at the 3 quarter mark reflects the relatively good performance of ex ante forecasts between 1970.3 and 1973.1, a steady period of expansion.

[21]Among the components of GNP, the econometric models generate their largest percentage errors with respect to relatively small magnitudes such as fixed investment and inventory investment. On the income side, the error in predicting profits is as large as that generated in predicting the much larger wage component. (See McNees (1976), Fromm and Klein (1975), and Zarnowitz (1978)).

## Bibliography

Alexander, Sidney S. and H. O. Stikler, "Forecasting Industrial Production - Leading Series Versus Autoregression," Journal of Political Economy 67 (Aug. 1959), 402-409.

Andrew, S. L. and H. M. Flinn, "Appraisal of Economic Forecasts," Journal of the American Statistical Association 25 (March 1930), 36-38.

Ash, J. C. K. and D. J. Smyth, "Who Forecasts the British Economy Best?," The Bankers' Magazine 216 (Oct. 1973), 153-159.

Babson, Roger W., Actions and Reactions (New York: Harper and Bros. Publishers, 1935).

Baker, John D. and Don Paarlberg, "Outlook Evaluation - Methods and Results," Agricultural Economics Research 4 (Oct. 1952A), 105-114.

_____, "How Accurate is Outlook," Journal of Farm Economics 34 (Nov. 1952B), 509-519.

Benner, Samuel, Benner's Prophecies of Future Ups and Downs in Prices (Cincinnati: R. Clark and Co., 1892).

Bratt, Elmer C., Business Cycles and Forecasting (Chicago: Business Publications, Inc., 1937).

_____, Business Cycles and Forecasting (Homewood, Ill.: Richard D. Irwin, Inc., 1961).

Brookmire, J. H., "Methods of Business Forecasting Based on Fundamental Statistics," American Economic Review 3 (March 1913), 43-58.

Cavin, James P., "Forecasting the Demand for Agricultural Products," Agricultural Economics Research 4 (July 1952), 65-76.

Christ, Carl F., "A Test of an Econometric Model for the United States, 1921-1947," in Conference on Business Cycles (New York: National Bureau of Economic Research, 1951).

_____, "Aggregate Econometric Models," <u>American Economic Review</u> 46 (June 1956), 385-408.

_____, "Judging the Performance of Econometric Models of the U.S. Economy," <u>International Economic Review</u> 16 (Feb. 1975), 54-74.

Cole, Rosanne, "Data Errors and Forecasting Accuracy," chapter 2 in Jacob Mincer (ed.), <u>Economic Forecasts and Expectations: Analysis of Forecasting Behavior and Performance</u> (New York: National Bureau of Economic Research, 1969).

Cooper, J. P. and C. R. Nelson, "The Ex Ante Prediction Performance of the St. Louis and FRB-MIT-PENN Econometric Models and Some Results on Composite Predictors," <u>Journal of Money, Credit and Banking</u> 7 (Feb. 1975), 1-32.

Cooper, Ronald L., "The Predictive Performance of Quarterly Econometric Models of the United States," in Bert Hickman (ed.), <u>Econometric Models of Cyclical Behavior</u> (New York: Columbia University Press, 1972).

Cox, Garfield V., <u>An Appraisal of American Business Forecasts</u>, Revised Edition (Chicago: University of Chicago Press, 1930).

Evans, M. K., Y. Haitovsky and G. Treyz, "An Analysis of the Forecasting Properties of U.S. Econometric Models," in Bert Hickman (ed.), <u>Econometric Models of Cyclical Behavior</u> (New York: Columbia University Press, 1972).

Fair, Ray C., <u>A Model of Macroeconomic Activity</u> (Cambridge: Ballinger Publishing Co., 1976).

_____, "Estimating the Expected Predictive Accuracy of Econometric Models," Cowles Foundation Discussion Paper No. 480, Jan. 17, 1978.

_____, "A Forecast from an Econometric Model and its Estimated Uncertainty," <u>Economic Outlook USA</u> 5 (Spring 1978), 19-21.

Fels, Rendigs and C. Elton Hinshaw, <u>Forecasting and Recognizing Business Cycle Turning Points</u> (New York: National Bureau of Economic Research, 1968).

Fisher, Franklin M., "On the Cost of Approximate Specification in Simultaneous Equation Systems," Econometrica 29
(April 1961), 139-170.

_____, "Dynamic Structure and Estimation in
Economy-wide Econometric Models," In J. S. Duesenberry et. al.
(eds.), The Brookings Quarterly Econometric Model of the United
States (Chicago: Rand McNally Co., 1965).

Fisher, Irving, "The Stock Market Panic in 1929," Journal
of the American Statistical Association 25 (March 1930),
93-96.

Frisch, Ragnar, "Propagation Problems and Impulse Problems
in Dynamic Economics," in Economic Essays in Honour of Gustav
Cassel (London: George Allen and Unwin, Ltd., 1933).

Fromm, Gary and Lawrence R. Klein, "The NBER/NSF Model
Comparison Seminar: An Analysis of Results," Annals of
Economic and Social Measurement 5 Winter 1976), 1-28.

Granger, C. W. J. and Paul Newbold, "Economic Forecasting"
The Athust's Viewpoint," in G. A. Rinton (ed.), Modelling the
Economy (London: Heinemann Educational Books, 1975).

Haitovsky, Yoel, George Treyz and Vincent Su, Forecasts
with Quarterly Macroeconometric Models, (New York: National
Bureau of Economic Research, 1974).

Hardy, Charles O. and Garfield V. Cox, Forecasting
Business Conditions (New York: The MacMillan Co., 1927).

Hirsch, Albert A., B. L. Grimm and G. V. L. Narasimhan,
"Some Multiplier and Error Characteristics of the BEA Quarterly
Model," International Economic Review 15 (Oct. 1974), 616-631.

Howrey, E. Philip, "The Use of Preliminary Data in
Econometric Forecasting," The Review of Economics and Statistics
60 (May 1978), 193-200).

Howrey, E. Philip, Lawrence R. Klein, and Michael D.
McCarthy, "Notes on Testing the Predictive Performance of
Econometric Models," International Economic Review 15 (June
1974), 366-383.

Hymans, Saul H., "On the Use of Leading Indicators to Predict Cyclical Turning Points," Brookings Papers on Economic Activity 1973:2, 339-375.

Kennedy, M. C., "How Well Does the National Institute Forecast?," National Institute Economic Review (Nov. 1969), 40-52.

Klein, Lawrence R., "A Post-Mortem on Transition Predictions of National Product," Journal of Political Economy 54 (Aug. 1946), 289-308.

_____, Economic Fluctuations in the United States, 1921-1941, Cowles Commission Monograph No. 11 (New York:  John Wiley and Sons, Inc., 1950).

_____, "The Precision of Econometric Prediction," in The Economic Outlook for 1973 (Ann Arbor, Mi.:  Research Seminar in Quantitative Economics, 1973).

Klein, L. R., E. P. Howrey, M. D. McCarthy, and G. R. Schink, "The Practice of Macroeconometric Model Building and its Rationale," Paper presented to the NSF Conference on Macro-Econometric Forecasting Models at the University of Michigan, October 26, 1978.

Koopmans, T. C. (ed.), Statistical Inference in Dynamic Economic Models, (New York:  John Wiley and Sons, Inc., 1950).

Liu, L. C., "Underidentification, Structural Estimation, and Forecasting," Econometrica 28 (Oct. 1960), 855-865.

Marshall, Alfred, Money Credit and Commerce (London: MacMillan and Co. Ltd., 1923).

McNees, Stephen K., "The Forecasting Performance in the Early 1970's," New England Economic Review (July/August 1976A), 29-40.

_____, "An Evaluation of Economic Forecasts: Extention and Update," New England Economic Review (Sept./Oct. 1976B), 30-44.

Moore, Geoffrey H., "Forecasting Short-Term Economic Change," Journal of the American Statistical Association 64

(March 1969), 1-22.

_____, "Economic Indicator Analysis During 1969-1972," in P. A. David and M. W. Reder (eds.), Nations and Households in Economic Growth (New York:  Academic Press, 1974).

Moore, Geoffrey H. and Julius Shiskin, Indicators of Business Expansions and Contractions (New York:  National Bureau of Economic Research, 1967).

Moore, Henry L., Economic Cycles:  Their Law and Cause (New York:  The MacMillan Co., 1914).

Newbold, Paul and C. W. J. Granger, "Experience with Forecasting Univariate Time Series and the Combination of Forecasts," Journal of the Royal Statistical Society, Series A 137 (1974), 131-146.

Okun, Arthur, "A Review of Some Economic Forecasts for 1955-1957," Journal of Business (July 1959), 199-211.

_____, "On the Appraisal of Cyclical Turning-Point Predictions," Journal of Business (April 1960), 101-120.

Polyani, George, Short Term Forecasting:  A Case Study, Background Memorandum #4, (London:  Institute of Economic Affairs, 1973).

Prothero, D. L. and K. Z. Wallis, "Modelling Macroeconomic Time Series," Journal of the Royal Statistical Society, Series A 139 (1976), 468-486.

Roos, Charles F. "Dynamics of Economic Growth:  The American Economy, 1957-1975," The Econometric Institute, New York, 1957.

Sapir, Michael, "Review of Economic Forecasts for the Transition Period," in Studies in Income and Wealth, Vol. II (New York:  National Bureau of Economic Research, 1949).

Sims, Christopher A., "Evaluating Short-Term Macro-Economic Forecasts:  The Dutch Performance," Review of Economics and Statistics 49 (May 1967), 225-236.

Stekler, H. O. Economic Forecasting (New York: Praeger, 1970).

Theil, Henri, Economic Forecasts and Policy (Amsterdam: North-Holland Publishing Col, 1961).

_____, Applied Economic Forecasting (Chicago: Rand McNally and Co., 1966).

Tinbergen, Jan, An Econometric Approach to Business Cycle Problems (Paris: Hermann et Cic., 1937).

_____, Statistical Testing of Business Cycle Theories (Geneva: League of Nations, 1939).

Vaccara, Beatrice N. and Victor Zarnowitz, "Forecasting with the Index of Leading Indicators," National Bureau of Economic Research Working Paper 244, May 1978.

Worswick, G. D. N., "National Institute Experience with Econometric Models," in G. A. Renton (ed.), Modelling the Economy (London: Heinemann Educational Books, 1975).

Woytinsky, W. S., "What Was Wrong in Forecasts of Post-war Depression?," Journal of Political Economy LV (April 1947), 142-151.

Zarnowitz, Victor, An Appraisal of Short-Term Economic Forecast (New York: National Bureau of Economic Research, 1967).

_____, "Forecasting Economic Conditions: The Record and the Prospect," in V. Zarnowitz (ed.), The Business Cycle Today (New York: National Bureau of Economic Research, 1972).

_____, "On the Accuracy and Properties of Recent Macroeconomic Forecasts," American Economic Reveiw 68 (May 1978), 313-319.

LARGE-SCALE MACRO-ECONOMETRIC MODELS
J. Kmenta, J.B. Ramsey (editors)
© North-Holland Publishing Company, 1981

AN EVALUATION OF THE FORECASTING PERFORMANCE OF
MACRO ECONOMIC MODELS, WITH SPECIAL EMPHASIS ON MODEL SIZE

Harry H. Kelejian and Bruce Vavrichek

Department of Economics
University of Maryland
College Park, Maryland
U.S.A.

The purpose of this paper is twofold:
First, we develop a theoretical framework
within which it is meaningful to compare
the forecasting performance of economic
models of varying sizes.  Second, we
compare the forecasting performance of
some of the major existing econometric
models and relate this to model size.  As
an implication of our theoretical analysis
we demonstrate that the issue of forecasting
performance should be separated from model
validation.

## 1. INTRODUCTION

The purpose of this research is to investigate the relationship between model forecasting accuracy and size for a
spectrum of macro economic models.[1] We begin our analysis by
defining simultaneous equations models in terms of the underlying distribution theory.  Within this framework, many model
formulations are possible which relate various sets of endogenous and predetermined variables to each other.  Therefore,
models of different sizes with respect to the number of endogenous and predetermined variables may be considered to be consistent with each other in that they are consistent with the
underlying distribution theory.

The issue is then raised as to which model will best predict a particular endogenous variable.  Assume that predictions
are derived from the models' reduced form equations.  Assume
also that each of the models considered is correctly specified
in that it is consistent with the underlying distribution theory
Finally, assume that the parameters of the models are known
or have been consistently estimates with an "infinite" sample.
Then our results imply that the forecasting performance

of a given model with respect to a given endogenous variable
will relate to its size only because the number of predetermined
variables is important; the number of endogenous variables is
irrelevant.  Under these circumstances, our results suggest
that the value of a simultaneous equations model for forecasting purposes is of a computational nature.  Our results are
less clear if the model's parameters have been estimated in
terms of a finite sample.  The reason for this is that a correctly specified model whose parameters are estimated need not
"outpredict" an incorrectly specified model whose parameters
are also estimated.

    This somewhat paradoxical result suggests that models
should not be validated in terms of their forecasts.  Instead,
if forecasting accuracy is desired, models should be viewed
as forecasting instruments and evaluated as such.

    In a manner consistent with our theoretical presentation,
we analyze evidence relating model size to forecast accuracy by
considering the recent predictive performance of several major
macro econometric models.  Although our sample of forecasts is
small, it suggests the lack of an empirical relationship between model size and predictive performance.

## 2.  THE BASIC FRAMEWORK OF ANALYSIS

    For purposes of illustration, consider quarterly time
series models and let $S_t = (Z_{1t}, Z_{2t}, ...)$ be a set of values
at time t of variables that economic model builders may potentially be interested in, or may use in their models.[2]  It will
typically not be possible to predict with perfect accuracy the
future values of most of these variables.  This will be the
case for variables which are typically assumed by economic
model builders to be exogenous, such as temperature and rain-
fall, as well as for variables which are more directly
related to the economic system, such as GNP.  Therefore, at
least in a Bayesian sense, it is reasonable to assume that a
majority of the variables of $S_t$ are stochastic.  Denote this
subset of the elements by the vector $S_{1t}$; let the vector $S_{2t}$
denote the subset of variables of $S_t$ which are not stochastic.
Variables which fit into this second category are the "dummy"-

type variables, such as time trend variables, seasonal dummy variables and, perhaps, some control variables. Control variables can be thought of as policy variables, or as variables whose values are set by researchers in their experimental designs. Although perhaps not all, one would expect most policy variables to be stochastic because the alternative implies that policy variables are set entirely by open loop procedures, or that the values of the objective functions are deterministic.

Assume that the set of variables $S_t$ is such that the conditional distribution of $S_{1t}$ given $S_{2t}$ is stationary in the sense that its form and parameters do not change over time.[3] Assume also that there are many researchers, and that the i-th researcher selects two mutually exclusive sets of variables from $S_{1t}$, and designates the first set, containing $N_{1i}$ elements, as endogenous variables, and the second set, containing $N_{2i}$ elements, as predetermined variables. The predetermined variables may include lagged values of the variables which are designated to be endogenous, as well as variables which are designated to be exogenous. We do not assume that all model builders agree as to which variables are exogenous, nor do we assume that they focus their analysis on the same subset of variables from $S_{1t}$.

Let $Y_{it}$ and $X_{it}$ be, respectively, the $N_{1i} \times 1$ and $N_{2i} \times 1$ vectors of values at time t of the endogenous and predetermined variables so designated by the i-th model builder. Let $D_{it} = D_i(Y_{it}, X_{it})$ be any $p_i \times 1$ vector of known functions $(p_i \geq N_{1i})$ whose elements have finite first two moments conditional on $X_{it}$ and $S_{2t}$. The assumption that the first two conditional moments are finite is reasonable in that most variables considered by economists have finite range. Now let $A_i D_{it}$ be any $N_{1i}$ linear combinations of the elements of $D_{it}$, where the rank of the $N_{1i} \times N_{1i}$ matrix $\partial(A_i D_{it})/\partial Y'_{it}$ is $N_{1i}$ for all permissible values of the variables involved. Then for every such selection of linear combinations, $A_i D_{it}$, there exists a model which is consistent with the underlying distribution theory. To see the nature of this model we first note that[4]

$$(1) \quad E(A_i D_{it} | X_{it}, S_{2t}) = \int_{R_y} A_i D_{it} dF_y (Y_{it} | X_{it}, S_{2t})$$

$$= H_i (X_{it}, S_{2t})$$

where $F_y (Y_{it} | X_{it}, S_{2t})$ denotes the conditional distribution of $Y_{it}$ given $X_{it}$ and $S_{2t}$, $R_y$ denotes the region of integration and $H_i (X_{it}, S_{2t})$ is an $N_{1i} \times 1$ vector of functions of $X_{it}$ and $S_{2t}$. In general, $H_i (X_{it}, S_{2t})$ will not be linear in $X_{it}$ and $S_{2t}$; its particular specification will depend upon the parameter matrix $A_i$, the vector of functions $D_{it}$, and the conditional distribution $F_y (Y_{it} | X_{it}, S_{2t})$.

It follows from (1) that

$$(2) \quad A_i D_i (Y_{it}, X_{it}) = H_i (X_{it}, S_{2t}) + \psi_{it},$$

where $\psi_{it}$ is an $N_{1i} \times 1$ vestor of stochastic terms such that $E(\psi_{it} | X_{it}, S_{2t}) = 0$. The system of equations in (2) is in the form of a simultaneous equations model. One could think of the linear combinations on the left hand side of (2) as a description of the interactions involving the endogenous variables; typically, these linear combinations, which could involve nonlinear forms of the endogenous variables, would be chosen in a manner which reflects economic hypotheses. These hypotheses also typically specify the form of the elements of $H_i (X_{it}, S_{2t})$.[5] For our purposes, however, we need only note that whatever the manner of determining the selection of the linear combinations, $A_i D_{it}$, there exists a vector of functions $H_i (X_{it}, S_{2t})$ in terms of which a model such as (2) can be specified, which is consistent with the underlying distribution theory. The suggestion is that there are many so-called "true models"[6] and that specification error analysis relating to omitted variables and functional forms should focus on the elements of $H_i (X_{it}, S_{2t})$[7]; the higher conditional moments of $\psi_{it}$ given $X_{it}$ and $S_{2t}$ should also be objects of specification analysis--$\psi_{it}$ may be heteroskedastic, for example.[8]

2.1  THE FORECASTING EQUATIONS: THE CASE OF KNOWN PARAMETERS

It is well known that the minimum mean squared error predictors of the elements of $Y_{it}$ are the corresponding conditional means. Denote these means by the vector $K_i (X_{it}, S_{2t})$.

Then

$$(3) \quad K_i(X_{it}, S_{2t}) = \int_{R_y} Y_{it} \, dF_y(Y_{it}|X_{it}, S_{2t}).$$

In (3) each element of the conditional mean vector is defined in terms of the conditional distribution of the corresponding element of $Y_{it}$ given $X_{it}$ and $S_{2t}$. The vector $K_i(X_{it}, S_{2t})$ can also be defined in terms of the simultaneous equations model (2). For example, assume that (2) uniquely defines $Y_{it}$ in terms of $X_{it}$, $S_{2t}$ and $\psi_{it}$ as

$$(4) \quad Y_{it} = G_i(X_{it}, S_{2t}, \psi_{it})$$

where $G_i(\cdot, \cdot, \cdot)$ is an $N_{1i} \times 1$ vector of functions of $X_{it}$, $S_{2t}$, and $\psi_{it}$. Denote the conditional distribution of the disturbance term, $\psi_{it}$, given $X_{it}$ and $S_{2t}$ as $F_\psi(\psi_{it}|X_{it}, S_{2t})$. Then

$$(5) \quad K_i(X_{it}, S_{2t}) = \int_{R_\psi} G_i(X_{it}, S_{2t}, \psi_{it}) \, dF_\psi(\psi_{it}|X_{it}, S_{2t})$$

where $R_\psi$ denotes the region of integration. As a point of interest we note that if $K_i(X_{it}, S_{2t})$ is linear in $X_{it}$ and $S_{2t}$, the vector of functions $H_i(X_{it}, S_{2t})$ in (2) will be linear in $X_{it}$ and $S_{2t}$ if $A_i D_{it} = B_i Y_{it}$, where $B_i$ is a matrix of parameters. This would correspond to the linear simultaneous equations model. However, note that even if $K_i(X_{it}, S_{2t})$ is linear in $X_{it}$ and $S_{2t}$ pseudo nonlinear models could still be considered--that is, $A_i D_{it}$ need not be linear in $Y_{it}$[9].

A few points concerning the prediction equations in (3) should be noted. First, since the elements of $K_i(X_{it}, S_{2t})$ are means of the corresponding endogenous variables conditional on $X_{it}$ and $S_{2t}$, they are completely defined by the marginal distributions conditional on $X_{it}$ and $S_{2t}$. Therefore, if two models differ only in their assumed sets of endogenous variables, they have the same conditional mean prediction equation for each endogenous variable they have in common. Thus, since these conditional means are minimum mean squared error predictors, the "limit" of the predictive ability of a model with respect to a given endogenous variable depends only upon the assumed predetermined variables; the number of endogenous vari-

ables is irrelevant.  Therefore, if the parameters are known,
or have been consistently estimated with a "large" sample, then
the usefulness of measures of model size which relate to the
number of endogenous variables, such as the number of equations,
is of questionable value for purposes of comparing model forecasts.[10]  In this framework, forecasting performance should relate to model size only because the number of predetermined
variables is important.[11]

## 2.2  COMPARISONS OF MULTIPLIERS: THE CASE OF KNOWN PARAMETERS

Consider now the policy response of a given model as
described by mean impact multipliers with respect to the
elements of $S_{2t}$ which are unlagged control variables, say $C_t$.
Assume that the current period is t, and the change in the
values of the control variables is scheduled for period t+1.
Then, we define the mean impact multipliers of the model (2)
by the matrix

$$(6) \quad MU_{i,t+1} = \frac{\partial E(Y_{i,t+1} | S_{2,t+1}, S_{2t}, Y_{it}, X_{it})}{\partial C'_{t+1}} .$$

In general, the elements of $MU_{i,t+1}$ will be functions of
the vectors $S_{2,t+1}, S_{2t}, Y_{it}$, and $X_{it}$ so that the multipliers
corresponding to an assumed endogeneous variable will be model
specific.  However, the multipliers from various models are
not inconsistent with each other because the given conditions
defining them differ.  In a sense the multipliers are model
specific because they are based on different levels of
information.  To see this note that[12]

$$(7) \quad E(MU_{i,t+1} | S_{2,t+1}, S_{2t}) = \frac{\partial E(Y_{i,t+1} | S_{2,t+1}, S_{2t})}{\partial C'_{t+1}} ;$$

that is, if the multipliers are averaged over the values of
$Y_{it}$ and $X_{it}$, which represents model information, the result is
the matrix of "unconditional" multipliers, as described by the
terms on the right hand side of (7).

## 3.  THE VALUE OF A SIMULTANEOUS EQUATIONS MODEL FOR FORECASTING PURPOSES

We now consider the value of a simultaneous equations

model in forecasting the endogenous variables in each of two cases. In the first case, the parameters of the model are assumed to be known; in the second case they are assumed not to be known. Our discussion will suggest that for both cases, if the sample size is large, the value concerning forecasting of the specification of a model such as (2) relates to computational issues. If the parameters are unknown and the sample size is not large, our results are less clear. They do, however, suggest that in this case models should not be validated (tested for correctness of specification) in terms of their forecasts. For notational simplicity, we will henceforth refer to both the predetermined variables $X_{it}$ and the nonstochastic variables $S_{2t}$ simply as predetermined variables.

## 3.1  PREDICTION:  THE CASE OF KNOWN PARAMETERS

In principle, the prediction equations of (5) can be determined if the specifications and the values of the parameters of a simultaneous equation model such as (2) are given. To see this, note first that if the model is a linear one, in that $A_i D_{it} \equiv B_i Y_{it}$, and $H_i(X_{it}, S_{2t})$ is linear in $X_{it}$ and $S_{2t}$, the prediction equations are linear and so are easily determined if the parameters of the system are known. For the more general case of (2), however, the prediction equations will be nonlinear and so, generally, numerical methods would be considered.

There are at least two model-oriented numerical methods for determining the prediction equations. The first is stochastic simulation.[13] In this method, the model is solved numerically for the values of the endogenous variables corresponding to a given vector of values of the predetermined variables, say $X_{it}^o$ and $S_{2t}^o$, and a randomly selected vector of values of the disturbance terms. This process is repeated, say L times, for L randomly selected values of the disturbance vector. The solution values for the endogenous variables are then averaged. Assuming (quite reasonably) that the endogenous variables have finite variances, it can be shown from the law of large numbers that the solution averages of the endogenous variables converge in probability to their

conditional mean, $H_i(X^o_{it}, S^o_{2t})$, as $L \to \infty$. These conditional
means are the minimum mean squared error predictors. For
finite values of L, the sample averages can be viewed as
estimates of the corresponding elements of $H_i(X^o_{it}, S^o_{2t})$.

Another model-oriented method for determining the prediction equations is that of numerical integration. Specifically, the values of the prediction equations corresponding
to the given values of the predetermined variables $X^o_{it}$ and
$S^o_{2t}$ may be defined as

$$(8) \quad H_i(X^o_{it}, S^o_{2t}) = \int_{R_\psi} G_i(X^o_{it}, S^o_{2t}, \psi_{it}) \, dF(\psi_{it} | X^o_{it}, S^o_{2t})$$

The vector of functions $G_i(X^o_{it}, S^o_{2t}, \psi_{it})$ can be evaluated for
all possible values of the vector $\psi_{it}$; consequently
$H_i(X^o_{it}, S^o_{2t})$ can, in principle, be estimated by numerical
integration procedures applied to (8).

The methods suggested above for determining the prediction equations require the specification of a simultaneous
equation model such as (2). Without such a model, the prediction equations could be approximated in terms of the
ordinary least squares regression of each assumed endogenous
variable upon polynomial (or other) functions of the predetermined variables. If the sample is large, and the
polynomials are of a high enough degree, the approximations
should be good. However, in practice the sample size may not
be very "large" relative to the number of predetermined
variables.[14] Under such conditions, low order polynomials
would be considered, and consequently the approximations to
the prediction equations may not be "satisfactory." Indeed,
for large macro models, the number of predetermined variables
may exceed the number of observations;[15] therefore, the
(model-less) direct least squares approach to the estimation
of the prediction equations would have serious shortcomings.
On the other hand, it should be noted that stochastic
simulation of large macro models involves "computational
costs."

To summarize, the predictive ability of a model with
known parameters relates to its size only because the number
of predetermined variables entering the prediction equations

is important. We have argued that in some cases it may be quite difficult to obtain reasonable approximations to these prediction equations if the specifications of a simultaneous equation model are not available. On the other hand, it should be pointed out that if the sample size is "large" relative to the number of predetermined variables, the direct least squares approach, which has obvious computational benefits, may also be accurate. For instance, the error in the approximation due to the finite degree of the polynomial may be of less importance than the error introduced by the finite number of stochastic simulations. In addition, the direct least squares approach may be more robust because it is not model specific and therefore would not be affected by specification errors. In light of these comments we conclude that for models with known parameters the value concerning forecasting of the model specifications relate to computational issues concerning the prediction equations primarily for the case in which there are a large number of predetermined variables relative to the sample size.

## 3.2 PREDICTION: THE CASE OF UNKNOWN PARAMETERS

Assume now that the parameters of the system in (2) are not known, and for purposes of illustration that the system is linear. Denote this system as

$$(9) \quad B_i Y_{it} = J_i P_{it} + \psi_{it}$$

where $P'_{it} = (X'_{it}, S'_{2t})$, and $J_i$ is a corresponding matrix of parameters. Under such conditions the above discussed computational issues and parameter estimation problems arise concerning the estimation of the prediction equations. The computational issues are identical to those discussed above. Consider the associated parameter estimation problems. Under typical specifications, it is well known[16] that if the reduced form parameter matrix $\pi_i = B_i^{-1} J_i$ is estimated as $\hat{\pi}_i^F = \hat{B}_i^{-1} \hat{J}_i$, where $\hat{B}_i$ and $\hat{J}_i$ are full information systems estimators of $B_i$ and $J_i$, $\hat{\pi}_i^F$ will be consistent and efficient relative to the least squares estimator of $\pi_i$, say $\hat{\pi}_i^{LS}$. Let the vector of forecast errors based upon $\hat{\pi}_i^F$ and $\hat{\pi}_i^{LS}$ corresponding to a period, say f, beyond the sample be defined as

$$(10) \quad \hat{e}_{if}^{F} = Y_{if} - \hat{\pi}_{i}^{F} P_{if}; \quad \hat{e}_{if}^{LS} = Y_{if} - \hat{\pi}_{i}^{LS} P_{if}$$

Then, under usual assumptions, because $\hat{\pi}_{i}^{F}$ and $\hat{\pi}_{i}^{LS}$ are both consistent, it is easy to show that the asymptotic variance-covariance matrices of $\hat{e}_{if}^{F}$ and $\hat{e}_{if}^{LS}$ are identical <u>if the sample size is large</u>.[17]  Therefore, in the large sample case, which is the case usually considered in systems estimation, the value of the model specification concerning forecasting reduces to the computational issues discussed above.

One would think that in the finite sample case forecasts based upon a correctly specified simultaneous equation model which has been estimated by a full information procedure would be efficient relative to those based upon the direct least squares estimates of the reduced form equations.  Our discussion below, however, will indicate quite clearly that this may not be the case.

Consider the general nonlinear form of (2), and the corresponding minimum mean squared error predictor vector $H_i(X_{if}, S_{2f})$.  This vector will generally not be known even in principle because each of its elements will typically be a function of the unknown parameters of (2).  Let $\Omega_i$ denote the set of all parameters of the system (2), and denote the dependence of $H_i(X_{if}, S_{2f})$ upon $\Omega_i$ as $H_i(X_{if}, S_{2f}|\Omega_i)$.  Let $\hat{\Omega}_i^F$ be the full information maximum likelihood estimator of $\Omega_i$. Then, unfortunately, it is not the case that $H_i(X_{if}, S_{2f}|\hat{\Omega}_i^F)$ is the minimum mean squared error predictor of $Y_{if}$ in the finite sample case.  Formally, the reason for this is that in the finite sample

$$(11) \quad E(Y_{if}|X_{if}, S_{2f}, \hat{\Omega}_i^F) \neq H_i(X_{if}, S_{2f}|\hat{\Omega}_i^F).$$

On a more instructive level, we give an example below which demonstrates that because (11) does not hold as an equality, forecasts based upon a misspecified model may be efficient relative to those based upon a correctly specified model even if its parameters have been estimated by a full information technique.  We give another example which suggests that if the parameters of a correctly specified model are not estimated by a full information technique, the resulting forecasts may be considerably inferior to those based upon a misspecified model. This is important because large macro models are not typically estimated by full information techniques.[18] We conclude for the unknown parameter finite sample case, that if forecasts based upon correctly formulated models need not be superior to those based upon incorrectly formulated models, models should not be validated in terms of forecast comparisons.

## 3.2.1 A FULL INFORMATION FORECAST ILLUSTRATION

Consider the model

$$(12) \quad Y_t = \exp(bX_t) - 1 + U_t, \quad t = 1, \ldots, T$$

where $Y_t$ and $X_t$ are the values of the dependent and independent variables at time t, and $U_t$ is the corresponding disturbance term. Assume that $U_t$ is normally distributed, is independent of $X_s$ and $U_r$ for all t, s and r $\neq$ t, and $EU_t = 0$, and $EU_t^2 = \sigma^2$. Assume that a sample of size T is available on $Y_t$ and $X_t$ for t=1,...,T, and for this sample period $X_t = 1$. Finally, the problem is to predict the value of the dependent variable in a future period, $Y_f$, under the assumption that the value of the independent variable for that period, $X_f$, is known. We consider three cases concerning the value of $X_f$, namely $X_f = 0,1,2$.

The above assumptions imply that

$$(13) \quad E(Y_f|X_f) \equiv Y_f^m$$
$$= \exp(bX_f) - 1$$

The maximum likelihood estimate of $Y_f^m$ is

$$(14) \quad \hat{Y}_f^m = \exp(\hat{b}X_f) - 1$$
$$= [\exp(\hat{b})]^{X_f} - 1$$

where $\exp(\hat{b})$ is the maximum likelihood estimator of b obtained via the data corresponding to (12):

$$(15) \quad \exp(\hat{b}) = \bar{Y} + 1, \quad \bar{Y} = \sum_{t=1}^{T} Y_t / T.$$

Our assumptions concerning $U_t$ imply that, conditional on $X_t = 1$, t=1,...,T, $\bar{Y} + 1$ is normally distributed with mean exp (b), and variance $\sigma^2/T$.  Therefore, the second and fourth moments, which will be needed to calculate the mean squared error of forecasts of $\bar{Y}+1$, are

$$E(\bar{Y}+1)^2 = \exp(2b) + \sigma^2/T$$

(16)

$$E(\bar{Y}+1)^4 = (3\sigma^4/T^2) + (6\sigma^2/T)\exp(2b) + \exp(4b)$$

The forecast error, $e_f$, is

(17)    $e_f = Y_f - \hat{Y}_f^m = [\exp(b)]^{X_f} + U_f - (\bar{Y}+1)^{X_f}$ ;

the mean squared error of forecast can be shown to be

(18)    $MSE = Ee_f^2 = \begin{cases} \sigma^2, & \text{if } X_f = 0 \\ \sigma^2(1+1/T), & \text{if } X_f = 1 \\ \sigma^2(1+3\sigma^2/T^2 + 4T\exp(2b)), & \text{if } X_f = 2 \end{cases}$

Assume now that an experimenter considers a linear approximation to the model in (12),

(19)    $Y_t = AX_t + V_t$, $t = 1,\ldots, T$

where A is viewed as a parameter and $V_t$ is the assumed disturbance term.  The least squares estimator of A is $\bar{Y}$.  In terms of this model, the forecasted value of $Y_f$ would be

(20)    $\hat{Y}_f^{LS} = \bar{Y}X_f$,

and so the forecast error would be

(21)    $e_f^{LS} = Y_f - \hat{Y}_f^{LS} = [\exp(b)]^{X_f} - 1 + U_f - \bar{Y}X_f$

It can be shown that the mean squared error of forecast is

(22)    $E(e_f^{LS})^2 = \begin{cases} = \sigma^2, & \text{if } X_f = 0 \\ = \sigma^2 + \sigma^2/T, & \text{if } X_f = 1 \\ = 1 + \sigma^2 + (4\sigma^2/T) - 4[\exp(b)] + \\ \quad 6[\exp(2b)] - 4[\exp(3b)] + \\ \quad \exp(4b), & \text{if } X_f = 2. \end{cases}$

In comparing (18) and (22) we see that the mean squared are different only for the case in which $X_f = 2$.  For this case, we note that $Ee_f^2$ will tend to be large relative to $E(e_f^{LS})^2$ if $\sigma^2$ is large, because of the fourth degree term; on the other hand this magnitude will tend to be relatively small if b is large. In the large sample, $T = \infty$, we see that $Ee_f^2 < E(e_f^{LS})^2$ for all finite value of $\sigma^2$ and b, except b = 0 which corresponds to a degenerate case of the model.

These results illustrate that, in finite samples, forecasts based upon a correctly specified model may not have smaller mean squared errors than forecasts based upon an incorrectly specified model if the parameters are unknown but efficiently estimated. We will now give an example which will illustrate that if the parameters of a correctly specified model are estimated inefficiently (but consistently) the forecasts based upon that model may be decidedly inferior to those of a misspecified model.

## 3.2.2  A LIMITED INFORMATION FORECAST ILLUSTRATION

Consider the regression model

$$(23) \quad Y_t = 1/(1-bX_t) + U_t, \qquad bX_t \leq .9, \; b \geq 0$$

where $Y_t$ and $X_t$ are the values of the dependent and independent variables at time t and $U_t$ is the disturbance term. We maintain the assumptions concerning $X_t$ and $U_t$ made in Section 3.2.1 but now assume that for the sample period $X_t = 1/2$, t=1,...,T; for the future period we take the value of the independent variable to be given but unspecified, $X_f$. The problem is again to forecast the value of the dependent variable in a future period, $Y_f$, corresponding to the given value $X_f$.

In practice, the forecast based on a nonlinear simultaneous equation model would be constructed by first estimating the parameters of the model and then dynamically simulating the endogenous variables forward to the future period. The simulation considered is typically deterministic and the estimation procedure is rarely a full information one which accounts for, among other things, all of the inequality constraints involved. For our single equation example, we will consider the less-than-optimal forecasts of $Y_f$ to be

$$(24) \quad \hat{Y}_f = 1/(1-\hat{b}X_f)$$

where $\hat{b}$ is the maximum likelihood estimator of $b$ based upon observations on $Y_t$ and $X_t$, $t=1,\ldots,T$. We assume that the maximization procedure accounts for the inequality constraint $bX_t \leq .9$, $t=1,\ldots,T$, but does not account for the constraint $bX_f \leq .9$ and thus is not quite a full information one.[19]

We first note that since $X_t = 1/2$, $t=1,\ldots,T$, the range of values of $b$ that would be considered are $0 \leq b \leq 1.8$ thus, the corresponding range of values of the conditional mean of $Y_t$, say $Y_t^m$, in (23) is $1 \leq Y_t^m \leq 10$. Therefore, the maximum likelihood estimator of $b$ can be defined as

$$(25) \quad \frac{1}{1-(\frac{1}{2})\hat{b}} = \text{Min}\,(\bar{Y},\, 10), \text{ if Min}(\bar{Y},10) \geq 1$$

$$= 0, \text{ otherwise.}$$

The range of values of $\hat{b}$ in (25) is $0 \leq \hat{b} \leq 1.8$; it follows that the variance of the forecast error based upon the forecast

$$(26) \quad \hat{Y}_f = 1/(1-\hat{b}X_f)$$

will be infinite if $X_f = 1/1.8$

Now consider the linear approximation to (23):

$$(27) \quad Y_t = \alpha + BX_t + V_t, \qquad t=1,\ldots,T$$

where $V_t$ is an assumed disturbance term. The corresponding forecast of $Y_f$ is

$$(28) \quad Y_f^* = \hat{\alpha} + \hat{B}X_f$$

where $\hat{\alpha}$ and $\hat{B}$ are the least squares estimators of $\alpha$ and $B$. Our assumptions imply that the variance of the forecast error based on the forecast in (28) is finite. It follows that, if $X_f = 1/1.8$, then the mean squared error of the forecast based upon the linear approximation will be less than that corresponding to the correctly formulated model for all finite values of the sample size, $T$. We note that this infinite variance problem would not arise if $b$, or if the conditional mean $1/(1-bX_f)$, were estimated by a full information technique.

However, even in this case, our discussion in Section 3.2.1 implies that forecasts based upon the correctly formulated model (23) need not dominate those based upon the linear approximation (27). We thus conclude that while the method of estimation may be quite important in determining the properties of forecasts, simpler methods applied to ad hoc models may yield forecasts with more desirable properties.

## 4. MODEL COMPARISONS AND FORECASTS

### 4.1 THE ARGUMENT FOR EX ANTE COMPARISONS

Our discussion above suggests that models should not be validated in terms of their forecasts. Instead, if forecasting accuracy is desired, models should be viewed as forecasting "instruments" and evaluated as such. In doing this a problem arises. It should be clear that the variance of the forecast error is a function of the predetermined variables used in constructing the forecasts. Therefore, unless all models have the same set of predetermined variables, comparison of model forecasts may not, at least in the large sample framework, reveal much about the "quality" or usefulness of the models involved. For example, in a large sample framework, <u>ceteris</u> <u>paribus</u>, the larger the list of predetermined variables the more accurate the <u>ex</u> <u>post</u> forecasts, but the more difficult will be the construction of the <u>ex</u> <u>ante</u> forecasts.

Our approach to the problem of evaluating models as forecasting instruments is to compare their forecasting performance only in terms of <u>ex</u> <u>ante</u> forecasts. The reasons for this are implicit in the discussion of Section 2. Specifically, ignore for the moment issues relating to costs of model operation, subjective adjustments and methods of estimation concerning the parameters of the model. Assume that a model which is to be used by a researcher as a forecasting instrument contains all of the variables and relationships the researcher assumes to be important. Finally, assume the non-confidentiality of the data. That is, assume that each researcher could obtain the data which is available to any other researcher.

Let $I_t$ denote the data which are available at time t to any of the researchers; then a comparison of ex ante forecasts enables us to compare the forecasting performance of the various models under the restriction that they are all based upon a common data base, namely $I_t$. In a sense, we are viewing each researcher's model as a filter which selects from $I_t$ the components which are deemed to be important. In such a framework, comparisons of ex ante forecasts should reveal whether one model is making better use of the common available data base, or is neglecting fewer important components than another.[20]

## 4.2 THE MODEL AS A MAPPING

Let $y_t$ be the value of a variable of interest at time t. Then consistent with the above method of comparison is the view that a forecasting model is a function which maps the available data into a forecast. The minimum mean squared error of forecast of $y_{t+j}$ (j >0) conditional on $I_t$ is

$$(29) \quad E(y_{t+j}|I_t) = h_j(I_t)$$

where $h_j(I_t)$ is the function of $I_t$ which describes the conditional mean of $y_{t+j}$.[21] One interpretation of each model's forecast is that it is an estimate of $h_j(I_t)$.

## 4.3 PARAMETER ESTIMATION AND SUBJECTIVE ADJUSTMENT ISSUES

In practice, the parameters of the model are not known and therefore must be estimated. Subjective adjustments of various sorts are also made in constructing forecasts. Continuing for the moment to ignore model cost issues, we view the method of estimation and the implicit relationships which underlie the subjective adjustments as part of the model. Our reason for doing this is that both of these "model components" are instrumental in mapping data into forecasts.

The subjective relationships which underlie the subjective adjustments are not objectively expressed[22] and may change in character from period to period. These subjective adjustments may also be specific to a researcher. This implies that for such cases, a complete and objective specification of the model over time is not available and that the researcher is an integral component of the model specification. The desire for objectivity and stability of model specification may lead one to consider only the objectively specified component of such models; we do not do this because these objectively defined components are not the models' mapping of data into forecasts, and in many cases may not even be of interest.[23]

We note that in evaluating econometric models as forecasting instruments in terms of ex ante forecasts we have driven another wedge between the issue of forecast evaluation and that of model validation. As one example, econometric models are typically formulated in such a way that only distributions which are conditional upon the model's exogenous variables are considered for the estimators of the parameters and disturbance terms of a model, or for beyond the sample values of endogenous variables. This implies that tests of a model's specification which are carried out in terms of forecasted values should be based upon the realized values of the model's exogenous variables -- that is, they should be ex post forecasts.[24] On the other hand, we have argued that ex post forecast comparisons may not be of interest in evaluating models as "forecasting instruments."

## 4.4   MODEL COSTS AND BENEFITS

Our discussion thus far has ignored issues relating to model costs and benefits. Assume that data collection is costly and that the costs vary from one datum to another and, perhaps, for a given datum, from one researcher to another. Assume also that each researcher has a benefit function whose value depends negatively upon forecast errors. The researchers need not have identical benefit functions.

Under these assumptions one would expect a variety of models if each researcher maximized his expected net returns. Forecast comparisons between models would not determine which of the models are best suited for their respective purposes. Instead, forecast comparisons of the ex ante variety would only reveal the extent to which the various models make use of the available data $(I_t)$.[25]

## 5.  THE RECENT PERFORMANCE OF SOME MACRO ECONOMIC MODELS

In order to assess the recent predictive performance of
the major models as well as to relate this performance to
model size we have compiled recent forecasts of some macro
economic models in use today.  Time restrictions, problems of
data comparability, and other reasons[26] have caused us to
restrict our compilations to a relatively short time period.
We have considered only quarterly forecasts generated since
the 1976 revision of the National Income and Product Account
data, resulting, therefore, in forecasts for 1976:1 through
1978:2.  As a result of our use of this small set of forecasts,
it should be noted that our comparison of models' performances
is an incomplete indicator of which model is best at forecasting particular economic variables.  A meaningful ranking of
these models would require evidence of significant differences
in predictive performance over a longer time period.  This
fact notwithstanding, we hope it is enlightening to consider
the forecasting records over even this limited period of time.

The models used in our comparisons are from the following
sources:  the Bureau of Economic Analysis, U. S. Department of
Commerce (BEA); Chase Econometric Associates, Inc. (Chase);
Data Resources, Inc. (DRI); the Research Seminar in Quantitative Economics of the University of Michigan (MQEM);
Wharton Econometric Forecasting Associates, Inc. (Wharton);
the Bergmann-Bennett Microsimulation of the U. S. Economy
(BB-Micro); the Fair Model (Fair); and the Research Department
of the Federal Reserve Bank of St. Louis (St. Louis).  With
the exception of the Bergmann-Bennett model, these forecast
sources base their predictions on simultaneous equations
econometric models.

The structure of the Bergman-Bennett model requires
special note since it is different from the other models and
because it is a new contributor of economic forecasts.  The
core of this model consists of 1000 worker-consumer units,
twelve private industries (including ten nonfinancial industries (including ten nonfinancial industries, one commercial
bank, and one financial intermediary), two governmental units

(federal, and state and local), and one foreign unit.  Each of
the economic decision makers has characteristics and an economic situation which remain with that agent throughout the
simulation.[27]  Agents' simulated actions are noted in balance
sheet format, and are replicated and aggregated to give macro
forecasts.  The model's structure is nonlinear and contains
265 estimated parameters.[28]

Table 1
Some Indicators of Model Size

| Model | Equations | Number of Stochastic Equations | Exogenous Variables | Predetermined Variables |
|-------|-----------|-------------------|---------------------|------------------------|
| BEA | 196 | 108 | 150 | 249 |
| Chase | 350 | 150 | 150 | 350 |
| DRI | 831 | 350 | 178 | 628 |
| MQEM | 81 | 47 | 76 | 105 |
| Wharton | 695 | 299 | 242 | 677 |
| BB-Micro | - | - | - | - |
| Fair | 97 | 29 | 83 | 139 |
| St. Louis | 7 | 5 | 3 | 7 |

Various indicators of size for the eight models are
presented in Table 1.  These indicators include the total
number of equations, including stochastic equations and identities, the number of stochastic equations, the number of
exogeneous variables, and the number of predetermined variables, including exogeneous and lagged endogenous variables.[29]
Absent from this list is the total number of predetermined variables (counting each different lag of an endogenous variable
as a different predetermined variable).  Typically, however,
many of these lagged values are constrained to lie along a
distribution, implying that the numbers of predetermined variables indicated in Table 1 may be an adequate measure of this
dimension of model size.  As the above measures of size are
generally related, it is not surprising to see in Table 1 that

models considered large (small) by one criterion are typically
large (small) by the other criteria as well.  This correlation
in size-measures makes an empirical determination of the
aspect of size most relevant to predictive performance a
difficult problem.[30]

    The forecasts from these models were compared for six
economic variables--Nominal GNP, GNP Deflator, Nominal Personal
Consumption Expenditures, and the three components of Personal
Consumption, namely Durables, Nondurables, and Services.  The
first three variables were selected because of their popularity and importance as measures of overall economic activity.
The second three were selected to compare the models' performances on somewhat disaggregated variables.  Mean squared
forecast errors for one to eight quarter horizon forecasts of
these variables appear in Tables 2a and 2b.  These tables
contain mean squared forecast errors for nine one period horizon forecasts, eight two period horizon forecasts, etc.[31]  As
noted earlier, while comparison of this small number of forecasts is strictly valid, a ranking of models on the basis of
these errors will be ill-advised.

    We were only partially successful in our attempt to re-
strict the analysis to ex ante forecasts.  Release dates of the
various model predictions differed significantly, so that
strictly comparable forecasts were not obtained.[32]  Of the
eight models compared, the only two that used completely ex
ante forecasts were the Fair model and Bergmann-Bennett Microsimulation model.  The other models differed in their use of
preliminary data, with Chase and DRI using earlier, more preliminary, information than BEA, Wharton, and MQEM.  The St
Louis forecasts were ex post.

    The information in Tables 2a and 2b indicate some in-
consistency in forecasting accuracy over various time horizons.
While the mean squared errors predominantly get larger the
farther into the future the forecasts are made, there are a
large number of cases in which prediction accuracy increases
with the forecast horizon.  This anomaly can likely be explained by the small number of forecasts being averaged; however, it does emphasize the difficulties in drawing too

Table 2a

Mean Squared Forecast Errors for Some
Quarterly Economic Models

Predicted Variable: <u>Nominal GNP</u>

Forecast Horizon (Periods Ahead)

| Model | 1 | 2 | 3 | 4 | 5 | 6 | 7 | 8 |
|---|---|---|---|---|---|---|---|---|
| BEA | 392. | 347. | 305. | 59. | 556. | 889. | 1644. | 2265. |
| Chase | 271. | 311. | 534. | 1088. | 1319. | 2050. | 3558. | 1943. |
| DRI | 91. | 204. | 337. | 538. | 543. | 455. | 658. | 582. |
| MQEM | 170. | 260. | 623. | 387. | 784. | 1764. | 2610 | - |
| Wharton | 244. | 261. | 364. | 573. | 479. | 116. | 755. | 579. |
| BB-Micro | 230. | 753. | 1285. | 1717. | 2544. | 2307. | 2369. | 2764. |
| Fair | 638. | 328. | 1044. | - | - | - | - | - |
| St Louis | 246. | 569. | 612. | 427. | 777. | 1517. | 1535. | 944. |

Predicted Variable: <u>GNP Deflator</u>

Forecast Horizon

| Model | 1 | 2 | 3 | 4 | 5 | 6 | 7 | 8 |
|---|---|---|---|---|---|---|---|---|
| BEA | 0.213 | 0.784 | 0.591 | 0.695 | 0.649 | 2.323 | 3.543 | 0.212 |
| Chase | 0.165 | 0.706 | 1.030 | 1.271 | 1.250 | 2.451 | 5.980 | 1.811 |
| DRI | 0.113 | 0.146 | 0.339 | 0.616 | 0.358 | 0.634 | 0.735 | 0.022 |
| MQEM | 0.248 | 1.040 | 1.200 | 0.301 | 1.811 | 2.502 | 3.927 | - |
| Wharton | 0.168 | 0.690 | 1.110 | 0.911 | 0.821 | 1.163 | 3.104 | 1.054 |
| BB-Micro | 0.917 | 2.280 | 2.711 | 5.440 | 12.055 | 27.428 | 24.530 | 30.001 |
| Fair | 1.887 | 3.604 | 7.860 | - | - | - | - | - |
| St Louis | 0.690 | 1.653 | 3.103 | 4.830 | 6.891 | 9.547 | 15.410 | 4.620 |

Predicted Variable: <u>Personal Consumption Expenditures</u>
(Nominal)

| Model | 1 | 2 | 3 | 4 | 5 | 6 | 7 | 8 |
|---|---|---|---|---|---|---|---|---|
| BEA | 268. | 213. | 287. | 403. | 696. | 720. | 915. | - |
| Chase | 207. | 218. | 241. | 339. | 393. | 546. | 821. | 841. |
| DRI | 59. | 142. | 109. | 129. | 50. | 32. | 26. | 78. |
| MQEM | 102. | 120. | 202. | 224. | 387. | 869. | 1213. | - |
| Wharton | 241. | 262. | 332. | 413. | 488. | 445. | 901. | 926. |
| BB-Micro | 55. | 141. | 237. | 288. | 607. | 1218. | 1816. | 2290. |
| Fair | - | - | - | - | - | - | - | - |
| St Louis | - | - | - | - | - | - | - | - |

Table 2b

Mean Squared Forecast Errors for Some
Quarterly Economic Models

Predicted Variable:   PCE-Durables (Nominal)

| Model | 1 | 2 | 3 | 4 | 5 | 6 | 7 | 8 |
|-------|-----|-----|-----|-----|-----|-----|-----|-----|
| BEA      | 23.5 | 12.2 | 30.7 | 17.5 | 39.2 | 24.4 | 31.1 | – |
| Chase    | 18.4 | 24.2 | 26.3 | 49.9 | 44.1 | 64.6 | 80.1 | 81.9 |
| DRI      | 14.0 | 30.3 | 40.5 | 45.4 | 49.9 | 56.6 | 65.0 | 16.0 |
| MQEM     | 24.9 | 23.4 | 44.2 | 17.6 | 18.2 | 42.4 | – | – |
| Wharton  | 24.7 | 25.0 | 21.8 | 35.2 | 22.8 | 24.6 | 15.7 | 60.8 |
| BB-Micro | 31.7 | 37.5 | 67.5 | 79.4 | 137.0 | 53.5 | 63.4 | 116.1 |
| Fair     | – | – | – | – | – | – | – | – |
| St Louis | – | – | – | – | – | – | – | – |

Predicted Variable:   PCE-Nondurables (Nominal)

| Model | 1 | 2 | 3 | 4 | 5 | 6 | 7 | 8 |
|-------|-----|-----|-----|-----|-----|-----|-----|-----|
| BEA      | 31.3 | 13.7 | 30.0 | 30.1 | 34.7 | 46.0 | 39.6 | – |
| Chase    | 10.3 | 22.6 | 21.5 | 27.5 | 44.0 | 105.3 | 177.0 | 175.4 |
| DRI      | 14.5 | 41.7 | 46.4 | 62.2 | 59.6 | 37.1 | 38.3 | 26.9 |
| MQEM     | 20.4 | 26.2 | 32.8 | 27.1 | 13.4 | 68.3 | 20.6 | – |
| Wharton  | 30.9 | 53.6 | 100.6 | 89.3 | 153.2 | 180.4 | 175.0 | 279.8 |
| BB-Micro | 14.8 | 21.2 | 34.3 | 35.0 | 61.0 | 174.6 | 207.2 | 141.0 |
| Fair     | – | – | – | – | – | – | – | – |
| St Louis | – | – | – | – | – | – | – | – |

Predicted Variable:   PCE-Services (Nominal)

| Model | 1 | 2 | 3 | 4 | 5 | 6 | 7 | 8 |
|-------|-----|-----|-----|-----|-----|-----|-----|-----|
| BEA      | 144. | 155. | 224. | 301. | 416. | 440. | 582. | – |
| Chase    | 121. | 153. | 214. | 273. | 357. | 431. | 577. | 726. |
| DRI      | 6. | 5. | 20. | 22. | 52. | 74. | 116. | 156. |
| MQEM     | 75. | 101. | 142. | 225. | 313. | 425. | 426. | – |
| Wharton  | 167. | 217. | 318. | 491. | 651. | 557. | 1244. | 1624. |
| BB-Micro | 43. | 88. | 180. | 313. | 451. | 692. | 1010. | 1418. |
| Fair     | – | – | – | – | – | – | – | – |
| St Louis | – | – | – | – | – | – | – | – |

specific of conclusions from this forecast set.

In order to diminish the importance of noncomparability of forecasts due to the release date problem and to facilitate interpretation of this body of information, consider two groups of forecast horizons--"short term" forecasts of one to four period horizons, and "medium term" forecasts of five to eight period horizons. Also, consider a categorization of the six economic variables being predicted into major "macro" variables, consisting of GNP, GNP Deflator, and Personal Consumption, and the somewhat "disaggregate" variables, namely Durables, Nondurables, and Services. According to this two-by-two breakdown of forecast horizons (into short and medium term) and aggregation of variables (into macro and disaggregate levels) we can summarize the performance of the models.[33] For the period and variables in question, the BEA model had more success relative to the other models considered in producing short term forecasts than medium term forecasts. Relative to the other models, BEA performed equally well on both macro and disaggregate predictions. The forecast errors[34] generated by the Chase model do not appear to have a systematic relation to those of the other models. Their forecasts range from best to worst with respect to both short and medium term forecasts, and macro and disaggregate variables. The DRI model exhibited the most accurate forecasts of the macro variables in both the short and medium term. Their forecasts of the disaggregate variables were comparatively less accurate however, than the other models. The MQEM model performed at about the average in predicting the macro variables, while being among the most accurate models in predicting both short and medium term disaggregates. Their medium term disaggregate forecasts were on average the best of the five models. Errors made by the Wharton model placed it from best to worst in forecasting the macro variables. Their performance on disaggregate forecasts was below the average except for predictions on Durables. Forecasts from the BB-Micro model ranked it predominantly at the bottom of the accuracy list. While this was expected considering that these were the first forecasts ever produced by this model, it was surprising to note the strength of some

of its disaggregate forecasts:  The BB-Micro forecasts were
more than competitive in predicting short term Nondurables and
Services.

To analyze the evidence relating model size to predictive
performance, we first ranked the models according to the
number of predetermined variables.[35]  We then compared that
ranking to the rankings of predictive accuracy for short and
medium term forecasts of each of the six economic variables.[36]
These relative rankings appear in Table 3.  Column one of this

Table 3

Rankings of Model Size and Predictive Performance

Predicted Variable and Term of Forecast

| Model | Size Ranking | GNP Short | GNP Medium | GNP Deflator Short | GNP Deflator Medium | PCE Short | PCE Medium |
|---|---|---|---|---|---|---|---|
| BEA | 4 | 1 | 3 | 2 | 3 | 4 | 4 |
| Chase | 3 | 5 | 5 | 5 | 5 | 3 | 2 |
| DRI | 2 | 2 | 2 | 1 | 1 | 1 | 1 |
| MQEM | 5 | 3 | 4 | 3 | 4 | 2 | 5 |
| Wharton | 1 | 4 | 1 | 4 | 2 | 5 | 3 |

| Model | Size Ranking | Durables Short | Durables Medium | Nondurables Short | Nondurables Medium | Services Short | Services Medium |
|---|---|---|---|---|---|---|---|
| BEA | 4 | 1 | 3 | 2 | 2 | 4 | 3 |
| Chase | 3 | 4 | 5 | 1 | 4 | 3 | 4 |
| DRI | 2 | 5 | 4 | 4 | 3 | 1 | 1 |
| MQEM | 5 | 3 | 1 | 3 | 1 | 2 | 2 |
| Wharton | 1 | 2 | 2 | 5 | 5 | 5 | 5 |

table contains model size rankings from largest ("1") to
smallest ("5").  The other columns contain rankings of the
models' forecasting accuracy for various variables and forecast horizons.  Rankings in these columns range from most
accurate ("1") to least accurate ("5").  The absence of a
strong relation between model size and predictive performance
is borne out in further calculations from this table:  the
average rank correlation between model size and short term forecast accuracy is -0.3 for the six variables considered, and the
average rank correlation between model size and medium term

forecast accuracy is +0.07. At least for the five models considered here--which do not differ dramatically by this measure of size--there is little evidence of a strong relation between size and forecast accuracy.

## FOOTNOTES

1. The authors wish to acknowledge, without implication, helpful comments from S. Goldfeld, A. Hirsch, L. Klein, J. Kmenta, and W.A. Spivey. Computer facilities were provided by the University of Maryland Computer Science Center.

2. Note that we are not ruling out the possibility that some elements of $S_t$ are lagged values of the other elements.

3. This stationarity assumption is made for ease of exposition; the central results of the paper do not depend upon this assumption.

4. For simplicity of notation, we are not distingushing between the random variables and the values they take on. We are also taking the structural equation approach to model formulation. For a nice discussion of this procedure see Goldberger (1964; pp. 380-388).

5. In a typical linear model, each element of $H_i(X_{it}, S_{2t})$ would be a linear combination of a subset of the elements of $X_{it}$ and $S_{2t}$.

6. Much of econometric theory is based upon the assumption that variables which are assumed to be exogenous are nonstochastic, and therefore there is a "true" model; any deviation from this model therefore leads to specification errors. See, for example, the discussion of specification errors in Goldberger (1964; p. 196), Johnson (1972; p. 168), or the more general analysis in Ramsey (1969). Also, see Fair (1978 b) for a complaint concerning a lack of agreement of the "true" specification of macro models.

7. Note that feedback control variables which are stochastic are not elements of $S_{2t}$, and therefore need not be considered as "potentially omitted variables" in model specification. For an excellent presentation of control theory as it relates to macro economic models see Chow (1975).

8. For an application of this framework of analysis to specification issues relating to aggregate macro models see Kelejian

(1978).

9.  For other presentations and analyses of nonlinear models see Fisher (1966) and Howrey and Kelejian (1971).

10.  Among others, measures of this sort were used by Fromm and Schink (1973) and Christ (1974).

11.  Let one model, say the first, incorporate the predetermined variables $X_{1t}$, and a second model incorporate the predetermined variables $X_{1t}$ and $X_{2t}$. Assume that both models incorporate a particular endogenous variable, $Y_{1t}$, and all relevant deterministic variables by the vector $s_{2t}$. Let $E_t$ denote the expected value operator given $s_{2t}$. Then, since

$$E_t(Var(Y_{1t}|X_{1t},X_{2t},s_{2t})) \le E_t(Var(Y_{1t}|X_{1t},s_{2t}))$$

the second model should "out predict" the first. The proof of this inequality is a straight forward generalization of the result given in Mood, Graybill and Boes (1974, page 159).

12.  Let $f_{t+1} = f(Y_{i,t+1}|S_{2,t+1},S_{2t},Y_{it},X_{it})$ be the conditional density of $Y_{i,t+1}$ given the indicated vectors. Denote the elements of $S_{2,t+1}$ which are not in $C_{t+1}$ as $W_{t+1}$. Then, for given values of the vectors $W_{t+1}$ and $S_{2t}$ the result in (7) will hold if $f_{t+1}$ and the elements of $\partial f_{t+1}/\partial C'_{t+1}$ are continuous in the elements of $Y_{i't+1}$, $C_{t+1}$, $Y_{it}$ and $X_{it}$ for the range of values considered. See Brand (1955, page 295).

13.  For a more detailed discussion of this procedure see Howrey and Kelejian (1971); see also Klein and Preston (1969), Cooper and Fischer (1975) and Fair (1978a) for applications.

14.  See, for example, the discussion given by Duesenberry and Klein (1965).

15.  See, for example, Fisher and Wadyck (1971) and Swamy and Holmes (1971).

16.  See, for example, Schmidt (1976, pp. 236-243).

17.  For example, let $\hat{\pi}_i$ be any consistent estimator of $\pi_i$, and define $\hat{e}_{if}=Y_{if}-\hat{\pi}_iP_{if}$. Since plim $(\hat{\pi}_i) = \pi_i$, $\hat{e}_{if}$ converges in distribution to $V_{if}=Y_{if}-\pi_iP_{if}$, where $V_{if}$ is the corresponding vector of reduced form disturbance terms. Thus, if the sample size is $T = \infty$, the variance-covariance matrix of the forecast error vector, $\hat{e}_{if}$, reduces to the variance-covariance matrix of the reduced form disturbance terms, $V_{if}$. Alternatively, set $T = \infty$ in Schmidt's (1971, p. 244) formula given for his problem

2C.

18. Another problem which may make the forecasts based upon a nonlinear model less effective is that deterministic simulation may be used to estimate the prediction equations. In the typical case the disturbance terms are set equal to zero and the model is solved numerically for the endogenous variables in terms of given values of the predetermined variables. See, for example, Howrey and Kelejian (1971). See Fair (1978a) for one of the few examples in which stochastic simulation is considered with respect to both the disturbance terms and parameter estimates.

19. It should be noted that the regularity conditions are not needed for the consistency of the maximum likelihood estimator. See Kendall and Stuart (1961, pages 39-41).

20. Although somewhat more formal, our views concerning ex ante vs ex post forecast evaluation are quite consistent with those expressed by McNees (1975, p. 5). Specifically, he states "using the ex ante record of forecasts acts as a sort of control for the degree of exogeneity, putting the different models on a more nearly equal footing." For a counter view see Stekler (1972).

21. See Bradford and Kelejian (1978) for an application of this view of forecasting to a value of information problem.

22. Our conclusions below would not be altered if the relationships which underlie the "subjective" adjustments were in fact objectively expressed but not revealed for a variety of reasons.

23. See, for example, Howrey, Klein and McCarthy (1974). As a point of interest, McNees (1975) argues that there is more stability in model proprietors than there is in objective components of the various models. Therefore, a desire for continuity of the analysis of forecasts over time would lead one to study the performance of proprietors and not their "objectively" specified models.

24. For a very nice discussion of some of the issues involved see Dhrymes, et al. (1972).

25. These considerations suggests that "rational predictions" can not be defined without reference to cost and benefit functions. See, for example McNees (1978).

26.  Not the least of which is the careful and thoughtful work
of McNees (1975, 1978) and others in analyzing the forecasting
performance of many of these same models.

27.  For example, demographic characteristics as well as the
wealth, employment status, etc., of the agents are used as
determinants of individual actions.  On-going case histories
are maintained.

28.  It should be noted that heretofore this model has not been
used to produce economic forecasts.  The proprietors generated
the included forecasts at our request.  Any lack of accuracy
might therefore be attributed as much to their lack of experience in making detailed forecasts as to any deficiencies in the
model.

29.  The number of lagged endogenous variables here refers to
the number of endogenous variables whose lags appear in the
relevant model, and not the total number of lags of the endogenous variables.

30.  A possible exception to this pattern is the Bergmann-
Bennett model, for which these standard measures of size seem
inappropriate.  This model could be viewed alternatively as
very large or very small by several criteria.

31.  For the Fair model only four one period horizon forecasts,
three two period ahead forecasts, etc., were used.

32.  See McNees (1975) for a discussion of release dates and
their relation to predictive performance.

33.  This information in summary form can be obtained from the
right-most six columns in Table 3.  There the models are ranked
by forecast accuracy.

34.  Over time and by macro/disaggregate classification.

35.  Recall that unfortunately this does not include the total
number of lagged endogenous variables, but includes the number
of endogenous variables whose lags appear in the model.

36.  For these comparisons we considered only the first five
models in Table 1.

BIBLIOGRAPHY

Bradford, D. and Kelejian, H., The Value of Information for Crop Forecasting with Bayesian Speculators, The Bell Journal of Economics, 9 (1978), 123-144.

Brand, L., Advanced Calculus (New York: John Wiley and Sons, Inc., 1955).

Christ, C., Judging the Performance of Econometric Models of the U.S. Economy, International Economic Review, 16 (1975), 54-74.

Chow, G., Analysis and Control of Dynamic Econometric Systems (New York: John Wiley and Sons, Inc., 1975).

Cooper, J. and Fischer, S., A Method for Stochastic Control of Nonlinear Econometric Models and an Application, Econometrica, 43 (1975), 147-162.

Dhrymes, P. et al., Criteria For Evaluation of Econometric Models, Annals of Economic and Social Measurement, 1 (1972), 291-324.

Duesenberry, J. and Klein, L., Introduction: The Research Strategy and its Application, in: The Brookings Quarterly Econometric Model of the United States, eds. J. Duesenberry et al., (Chicago: Rand McNally and Co., 1965).

Fair, R.C., An Evaluation of a Short-Run Forecasting Model, International Economic Review, 15 (1974), 285-304.

_____, The Sensitivity of Fiscal-Policy Effects to Assumptions About the Behavior of the Federal Reserve, Cowles Foundation Discussion Paper (1977), Yale University.

_____, Estimating the Expected Predictive Accuracy of Econometric Models, Cowles Foundation Discussion Paper No. 480R (1978a), Yale University.

Fisher, F., The Identification Problem in Econometrics (New York: McGraw-Hill Book Co., 1966).

Fisher, W. and Wadyck, W., Estimating a Structural Equation in a Large System, Econometrica, 39 (1971), 461-466.

Fromm, G. and Klein, L., A Comparison of Eleven Econometric Models of the United States, Papers and Proceedings of the American Economic Association, 63 (1973), 385-393.

Fromm, G. and Schink, G., Aggregation and Econometric Models, International Economic Review, 14 (1973), 1-29.

Goldberger, A.S., Econometric Theory (New York: John Wiley and Sons, Inc., 1964).

Howrey, E.P. and Kelejian, H.H., Simulation Versus Analytical Solution: The Case of Econometric Models, in Computer Simulation Experiments with Models of Economic Systems, ed. T.H. Naylor (New York: John Wiley and Sons., Inc., 1971).

Hurwicz, L., Aggregation in Macroeconomic Models, Econometrica, 20 (1952), 489-490.

Hymans, S. and Shapiro, H., The Structure and Properties of the

Michigan Quarterly Econometric Model of the U.S. Economy, International Economic Review, 15 (1974), 632-653.

Johnston, J., Econometric Methods (New York: McGraw-Hill Book Co., 1972).

Kelejian, H., Aggregation and Disaggregation of Nonlinear Econometric Equations, in Evaluation of Econometric Models, eds., J. Kmenta and J. Ramsey (New York: Academic Press, Inc., 1980).

Kelejian, H. and Madan, D., The Estimation of a Policy Response in a Nonlinear System, Economic Statistics Papers (1977), University of Sydney.

Kendall, M. and Stuart, A., The Advanced Theory of Statistics, Vol. 2, (New York: Hafner Publishing Co., 1961).

Klein, L. and Preston, R., Stochastic Nonlinear Models, Econometrica, 37 (1969), 95-106.

Lahiri, K., Multiperiod Predictions in Dynamic Models, International Economic Review, 16 (1975), 699-711.

Liebling, H., Bidwell, P. and Hall, K., The Recent Performance of Anticipation Surveys and Econometric Model Projections of Investment Spending in the United States, The Journal of Business of the University of Chicago, 49 (1976), 451-477.

McCarthy, M., Howrey, P. and Klein, L., Notes on Testing the Predictive Performance of Econometric Models, International Economic Review, 15 (1974), 366-383.

McNees, S., An Evaluation of Economic Forecasts, New England Economic Review, (1975), 3-39.

_____ , The 'Rationality' of Economic Forecasts, Papers and Proceedings of the American Economic Association, 68 (1978), 301-305.

Ramsey, J., Tests for Specification Errors in Classical Linear Least-Squares Regression Analysis, Journal of the Royal Statistical Society, Series B, 31 (1969), 350-371.

Schmidt, P., Econometrics (New York: Marcel Dekker, Inc., 1976).

Stekler, H., Studies in Income and Wealth, in B. Hickman, ed., Econometric Models of Cyclical Behavior, National Bureau of Economic Research, 1972.

Su, V., An Error Analysis of Econometric and Noneconometric Forecasts, Papers and Proceedings of the American Economic Association, 68 (1978), 306-312.

Swamy, P. and Holmes, J., The Use of Undersized Samples in the Estimation of Simultaneous Equation Systems, Econometrica, 39 (1971), 455-460.

Tsurumi, H., A Comparison of Econometric Macro Models in Three Countries, Papers and Proceedings of the American Economic Association, 63 (1973), 394-401.

Zarnowitz, V., On the Accuracy and Properties of Recent Macroeconomic Forecasts, Papers and Proceedings of the American Economic Association, 63 (1978), 313-319.

LARGE-SCALE MACRO-ECONOMETRIC MODELS
J. Kmenta, J.B. Ramsey (editors)
© North-Holland Publishing Company, 1981

# THE COMPARISON OF TIME SERIES
# AND ECONOMETRIC FORECASTING STRATEGIES

C. W. J. Granger

The basic forecasting situation is easily stated. Suppose that, at time n, one wants to forecast the next value of the series $x_t$, which will be $x_{n+1}$. Further suppose that there is an information set $I_n$ available at time n and that a cost function $C(e)$ is specified, so that $C(e)$ is the cost to the user of the forecast if a forecast error of size e is made. To produce an optimum forecast one merely has to produce a function $f_{n,1}(I_n)$ of the contents of $I_n$ so that the expected value of $C(e_{n,1})$, where

$$e_{n,1} = x_{n+1} - f_{n,1}(I_n)$$

is minimized. Having stated this, there is plenty of scope for alternative forecasting strategies as the form of the function $f_{n,1}(I_n)$ and the selection of the contents of $I_n$ are not pre-determined and are at the choice of the forecaster. There is by no means just a pair of major strategies, which might be labelled the time-series analyst's and the econometrician's approaches, but rather a whole spectrum of methods ranging from an unsophisticated, classical time-series approach to that of an unrepentant old-fashioned econometrician. Nevertheless, for purposes of exposition, it is easier to start by considering two strategies, which will be called the time-series and the econometric, to give some structure to the discussion.

The time-series analyst's basic strategy is to try to let the data suggest the appropriate specification of a model. By looking at a variety of summary statistics an attempt is made to "identify" one, or just a few models, which are then estimated and a simple diagnostic check is applied to see if the resulting model does satisfactorily fit the data. This procedure is rather well developed when the information set consists of only the past and present of the series to be forecast. These methods, which have been popularized by Box and Jenkins (1970), frequently lead to rather complex lag structures (both autoregressive and moving average) even though the techniques are biased towards low and seasonal lags. The methods are much less developed for larger information sets. When there are a (small) number of pure causal variables available for the series to be forecast, techniques are available to form unconstrained transfer functions, but the quality of the models so achieved is still unclear. When a pair of two-way causal variables are involved, Granger and Newbold (1977) have suggested a method for identifying models, but this method is complicated to apply and it is doubtful if it can be successfully generalized to much larger information sets.

Because the time-series analysts are not constained by any theory, their models are usually either reduced forms or triangular recursive forms and so may be estimated by least squares. There is currently a move to introduce exogenous variables into the models but little actual experience in doing this has been accumulated. Once a model has been derived, forecasts are easily formed because the models are linear; one specifies how the future value of interest will be generated according to the model and then replaces all variables known at time n with their observed values and all other variables with their forecast values.

The econometrician's approach to specifying a model is, of course, quite different, at least at first glance. Their models consist of many equations and plenty of variables, but the equations are relatively sparse since most variables do not enter into most equations. The inclusion or exclusion of a variable is usually determined by the application of a theory rather than any message contained in the data. In practice, of course, when a "moderate"-size econometric model of 400 or so equations is specified, it is beyond the scope of current macroeconomic theory. The theory is hardly capable of specifying all of these equations in any kind of detail; at most it may indicate potentially relevant variables for inclusion in each equation. Frequently the theory is little more than a plausible story, and only rarely does the theory being applied help to specify the lag structure of the variables.

It is perhaps curious that the econometric model builders lay quite a bit of emphasis on the use of economic theory yet virtually seem to ignore econometric theory. According to the Howrey, Klein, McCarthy and Schink survey, the builders of big models still use ordinary least squares and Durbin-Watson statistics, despite the presence of lagged dependent variables and simultaneous relationships. One wonders what has been the purpose of the work of the majority of theoretical econometricians for the last twenty years, or of a third of the pages of Econometrica.

To the eyes of an econometrician, the time-series models involve far too few variables and ridiculously few equations for them to be of any value. To the eyes of a time-series analyst the model specified and used by an econometrician displays a surprising lack of lags of both dependent and "independent" variables, except possibly in an over-constrained distributed lag form. I have said elsewhere that when a time-series analyst finds that his model is not forecasting very well, he is inclined to add further lagged terms, but when an econometrician is unhappy with his model, he adds further equations. This may not be totally true, but I do believe that the statement contains more than an element of truth and also that it reflects basic attitudes.

Before discussing the merits of the two strategies, it is worthwhile mentioning the relationship between forecasting ability and various information sets. Suppose, for convenience, that a mean-square measure is used to compare the forecasting abilities of alternative models. Let $f_{n,k}(I_n)$ and $g_{n,k}(I'_n)$ be forecasts of $x_{n+k}$ , both made at time n. If $I_n$ is included within $I'_n$ and if both forecasts are optimal (that is, they use the information in their sets in the best possible fashion and completely) then $g_{n,k}$ will not be inferior to $f_{n,k}$ ; and if the other extra information in $I'_n$ but not in $I_n$ is relevant, g should be superior.

This fact was stated by Kelejian and Vavrichek in their paper. However, a rather stronger result is available which states that any combined forecast $\lambda f_{n,k} + (1-\lambda)g_{n,k}$ cannot out-perform $g_{n,k}$ for any $\lambda$ if $g_{n,k}$ is optimal. Thus the optimal $\lambda$ is zero. A further result is that $x_{n+k} - f_{n,k}$ and $x_{n+k} - g_{n,k}$ will each be MA(k-1) if the forecasts are optimal; thus the one-step forecast errors become white noise provided that the infor mation sets are proper (that is, they contain the past and present of the series being forecast). It seems very unlikely to find in economics sufficiently broad information so that the forecast error variance is zero. I believe that economic series are never deterministic.

Finally, if $f_{n,k}$ is an optimal forecast based on a proper information set, then the variance $V_k$ of the k-step forecast error $x_{n+k} - f_{n,k}$ will be a non-decreasing sequence as k increases. If the forecast errors are not stationary, in their variances change through time, $V_k$ has to be replaced by "average variance" over a suitable time period. Variance is used here, rather than the mean-squared error, because I assume unbiased forecasts are used. It is of course sometimes possible to obtain a lower mean square by accepting some bias.

When evaluating forecasts, these various properties are useful in ranking alternative methods and in judging when an individual method produces optimum forecasts. For example, if forecasts do not make optimal use of an information set, the forecast error variances need not increase as one forecasts further ahead. The figures given in Kelejian and Vavrichek's paper are thus revealing; for example the BEA model forecasts GNP deflators eight steps ahead much better than a lesser number of steps (e.g. a mean-square error of 0.21 for eight-step fore-cast errors and 3.54 for seven steps) and the DR1 model forecasts seven steps much better than two steps (MSE of 26 compared to 142). There are many other examples, all of which suggest that

the models are capable of improvement in their specifications,
particularly if these observed differences are significant.

    If expanding the information set produces improved fore-
casts it means simply that econometric models based on large
information sets should always outperform time-series models
based on very limited information sets.  The fact that the two
types of models perform in comparable ways indicates that the
econometricians use the information sets much less intensively
than do the time-series analysts.  As has been said before, the
econometricians cannot be satisfied until a combination of forecasts from the two types of models gives (virtually) zero weight
to the forecasts based on the smaller information set.  Unfortunately this more powerful test has not been applied very
frequently, but I am certain that if an optimal combined forecast were to be constructed using econometric and time-series
forecasts, the average weights would be nearly equal.  The econometricians should take little pleasure from being told that their
models can now just outforecast simple ARMA models, both for the
reasons given above and also because the time-series analysts
are developing a number of new models which make yet more intensive use of their limited information sets.  Vector autoregressive, bilinear, and other nonlinear, long-memory and state-space
(time-varying parameters using the potentially very powerful
Kalman filter algorithm) models are the most obvious examples.

    The rules for comparing forecasting methods cannot be used
when the information sets are not nested.  Thus a bivariate
time-series model, using the past of the series to be forecast
plus results from a series of anticipations surveys, cannot be
theoretically compared to an econometric model that does not
utilize these anticipations.  The mean-squared errors of the two
sets of forecasts can be compared and a combined forecast formed,
but one has no a priori expectations about the results.  If a
combined forecast proves superior then it suggests that a superior econometric model is possible, once more.  However, this
better model may not completely satisfy the prescribed economic
theory that the original model used.

    This problem of making theory and the data more compatible
is easily solved, at least in theory.  The reason that the econometrician requires the use of a theory is clear.  As he is dealing
simultaneously with lots of variables, the number of possible
alternative models becomes immense and the quantity of data
available is insufficient for a proper selection process to be
applied.  By incorporating a theory, he is essentially adding
to his information set--and in a particularly useful fashion,
if the theory gives many zero restrictions.  Of course a bad
theory will be effectively adding irrelevant data, or worse.
The weakness of the approach is that, at least in theory, the
evidence from the data cannot be used to overturn the poor
theory because the theory is not being tested.  In practice,
some data mixing certainly occurs.  To my mind a partial Bayesian
approach would be better here.  For coefficients in the model
that are put at zero by one theory but which other theories
would not put at zero (that is, the more controversial coeffi-

cients) a fairly tight Bayesian prior distribution could be used, such as a normal with zero mean and a small standard deviation $\sigma$ . Thus the present method, which would put $\sigma = 0$, is replaced by a more flexible technique that would allow any nonzero coefficient value to be reached if there were enough data. However, the use of such techniques is the fight of the Bayesian rather than the time series analyst and, of course, this fight is already well under way.

The eventual objective of both classical econometricians and classical time-series analysts is to produce a good approximation to the true underlying generating process for the macro-economy. It is clear that both sides have something to contribute to the discovery of such a model, assuming that it exists. It is also clear that neither group has so far come anywhere near this model. It also seems obvious that worthwhile progress has been made in recent years in learning from each other. Time series analysts are worrying about how to build models involving more variables and the econometricians are now worrying much more about lags. Nevertheless, the gap between the two strategies is still considerable.

A modest attempt at a synthesis of the two approaches has recently been discussed in Ashley and Granger (1979). There, the residuals from equations of an econometric model are subjected to time-series analysis, both for individual series of residuals and for pairs of such series. The result is a suggested re-specification involving a more complicated residual temporal structure, greater use of lagged dependent and independent variables and a re-classification of variables between endogenous and exogenous. To the time-series analyst's eye, the assumption by econometricians that their residuals are either white noise or AR(1) is a very curious one. Having analysed many such residual series, I have to say that I have only rarely identified such simple models. However, yet more curious are those models which attempt to explain one variable only in terms of other variables, ignoring the past of the dependent variable.

Two further points need to be made. Howrey, Klein, McCarthy and Schink point out that time-series models are irrelevant for policy considerations. This is obviously quite correct, but exactly the same remark can be made about a poorly specified econometric model. However, a badly specified econometric model is even more dangerous because it may appear to have something to say about alternative policies and yet actually may be very misleading.

Finally, there is the topic of structural change. One frequently claimed virtue and advantage of a structural econometric model over a reduced form model is that when a change in the economic structure occurs, this is easily assimilated and thus improved forecasts results. It would be interesting to see evidence of this advantage actually occurring. To the outsider it appears that after periods such as 1974, econometric models that have performed poorly are then "fixed up" to allow for the new circumstances. Once more, if and when a really good struc-

tural model is found, it will have the advantage of incorporating structural changes, but so far the models appear not to be
adequate for this occur.  This is hardly suprising when some
of the better known of these models contain dummy variables to
"mop up" periods when the model did not fit the data adequately.
Surely, a properly specified structural model would not need
to use such dummies.


REFERENCES


Ashley, R. A. and Granger, C. W. J., "Time Series Analysis of
     Residuals From the St. Louis Model", Journal of Macroecono-
     mics, v. 1 1979  pp.  373-394.

Box, G. E. P. and Jenkins, G. M., Time Series Analysis, Fore-
     casting and Control,  San Francisco: Holden Day, 1970.

Granger, C. W. J., Forecasting in Business and Economics,
     Academic Press, 1980.

Granger, C. W. J. and Newbold, P., Forecasting Economic Time
     Series, Academic Press, 1977.

LARGE-SCALE MACRO-ECONOMETRIC MODELS
J. Kmenta, J.B. Ramsey (editors)
© North-Holland Publishing Company, 1981

THE PROBLEM WITH WHAT THEY DO AND WHY THEY DO IT:  A COMMENT ON
THE PAPER PREPARED BY LAWRENCE R. KLEIN, E. PHILIP HOWREY,
MICHAEL D. McCARTHY AND GEORGE R. SCHINK

Karl Brunner

Graduate School of Management
University of Rochester
Rochester, New York
U.S.A.

The comments offer an explanation of the authors' rationale for
"why they do what they do".  A Laplacian vision of the world
seems to yield quite naturally the major emphasis and
interpretation offered by the authors.  A critical examination of
this cognitive vision leads in the last section to a restatement of
a "classical program" as an alternative to the large-scale
modelling effort.

Almost half a century ago Jan Tinbergen published his pioneering study exploring the
nature of economic fluctuations in the USA.  The evolution initiated with this endeavor
was suspendend for a decade by the political storm of the second world war.  But the
momentum of the "Keynesian Revolution" created new impulses driving the
econometric exploration of an economy's global behavior.  The isolated endeavors
swelled over the decades to a broad stream including an expanding range of scholars
over the whole world.  The modelling of economic activity became moreover ever
more ambitious.  The size of the equation system expanded and models containing at
least 500 equations with hundreds of exogenous variables emerged during the 1970's as
a standard product.  The level of sophistication achieved over the years in this pursuit
is certainly impressive.  Similarly impressive is the accumulated investment of
resources reflected at this time by a massive "technological" and organizational
apparatus.  Lastly, even more impressive are the opportunities for effective exercises
in wealth maximizing behavior centered on the use and sequential development of
large (and larger) scale econometric models purporting to explain the interaction
between global movements and allocative processes characterizing an economy.  This
success on the marketplace, within the profession and also beyond the profession
devoted to users in business and government, yields by itself no information about the
cognitive returns on the investment made or the cognitive role of the whole endeavor.
The "sociology" of large scale econometric model construction may be a fascinating
subject and offers some intriguing information.  The nature of this market fostering
this allocation of resources over the postwar period could form an interesting subject
of research in its own right.  The Conference sponsored by the National Science
Foundation was however not designed to address these aspects, important as they may
be in order to understand the avalanche of large scale modelling with all their links and
satellite systems.  Our attention is directed to essentially cognitive issues and
cognitive aspects of large scale econometric model building and model use.  This
activity is purported to yield (eventually) superior formulations of hypotheses or
theories bearing on the operation of economic systems.  Given the real cost of the
intellectual investment, the cognitive returns should be correspondingly high in order
to justify the survival of this activity within the intellectual market.  The paper
presented by the four authors at the Conference describes "why they do what they do",
at least in the realm of large-scale econometric modelling.  It offers thus the
professionals' deliberate reflection bearing on the question addressed by the
Conference.  My comments examine "what is done and why it is done" in the context of

the arguments and views advanced by the authors.

## THE RATIONALE OF LARGE-SCALE MODEL CONSTRUCTIONS

The authors provide an informative summary of the rationale underlying the massive research effort expressed by large scale modelling.  The following assembly covers probably most of the arguments addressed in the paper:

a) Larger models provide better approximations to the ideal Walrasian model representing the full reality of the world.  An inherent complexity of the world cannot be adequately grasped analytically in the context of small-scale hypotheses.  We also hear that "everything depends on everything else".  It appears to follow under the circumstances that "optimal forecasting" requires larger models.  Alternatively, we are told that the nature of the economic process naturally imposes the requirement of a large model size.  There occurs also a strong belief that a minimal, but substantial, disaggregation is unavoidable for the purposes addressed with model constructions.

b) Larger models offer a ready made framework to integrate "special events" occurring in shifting locations of the economy.

c) The users of the model respond positively to an ever increasing supply of detailed data.

d) The accuracy of the forecasts will increase with the model size.

e) An increasing array of policy instruments requires a corresponding extension of the model in order to proceed with the policy analysis required.

f) The formulation of a large model forces the researcher "to lay down his bets explicitly".  It compels him to an objective, interpersonally intelligible formulation contrasting with the perils inherent in an essentially judgmental approach to policy problems.

g) The expanding potency of computers encourages a matching expansion of computational demands.  The supply of computer services creates its own demand in the form of large-scale models.

h) Larger models improve our understanding of an economy's mode of operation. They improve most particularly our understanding of turning points in the evolution of economic fluctuations.

## THE COGNITIVE VISION OF THE RATIONALE

The array of views motivating the construction of large scale econometric models reflects basically a specific cognitive vision.  The diverse arguments form a coherent story conditioned by a pervasive "Laplacian tradition".  This tradition may be characterized by two connected strands woven into a single program expressed by the idea of a deterministic and encompassingly interdependent world.  It appears that in the authors' minds the world is best represented as an enormous Walrasian model including the full richness of all the detailed transactions evolving over time.  This encompassing model reflects the pervasive interdependence of all events and processes ever observed.  Once we recognize that "everything depends on everything else" an encompassing model becomes the only acceptable paradigm.  But more or less uniform interdependence stretching in all directions is supplemented by another strand in order to constitute the "Laplacian tradition".  This strand involves the conception of an essentially deterministic world.  Not only does everything depend on everything else, but everything is fully determined without any loose ends by an encompassing process of social interaction.

This cognitive vision effectively explains the diverse components of the rationale summarized above.  The underlying vision controls the search for ever expanding models.  It also guides the search for ever more detail expressed by the aspects of economic life incorporated into the models and the linkage and satellite programs developed.  Two major implications of the basic vision should be noted for our purposes.  They bear on the use and interpretation of measures revealing goodness of fit and accuracy of forecasts.  They also affect the interpretation of the stochasticity built into the models actually used.  Once we accept the Laplacian view we are committed to interpret the probability concept as an expression of our comparative ignorance about the full and (non-stochastically) systematic detail of a deterministic process.  The German logician and philosopher of science Stegmüller emphasized in particular the association between a "subjective" or "personal" probability concept and a deterministic vision of the world.  A subjective interpretation of probability emerges in this context as a necessary and sufficient condition of a deterministic conception.  It follows under the circumstances that forecast accuracy and goodness of fit form the natural and relevant criterion guiding the search for larger models and controlling the evaluation of imperfect approximations to the encompassing true "Walrasian model" incorporating the full reality.  The construction and evaluation of large (and larger) models in accordance with a goodness of fit criterion converges on the average towards the true underlying model.  This convergence seems assured by the cognitive vision motivating (or justifying) the rationale expressed and the associated activities.  All revisions in existing models raising the goodness of fit thus lower the remaining subjective ignorance about aspects of a full and deterministic reality.

The two strands of the basic cognitive vision also explain the pervasive appearance of instrumentalist and descriptivist aspects and attitudes in the large scale modelling game.  Instrumentalist interpretations of science occurred ever since Copernicus and Galileo threatened the interpretation monopoly of the Christian tradition.  The emerging science could hardly be faulted in terms of its evident success to "reproduce" intellectually important and occasionally puzzling observations.  But the hypotheses and theories advanced could not be accepted as cognitive interpretations of our universe.  Such cognition beyond the control of an institutionalized faith threatened the understanding offered by a theological inheritance.  This competition by an alternative interpretation could hardly be tolerated.  Still, the "technical achievements" of the new science were difficult to contest.  This intellectual dilemma was resolved with an instrumentalist and thus essentially non-cognitive interpretation of scientific activities with the resulting product.  Hypotheses and theories offer under this interpretation no cognitive representation of the world.  They contain no meaningful statements and yield no understanding about structure or operation of our environment.  This understanding and meaning is only supplied by the philosophical or theological heritage.  Hypotheses and theories advanced in the context of scientific endeavors subsume under the circumstances no cognitive dimension.  They are but tools for efficient computation or devices for conveniently tracking in one sense or another useful observations.  They are but instruments effectively summarizing observational patterns.  No cognitive claim is associated with such instruments.  The cognitive claim remains the monopoly of the philosophical-theological tradition.

The descriptivist attitude emerges from a very different background.  It was not launched by the attempts of an endangered monopolist to protect the accustomed controls over prevalent beliefs and cognitive claims.  A descriptivist attitude reflects the view that an understanding of any process or phenomenon is fostered by a massive attention to all possible observational detail.  It conditions, for instance, the view that no understanding of inflation can be achieved without systematic attention to all the detail of price-setting among the variety of suppliers or demanders.  It also conditions the view that we will never understand adequately the nature of monetary processes without tracing the fullest detail of all the channels in a nation's credit markets.

We can easily recognize that a descriptivist position occurs as a natural by-product of the basic cognitive vision motivating large scale modelling.  The commitment to a deterministic world with an encompassing interdependence produces the descriptivist interest as an unavoidable consequence. This descriptivist attention does not enter the econometric game under consideration as an independent condition shaping the approach to work. Descriptivism emerges thus as a natural product of the underlying cognitive vision. This is however not the case for instrumentalism. The cognitive vision described above does indeed produce a habit emphasizing forecasts and their accuracy. We find no doubt some strands of instrumentalist tradition or overtones permeating the large scale modelling endeavor. But these strands are not accompanied by the usual instrumentalist interpretation of the analytic constructions advanced. The cognitive vision underlying the econometric endeavor *appears* to suggest, with the resulting emphasis on forecastability, accuracy, etc., an instrumentalist disposition. This may be reinforced by the language occasionally used to describe the general nature of the ongoing work. But this emphasis on forecastability, accuracy, computability, and quantifiability is a natural consequence of the basic vision. This vision also justifies a general *cognitive* claim to the endeavor not reconcilable with the instrumentalist tradition.

## SOME CRITICAL EXPLORATION OF THE COGNITIVE VISION

An implicit assumption of the cognitive vision needs to be clearly discerned for our purposes. It suggests that the underlying Walrasian model offers somehow a representation of *full* reality. This representation is apparently characterized by the limit of the goodness of fit values with a complete forecast accuracy. This limit expresses a total endogeneity of all aspects in reality. The occurrence of exogenous variables and stochastic disturbances in the context of any analytic representation determines its essentially incomplete construction offering a more or less adequate approximation to the full reality aspired to. In the context of an encompassing interdependence no exogenous magnitudes can remain. There seems, however, no evidence available suggesting that we approach the limit in our lifetime or even ever at all in the future. There are on the contrary good grounds to argue that we will not move ever closer to this limit.

We are indebted to Robert Lucas for an explicit recognition that the structure of economic processes are not invariant with respect to variations in policy regimes. Lucas emphasizes the effect of changing policy regimes on agents' behavior via the formation of expectations bearing on the stance of policy. The information process underlying the "Lucas effect" needs to be broadened however. The market mechanism operates, beyond the determination of prices and transactions, a vast communication system disseminating information. The information conveyed modifies over time the agents' opportunity sets. It follows that the social interaction expressed by the market process generates drifting changes in an economy's detailed response structure. The basic patterns established by economic analysis, e.g. the responsiveness of agents' behavior to variations in relevant costs and yields, remains indeed invariant. But the markets' communication and information process changes the range of relevant costs and yields affecting the agents' behavior. The underlying Walrasian model motivating or justifying large scale econometric modelling offers thus no resting place or natural fix point for the analysis. It is, if we insist on its existence, an entity drifting over time according to an unknown stochastic process. But this implication destroys any real significance of an encompassing Walrasian model operating as a convergence limit with respect to actual model constructions guided by measures of goodness of fit. The vision of an underlying determinacy appears under the circumstances as a metaphysical dream. We will remain forever confronted with a pervasive and ineradicable stochasticity enmeshed in the patterns of social interactions.

This ineradicable stochasticity lowers the significance and weakens the rationale of judging the cognitive status of an econometric model in terms of any set of goodness of fit measures. This implication raises the importance of potential evaluations beyond the standard goodness of fit and forecast accuracy procedures. We note that the range of propositions bearing on important response patterns vary substantially between alternative large-scale models even against the background of comparatively similar global forecast performances. These differences were hardly exploited for the benefit of systematic evaluations bearing on the cognitive status of alternative models. More detailed evaluations centered on implied economic propositions offer little attraction so long as we consider the array of existing models as stepping stones to ever better approximations. The major incentive directs intellectual efforts under the circumstances toward an endless sequence of restructuring, enlarging or reestimating the analytic construction in diverse modes.

The attention directed by the authors to "validation and tests" in econometric modelling seems to falsify the statement made in the previous paragraph. But the meaning of these validation and test exercises needs to be examined more carefully. Eckstein describes the content of the validation procedure with particular explicitness. Two aspects are involved: simulation analysis and the standard test statistics applied to the single equations of the model. The use of the standard test statistics clearly reveals their role. They are dominantly used in the context of search for a hypothesis. They are devices used to sort alternative contenders among potential components constituting the model on the way to a "final" formulation. The test statistics are moreover usually applied in the context of an assessment against the permanent chance alternative. On either count the standard test statistics offer no relevant information bearing on the comparative cognitive status of the end product emerging from the search. The use of these statistics in the context of search could at best be interpreted to condition the prior probabilities assigned to alternative hypotheses in preparation of Baysian test procedure.

The simulation analysis proposed covers single equations, historical dynamic simulation of the full system, implications of states with extreme input values, and ex ante long-run simulations in order to explore implicit growth patterns. All this is supplemented by simulations directed to compare crucial response patterns (e.g. multipliers) built into the model with the patterns customarily associated with Keynesian theory. Validation expressed by such simulation analysis thus involves two activities. The last strand of these activities mentioned above, i.e. the comparison with theoretically expected patterns, simply functions as a control over the emerging construction. The latter should satisfy some initial constraints on the response patterns and the global performance. These constraints express the researcher's prior commitments guiding his search activities in the formulation of the model. This portion of the simulation procedures thus operates similarly to the standard test statistics as a criterion guiding the researcher to the final formulation. The criteria used appear as implicit constraints on the search activities and thus ultimately on the class of emerging hypotheses. They offer however no information about the comparative cognitive status of the completed hypotheses (i.e. the fully specified model).

The other simulation activities listed above serve another function. They are essentially explorations of the logical content of the completed hypothesis. They form an important preparation for any cognitive assessment of the analytic construction. This simulation uncovers the major patterns implied by the hypothesis. It also uncovers crucial implications which could be exploited for an assessment against systematic alternatives. Simulations and the usual application of standard statistics in standard modes are certainly not useless exercises. They both perform a relevant function. But the term "validation" badly mis-labels this function and misleads the unwary reader and very often, apparently, also the researcher coping with the large modelling efforts. "Validation" in the econometricians sense refers to potentially useful examinations proceeding in the context of search with little, if any, spillover to the context of systematic evaluation assessing the comparative cognitive status of competing hypotheses.

Eckstein elaborates with similar clarity the meaning of the "tests" carried out in the context of large-scale modelling efforts. Such tests involve two components. One component addresses again "the standard statistical tests" expressed by a "corrected R-square, Durbin-Watson statistic etc.". These are, moreover, supplemented by the computation of the root mean square based on a "full dynamic history". The last component of the "tests" invokes an examination of "consistency with economic theory". This examination of "consistency" should again be understood as a screening device guiding the construction process. But this screening device, as any criterion used in the context of search, offers no relevant information bearing on the comparative cognitive status of the finished hypothesis. The first component essentially coincides, moreover, with the role of the standard test statistics occurring in the context of "validation". They provide at this stage, however, additional information about the degree of approximation to the full reality of our world achieved with any given construction. This "test component" thus forms an essential feature of the cognitive vision underlying this intellectual endeavor.

Our examination of the activities pursued under the heading of "validation and tests" establishes the following result: Some are immediate consequences of the cognitive vision enunciated above and most involve useful and even necessary steps constituting the context of search or analysis of a hypothesis. But the validation and tests summarized are not addressed to the systematic evaluation of the completed hypothesis expressed by the full construction of the model. This neglect of a meaningful evaluation of alternative constructions is most probably conditioned by the underlying cognitive vision. This vision tends to assign more importance to the persistent restructuring, expansion, and complication of an ever more encompassingly interrelated model than to the systematic evaluation of the cognitive status of *existing* models. This statement does not deny the occurrence of detailed examinations, even competitive examinations, of large-scale econometric models. But all these examinations were controlled by the same cognitive vision guiding the whole endeavor. Such examinations concentrated under the circumstances on goodness of fit and relative accuracy of forecasts. There remains a further dimension to be considered, however. A systematic evaluation bearing on the comparative cognitive status of competing constructions can only proceed in case the contending constructions satisfy a minimal requirement for the occurrence of an empirical hypothesis. This minimal requirement can be expressed in terms of a positive empirical context. This content is constituted by the set of all possible observations which are either inconsistent or highly unlikely under the hypothesis to be considered. This empirical content determines the extent and degree of information conveyed by the hypothesis. The information offered by a hypothesis rises with its empirical content. The occurrence of empirical contents with non-overlapping subsets also assures us that discriminating tests can in principle be applied to contending models. The constructions under consideration are empirical hypotheses amenable to systematic evaluation on the basis of relevant observation.

The question whether or not the product of large scale modelling efforts do satisfy the requirements of an empirical hypothesis has been repeatedly raised for discussion. It has also been repeatedly answered in the negative. Two major aspects of the modelling effort need be examined in this context. They involve the degree of freedom problem and the fine-tuning activities applied to the model. The degree of freedom problem emerged in the context of simultaneous equation estimation procedures. It is not a problem inherent in such procedures. It is typically produced however, by the expanding size of the models. The model size demanded by the underlying cognitive vision creates an excessive number of exogenous variables, frequently lowering the available degrees of freedom to a *negative* number. This problem is resolved within the context of simultaneous equation estimation with the aid of a variety of techniques. Such procedures essentially involve the imposition of additional constraints on the joint behavior of exogenous magnitudes. But this means that exogenous variables are implicitly asserted to be governed by a systematic process. The nature of this process remains, however, somewhat of a mystery and is not explicated with an adequately formulated auxiliary hypothesis supplementing the central model. In the absence of an explicitly stated auxiliary hypothesis, this resolution of the degree of freedom problem produces ultimately a construction with an indeterminate empirical content. The resulting construction, however impressive its analytic features and sweep, does not satisfy the requirement of an empirical hypothesis. It involves but a pretension at scientific hypothesis formulation. The four authors seem to acknowledge the degree of freedom problem and avoid it by sacrificing any attempt at simultaneous equation estimation. The authors' argument is most forthright in this respect. The choice of an OLS procedures indeed exorcises the degree of freedom problem. It also appears, after all, that the statistical properties of the simultaneous equation estimators are not necessarily so superior once we proceed beyond the first two moments.

The choice of estimation technique does not resolve the "fine-tuning" problem, however. The nature of the procedure is well known and clearly described by the authors. It is customary among practitioners of the large scale modelling game to impose some constraints on both exogenous variables and stochastic disturbances in the usual preparation of forecasts. The researcher typically develops unconditional or conditional projections of all the exogenous variables occurring as inputs into the model. These projections implicitly express a set of hypotheses about the behavior of relatively exogenous processes. These hypotheses may actually violate the basic exogeneity assumption and recognize a feedback from the endogenous process to the projected profile of some policy variable. Such inconsistency would, of course, destroy the originally formulated hypothesis and produce a vanishing empirical content.

The imposition of constraints on the behavior of residuals occurs probably as a more pervasive problem. Such constraints may be formulated on the basis of observed serial correlation, or may be introduced on the basis of ad hoc mechanical procedures or judgment. All three procedures formulate supplementary conjectures about the economy's operation. These conjectures may be formulated in a mode which yields a definite content and allows thus a critical assessment. The judgmental procedure relies, however, on a personal guessing game controlled by an unspecified hypothesis inaccessible to interpersonal evaluation. With the properties of the disturbances not specified by an explicit hypothesis, the empirical content of the model remains quite indeterminate. We can hardly accept it under the circumstances as an empirical hypothesis. The model appears as a numerological instrument producing numbers to be sold on the forecasting market. The numerological denial of an empirical hypothesis is reinforced by the custom of sequentially adjusting the expected residual value in order to move the forecast values within a predetermined "reasonable" range. We observe in this context how the incentives of the forecast market foster an instrumentalist behavior not inherent in the "Laplacian tradition". But this behavior empties the massive constructions even more effectively of all cognitive claims than the Inquisition.

## AN ALTERNATIVE APPROACH

My critique is not addressed to econometric theory or its use in empirical work. It is addressed to a particular mode of work represented by large scale econometric modelling. But critique remains empty without an alternative idea to be ultimately assessed in terms of the original critique. This alternative is hardly a secret and has been more or less successfully practiced by the profession over a considerable time span. This alternative rejects both components of the Laplacian tradition. It acknowledges the objective reality of stochastic processes as an inherent property of nature and society. It also recognizes substantial and usefully discernible differences in the order of magnitude of dependencies in various directions. The alternative vision thus rejects a deterministic concept of the world and emphasizes the essential emptiness of slogans asserting that "everything depends on everything else". It rejects thus in particular the view of a more or less uniformly encompassing interdependence.

The rejection of the Laplacian tradition yields for our purposes two important implications. The acceptance of a pervasive indeterminacy built into the core of nature changes our interpretation bearing on goodness of fit measures of forecast accuracy. These measures lose their central position as guiding beacons in the construction of hypotheses. But most particularly, they offer per se, used in the usual manner, no information about the comparative cognitive status of alternative hypotheses. The standard goodness of fit comparisons do not satisfy the logical requirement of an adequate test procedure bearing on contending claims. We note that for every stochastic hypothesis there exists a range of very high or very low R-square values which appear unlikely under the specified stochastic properties. Sample values of R-square beyond some benchmark levels must be interpreted under the circumstances as negative evidence with respect to the hypothesis under consideration.

The binding character of a test statement depends on a specific logical relation between a test statement and the hypothesis to be tested. Within the class of non-stochastic hypotheses, test statements appear as logical implications of a conjunction formed by the hypothesis and appropriate boundary conditions as component statements. The falsehood of the test statement, established by its incompatibility with critical observation, unavoidably falsifies the antecedent conjunction. With good reasons to maintain the statements summarizing the boundary conditions, falsification is concentrated on the hypothesis. The situation differs somewhat in the case of stochastic hypotheses. The hypothesis supplemented with appropriate boundary conditions logically implies a probability statement. The test statement occurs as a clause in this probability statement. Two simple schematic examples may illustrate the issue. Let $h(y,x,\pi,u)$ describe a class of definite statements explaining the behavior of a vector y in terms of exogenous variables x, fixed parameters and a stochastic term u satisfying specified stochastic properties. This general specification assures that h represents a hypothesis with positive content. We can then write

$$h(y,x,\pi,u).x = x_o \supset P\left[y \epsilon R(y_o)\right] \geq 1 - \alpha$$

where $x_o$ is a definite value of x, $y_o$ the value determined by $h(y,x_o,\pi,0)$ and y the observed value; R refers to an admissible range of y-values centered on $y_o$ corresponding to the benchmark probability $\alpha$. This probability is selected to represent the researcher's assessment of "almost certain event". With $\alpha$ sufficiently small, y is in R "almost certainly". An inductive step yields thus the test statement $y \epsilon R(y_o)$. This test statement can be confronted by appropriate computations derived from a sample and falsified or verified. Its falsification does not falsify the logical implication $P[y \epsilon R(y_o)] \geq 1 - \alpha$ derived from the hypothesis and the boundary condition. The falsification of the test statement provides, however, good grounds, based on the researcher's inductive commitment expressed by $\alpha$, for rejecting the statement $P[y \epsilon R(y_o)] \geq 1 - \alpha$ and thus for rejecting the hypothesis h (assuming good grounds to accept the boundary condition).

A second example reveals alternative test opportunities associated with the identification problem. Suppose that the formulation of the hypothesis h does not uniquely fix the parameter $\pi$. Three cases have usually been distinguished:

underidentification, exact and overidentification. It has been argued on occasion in the past as if these states were inherent in the nature of things. They are not. They are our creations emerging in the context of search for a hypothesis. Underidentification simply means that we suspended our task to formulate a hypothesis. We fail under the circumstances to provide the conditions necessary for the successful termination of hypothesis construction. Exact identification means, in contrast, that we provided sufficient conditions to terminate successfully the construction of a hypothesis with the aid of estimation techniques applied to a sample. Overidentification ultimately means that we have constructed a hypothesis (or a class of hypotheses) before application of statistical inferences. The sample can be used under the circumstances both for estimation and a relevant test. Overidentification appears on a first impression as a kind of overdetermination. But this would be a misleading impression. The degree of apparent overdetermination describes the range or number of test statements available. These test statements occur within linear systems as rational expressions $R(\pi)$ of the parameter vector $\pi$. The test situation can be formulated in this case as follows

$$h[\,h,x,\pi,u\,].S \supset P[\,R(\pi,S)\,\epsilon C\,] \geq 1 - \alpha$$

The conjunction of the hypothesis with the sample statement S logically implies a probability statement involving the rational expression based on $\pi$. This expression must lie with probability at least $1 - \alpha$ in a configuration C. An inductive step yields the test statement $R(\pi,S)\epsilon C$ to be confronted with computational implications from a given sample. We note that the variation in the game does not modify the basic logical structure of the test situation.

The crucial condition associated with this aspect of the alternative approach must be recognized in the attention to testability. Such testability requires that test statements can be derived, and this requires a sufficiently developed construction of the underlying idea into an empirical hypothesis. We may interpret in this context an objection occasionally advanced to the standard game as a somewhat misleading formulation of a relevant emphasis. Some economists object to the usual econometric practice as an expression of "ad hoc procedures". Such objections are usually not connected with the logician's reference to ad hocery. The objection usually means in this context that a particular formulation has not been derived from a higher level hypothesis. Such objections are however by themselves, without further investigation, without force. The cognitive status of an empirical hypothesis is not necessarily affected by having it subsumed under a higher level hypothesis. The argument should be understood as a methodological device suggesting the exploitation of higher level hypotheses as a means to tighter conditions with specific economic interpretations for the formulations eventually advanced as an empirical hypothesis. We should refrain, however, from legislating that all empirical hypotheses at any given time must be constructed in this manner.

The rejection of the Laplacian tradition also bears on its second strand. We may continue to accept the occurrence of an encompassing interdependence. But we do insist in this case that such interdependence is far from uniform and varies widely in the order of magnitude of its relevant operation. One wonders in this respect what the explanatory value of the multi-hundred of exogenous variables really is when attempting to explain the observable behavior of major aggregate patterns. Are these multi-hundred exogenous variables uniformly relevant in a model's explanation of inflation, of the movement in interest rates or of nominal GNP? Or could it be that a small subset of all the exogenous variables actually explains quite adequately major aggregate phenomena with little contribution from the mass of exogenous variables? I conjecture that these questions would be answered affirmatively by a detailed examination of all the available models.

Major scientific advances are achieved by disregarding the injunction that "everything depends on everything else" with a felicitous simplification. The classical program clearly expressed this attitude. It more or less implicitly separated global and allocative aspects of an economy. The program essentially asserts that major global phenomena, as for instance the inflation rate, can be adequately explained without invoking a host of allocative processes. Many important problems, on the other hand, pose dominantly allocative issues with comparatively minor global feedbacks. Such problems are most usefully approached in the context of an allocative hypothesis specified for this purpose. The basic idea should not be interpreted as an ontological principle about the "deepest reality". It is offered as a methodological rule guiding our approach to cope with a wide array of problems. It is a rule essentially designed to direct our attention to the construction of manageable formulations satisfying the requirement of an empirical hypothesis with an intelligible interpretation. The rule is certainly not beyond an assessable challenge. It could be successfully violated. And if it is, so be it; we would have gained an interesting hypothesis. Large scale modelling has offered so far no useful evidence suggesting that we abandon the rule. The problems associated with this particular econometric practice and conditioned by its underlying vision still indicate to me, at least in the range of our cognitive endeavors, the viability, if not superiority, of the classical program.

LARGE-SCALE MACRO-ECONOMETRIC MODELS
J. Kmenta, J.B. Ramsey (editors)
© North-Holland Publishing Company, 1981

DISCUSSION

Stephen M. Goldfeld

Princeton University

Princeton, New Jersey, U.S.A.

The papers in this session analyze the role of macroeconometric
models in forecasting from a variety of perspectives.  The most
formal approach is contained in the interesting paper by  Kelejian and Vavrichek (KV).  This paper advances two somewhat controversial themes:  (i)  forecast accuracy is not a useful way
to "validate" econometric models;  and (ii) the main value  of
an econometric model in forecasting is as a computational device.  The restrictive nature of the assumptions necessary to
yield these conclusions, however, would seem to limit dramatically their practical relevance.  To see why this is so it may
help to review briefly the essence of the formal argument.

KV consider a situation where we are confronted with a number
of alternatively but properly specified models.  These models
may differ in size and in terms of which  variables are treated as exogenous or endogenous.  While this situation may sound
puzzling,  it is the definition of model "properness"  which
makes it formally possible. More specifically, in its most extreme version, for any particular choice of endogenous and exogenous variables,  the model builder is assumed to know  the
correct form and the parameters  of the conditional distribution of the endogenous variables,  given the exogenous  variables.  Armed with this information, forecasting in principle
becomes a rather simple matter because one can calculate the
expected value of the endogenous variables conditional on the
exogenous ones.   As KV characterize it, the main role for an
econometric model in such a framework  is as a computational
device.  In particular, a model may be used as a substitute
for the relevant conditional distribution in calculating the

expected values of the endogenous variables (i.e., the forecasts), either through the use of stochastic simulation or numerical integration.

As should be apparent from this description, in realistic situations model builders have considerably less information than is necessary to specify a proper conditional distribution or a proper model. Indeed, the form of this distribution will vary depending upon the choice of endogenous and exogenous variables. For example, one could well imagine a "proper" model in which one endogenous variable is a function of a single exogenous variable. However, despite its apparent simplicity, calculating the relevant conditional distribution for such a model is likely to require an incredible degree of a priori information. In a more plausible setting, the model builder or forecaster is likely to face considerable uncertainty as to the proper or correct form of the model as well as to the relevant underlying parameter values. In such an environment model building takes on a more search-like nature -- one in which forecasting accuracy may well have a useful role to play in model validation. Furthermore, in the absence of knowledge of needed model parameters, these must be estimated and the model itself becomes more than a computational convenience.

KV are, of course, aware of these issues but they tend to downplay their relevance. They do this in part by considering two examples where good models forecast less well than misspecified ones. While the examples are clever, I don't think they are sufficiently general to really establish their case. Indeed, one doesn't need econometrics to make the same point. One can simply contrast a clock which is randomly off by a minute at each instant with another clock which is stopped. There are clearly certain time intervals when the stopped clock is the better forecaster but few would advocate using the stopped clock for general forecasting. While the analogy to the KV examples may not be perfect, their rather specific nature leaves me unconvinced that forecasting as a validation technique is not worthwhile.

The papers by Howrey, Klein, McCarthy and Schink and by Shapiro and Garman provide an interesting overview of model building and forecasting, both past and present.  The Howrey et.al.
paper contains a survey of model building practices and  a
plausible subtitle for the paper might be "the five little models and how they grew." The survey responses come from eminently reasonable people and consequently yield reasonably but
hardly surprising results.  (To some extent the paper has the
air of a group of distinguished economists retaking their general examinations and at least this discussant votes to pass
them.)

Rather than attempt to summarize the consensus of the survey,
it will be more useful if we ask how model-building practices
have changed in the last 20 years, say, and to identify those
areas where more progress is still needed.  (The Shapiro-Gar-
man paper asks another interesting question -- the extent to
which models have contributed to improved decision-making in
economic policy -- but anything other than a flip answer to
this question would take us too far afield.)

Model building has, in many obvious ways, changed noticeably
in the past few decades. Due in substantial part to advances
in computing, models have gotten larger as more and more sectoral detail has been incorporated. Some of this reflects the
demand for detail on the part of model users, a factor which
accounts for another new development -- the commercial profit-
ability of econometric model services. Computing advances have
also made practical the use of nonlinear models and a host of
other sophisticated statistical techniques (e.g., for dealing
with limited or truncated dependent variables). One slight bit
of negative fallout from the computer revolution has been the
ease of data mining but it would be churlish to overemphasize
this point.

Despite the many advances in model building, there are those
who would argue that not all is well with macroeconometric
models.   To a certain extent, this feeling stems from the

more general disagreements which currently pervade macroeconomics.  I have in mind here the recent supply-side debate and
questions pertaining to the importance and treatment of expectations.   These somewhat cosmic issues aside, there remain a
number of ways in which model-building practices have not really changed much in the last two decades which may well deserve
attention.  Some examples of this include the following:

-- Despite econometric and computing advances, ordinary
   least squares remains the most prevalent estimating
   technique for large models.

-- Model builders still tend to wave their hands at
   aggregation problems, of either the conventional
   or temporal sort.

-- Excessive reliance is placed on quarterly postwar
   time series data.

-- Insufficient attention is paid to integrating the
   various financial and nonfinancial aspects of firm
   and household behavior.

-- Model dynamics and lag structures are generally
   treated as empirical matters with theory providing only limited guidance.

While others would undoubtedly offer a somewhat different list,
I trust few would quarrel with the notion that  there remains
ample room for further advances in model building practices.

One final point I would like to address concerns the virtue of
model size for forecasting purposes.  In some crude sense, it
might be hoped that larger models would diversify the forecaster against the possibility that some important equation would
go off track.  While to some extent this may have taken place,
I continue to be impressed with the vulnerability of the performance of large models to individual equations.   In recent

years, for example, errant money demand equations have created
substantial problems for forecasting and policy analysis.[1]
What this suggests, is that the issue of big vs. small models
may be a bit of a red herring as far as forecasting is concerned. Put another way, while large models are useful for
many purposes, it is hardly a foregone conclusion that ever
larger models will contribute to improved forecasting.

---

[1] For an earlier example involving a malfunctioning housing
equation see my comments in The Brookings Model: Perspective
and Recent Developments, edited by G. Fromm and L. R. Klein,
Amsterdam, North-Holland Publishing Co., 1975, pp. 353-358.

LARGE-SCALE MACRO-ECONOMETRIC MODELS
J. Kmenta, J.B. Ramsey (editors)
© North-Holland Publishing Company, 1981

MODEL SIZE AND THE EVALUATION OF THE FORECASTING
PERFORMANCE OF MACROECONOMIC MODELS

A Discussion

W.Allen Spivey

Professor of Statistics
Graduate School of Business Administration
University of Michigan
Ann Arbor

At various points in this session the vexed questions of model
size and of the assessment of model forecasting performance
have been touched upon. It is interesting that although there
is some agreement that bigger does not necessarily mean better,
we are unable as yet to state clearly what big means and many
attempts at assessing model performance are really descriptive
in nature and refer to past realizations only. Moreover, we
are unable at this time to inject any useful inference toward
future forecasting performance on the basis of past forecasting
performance. These observations can be elaborated upon in discussing the presentation of Kelejian and Vavrichek in some detail.

These authors develop a formalism which shows, under some restrictive conditions which are discussed further below, that
the number of endogenous variables in a simultaneous equation
system appears to have little influence on the forecasts made
by these models. They present some simple examples in which
the use of asymptotically justified estimators (to use
Zellner's apt term) produces anomalies when forecasts of incorrectly specified and correctly specified simultaneous equation models are compared. The authors then assert that these
findings make a case in favor of using ex ante forecasting
performance for model validation purposes rather than ex post
forecasts. They conclude their paper with a descriptive study
of ex ante forecasts of a selection of major large-scale U.S.
econometric models.

Some comments with respect to the author's formalism, the

central part of their interesting paper, must first be made.
They introduce the set $S_t = \{Z_{1t}, Z_{2t}, \ldots\}$ of values of variables at time t that a collection of economic model builders
either have in their models or may be interested in including
in their models.  Some of the elements in $S_t$ are random variables and some are nonrandom or deterministic.  Let the random
variables in $S_t$ be the components of the vector $S_{1t}$ and the
deterministic variables in $S_t$ be the components of the vector
$S_{2t}$.  For the $i^{th}$ model builder $S_{1t}$ is split into the $N_{1i}$ by 1
vector $Y_{it}$ of values at time t of the endogenous variables and
the $N_{2i}$ by 1 vector $X_{it}$ of values at time t of the predetermined variables.

In developing their formalism the authors make a number of
assumptions.  The following four assumptions or conditions are
important features of their argument and they expose some of
the restrictive conditions that the authors have incorporated
into their formalism.
   --Each model builder selects the same predetermined vari-
     ables $X_{it}$ and the same deterministic variables $S_{2t}$.
   --The conditional densities of $Y_{it}$ given $X_{it}$ and $S_{2t}$ must
     be the same for each of the endogenous variables that the
     model builders have in common.
   --Each model builder either knows the values of the param-
     eters of his model or, if parameters are unknown, each
     uses consistent estimators calculated from an infinite
     sample.
   --Although the formalism does not require that $X_{it}$ and $S_{2t}$
     be the same, the forecasting discussion does require this
     condition.
Each model builder also uses the minimum mean squared error
predictor which is denoted
$$K_i(X_{it}, S_{2t}) = \int_{R_y} Y_{it} dF_y(Y_{it} \mid X_{it}, S_{2t}).$$

The authors then conclude that the model builders will produce
the same forecasts for each of the endogenous variables they
have in common, and that the number of variables is less important than the selection of and number of predetermined

variables.

In addition to the restrictions that these four assumptions or
conditions entail, the authors' formalism has several other
problems which severely limit its importance and potential usefulness. First of all, their development requires that all
model builders have the same umbrella joint density function
$F_y$. Exactly what this would mean in practice is unclear.
Secondly, even in the case in which each model builder knows
the values of the parameters of his model, the prediction equation in this formalism, given by the authors as

$$H_i(X^0_{it}, S^0_{2t}) = \int_{R_\psi} G_i(X^0_{it}, S^0_{2t}, \psi_{it}) \, dF(\psi_{it} \mid X^0_{it}, S^0_{2t}),$$

may be very difficult to obtain. It is one thing to say, as
the authors do, that the vector of functions $G_i(X^0_{it}, S^0_{2t}, \psi_{it})$
can be evaluated for all possible vectors $\psi_{it}$ so that "in
principle" one can estimate $H_i(X^0_{it}, S^0_{2t})$; it is quite another
matter to carry this out. If the simultaneous equation models
of the model builders are nonlinear, then the prediction equations would be nonlinear also. Moreover, the number of possible vectors $\psi_{it}$ may be very large. In any case, deep problems of convergence and numerical analysis would doubtless
arise. Thirdly, in the case in which the model parameters are
unknown, these equations would be still more difficult to obtain and it appears reasonable to expect that for a wide class
of realistic cases they would be altogether impossible to determine or to approximate. Nor does stochastic simulation with
its peculiar difficulties offer an attractive alternative.
Lastly and perhaps most important, the authors' paper tells us
nothing about the situation when the $X_{it}$ and the $S_{2t}$ are not
the same for all model builders. Unfortunately, this is the
situation one finds most often in model building and model comparison; it thus appears that the conclusions of Kelejian and
Vavrachek, intriguing though they seem to be on first sight,
cannot be applied to the major simultaneous equation models in
use today.

I pass on to comments on the section in the paper of Kelejian
and Vavrichek in which they consider the recent forecasting

performance of some of the better known U.S. econometric models.
Their work, as is the case with so many of the comparative
studies in the literature such as that of Christ [1], Fromm and
Klein [2], McNees [3], Zarnowitz [6], and many others, suffers
from the standard and excessive reliance on the root mean
squared error (RSME) statistic.  Kelejian and Vavrichek com-
pound the interpretation problem relating to RSMEs by using
them to rank model forecasting performance.  The authors state:

> "A meaningful ranking of these models would require evi-
> dence of significant differences in predictive performance
> over a longer time period.  This fact notwithstanding, we
> hope it is enlightening to consider the forecasting records
> over even this limited period of time."

Unfortunately, their study of forecast performance is not enlightening and it is important to state why this is the case.
First of all, the work of the authors is vitiated by the
severely limited number of observations (forecasts) from the
models they have chosen to consider.  As the authors point out,
there were 9 one quarter ahead forecasts from each model included in their study, 8 two quarter ahead forecasts, etc.,
and finally, only 2 eight quarter ahead forecasts.  I think we
can all agree that sample sizes varying from a minimum of 2 to
maximum of 9 are quite small.  With respect to time series
forecasts these sample sizes are virtually microscopic because
RSMEs calculated from small sets of observations which are realizations of stochastic processes having complicated correlation structures cannot yield reliable statistical inferences.

The basic problems with the RSME statistic are many and they
are rarely stated explicitly in the forecast evaluation literature (which by now is extensive).  Although one can rank
models in terms of forecast error performance by using descriptive measures such as RSME, as Kelejian and Vavrichek have
done, such rankings relate only to the specific time period of
the data set used.  Performance rankings can and usually do
change when different time periods are considered or when forecasts of other variables are considered over the same time
period.  Thus although a given model may, over a given time

horizon, predict a given variable best in terms of RSME, it is almost always the case that if the time horizon or variable changes this no longer holds. It is a melancholy truth that it is impossible to determine with reasonable confidence which model will forecast a given variable best in the future on the basis of descriptive measures of past forecast performance. The reason is that the evaluation of forecast performance is really a problem of statistical inference concerning parameters of distributions of forecasts over time and these inferences must take account of correlations among the forecasts from a given model as well as across models. This is exceedingly difficult to do even if long forecast histories are available. Because of the extensive correlation structure between forecasts, one can pass from descriptive measures to inferences only with enormous difficulty at the present time.

If one were to make an assumption that model forecasts are covariance stationary processes, then estimation of this correlation structure could be carried out in two ways, at least in theory. One could use the standard asymptotic results associated with autocorrelation and cross-correlation structures in either the time or frequency domains. Alternatively, one could exploit the Wold decomposition and model the forecasts as multivariate moving average processes and then estimate the parameters of these processes by means of appropriate large sample methods. These estimators could be used in turn to estimate the covariance structure. However, neither of these approaches can be employed because of the small size of the forecast data bases currently available. The most complete data base presently known to this writer is that of McNees [3]; he compiled 20 correlated one quarter ahead forecasts, 19 correlated two quarter ahead forecasts, etc., and finally, 13 correlated eight quarter ahead forecasts. Moreover, McNees had only 13 replications of complete sets of 1 through 8 quarter ahead forecasts for each econometric model he considered, and the elements of these were themselves correlated.

Attempts at parametric estimation of the complete correlation structure of forecasts by either of these methods would lead to

results having unsatisfactory small sample properties. Estimators would have low precision and hypothesis tests would have
low power. Thus statistical inferences that would lead to useful delineations between models on the basis of forecast performance cannot be made at the present time.

This inconclusive state of affairs will continue until data
sets of comparable forecasts for longer periods of time are
made available by the major econometric model proprietors or
until adequate small sample inference procedures are developed.
The former is more of a problem than it appears to be; model
builders, when confronted by requests for longer forecast
histories, often reply that their models are being updated,
changed, and reestimated sometimes several times per year.
Thus larger data sets would not necessarily provide larger
numbers of comparable forecasts, and there may be no real
alternative to living with small sets of dependent forecast
observations. We may not be able to move out of a zone of
indeterminacy with respect to comparisons of forecasting performance until more research is given to the underlying statistical theory of dependent time series observations. In the
meantime there are, at the very least, other descriptive statistics that economists could use to their advantage in the
study of forecast performance. The rapidly expanding collection of exploratory data analysis procedures of Tukey and
others, which include  visual devices such as box plots as well
as order statistics, can be useful descriptive supplements to
the ritualized but only partially informative RSME.

REFERENCES

[1] Christ, C., Judging the Performance of Econometric Models
    of the U.S. Economy, International Economic Review, 16
    (1975) 54-74.
[2] Fromm, G., and Klein, L., The NBER/NSF Model Comparison
    Seminar: An Analysis of Résults, Annals of Economic and
    Social Measurement, 5(1976) 1-27.

[3] McNees, S.K., An Evaluation of Forecasts, New England Economic Review, Nov/Dec 1975, 3–39.

[4] Mosteller, F., and Tukey, J., Data Analysis and Regression (Addison-Wesley Pub. Co., Reading, Mass., 1977).

[5] Spivey, W.A., and Wrobleski, W.J., An Analysis of Forecast Performance, Proceedings of the American Statistical Assn., 1977, 31–40.

[6] Zarnowitz, V., Forecasting Economic Conditions: The Record and the Prospect, in: Zarnowitz, V. (ed.), The Business Cycle Today (National Bur. Econ. Res., New York, 1972).

III.   ADVANCEMENT OF ECONOMIC KNOWLEDGE
      AND THE SIZE OF MACRO-ECONOMETRIC MODELS

LARGE-SCALE MACRO-ECONOMETRIC MODELS
J. Kmenta, J.B. Ramsey (editors)
© North-Holland Publishing Company, 1981

ECONOMIC THEORY AND ECONOMETRIC MODELS

Otto Eckstein*
President, Data Resources, Inc., and
Paul M. Warburg Professor of Economics, Harvard University

The relation between the theoretical and empirical branches of economics has never been an easy one. Our discipline has not followed the model of the natural sciences in which theories are a response to previously unexplained phenomena and enter the body of accepted doctrine only after empirical testing. In economics, theory is the property of the neoclassical school, deriving its principal ideas from Smith, Ricardo, Marshall and Walras. Fortunately, the impetus from Keynes' attempt to shift mainstream economics into different channels is not yet fully spent, and macroeconomic theory retains a role for psychological, expectational and disequilibrium elements in behavior.

Empirical economics, on the other hand, has resided mainly in the applied branches of our discipline. Such fields as public finance, international economics, labor economics, monetary economics and industrial organization have always considered empirical data their basic material for research and analysis. In recent years, these fields have assimilated the advances in econometric methods and have made intensive use of theory, creating a rapprochement between the two camps.

The development of macroeconometric models has created a new source of tension between the theoretical and empirical wings. The models are a check on the delivered doctrine of economic theory. They describe the behavior of the economic system, and on some issues are an alternative theory. The writings of Robert Lucas (1972, 1976) show that theorists are aware of this challenge. As government relies heavily on the macroeconometric models for policy analysis and the models become an important source of expectations for both the private and public sectors, controversy must be expected.

The intellectual origins of macroeconometric models contained some anti-classical strands in economic thought. It is no accident that Jan Tinbergen is the father of both the macro

*I am grateful to Stephen Brooks who developed the crowding-out simulations and to Frank Cooper who conducted the rational expectations experiments. I also thank Jerry Green of Harvard University, Allen Sinai and Roger Brinner, who commented on the manuscript and improved it.

econometric model and the theory of economic policy (1939, 1952). The development of models appeared to create the possibility of a high degree of intervention by the state: if the future could be calculated and the impact of instruments be known, it should become possible to use the tools of government to achieve rather precise and numerous goals. While the neoclassical tradition of economic theory has most commonly served as an elaborate rationale for government in-action, the macroeconometric models appeared to be a founda-tion for interventionism.

The present paper puts the current relation between economic theory (mainstream-branch) and macroeconometric models, as illustrated by the DRI model, into a factual perspective. The paper will deal principally with these issues: (1) Are the micro foundations of the models consistent with economic theory? (2) In what ways have the models gone beyond delivered doctrine to incorporate aspects of the microeconomic world which have never received much attention from economic theory? (3) What are the principal behavioral characteristics of the economy as represented in the models with regard to such currently live theoretical matters as Phillips Curves, crowding out, rational expectations, cyclicality and growth?

The disagreements between the model and economic theory are quite narrow, and mainly due to the empirical necessities created by explicit representation of the dynamics of learn-ing, expectations, errors and adjustment. Much of the apparent controversy is based on a distorted and obsolete picture of the nature of the models. Both theorists and modelers are blown by the same intellectual winds. Differences are related less to intellectual origins than to styles of research, values and choice of problems.

MICRO FOUNDATIONS

The quarrel between the econometricians and the theorists is about the micro foundations of the models. The wave of innovations in the 1950's and the early 1960's, including the work on investment by Jorgenson (1963), Modigliani-Brumberg (1954) and Ando-Modigliani (1963) on consumption and DeLeeuw's formulation of a financial sector (1965-in the Brookings Model), brought solid theoretical underpinnings to the model equations. Indeed, even the early Klein model (1950) provided a microeconomic basis for its equations. Differences in emphasis remain, of course. Theory has mainly a micro-orien-tation, and usually assumes price flexibility without lags, limiting the effect of random factors (white noise) to similar uncorrelated noise in prices and quantities. The models accept the time lags the data appear to imply, and thereby leave room for random factors to affect the system's behavioral properties.

Chart 1 shows the theoretical foundations of the principal be-havioral sectors in the DRI model, as well as some of the

**Chart 1**
**Economic Theory and Specifications in DRI Model**

| | Bases and Variables Drawn from Economic Theory | Extensions |
|---|---|---|
| **Households** | Utility maximization | |
| Consumption | Temporary and permanent income, assets, relative prices | Variance of income, debt burden, demographic structure, consumer confidence (modeled from macro risks of inflation and unemployment) |
| Labor Supply | Unemployment rate, wages | Demographic composition of the labor force |
| Wages | Price expectations, unemployment | Temporary and permanent price expectations |
| **Firms** | Profit maximization | |
| Fixed Investment | Rental price of capital, stock adjustment | Pollution abatement requirements, long versus short-term output expectations, surprises in output, cost of capital by financial sources, debt burden, balance sheet optimum |
| Inventory Investment | Stock adjustment to sales expectations | Errors in sales expectations, capacity utilization, delivery conditions, debt burden |
| Production | Variable coefficient input-output relations | Cyclical supply-demand disequilibrium |
| Employment | Output, wage rates, productivity trends | Cyclical productivity swings |
| Pricing | Material cost, unit labor cost, demand-supply disequilibrium, exchange rate | Vendor performance, stage of processing |
| **Financial Institutions** | | |
| Portfolio Decisions | Profit-maximizing portfolio behavior Balance sheet, relative rates of return and costs, opportunity costs | Modeling of flow-of-funds of households, corporations, financial institutions |
| Interest Rates | Price expectations, supply and demand of liquidity, sectoral borrowing demands | Segmented short and long-term markets, competitive equity returns |
| **Central Bank** | Exogenous in policy parameters | |
| **State & Local Governments** | Utility maximization for spending and taxes subject to budget constraint | Optimal revenue combination, demographic structure |
| **Federal Government** | | |
| Spending | Real full employment values as policy variables | Policy levers for major fiscal instruments |
| Taxes | Income distribution, activity levels | Rates as policy variables |
| **Rest-of-World** | | |
| Exports | Activity levels and relative prices abroad, exchange rate | World grain reserves, exchange rate response to balance of trade constraint |
| Imports | Relative prices, exchange rate, input-output relations | Capacity utilization, excess demand, real income |

extensions which further research, changing times, and experience have added. Ten years of data of increased varia- bility produced by a shock-ridden economy have required some modifications in the representation of behavior. Spending decisions are affected by risks originating in the macro- economy. While theory has rushed to embrace a concept of rational expectations in which only unbiased expected values enter decisions, the model shows the effects of economy-wide errors in expectations and changing variances. The interplay of its financial and real sectors has become tighter as the economy's liquidity position has deteriorated. The represen- tation of cost and supply factors has become more elaborate: price controls, a world food shortage and the energy revolution have made the management of production, which had been a solved problem for advanced industrial societies, a central concern and a force for inflation once more.

VALIDATION

The validation procedures developed in the last ten years help assure a general consistency between model and theory. A model may consist exclusively of esthetically and scientific- ally pleasing equations which will act poorly in full model simulation. It may prove too sluggish, unable to reproduce actual business cycles, or oversensitive, triggering subsector loops that have not been observed. Multipliers may be inconsistent with the general body of knowledge; the Phillips Curves may be unrealistically flat; or the model may have invalid growth properties. A single equation appearing to be reasonable enough on every theoretical and statistical criterion can destroy the simulation properties of a model.

Besides the standard single-equation statistical tests, the validation procedures used in the annual respecification of the DRI model include the following:

(1) A full-dynamic simulation over a period of longer than a decade to assure a close correspondence to the actual historical record. This correspondence is measured by a historical error function,

$$E_h = \Sigma \, \alpha_i \, \%RMSE_i$$

where $\%RMSE_i$ is the percent root-mean-square error in the full-dynamic simulation for a particular variable, and $\alpha_i$ reflects the importance of the variable. Because the economy is a single system, good simulation requires that all the principal elements, including final demands, production, supply, inflation and interest rates, show small errors.

(2) Tests of all policy levers. Counter-intuitive results, which are considered appealing in noneconomic models of social systems behavior, are treated as suspect in the econometric

models, and usually found to be inadvertent byproducts of eccentric specifications.

(3) Tests of various other significant features of the economy. Are the effects of foreign trade on domestic activity and prices consistent with the price and income elasticities of exports and imports reported in the specialized literature? Does potential output react properly to variations in capital formation, and are the various productivity and capacity responses mutually consistent? Do income shares stay within historical ranges and display realistic elasticities? Are the Engel Curves consistent with long-term historical studies?

(4) Ex ante simulations, using conventional assumptions about exogenous variables, to assure the model can follow a balanced-growth path. Labor force growth and factor productivity trends change over the decades and the step-up of inflation can produce previously unobserved behavioral reactions, particularly in the financial system. But inexplicable breaks with the past are treated with suspicion.

(5) Destructive tests. Will the model produce hyperinflations if shocks are large enough and monetary policy is accommodating? Will the model produce a real downturn if stimulus presses activity against the full-employment ceiling? Is a depression possible if fiscal and monetary policies react perversely to the initial declines? These tests also provide the opportunity to verify the detailed structural properties of the model, to make sure that the highly disaggregated demand, production, employment and flow of-funds equations respond as economic theory and common sense would dictate.

One of the challenges to economists, both theorists and econometricians, is to define the full list of questions which they must be prepared to analyze. New issues have arisen with great rapidity, and the model builders have scrambled to include them in their work and to offer a serious treatment in time for the policy decisions that the society had to make.


THE CROWDING-OUT FUNCTION

While there is a commonality of ideas, there are apparent disagreements between economic theory and econometric models about a number of critical issues at this time. The remainder of this paper treats several such cases.

Does fiscal policy work? Or does the financing of deficits "crowd out" private activity? This has been one of the more durable controversies in macroeconomic theory, and is also reflected in the model counterparts. The purely "fiscalist" model must assume monetary policy to be fully accommodating so that the multiplier mechanism can occur without negative feedback from the money market. The monetarist position, on the

other hand, assumes that the financing of fiscal stimulus
fully displaces private spending, leaving fiscal policy power-
less, regardless of the degree of resource utilization.

Like most empirical implementations of theoretical ideas, the
DRI model requires some sharpening of the issue of "crowding
out" and provides answers both conditional and variable.  The
amount of crowding out can be determined by comparing the
stimulative effects of a fiscal policy in which monetary
policy is nonaccommodating with one in which monetary policy
is accommodating.  At least four different degrees of monetary
accommodation can be defined within the model.  The least
accommodating policy keeps the pattern of money supply (M1)
growth unchanged.  This policy requires the Federal Reserve to
operate according to a model which allows it to calculate the
effect of fiscal stimulus on the demand for money and to
reduce the growth of nonborrowed bank reserves sufficiently to
leave the actual amount of money in circulation unaffected.  A
looser definition of nonaccommodating monetary policy leaves
the growth of nonborrowed bank reserves unchanged.  The actual
amount of money in circulation would be slightly higher in response to the fiscal stimulus because of the increased demand
for money.  One level of monetary accommodation increases bank
reserves to leave real interest rates unchanged.  A fuller
accommodation leaves nominal interest rates unchanged, a
policy which could be defined to be overaccommodation since it
would reduce the real cost of borrowing through the inflation
created by the fiscal stimulus.  Both of the interest rate
criteria must be made specific in terms of a particular rate,
since the fiscal stimulus will alter the relative rates
between Treasury and private securities and between long and
short-term maturities.

To illustrate the empirical representation of crowding out in
the DRI model, two sets of exercises were run.  The first
takes the economy in a normal period, well short of full
resource utilization and with a stable history of inflation,
and applies a sustained increase of $10 billion in real non-
military purchases of goods and services.  Chart 2 summarizes
the results under the four monetary policies sketched above.
In the polar fiscalist case, where nominal interest rates are
left unchanged, nominal GNP grows without limit since the
monetary aggregates and the price level will advance together.
In real terms, however, the peak multiplier is reached after
nine quarters, at a value of 2.3.  Thereafter, the damage of
inflation, even with unchanged nominal interest rates, brings
the multiplier down to zero after eight years.  For the case
of constant real interest rates, the multiplier is still
large, peaking at 1.9 in years two and three, and remaining a
positive 0.4 after eight years.

A policy of unchanged nonborrowed bank reserves, DRI's usual
definition for a nonaccommodating monetary policy, shows a
peak multiplier of 1.9 after five quarters, with inflation and
the effects of higher interest rates fully crowding out the
stimulus after five years.  The early restraining effect is

**Chart 2**
**Fiscal Policy Multipliers Under**
**Different Monetary Policy Assumptions\***

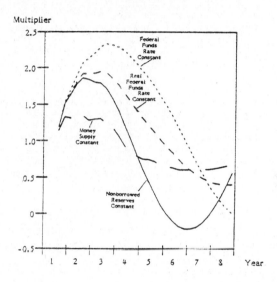

\*In each of the simulations real
nondefense purchases of goods and
services were increased by $10
billion from their baseline value.
In the first, nonborrowed reserves
were held constant. In the second,
nonborrowed reserves were increased
by enough to hold the nominal
Federal Funds rate at its baseline
value. In the third, nonborrowed
reserves were changed enough to hold
the real Federal Funds rate, the
nominal Federal Funds rate minus the
annual rate of increase in the GNP
deflator, constant. In the fourth,
nonborrowed reserves were adjusted
to leave the nominal money supply
unchanged.

accentuated in the final case, where the nominal money supply is held unchanged: the multiplier reaches a peak of 1.4 in the second year, drops to 0.7 in the fourth year, but then remains near that value.

Paradoxically, complete crowding out is only achieved in the two cases of monetary accommodation, where the economy becomes too strong, bounces against the full-employment ceiling and turns down. In the nonaccommodating cases, where the peak effects are smaller, the economy heads toward a new equilibrium where the sustained stimulus has a modest permanent effect.

The size of the crowding-out effect also depends upon the choice of fiscal instrument. For example, a reduction in corporate income tax rates directly enhances the liquidity of business. An investment tax credit, on the other hand, adds a strong stimulus to spending, thereby creating two opposing effects on business liquidity. Similar variations can be found among types of personal tax reductions and among spending programs.

Finally, the extent of crowding out depends upon the condition of the economy. When the financial situation is very strong, with households having large liquid savings and light debt burdens, with business firms possessing strong balance sheets and local governments experiencing operating budget surpluses, crowding out will be less than in periods of financial stringency.

Crowding out develops through two channels: "financial" crowding out through higher interest rates and portfolio displacement effects created by increased public debt issues, and "real" crowding out from higher prices, wages and interest rates which reduce demands of businesses and households. Because some price effects occur at all levels of activity, real crowding out occurs even when the economy is far from the full-employment ceiling. The extent of crowding will depend upon the initial conditions of the economy in terms of inflation, the degree of resource utilization, the liquidity position of the financial system, the willingness of foreigners to buy government debt, particular shocks during the period of stimulus and other factors.

According to the traditional fiscalist position, real crowding out should not occur until the economy is near full employment. At that stage, it is generally recognized that public stimulus simply serves to displace other demands. But the empirical representation of the DRI model shows that the distinction between full employment and under-employment cannot be made rigidly. There are significant displacement effects even under conditions of substantial resource underutilization. Prices respond to demand in a continuous fashion, and not according to the presence or absence of an inflationary gap.

A crowding-out coefficient can be defined as

$$COC = 1 - \frac{GNP72'}{GNP72''} = 1 - \frac{k'}{k''},$$

where COC is the crowding-out coefficient, k' is the multiplier under nonaccommodating monetary policy and k" with accommodation. A crowding-out function can be defined as the variation of COC with particular other economic variables.

Financial crowding out varies particularly with the extent of inflation before and during the period of stimulus. Therefore, the fiscal stimulus exercises were performed on twelve baseline simulations, each with a different underlying historical rate of wage inflation. The wage rate determines the price level through price-wage interactions, and this in turn determines the state of the financial system at the time of the fiscal stimulus. To minimize the effects of real crowding out, the simulations in this experiment were designed so that real activity was the same prior to the stimulus. During the simulation, however, inflation was allowed to affect real activity.

Twelve alternative histories were created going back three years, by varying the rate of wage increase from 4 to 10.5%. Applying the fiscal stimulus under the two alternative monetary assumptions yields twelve paths of crowding-out coefficients, shown in Chart 3 and Table 1. These paths show that crowding out varies with the inflation rate. They also show that it takes about three quarters for half the crowding out to occur, and three years for it to approach its maximum. The crowding-out function is plotted by comparing the crowding-out coefficients after three years of stimulus across the twelve solutions with varying inflation assumptions. It can be seen that crowding out is as low as 0.6 when wage inflation is 4%, and is complete at 1.0 when wage inflation is as high as 10.5%. The particular values of the crowding-out function depend on the specifics of the initial conditions, of course. For example, because the financial system adjusts to steady inflation, the function depends partly on the change in the inflation rate. To an extent, therefore, worsened inflation creates a nonlinear crowding-out response, and produces the monetarist, full crowding-out answer if inflation moves 4% above the "core" rate to which the economy has adjusted.

The conclusions of the econometric model on this issue are probably closer to the monetarist than to the fiscalist position. Real crowding out occurs over a much broader range of resource utilization than the traditional Keynesian analysis would have suggested. Financial crowding out is sizable even in the short-run so long as the central bank is not fully accommodating. Further, if the central bank is fully accommodating, the absence of financial crowding out is converted into real crowding out a year or two later. Thus, the DRI model, with its simultaneous real and financial sectors including flows of funds and balance sheets, and with

**Table 1**
**Crowding-Out Coefficients**

| Wage Increase In Base Period | Quarters | | | | | |
|---|---|---|---|---|---|---|
| | 1 | 2 | 3 | 4 | 5 | 6 |
| 4.0% | 0.008 | 0.029 | 0.070 | 0.115 | 0.155 | 0.204 |
| 5.0% | 0.127 | 0.252 | 0.384 | 0.469 | 0.527 | 0.586 |
| 6.0% | 0.204 | 0.367 | 0.511 | 0.594 | 0.648 | 0.702 |
| 6.5% | 0.235 | 0.407 | 0.551 | 0.632 | 0.683 | 0.734 |
| 7.0% | 0.262 | 0.440 | 0.582 | 0.659 | 0.709 | 0.758 |
| 7.5% | 0.286 | 0.467 | 0.607 | 0.682 | 0.730 | 0.778 |
| 8.0% | 0.307 | 0.490 | 0.627 | 0.700 | 0.747 | 0.794 |
| 8.5% | 0.326 | 0.510 | 0.645 | 0.715 | 0.761 | 0.806 |
| 9.0% | 0.341 | 0.526 | 0.658 | 0.726 | 0.771 | 0.816 |
| 9.5% | 0.356 | 0.541 | 0.670 | 0.736 | 0.780 | 0.824 |
| 10.0% | 0.369 | 0.554 | 0.681 | 0.745 | 0.787 | 0.832 |
| 10.5% | 0.381 | 0.566 | 0.690 | 0.753 | 0.795 | 0.839 |
| | 7 | 8 | 9 | 10 | 11 | 12 |
| 4.0% | 0.252 | 0.296 | 0.350 | 0.421 | 0.502 | 0.601 |
| 5.0% | 0.636 | 0.674 | 0.715 | 0.763 | 0.806 | 0.846 |
| 6.0% | 0.746 | 0.777 | 0.808 | 0.842 | 0.872 | 0.899 |
| 6.5% | 0.776 | 0.804 | 0.833 | 0.865 | 0.891 | 0.913 |
| 7.0% | 0.798 | 0.825 | 0.853 | 0.882 | 0.905 | 0.924 |
| 7.5% | 0.817 | 0.844 | 0.867 | 0.893 | 0.915 | 0.934 |
| 8.0% | 0.832 | 0.857 | 0.877 | 0.901 | 0.923 | 0.941 |
| 8.5% | 0.844 | 0.865 | 0.885 | 0.909 | 0.931 | 0.948 |
| 9.0% | 0.853 | 0.873 | 0.892 | 0.917 | 0.938 | 0.955 |
| 9.5% | 0.861 | 0.879 | 0.899 | 0.925 | 0.947 | 0.967 |
| 10.0% | 0.867 | 0.886 | 0.907 | 0.934 | 0.960 | 0.987 |
| 10.5% | 0.873 | 0.893 | 0.916 | 0.947 | 0.983 | 1.033 |

*Twelve baseline simulations were created, each with identical real
activity in the preceding three years, but with different rates of
wage growth as indicated, ranging from 4% to 10.5%. Nominal
incomes, interest rates, prices, etc. were all different among
these baseline simulations. A fiscal stimulus of a $10 billion
sustained increase in real nondefense purchases was applied to each
of the twelve baselines leaving nonborrowed reserves unchanged—the
nonaccommodating case. A second set of twelve simulations combined
the fiscal stimulus with changes in nonborrowed reserves sufficient
to hold the Federal Funds rate at its baseline value.

**Chart 3**
**Crowding-Out Coefficients**

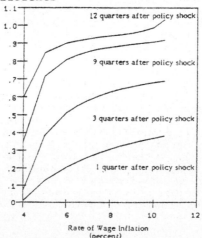

Rate of Wage Inflation
(percent)

its more sensitive responses of prices to variations in demand and supply, shows the power of fiscal policy to be quite circumscribed.

RATIONAL EXPECTATIONS?

The current gulf between the theoretical (mainstream) and empirical branches of economics appears to be greatest in the treatment of expectations and errors. The concept of rational expectations developed by Muth (1961) and made central to macroeconomics by Friedman (1968) was honed into a sharp critique of econometric models by Lucas (1972, 1976). Rational expectations are an extension of the theory of individual decisions of households and firms to include a specific pattern of behavior under uncertainty: the individual decision maker has a coherent (usually monetarist) view of the economic system, and interprets all the information available to him without systematic bias in reaching his own decisions.

The rational expectations school has advanced four propositions that are pertinent to econometric models. They deal with the "natural" rate of unemployment, the definition of rationality, the learning rate in expectation formations and the potential of policy.

First, the economy possesses a "natural" rate of unemployment. This rate is determined by the normal period of search of individuals as they change from one job to another in a world of imperfect information. In the absence of policy disturbance, the economy moves toward the natural rate. There is no trade-off between inflation and unemployment in the long run, and it would require accelerating and surprising inflation to hold unemployment below its natural rate.

While this lack of trade-off, the absence of a permanent Phillips Curve, is the most commonly cited disagreement between theory and models, the DRI model has shared this long-term property for some time. The wage equation is "near-accelerationist" with a price coefficient near unity (Eckstein-Brinner, 1972). The remainder of the wage price sector contains sufficient additional demand effects to gradually convert real stimulus into inflation, as Chart 2 showed. The natural rate of unemployment is quite high in the model, though the precise definition is dependent on elaborate specifications of initial conditions and assumptions for exogenous variables.

While the general conclusion in the DRI model has much similarity to the natural rate-rational expectations school, the mechanisms which produce the result are not the same. The difference lies mainly in the speed of adjustment. There are adaptive expectations mechanisms in individual equations, some of which reflect learning processing stretching over more years than a tough-minded rationalist would consider within the bounds of his definition of rationality. Both businesses and households learn only gradually from experience and form their expectations of the future principally from objectively observed conditions of the past.

The DRI model also rejects the definition of rationality which bases decisions only on the expected values of the variables, ruling out the higher moments of their distribution. The variance of income and other measures of macro and financial risk also affect spending decisions, introducing a bias below expected values if uncertainty is great. The data suggest that the aggregate consumer is averse to risk.

The length of the period of adjustment is perhaps the biggest difference between the DRI model and the rational expectations viewpoint. The school looks for a quicker approach to the no-trade-off condition because of the semantic problem created by its use of the concept of "money-illusion." Since learning processes are not treated explicitly nor a formal mechanism shown by which information modifies expectations, quick adjustment is necessary to keep out the irrationality of money illusion (see B. Friedman, 1975). But in the actual world, it takes years of experience to disentangle temporary from permanent changes and to assess in what ways the fundamental movements of the economy have been altered. A society which can assess its true state over a space of a few years is doing very well. Even after matters are understood, adjustment processes are slowed by the existence of long-term contracts including three-year wage agreements, by the slow, bureaucratic pricing processess which characterize some con-centrated, capital-intensive industries, by the regulatory lag for utilities, by slow turnover of portfolios, and other rigidities.

To test the potential role of a "quick rational expectations" approach in the DRI model, a wage equation was developed which embodies a quick price adjustment term and leaves only fleeting room for money illusion. The equation in the model, in contrast, applies two concepts of price expectations: a "permanent" expectation generated by a second order Pascal lag with an average lag of nearly two years, and a "temporary" price expectation based on the price increases of the last four quarters. These terms are combined with a demand measure, the ratio of actual to potential GNP, and with dummies for the mid-1960's guideposts, Phase I of the Nixon Controls, and the data break of 1964. The sum of the price coefficients in this equation is 0.88, or near-rational in the sense of being free of bias and money illusion in the long run. But because of the weight on the permanent price term with its long lag structure, the adjustment process is slow. This is the principal factor which creates the long lags between variations in real activity and the response of the price level.

The "quick rational expectations" alternative uses only the last quarter's behavior as the basis for price expectations. In this experiment, an attempt was made to see if a statistically adequate equation could be derived with so brief a price expectations process, and whether the DRI model would show shorter adjustment periods if such a wage equation were substituted.

Since price expectations cannot be observed, an instrumental variable approach must be used (McCallum, 1976). Using theoretical harmony with the rational expectations–monetarist viewpoint as one of the criteria for choosing the instrumental variables, the increase in the money supply for each of the preceding three quarters and the level of the long-term interest rate on high quality bonds in the current and the preceding two quarters were used. The bond yields incorporate price expectations of the participants in the bond market which themselves may or may not be rational. The DRI model equation for bond yields has a high price coefficient, but its adaptive expectations process is also long, with an average lag of almost two years.

Table 2 presents several wage equations. Clearly, the statistical quality of the quick equation is inferior. This, in itself, is not a surprising result, since the earlier wage studies had explored in detail whether the lags could be shorter. But two other conclusions were more surprising. First, insistence on a quick formation of price expectations produces an equation in which the demand measure plays a smaller role and the price coefficient drops to 0.80, both weakening the response of inflation to stimulus. As a result, when this equation is embedded in the model, the dynamic simulation properties show a weaker response of the price level to a policy stimulus (Chart 4).

The substitution of the "quick" wage equation in the model also damages the historic simulation quality of the model.

## Table 2
## Wage Equations With Four Kinds of Price Expectations

| Dependent variable: ln $(w/w_{-1})$ | "Quick Expectations" | | "Less Quick" | | "M 1 Expectations" | | Model | |
|---|---|---|---|---|---|---|---|---|
| | Coefficient | t-stat | Coefficient | t-stat | Coefficient | t-stat | Coefficient | t-stat |
| Constant | .007 | 7.12 | .008 | 11.27 | .004 | 6.35 | .008 | 16.02 |
| ln $(P_{-1}/P_{-2})$ [1] | .80 | 10.11 | -- | -- | -- | -- | -- | -- |
| ln $(P_{-1}/P_{-5})$ [1] | -- | -- | .81 | 13.50 | -- | -- | .444 | 6.59 |
| PEXP79 [2] | -- | -- | -- | -- | -- | -- | .441 | 4.71 |
| MONEYEXP90 [3] | -- | -- | -- | -- | 1.08 | 15.59 | -- | -- |
| ln $(\frac{\text{real GNP}}{\text{Potential GNP}})$ | .019 | 1.63 | .045 | 4.98 | .013 | 1.76 | .059 | 7.77 |
| Controls Dummy | .007 | 2.58 | .006 | 2.92 | .006 | 3.09 | .006 | 3.34 |
| Guidepost dummy | .0018 | 1.87 | .0021 | 2.94 | .0016 | 2.62 | .0020 | 3.76 |
| Data Dummy (64:1) | -.0068 | -2.15 | -.0058 | -2.44 | -.0055 | -2.54 | -.0057 | -2.95 |
| $\bar{R}^2$ | .645 | | .801 | | .802 | | .847 | |
| DW | 1.20 | | 1.23 | | 1.49 | | 1.90 | |

[1] The instruments are the bond yield (current, lagged once and lagged twice) and the growth in M1 (current, lagged once, twice, and three times).

[2] This is a second degree Pascal lag on p, the deflator for consumer spending with speed of adjustment of .79 and an average lag of 2 years.

[3] This is a second degree Pascal lag on the growth of M1 with speed of adjustment of .9 and an average lag of 4½ years.

**Table 3**
**Percent Root-Mean-Square Errors of**
**DRI Model With Four Wage Equations**

|            | Quick | Less Quick | M1 Expectations | Model |
|------------|-------|------------|-----------------|-------|
| Real GNP   | 1.30  | 0.96       | 1.10            | 0.86  |
| Deflator   | 1.52  | 1.12       | 1.89            | 0.51  |
| GNP        | 0.98  | 0.92       | 1.63            | 0.81  |
| Wage Rate  | 2.16  | 1.47       | 2.47            | 0.59  |
| WPI        | 1.09  | 1.15       | 1.45            | 0.75  |
| Bond Yield | 8.15  | 5.73       | 7.15            | 5.86  |

Table 3 shows the percent root-mean-square errors for the two versions of the DRI model in full historical simulation, 1966 to 1977. The difference in the errors for nominal GNP is not dramatic, but the difference is great in real terms. The increased error originates in the wage equation; its full system simulation error is greater by a factor of four, with a strong downward bias. This produces a negative bias for the whole wage-price sector which creates a positive bias in real activity.

To explore the territory of intermediate speeds of adjustment, a wage equation was developed with the most recent one-year change in prices as the basis for expectations, using the same instruments of bond yields and M1. The results are much better, but still inferior to the model (Tables 2 and 3). The speeds of adjustment are fairly slow, so the distinctions become small.

The above equations all use actual historical prices as the basis for price expectations. The instrumental variables employ the monetarist model to help estimate the relationship between price expectations and observed prices, but the monetarist mechanism is missing in simulation.

If price expectations are really derived from the behavior of M1, better results should be achieved by directly using money in the wage equation, using a reduced form which short-cuts the nonobservable price expectations variable. Using past money growth as the measure for expected price growth, a wage equation was developed (Table 2). Statistically acceptable results could only be obtained with long lag structures; correlations became weak and demand variables turned perverse with short lags on money. The simulation results were generally worse than the other experiments. This result is not conclusive, to be sure. Pure monetarism was applied to only one equation, and since M1 is not all-pervasive in the model, the wage-price loop becomes too weak if M1 replaces prices in the wage equation (Chart 4).

**Chart 4**
**Price Responses to Stimulus,**
**Four Wage Equations**

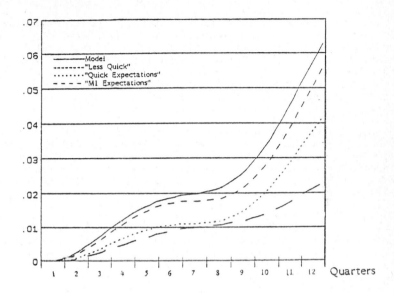

Rational expectations have arrived on the scene quite recently
and will be tested in many equations of the model as they are
re-estimated in future annual revisions. The "quick rational
expectations" version is unlikely to score many victories in
this contest of ideas. The three sets of equations with
particularly long lags—wages, bond yields and business fixed
investment—are not yielding readily to the new concepts. The
data try to tell us that it takes workers, investors and
businessmen several years to accept conditions of inflation or
output growth as "permanent." Indeed, given the volatility of
the variables which they confront, they would be irrational to
take the evidence of short periods as sufficient indication of
the future environment. The rational expectations school
needs to specify the learning processes by which information
enters decisions more explicitly, particularly to show how individuals form permanent expectations from temporary data and
how they modify their behavior in response to changes in
economic structure.

## THE ROLE OF ERRORS-IN-EXPECTATIONS

While recent theoretical discussion has emphasized
rationality under incomplete information, the highly cyclical
behavior of the economy has produced quite a different line of
empirical model research, seeking to identify how the expectations of businesses and households can be brought systematically into error.  False expectations create decisions which
produce incorrect stocks of fixed and variable capital and
excessive employment.  These errors are a critical ingredient
in the development of recession.  At several critical points
in the postwar years, business and household expectations were
in error, whether rationally arrived at or not, with events
falsifying the assumptions on which decisions had been based.

The DRI model contains expectations mechanisms which can
produce systematic error.  Let me illustrate for the case of
inventory investment.  In the model's equations, the measure
of sales expectations is based on the Metzler formulation
(1944), in which future sales expectations are equal to the
level of recent sales plus the recent change in sales
multiplied by an elasticity of expectations.  The Metzler
formula can be used to calculate the systematic errors in
sales expectations of business by contrasting its estimates
with the sales that occurred (Chart 5).  It can be seen that
the actual errors in expectations are erratic for most of the
interval, but at the critical turning points of the business
cycle, sales were grossly in error, and most extremely so in
the most severe of the postwar recession.

Systematic error is also important in the determination of
business fixed investment.  While the Jorgenson theory is
still serviceable as a general structure, the violence of the
recent record produces two important modifications, a more
elaborate treatment of business liquidity, and the explicit
introduction of systematic errors.  For example, the model
equation for producers' durable equipment contains a term
which shows the surprise element in production, defined as the
difference between actual production and a Koyck Lag on past
production which approximates an adaptative expectations process.

**Chart 5**
**Errors in Expectations:  Difference Between**
**Sales and Expected Sales, 1950-1978**

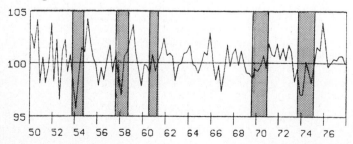

In the case of households, no systematic element of errors-in-expectations has been found. The reaction to risk is sufficient to create quick spending adjustments. The savings rate has leaped at the onset of macro difficulties. Apparently households are more sensitive than business, and can move more quickly. Of course, sharp changes in the economy do produce destabilizing stock adjustments in the household sector that would not occur if the future were fore-seen correctly.

Expectations processes capable of producing systematic errors are not in contradiction to the rational expectations theory. With incomplete information, external shocks, a stochastic economy, and unpredictable elements in policy all producing sizable surprises in the economic environment, even the most rational individual will make errors. But the models are closer to the older business cycle theories than to recent economic theory in their explicit modeling of errors that are critical to the economy's cyclic path.

POLICY ANALYSIS

The rational expectations school has asserted that econometric models are unsuitable for policy analysis because the policies change the parameters of the economy (Lucas 1972, 1976). This proposition has been specialized to become an argument against all demand management policies: the private sector, being rational and understanding the lack of permanent trade-off, recognizes that stimulus will be converted into inflation, will create no real gains, and therefore deserves no positive private spending response.

The empirical method of the large-scale econometric model puts this proposition in a quantitative perspective. Given that the "no-trade-off" equilibrium is reached only after several years and that the business cycle moves more quickly, rational private decisions must consider the short-run impact of stimulus.

Whether short-term demand management yields a positive benefit is also an empirical question which can be assessed through stochastic simulations of the model, and through control-theoretic searches for optimal demand management (Kelley, 1977). The conclusions of studies with the DRI model suggest that the potential expected benefit is modest but its variance great (Kelley, 1978a).

On the narrower issue raised by Lucas, it is an irrefutable theoretical proposition that policies can affect parameters, but the actual impact is an empirical question. Policy approaches have changed in the past, and deliberate policy moves have been among the major sources of variations in incomes, prices, interest rates, etc. The model's spending equations include the variability of incomes and the degree of leverage created by balance sheets, thus giving empirical expression to the effect of variability—whether from policy or other sources—on the behavior of the system.

If the approach to policy is changed so drastically that the economy operates under a new regime, the model may, indeed, cease to be applicable. But in this regard, policy is no different from any other major source of change. If the modelers are alert, they will quickly incorporate the changes in structure; if they are not, they will go astray. Probably the biggest single innovation in policy of the last thirty years was the imposition of wage and price controls in 1971. Although the DRI model was not built in anticipation of controls, this was one policy change that it handled well, correctly calculating the effects on inflation rates and the short-term benefits to real activity.

Compared to such exogenous shocks as wars and the oil and food crises, the changes in policy approaches have been small in the last decade. Policy is a source of stochastic variation, but no more so than other sources to which households and businesses must respond. There is no empirical basis to the assertion that the models are invalid because policies change parameters. So far, the evidence suggests that changes in policy regimes are among the lesser causes of simulation error.

ORIGINS OF THE BUSINESS CYCLE

Since the theoretical analysis of the business cycle reached its climax in the works of Hicks (1950), Duesenberry (1958) and Matthews (1959), economic theory has advanced no strong hypothesis about the origins of cyclical behavior. Indeed, theory has always been uneasy in its treatment of the business cycle and has never placed it at the center of concern.

Econometric models, on the other hand, represent cyclical behavior and can be used to reach conclusions about the nature and origins of business cycles. It has long been recognized that cycles can originate from: (1) irregular exogenous shocks acting on a nonlinear system; (2) error terms of individual equations in a nonlinear system; (3) stock-flow or other nonlinear adjustment processes which can produce damped, repeating or explosive oscillations; and (4) variations in public policies which are magnified in the private sector and which ultimately create reversing, hence cyclical, tendencies.

Without attempting a full-scale review of the literature, let me summarize the present conclusions. First, according to models such as DRI's, the economy would experience stable growth or strongly damped cycles in the absence of shocks if policies are neutral. Second, the stochastic elements in the models and in policies do produce cyclic behavior as they act on the nonlinear features of the models such as the physical stock-flow adjustment processes and portfolio effects

(Adelman and Adelman, 1959 and Kelley, 1978b). Exogenous shocks have been the biggest source of variation, of course, if one considers Korea, Vietnam, OPEC and the world food crisis to be exogenous events. Demand management policies have added to instability at some times and helped moderate it at others, producing a net effect which was probably somewhat destabilizing (Eckstein, 1973, 1978).

CONCLUDING COMMENT

Economists, including modelers and theorists, share a common training and intellectual heritage. Econometricians emphasize the empirical representation of the economic process through dynamic structures with specific quantitative parameters and with representation of the stochastic elements. Theorists represent the economic process that can be derived from a minimum of behavioral assumptions, but are willing to pursue logical ramifications a good deal further. Given these differences in method and attitude, it is not surprising that the conclusions are not always identical. However, I hope my discussion has made clear that both camps are subject to the same intellectual influences and respond to the same challenges in the economy. The gap between the two views of the economy is quite small, far smaller than the simplistic contrast between an extreme, fiscalist-dirigiste viewpoint and an extreme monetarist-quick rational expectations position. The models do not argue for large multipliers, weak monetary effects, successful fine-tuning, or the predictability of the future. They do argue against quick responses to demand management and therefore low costs to disinflation, against the use of a simple monetarist rule to policy, against discontinuous jumps in aggregate supply and, indeed, against every form of economic magic. The four principal positive conclusions from the models as opposed to the dominant theory are these:

1) Learning is slow, and it takes several years for the society to correctly assess the fundamentals of the economic environment in terms of inflation and longterm growth.

2) The expected variance of output and prices matters to decisions along with the expected values themselves. Businesses and households are risk-averters, and consequently reduce their spending behavior when expected variance increases.

3) Errors-in-expectations are an important element in the business cycle mechanism and must be modeled to account for inventory, employment and fixed investment cycles. Errors-in-expectations are not necessarily evidence of irrationality, but a correct theory must make room for the effects of errors. This is evidence that observed errors in expectations have sufficient autocorrelation to reject the "white noise" hypothesis.

4)  Detail    matters    even    in    macroeconomic    modeling.
    Particularly   in   a   world   of   exogenous   disturbances,
    differential    availabilities    of    industrial    capacity,
    institutionally  determined  variations  in  the  portfolio
    policies   of   different   participants   in   the   financial
    sector,   and   the   mix   of   economic   activity   affects   the
    behavior  of  the  economy  in  major  ways.   Hence,  the  size  of
    today's  models  is  largely  determined  by  the  necessity  to
    disaggregate    sufficiently    to    take    account    of    these
    financial,  supply,  and  stock  adjustment  effects.

Models  rub  our  noses  in  the  day-to-day  reality  of  empirical
relationships.   In  today's  environment,  the  models  are  playing
much  of  the  role  traditionally  played  by  economic  theory,  a
perpetual  warning  against  quick,  cheap  results,  a  constant  reminder  that  there  are,  indeed,  trade-offs  which  are  worse  than
we  would  like.

REFERENCE LIST

(1) Adelman, I. and Adelman, F.L., "The Dynamic Properties of the Klein-Goldberger Model," Econometrica, 1959, pp. 596-625.

(2) Ando, A.K. and Modigliani, F., "The 'Life-Cycle' Hypothesis of Saving: Aggregate Implications and Tests," American Economic Review, 1963, 55-84.

(3) DeLeeuw, F.F., "A Model of Financial Behavior," The Brookings Quarterly Econometric Model, Rand McNally, 1965, pp. 465-530.

(4) Duesenberry, J.S., Business Cycles and Economic Growth, McGraw-Hill, 1958.

(5) Eckstein, O. and Brinner, R., "The Inflation Process in the United States," Joint Economic Committee, U.S. Government Printing Office, Washington, D.C., February 1972, reprinted in Parameters and Policies in the U.S. Economy, North-Holland, 1976, pp. 99-158.

(6) Eckstein, O., "Instability in the Private and Public Sectors," The Swedish Journal of Economics, 1973, pp. 19-26.

(7) Eckstein, O., The Great Recession, North-Holland, 1978.

(8) Friedman, B., "Rational Expectations are Really Adaptive After All," Harvard University Discussion Paper No. 430 (1975).

(9) Friedman, M., "The Role of Monetary Policy," American Economic Review, 1968, pp. 1-17.

(10) Hicks, J.R., A Contribution to the Theory of the Trade Cycle, Oxford University Press, 1950.

(11) Jorgenson, D.W., "Capital Theory and Investment Behavior," American Economic Review, Proceedings, May, 1963, pp. 247-59.

(12) Kelley, J., "Forecast Risk—A Stochastic Simulation Analysis," DRI Review, November 1977, pp. 17-30.

(13) Kelley, J., "Optimal Macroeconomic Policy: Some Control Theory Experiments," DRI Review, September 1978, pp. 9-23.

(14) Kelley, J., "The American Business Cycle: Evidence from the DRI Model," DRI Review, February 1978, pp. 25-34.

(15) Klein, L.R., Economic Fluctuations in the United States: 1921-1944, Wiley, 1950.

(16) Lucas, R.E., "Econometric Testing of the Natural Rate Hypothesis," The Econometrics of Price Determination, Federal Reserve Board, 1972, pp. 50-59.

(17) Lucas, R.E., "Econometric Policy Evaluation: A Critique," in R. Brinner and A.H. Meltzer, eds., The Phillips Curve and Labor Markets, Carnegie-Rochester Series on Public Policy, 1976, pp. 19-46.

(18) McCallum, B.T., "Rational Expectations and the Natural Rate Hypothesis: Some Consistent Estimates," Econometrica, 1976, pp. 43-52.

(19) Matthews, R.C.O., The Trade Cycle, Cambridge, 1959.

(20) Metzler, L.A., "The Nature and Stability of Inventory Cycles, Review of Economics and Statistics, 1944, pp. 113-29, reprinted in Metzler, Collected Papers, Harvard University Press, 1973.

(21) Modigliani, F. and Brumberg, R., "Utility Analysis and the Consumption Function: An Interpretation of Cross-Section Data," in K.K. Kurihara, ed., Post Keynesian Economics, Rutgers University Press, 1954.

(22) Muth, J.F., "Rational Expectations and the Theory of Price Movements," Econometrica, 1961, pp. 315-35.

(23) Tinbergen, J., Business Cycles in the United States: 1912-1932, League of Nations, 1939.

(24) Tinbergen, J., On the Theory of Economic Policy, North-Holland, 1952.

LARGE-SCALE MACRO-ECONOMETRIC MODELS
J. Kmenta, J.B. Ramsey (editors)
© North-Holland Publishing Company, 1981

ECONOMIC THEORY, MODEL SIZE, AND MODEL PURPOSE

John B. Taylor *

Princeton University

I.  INTRODUCTION

The purpose of this paper is to discuss several issues pertaining to the specific question, "Does economic theory have a practical role to play in determining the appropriate size of a macroeconometric model?"  For the purpose of this discussion "size" will be defined simply as the number of stochastic equations in a model, although the number of parameters might in some cases provide a better definition.  Based on this definition, Table 1 illustrates the variation in model size for a representative group of macroeconometric models developed since Tinbergen's (1939) study.  Even if we allow for advances in computer technology, the variation in model size is quite large and appears to be growing.

The term "economic theory" as used in the above question cannot, of course, be defined so simply, and this is one of the reasons why the question is controversial.  For the purpose of this discussion, economic theory will be defined broadly as a method of reasoning based on models describing the interaction of utility maximizing individuals subject to budget, technological, and legal constraints.  Although very broad, these definitions narrow the scope of discussion considerably.  For example, the paper is not concerned with the role of statistical theory in determining model size, nor is it concerned with the research funding constraint which is clearly a practical limitation to model size in many cases.  And finally the paper does not attempt to determine which of the many strands of economic theory--for example, market clearing versus disequilibrium methods--are more appropriate microtheoretic foundations for macroeconometric models.[1]/

II.  TEXTBOOK THEORY AND ECONOMETRIC PRACTICE

Most textbook discussions of econometric methods appear to answer the above question in the affirmative.  Consider, for example, the static linear simultaneous equations system

(1) $\qquad By_t + \Gamma x_t = u_t$ ,  $t = 1, 2, \ldots T.$

where $y_t$ is a vector of $G$ endogenous variables, $x_t$ is a vector of $K$

---

I wish to thank Jan Kmenta and Edward Prescott for helpful comments.
A grant from the National Science Foundation is gratefully acknowledged.

exogenous variables, and $u_t$ is a vector of $G$ unobservable disturbances. Let $Eu_t u_t' = V$ and $Eu_t u_s' = 0$ for $t \neq s$. According to our definition, the size of model (1) is $G$. However, if the last $G - G_1$ elements of the first $G_1$ rows of $B$ and $V$ are known to be a zero, then the first $G_1$ equations of the system can be considered in isolation from the rest, and for the purpose of explaining these endogenous variables, the model can be reduced to size $G_1$. That is, if $B$ and $V$ can be written

$$B = \begin{pmatrix} B_{11} & B_{12} \\ B_{21} & B_{22} \end{pmatrix} \qquad V = \begin{pmatrix} V_{11} & V_{12} \\ V_{21} & V_{22} \end{pmatrix}$$

with $B_{12} = 0$ and $V_{12} = 0$, then the first $G_1$ elements of $y_t$ are exogenous to the last $G - G_1$ elements and for forecasting, multiplier analysis, and a general examination of the dynamic stochastic properties of these variables, one only needs to estimate $B_{11}$, $V_{11}$ and the appropriate elements of $\Gamma$.

The question is whether economic theory can tell us whether $B_{12} = 0$ and $V_{12} = 0$. The type of information we need, therefore, is similar to the standard "zero restriction" information normally used for identification of the structure of the model. According to most textbook discussions, economic theory can be used to determine whether a model is identified or not, and by this analogy theory can also be used to tell us whether a model of size $G$ or $G_1$ is sufficient for explaining the first $G_1$ elements of $y_t$. Johnston's (1972, p.352) description of the role of economic theory is representative of this textbook view and would apply both to the identification problem and to model size. "A priori knowledge thus results in a specific configuration for $B$ and $\Gamma$ and a specific set of assumptions about the distributions of the disturbances."

In practice, however, we usually find that economic theory is not precise enough to provide restrictions which are this strong. Identification restrictions are difficult enough to find,2/ let alone the additional restrictions necessary in order to eliminate equations. Koopmans (1950, p. 402) points out the enormity of the problem:

> Which factors in man's physical and historical environ-
> ment are not influenced by his economic activity? If the
> question is put in this way one can think of little else
> besides changes in weather, climate, geology, and geography
> that are brought about by natural causes. There remains a
> host of sociological, political, and psychological factors
> that are in continuous interaction with economic activity,
> and therefore cannot, on any grounds so far adduced, be
> accepted as they come without incorporating the explana-
> tion of their fluctuations in the system of equations.

And in his applied econometrics textbook Klein (1962, p. 180) writes:

> In some studies, theory has been used to make more explicit
> specifications about the form of the relationship. Macro-
> economic models are, however, more intuitive and less rigid-

Table 1


ECONOMETRIC MODEL SIZES FOR THE U.S., 1939 - 1975


| Model | Date | Size |
|-------|------|------|
| Hickman-Coen | 1975 | 50 |
| DRI | 1974 | 379 |
| Liu-Hwa | 1974 | 51 |
| Chase Econometrics | 1974 | 125 |
| Wharton III, Anticipations | 1974 | 79 |
| Wharton Annual | 1972 | 155 |
| Wharton Mark III | 1972 | 67 |
| Morishima-Saito | 1972 | 7 |
| Brookings (Fromm et. al.) | 1971 | 156 |
| Fair | 1971 | 14 |
| Michigan Quarterly | 1970 | 35 |
| St. Louis | 1968 | 5 |
| MPS | 1968 | 75 |
| Wharton | 1967 | 47 |
| OBE/BEA | 1966 | 58 |
| Brookings (Duesenberry et. al.) | 1965 | 101 |
| Liu | 1963 | 19 |
| Suits | 1962 | 16 |
| Duesenberry et. al. | 1960 | 10 |
| Valvanis | 1955 | 12 |
| Klein-Goldberger | 1955 | 15 |
| Klein | 1950 | 3 |
| Tinbergen | 1939 | 32 |


Source: Intriligator (1978, pp. 454-456). Model sizes refer
to the number of stochastic equations.

ly tied to a theory of rational behavior...There are
few acceptable rules limiting the scope and variety
of such systems.

Even when we take into account the important recent advances in micro-
economic foundations of macroeconomics, the use of theory to limit the size
of the models still appears quite limited.  Moreover, if we were successful in building up a complete aggregate model from explicit individual
maximization postulates--a goal toward which much macrotheory is now aim-
ing--it is not clear why the interdependences which Koopmans refers to
would be weakened, or that the role of theory in determining the appropriate size of the model should be any stronger.

One objection to this conclusion that economic theory has such a limited
role to play in determining model size, is that the zero restrictions
should not be taken so literally.  Accordingly economic theory can be used
to determine which equations are relatively unimportant and can safely be
omitted.  However, if one is interested in forecasting or multiplier analysis even relatively unimportant variables can in principle be of great
assistance in reducing error (recall that we are abstracting from problems
of statistical estimation error), and cannot therefore be omitted from the
model on economic theory grounds alone.

The conditions required for limiting model size are even stronger for
dynamic models which are the rule rather than the exception in macro-
econometric work.  A dynamic linear simultaneous equations system which
generalizes (1) is

(2)        $By_t + C(L)y_t + \Gamma x_t = u_t$

where  $C(L) = C_1 L + ... + C_p L^p$  is a matrix polynomial in the lag operator
L,  and where the error term  $u_t$  has the same distribution properties as
were assumed for (1).  The matrix polynomial  $C(L)$  can be partitioned as

(3)        $C(L) = \begin{pmatrix} C_{11}(L) & C_{12}(L) \\ C_{21}(L) & C_{22}(L) \end{pmatrix}$

Now the first  $G_1$  equations can be considered in isolation if  $B_{12} = 0$,
$V_{12} = 0$,  and  $C_{12}(L) = 0$.  Then, the first  $G_1$  elements of  $y_t$  are exogenous to the last  $G - G_1$  elements.  For dynamic models, the number of
a priori conditions required for reducing model size increases with the
order of the dynamic model, that is, with the order of the polynomial
$C_{12}(L)$  in (3).

III.  MODEL PURPOSE AND MODEL SIZE

An oversimplified empirical demonstration of this limited role of economic
theory in determining model size is to assume--as a first order approxima-
tion--that all the builders of the macroeconomic models represented in
Table 1 had about the same access to economic theory and were equally
adept at using this theory in constructing their models.  If this assump-

tion is at all accurate, then after controlling for changes in computer technology, there should be relatively little variation in model size. Table 1 illustrates how far from the truth this is. Evidently there are some important missing variables.

The most obvious candidate for explaining this observed variation in model size is the model-builder's purpose of model construction. To put things simply: for some purposes large models are necessary, but for other purposes small models are necessary, or at least sufficient. For example, a large model with a detailed investment sector and a detailed government tax sector is necessary to examine questions about the quantitative impact of an investment tax credit; a large model with a detailed interindustry structure is necessary for forecasting steel shipments; and a large financial sector is necessary for determining the likely outcome of a change in one of the many Federal Reserve policy instruments. On the other hand, a very small model might be sufficient for determining the relative effectiveness of broadly defined monetary and fiscal variables. An examination of the econometric models represented in Table 1 shows that much of the variation in model size can indeed be traced to the underlying purpose of the model.

The implication of these simple observations is that it is a mistake to examine the role of economic theory in the context of macromodels in general, rather than in the context of models of a given purpose. Although economic theory may have a small role in limiting the size of general multipurpose models, this is not the case for models designed for a specific purpose. The remarks of Koopmans and Klein mentioned above are clearly directed at models in the abstract without a specific purpose in mind.

IV. ALTERNATIVE MODEL PURPOSES: PREDICTION vs. STABILIZATION

Two alternative purposes of econometric models which have been widely discussed in the literature are prediction and stabilization. In this section we show how the appropriate size of a model depends on which of these two purposes the model builder has in mind. We consider the reduced form of the dynamic model introduced in equation (2) above, but specialized to the case of one lag. By suitable stacking of vectors, higher order systems can be represented as such a first order system. The model takes the form:

$$
(4) \qquad \begin{pmatrix} y_{1t} \\ y_{2t} \end{pmatrix} = \begin{pmatrix} A_{11} & A_{12} \\ A_{21} & A_{22} \end{pmatrix} \begin{pmatrix} y_{1t-1} \\ y_{2t-1} \end{pmatrix} + \begin{pmatrix} C_1 \\ C_2 \end{pmatrix} x_t + \begin{pmatrix} v_{1t} \\ v_{2t} \end{pmatrix} .
$$

We assume that the vector $(v_{1t} \; v_{2t})$ is serially uncorrelated with mean zero and covariance matrix $\Omega$. The system (4) could be constructed with the aim of forecasting $y_{1t}$ or of stabilizing $y_{1t}$. In the stabilization case we assume that the vector $x_t$ is a control variable which can be used to control or stabilize $y_{1t}$. In the forecasting case we assume that $x_t$ is exogenous and that the path of $x_t$ is known for all t. We assume in both cases that the model builder is not directly interested in the behavior of $y_{2t}$ except through its influence on $y_{1t}$ and thereby on the forecasting and stabilization goals. The question is whether knowledge of

$A_{21}$ or $A_{22}$ is necessary for predicting or stabilizing $y_{1t}$.

Consider the problem of forecasting $y_{1t+s}$ for $s > 0$ based on information through period $t-1$; that is, given $y_{t-1}, y_{t-2}, \ldots,$ and $x_t$ for all $t$. Under the minimum mean squared error criterion, we must choose a function $y_{1t+s}$ of these observations so that the prediction error covariance matrix $E(y_{1t+s} - \hat{y}_{1t+s})(y_{1t+s} - \hat{y}_{1t+s})'$ is a minimum in the positive definite sense. It is easy to show that the conditional mean of $y_{1t+s}$ given the observations, is the best predictor and that if $A_{12} \neq 0$ this conditional mean depends on both $A_{21}$ and $A_{22}$. Hence, if one is interested in predicting the vector $y_{1t}$ it is necessary to estimate the complete model; unless of course $A_{12} = 0$.

Next consider the problem of stabilizing $y_{1t}$, using a quadratic criterion function. That is, we attempt to minimize $Ey'_{1t} \Lambda_1 y_{1t}$ in the steady state (where $\Lambda_1$ is a symmetric weighting matrix) by choosing $x_t$ to be a function of observables $y'_s = (y'_{1s}, y'_{2s})$, where $s < t$. Since we are not concerned with the behavior of $y_{2t}$ the implicit weights on the elements of $y_{2t}$ in the weighting matrix are 0. Hence in terms of the full model the objective is to minimize

$$
(5) \qquad Ey'_t \begin{pmatrix} \Lambda_1 & 0 \\ 0 & 0 \end{pmatrix} y_t
$$

subject to the stochastic constraints

$$
(6) \qquad y_t = Ay_{t-1} + Cx_t + \nu_t
$$

with respect to the elements of the matrix $G$ where $x_t = Gy_{t-1}$. (The system (6) is identical to (4) without explicit partitioning.) If $C_1$ is <u>invertible</u>, then the optimal value of $G$ takes the form $G = (G_1 \ G_2)$ where

$$
(7) \qquad
\begin{aligned}
G_1 &= -C_1^{-1} A_{11} \\
G_2 &= -C_1^{-1} A_{12}
\end{aligned}
$$

(see Chow (1975), for example). Hence, the optimal stabilization rule does not depend on either $A_{21}$ or $A_{22}$. Since $C_1$ is invertible it is possible to isolate $y_{1t}$ from the extra fluctuations due to the $y_{2t}$ dynamics. In terms of model size this isolation implies that we can ignore the equations which describe the behavior of $y_{2t}$.

If $C_1$ is <u>not invertible</u>, then in general $G_1$ and $G_2$ will depend on $A_{21}$ and $A_{22}$ so that we cannot reduce model size in this simple way. Intuitively, if $C_1$ is not invertible then $y_{1t}$ cannot be completely cut off from the influence of $y_{2t}$. Hence, the way in which $y_{2t}$ influences $y_{1t}$ matters for the choice of feedback rule. There are some special cases, however, where the influence of $y_{2t}$ can be eliminated even though

$C_1$ is not invertible. For example, if $A_{12}$ can be written as a product of $C_1$ and an invertible matrix, then the feedback of $y_{2t}$ on $y_{1t}$ can be stopped. This type of situation arises in the application considered in the next section.

The importance of model purpose in determining model size is readily apparent from this comparison of prediction and stabilization. For prediction the complete model is needed. For stabilization the necessary size of the model depends on the invertibility of a certain matrix which describes the impact of the instruments on the variables to be controlled. However, economic theory does have a role to play in determining model size once the purpose of the model has been stated. If the purpose is stabilization, for example, then economic theory might be used to determine whether $C_1$ is invertible. A necessary condition is that $C_1$ be square (an order condition) which simply means that we have enough policy instruments to cut off the influence of $y_{2t}$ on $y_{1t}$. Economic reasoning certainly seems potentially useful in determining whether this order condition is satisfied. The sufficient rank condition may be more difficult to establish on theory grounds, but could be tested using statistical techniques.[3/]

Although these policy examples may represent special types of economic problems, they illustrate how simple theoretical considerations might be combined with a statement of model purpose to determine the appropriate size of a model. In the next section we consider an application of this principle to a particular macroeconomic problem--estimating the long-run policy tradeoff between inflation and unemployment. As will be shown, a small model may be sufficient for this purpose, even though a large scale model would be necessary for other purposes such as forecasting.

V.  DECOMPOSING A LARGE-SCALE MODEL FOR ESTIMATING THE OUTPUT-INFLATION
     TRADEOFF

One of the appealing features of the old-style Phillips curve--the apparent static tradeoff between the level of unemployment (or the output gap) and the rate of inflation--was that it presented a simple list of options to policymakers. However, the realization that the Phillips curve in fact presented no such tradeoff has invalidated this simple list and unfortunately has left a much more complex list of intertemporal tradeoffs in its place. In this section we focus on a procedure for constructing a list of output-inflation options which has many of the advantages of a simple static tradeoff, yet is based on the modern dynamic theory of wage and price determination. The approach is to represent the output-inflation tradeoff as a negatively sloped relationship between the standard deviations, rather than the levels, of the output gap and inflation. With a vertical long-run Phillips curve there is no long-run tradeoff between the levels of output and inflation. And while in principle we should be interested in all aspects of the behavior of output and inflation, we focus on the standard deviations for convenience and because of their frequent use in the evaluation of macroeconomic stabilization policies. Moreover, optimal control techniques are particularly well-suited to computing such tradeoffs. For example, a tradeoff between the standard deviations of output and inflation was developed empirically by applying optimal control techniques to an estimated quarterly model with rational expectations in Taylor (1979).

The question which we wish to examine is whether economic theory can serve
as a guideline for determining how large a macroeconometric model we need,
given that the purpose of constructing this model is to estimate this tradeoff between output and inflation stability.  The problem is a special case
of that examined in the previous sections.  Consider therefore the following representative "large scale" macroeconometric model:[4]

$$(8) \qquad y_{1t} = e'y_{2t} + x_t \qquad ,$$

$$(9) \qquad y_{2t} = \sum_{i=1}^{L} (a_i y_{1t-i} + A_i y_{2t-i}) + u_{2t} \qquad ,$$

$$(10) \qquad y_{3t} = \sum_{i=1}^{M} \Theta_i y_{3t-i} + \beta(y_{1t} - y_{1t}^*) + u_{3t} \qquad ,$$

where $y_{1t}$ = real GNP,

$y_{2t}$ = a  K  dimensional vector containing the disaggregated com-
        compents of GNP,

$y_{3t}$ = the rate of inflation in terms of the GNP deflator,

$y_{1t}^*$ = potential or full capacity GNP,

$x_t$ = federal government expenditures,

$e$ = a  K dimensional vector of ones,

$a_i$ = arbitrary  K  dimensional column vectors of parameters,

$A_i$ = arbitrary  K x K  dimensional matrices of parameters,

$u_{2t}$ = a  K  dimensional vector of disturbances,

$u_{3t}$ = a scalar disturbance.

We assume for simplicity that the model is linear, though similar methods
could be used for nonlinear models.  We also assume that the vector
$(u_{2t}, u_{3t})$  is serially uncorrelated, with a diagonal covariance matrix.

Equation (8) is simply the national income identity.  By permitting the
vector  $y_{2t}$  to be quite large we are implicitly considering a large-scale
model.  For example, available data would permit consumer expenditures to
be disaggregated into over 30 categories, and the potential range of disaggregation for net exports is even larger.  Without a statement of a particular purpose for the model, economic theory does not appear to be of
much use in limiting this disaggregation.  The variable  $x_t$,  government
expenditures, will be the sole aggregate demand policy instrument, although monetary policy would also be considered in a similar fashion.

Equation (9) is a reduced form representation for the individual components

of GNP. Equation (1) represents the wage-price sector of a typical econometric model. While more disaggregation may be useful for estimating the
output-inflation tradeoff, many econometric models can be reduced to such
a representation if some of the exogenous variables, such as fluctuations
of the minimum wage about trend, are considered as part of the disturbance
$u_{3t}$. Since the main purpose of this section is to examine whether expenditure and production decomposition is necessary we will not pursue the adequacy of the approximation implicit in equation (1). (If a small model of
the expenditure side is sufficient, more effort might be placed on developing the wage and price sectors.)

The output-inflation policy problem can be stated formally by substituting
(9) into (8) and (10) to get

$$(11) \quad y_{1t} = e'[\sum_{i=1}^{L} (a_i y_{1t-i} + A_i y_{2t-i}) + u_{2t}] + x_t \quad,$$

$$(12) \quad y_{3t} = \sum_{i=1}^{M} \Theta_i y_{3t-i} + \beta[e'[\sum_{i=1}^{L} (a_i y_{1t-i} + A_i y_{2t-i}) + u_{2t}]$$

$$+ \beta(x_t - y_{1t}^*) + u_{3t} \quad.$$

The policy objective is to find a feedback rule for $x_t$ to minimize the
expected squared deviations of $y_{1t}$ and $y_{3t}$ about given target levels.
We take $y_{1t}^*$ to be the target for $y_{1t}$ and, to save on notation, we assume that the target inflation rate is zero. We also assume that the rule
for $x_t$ should be chosen to minimize $\lambda E(y_{1t} - y_{1t}^*)^2 + (1 - \lambda)Ey_{3t}^2$ in
the steady state. This criterion corresponds to equation (5) in the pre-
vious section. For this problem, the rule is always of the form:

$$(13) \quad x_t = y_1^* - e'\sum_{i=1}^{L} (a_i y_{1t-i} + A_i y_{2t-i}) + \sum_{i=1}^{M} g_i y_{3t-i}$$

where the $g_i$ coefficients depend on the weights in the objective function. Hence, equations (11) and (12) reduce to

$$(14) \quad y_{1t} = y_{1t}^* + \sum_{i=1}^{M} g_i y_{3t-i} + e'u_{2t} \quad,$$

$$(15) \quad y_{3t} = \sum_{i=1}^{M} (\Theta_i + \beta g_i) y_{3t-i} + \beta e'u_{2t} + u_{3t} \quad.$$

The important thing to note about equations (14) and (15) is that neither
$y_{1t}$ nor $y_{3t}$ depend on the parameters $a_i$ and $A_i$ which describe the
behavior of the GNP components $y_{2t}$. Hence, the optimal tradeoff curve
between the mean square deviations in $y_{1t}$ and the mean square deviations
in $y_{3t}$ (which is a two-dimensional plot of the best pairs of deviations

for alternative values of λ) does not depend on the behavior of the GNP components. If the purpose of the model is to estimate this tradeoff then we do not need to disaggregate GNP.

To illustrate the practical implications of this result we have calculated a tradeoff curve between the standard deviation of output (real GNP) and the standard deviation of inflation (the first difference in the logarithm of the GNP deflator) using annual data from 1954-76 in the U. S. Equation (10) was estimated using several values of M, the length of the lag in the inflation equation. Somewhat surprisingly it was found that the simple equation

$$(16) \qquad y_{3t} = y_{3t-1} + \underset{(3.36)}{.303}[(y_{1t} - y_{1t}^*)/y_{1t}^*] + \underset{(2.55)}{.0081} + \varepsilon_t$$

could not be rejected in favor of the less constrained models represented in (10). For these estimates the impact of aggregate demand is to reduce inflation by about 1 percentage point for each year that the GNP gap is 3 percent below its equilibrium value. For computing the efficiency locus we therefore set $\theta_1 = 1$, $\theta_i = 0$ for $i > 1$ in equation (10). The estimated standard error of this equation is 1.2 percent. (Note that in estimating this equation we have used the percentage GNP gap rather than the absolute gap; this does not change the earlier discussion and permits us to consider percentage fluctuations in GNP as our welfare measure.) Note that the significant constant term in equation (16) indicates that inflation will be rising when GNP is equal to potential GNP as currently estimated by the Council of Advisers. The "no change" inflation point appears to occur at the GNP gap of about 2-2/3 percent.

Using the estimates given in equation (16), the two relationships (14) and (15) reduce to

$$(17) \qquad y_{1t} = y_{1t}^* + g_1 y_{3t-1} + e'u_{2t}$$

$$(18) \qquad y_{3t} = (1 + \beta g_1)y_{3t-1} + \beta e'u_{2t} + u_{3t}$$

where we have adjusted $y_{1t}^*$ to represent potential GNP less 2-2/3 percent, (so that the output target does not entail increasing inflation), and where we now interpret the output variable in percent. Given $\beta$, the variance of $u_{3t}$, and the variance of $e'u_{2t}$ the steady state variance-covariance matrix of $y_{1t}$ and $y_{3t}$ depends only on $\beta$.

In Figure 1 the curve labeled $\beta = .3$ represents the estimated output-inflation tradeoff curve assuming that the standard deviations of $u_{1t}$ and $u_{3t}$ are 1 and 1.2 percent respectively, in terms of the standard deviation of $y_{1t} - y_{1t}^*$ and $y_{3t}$. It is obtained by plotting the square roots of the diagonal elements of the variance covariance matrix of these variables for values of $g_1$ between 0 and 3.3. According to these estimates the aggregate demand accommodation parameter, $g_1$, should be slightly less than 1 but not as small as .7 if inflation fluctuations and output fluctuations would have to be 3 times more costly than inflation fluctuations (assuming linear indifference curves).

There is little that can be shown in general about how this graph will depend on β. This depends on the empirical values of the other parameters. We therefore consider the effect of β on the tradeoff curve, holding the variances constant at the values stated above. Figure 1 also shows two other tradeoff curves corresponding to two different values of β. The two curves are based on the estimated value of β plus or minus two estimated standard errors. The range between these two curves seems to cover most current estimates of the effect of aggregate demand on prices. Note that a <u>steeper</u> short-run curve makes the output-inflation tradeoff <u>more</u> favorable. As β increases, the opportunity set tends to encompass more points which are relevant policy choices, while eliminating points which would never be chosen anyway. Of course, as β increases above 1/2 we may begin to lose some relevant points, but values of β in this range are unrealistic.

Other comparative static questions could be examined by changing some of the other parameters of the model. An important question is the sensitivity of these results to changes in the wage and price dynamics implicit in the model, and in particular whether a more detailed wage-price sector would alter Figure 1. Recent research on rational expectations suggests, for example, that the tradeoffs represented in this figure are too pessimistic in the sense that greater efforts to stabilize inflation will not result in as great an increase in employment fluctuations as the tradeoffs suggest. The main point of the discussion of this paper is that these questions can in principle be investigated within the context of a model with a highly aggregated demand sector. The policy analysis is independent of the complex equation system which generates the components of GNP, and therefore it is sufficient to focus on the wage and price dynamics. On the other hand, if the purpose of the model changes to forecasting GNP, for example, then the detailed disaggregation again becomes potentially useful. This latter statement is a reminder that the arguments of this section apply only to models which have a limited number of purposes. The approach is not likely to have much of a role in limiting the size of multipurpose models.

It should also be emphasized that the decomposition procedure suggested here is more widely applicable than the particular example of this section may indicate. In general terms the procedure simply determines quantitatively whether the aims of an econometric model depend on certain economic relationships. If they do not, then we can eliminate these economic relationships. If they do not, then we can eliminate these economic relationships from consideration. While this principle is undoubtedly followed to some degree by most model builders, this paper has suggested how it might be formalized quantitatively when the objective of research is the estimation of optimal policy tradeoffs. It would be of interest to investigate whether other goals of economic modelling can be similarly quantified in order to weed out econometric relationships which are not essential.

VI. CONCLUDING REMARKS

The central themes of this discussion have been: (1) that the research objective of a model-building effort is the most important determinant of

the appropriate size of a macroeconometric model, (2) that the role of
economic theory in determining model size becomes significant only when
a well-specified set of objectives is known, and (3) that the appropriate
decomposition of a model into smaller isolated parts depends on the purpose to which the model is put.  To illustrate these points, quantitative
results were presented showing that a relatively small model could be used
for estimating macroeconomic policy tradeoffs between output and inflation
stability, while a large-scale model would be necessary for prediction
purposes.

Given this apparent importance of model objectives, it would be interesting to extend this research to statistical methods of model selection.
These methods have been generally based on <u>prediction</u> criteria; the results of this paper indicate that their power might be enhanced by basing
them on other model objectives such as optimal policy formation.

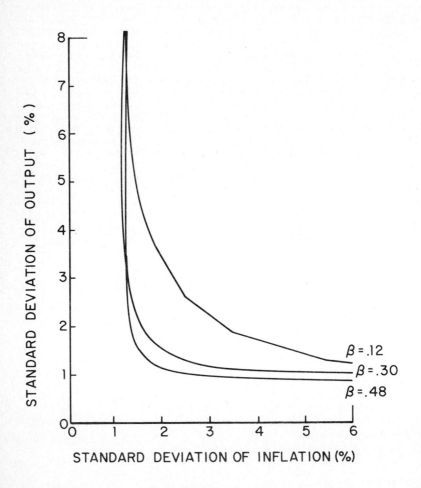

Figure 1

Notes

1.  Previous methodological discussions which have touched upon issues related to economic theory and model size are found in Fromm and Klein (1975) and the collection of papers in Brunner (1972). Kmenta's (1972) summary of the discussions held at two conferences during 1967 and 1968 is particularly useful.

2.  Sims (1979) argues that we rarely have enough theory to obtain identification. The same arguments would apply with greater force to the model decomposition problem.

3.  It should be noted that some of the results in this section on stabilization policy will not carry over to rational expectations models. In these models, prediction is an integral part of the structure and usually takes the form of cross equation constraints. This generally makes decomposition more difficult, and suggests that models need to be bigger when expectations are assumed to be formed rationally.

4.  It should be emphasized that these results are provided in order to illustrate a particular decomposition technique for a "representative" econometric model. No attempt is made here to incorporate rational expectations effects or explicit wage and price contracts as in Taylor (1979). Hence, although the results serve as a useful illustration, they are in principle subject to the potential criticism that the parameters are not stable across different policy regimes.

References

Brunner, K. (Ed.) (1972) Problems and Issues in Current Econometric
    Practice, Ohio State University Press, Columbus.

Chow, G. C. (1975) Analysis and Control of Dynamic Economic Systems,
    Wiley, New York.

Fromm, G. and L. R. Klein (Eds.) (1975) The Brookings Model: Perspective
    and Recent Developments, North-Holland, Amsterdam.

Intriligator, M. D. (1978) Econometric Models, Techniques, and Applications,
    Prentice-Hall, New Jersey.

Johnston, J. (1972) Econometric Methods (2nd Ed.), McGraw-Hill, New York.

Klein, L. R. (1962) An Introduction to Econometrics, Prentice-Hall, New
    Jersey.

Kmenta, J. (1972) "Summary of the Discussion," in Brunner, K. (Ed.),
    Problems and Issues in Current Econometric Practice, Ohio State Uni-
    versity Press, Columbus.

Koopmans, T. C. (1950) "When Is an Equation System Complete for Statistical
    Purposes," in Koopmans, T. C. (Ed.) Statistical Inference in Dynamic
    Econometric Models, Wiley, New York.

Sims, C. A. (1979) "Macroeconomics and Reality," Econometrica, 48, 1-48.

Taylor, J. B. (1979) "Estimation and Control of a Macroeconomic Model with
    Rational Expectations," Econometrica, 47, 1267-1286.

LARGE-SCALE MACRO-ECONOMETRIC MODELS
J. Kmenta, J.B. Ramsey (editors)
© North-Holland Publishing Company, 1981

STATISTICAL INFERENCE IN RELATION TO
THE SIZE OF THE MODEL

G. S. Maddala
University of Florida[*]

The term 'statistical inference' is very broad and the
term 'size' is very vague.  In this paper, I will survey
some aspects of statistical inference relating to what
are customarily called 'large econometric models'.  The
purpose of this survey is to focus the discussion on what
we know and where more work needs to be done.

## 1.  WHAT IS MEANT BY SIZE?

When we talk of 'size' of a model, clearly we mean only some magnitude
in relation to the questions we are asking.  This question of magnitude in
relation to the questions being asked can be an economic problem or a
statistical problem or both.  We can say a model is large if it is too
complicated and contains a lot more detail than necessary for the purpose
of the questions that are being asked.  This is more an economic problem
rather than a statistical problem.  Or alternatively, we can say a model is
large if we have the purely statistical problem of there being not enough
degrees of freedom or not enough precision in the estimated parameters.
The latter point is illustrated in the following examples:

Consider two regression models - one with 100,000 observations and another
with 60 observations - both with 50 explanatory variables.  Obviously, the
former is larger in dimensions but it makes more sense to term the latter
a 'larger' model.  Similarly, consider two regression models both with 50
observations and 30 variables.  In one case the 30 variables are more or
less orthogonal to one another and in the other case the 30 variables are
highly collinear (as in a distributed lag model with unrestricted
coefficients).  Again, it makes sense to call the latter model the larger
model.  When we move to simultaneous equations models we have to discuss
an additional dimension - the number of endogenous and exogenous variables.
Consider two models both with 80 observations and 60 variables.  In one
there are 20 endogenous and 40 exogenous variables and in another there
are 40 endogenous and 20 exogenous variables.  Again it makes sense to
consider the latter model a larger model.

Many macro-economic models have a large number of both exogenous and
endogenous variables in relation to the number of observations.  Further,
the data sets exhibit strong multicollinearity.  Table 1 lists the number
of observations and the number of exogenous and endogenous variables for
some macro-models.  The data are extracted from two sources which are not
too far apart in time.  It is interesting to note the trend in model size.
In the case of the DRI model the number of stochastic equations actually
fell whereas in the case of the Wharton model, it increased enormously.

## TABLE 1

### SOME INDICATORS OF MODEL SIZE

| Model | Observations | Number of | | Exogenous Variables |
| | | Stochastic Equations | Equations | |
|---|---|---|---|---|
| BEA | 72 | 67 | 117 | |
| Fair | 70 | 14 | 19 | 20 |
| DRI | 48 | 477 | 698 | 184 |
| MQEM | 68 | 35 | 59 | 63 |
| Wharton III | 67 | 68 | 191 | 92 |

Source:   Table 1, Christ (1975)

| Model | Equations | Number of | | Predetermined Variables |
| | | Stochastic Equations | Exogenous Variables | |
|---|---|---|---|---|
| BEA | 196 | 108 | 150 | 249 |
| Chase | 350 | 150 | 150 | 350 |
| DRI | 831 | 350 | 178 | 628 |
| MQEM | 81 | 47 | 76 | 105 |
| Wharton | 695 | 299 | 242 | 677 |
| BB-Micro | - | - | - | - |
| Fair | 97 | 29 | 83 | 139 |
| St Louis | 7 | 5 | 3 | 7 |

Source:   Table 1, Kelejian and Vavrichek's paper in this volume.

There are different definitions of size one can adopt based on the relationship of sample size and number of endogenous and exogenous variables. This distinction is important for the discussion of what methods of estimation are theoretically possible.  Of course what is theoretically possible need not be empirically feasible.  For instance, it is theoretically possible to estimate by FIML a Sixty-equation model with 20 exogenous variables and 90 observations.  Empirically it would pose  enormous problems.  The discussion of what requirements on size are necessary for the different estimation methods to be possible at least theoretically is however interesting.

Let T be the toal number of observations

    n the number of endogenous variables
    m the number of exogenous variables
    $n_1$ the number of stochastic equations
    $n_2$ the number of non-stochastic equations ($n=n_1+n_2$).

Then, we can say a model is large if

(a)  $n_1 > 1$
(b)  $n > T$
(c)  $m > T$
(d)  $m + n > T$

Very often, a model is defined to be large if condition (c) is satisfied.
But this is a very narrow definition. Intuitively, it is clear that the
four cases ought to pose different sorts of problems. For instance, (a)
would raise problems with those methods that depend on the inverse of the
covariance matrix of the residuals. Case (c) would raise problems in the
estimation of the unrestricted reduced form. Case (d) would raise problems
with the FIML method.

In the case of models like the DRI model, and Wharton III model, all the
different definitions lead to the conclusion that the model is large.
But the same is not the case with some other macro-models. For instance,
the MQEM model is large by only the definition (d).


## 2.  SAMPLE SIZE REQUIREMENTS FOR DIFFERENT SIMULTANEOUS EQUATIONS METHODS

Klein (1969, 1971) conjectured that the FIML method is feasible only if the
number of observations T is not less than (n + m), the total number of
variables in the system, i.e., the data matrix is of full column rank.
Sargan (1975) has proved that this condition is indeed correct when the
identifying restrictions are of the exclusion type.[1]  Brown (1978) extends
Sargan's analysis to a simultaneous equations system subject to linear
homogenous restrictions on the coefficients of single equations. He proves
in this case that FIML estimation is sometimes possible when T < n + m and
that this can only occur when the system can be transformed into an
equivalent system with fewer variables and the data matrix of the reduced
system is of full column rank. With more complicated models involving
cross-equation restrictions and non-linearities, the conditions for
existence of FIML estimates are expected to be weaker but are not yet known.

The sample size requirements for 2SLS and LIML are of course well known.
These are that the number of observations T is greater than the number of
exogenous variables m. For the existence of 3SLS estimates, the sample
size requirements are less stringent than for the FIML estimates. Court
(1974) shows that even the condition T > n is not necessary for the
existence of 3SLS estimates. However, the method Court suggests involves
the inversion of a matrix that is of a much higher dimension than that
in the usual 3SLS. If N is the total number of parameters in the system,
the usual 3SLS method involves the inversion of an (N x N) matrix whereas
the method that Court suggests involves the inversion of an (mn + N) x
(mn + N) matrix. Thus, though the 3SLS estimates are defined even when
T < n and hence the estimated covariance matrix of the residuals is
singular, the computational burden in computing them is much higher than
when this covariance matrix can be inverted.

Sample size requirements for the instrumental variable methods based on
restricted reduced forms like the LIVE and FIVE methods suggested by

Brundy and Jorgenson (1971) are much weaker than those of 2SLS and 3SLS. The first step in these methods is the construction of a consistent estimate of the structural parameters. These initial consistent estimates may be obtained by the use of consistent but possibly inefficient instrumental variable estimators. This is always possible so long as $T > m_i + n_i - 1$ where $m_i$ and $n_i$ are respectively the exogenous and endogenous variables in the i-th equation. For the FIVE method since the covariance matrix of the residuals is also estimated and inverted, we require $T > n$ (assuming that different instruments are used to estimate different equations) or $T > n + m^*$ where $m^*$ is the number of common instruments used in the estimation of <u>all</u> equations. Brundy and Jorgenson do not suggest any further iterations on their procedures but Dhrymes (1971) does. Hausman (1975) shows that the FIVE procedure when iterated gives the FIML estimates. Thus, the sample size requirements of the FIVE method, if iterated, are the same as those of FIML. Dutta and Lyttkens (1970) and Lyttkens (1974) suggest iteration on the LIVE estimator. However, it is not clear what this iteration converges to. It surely does not converge to the LIML estimator, nor does it converge to the FIML estimator with a diagonal covariance matrix.[2] Thus, the sample size requirements for the iterated version of the LIVE estimator are not yet known. Dutta and Lyttkens (1970) report the convergence of the iterated LIVE estimator. Their model has 17 annual observations, 36 equations of which 13 are identities and 22 predetermined variables of which seven are lagged endogenous. Since $T < m$, clearly 2SLS is not applicable. If their results are correct, it appears that the sample size requirements of the iterated LIVE estimator are weaker than those of 2SLS.

The reason why one might consider iterating on LIVE and FIVE is that the first round estimates will be highly sensitive to the initial instruments chosen. But the results, at least for the iterated FIVE (which has been shown to lead to FIML) indicate that once we start iterating, the sample size requirements are the same as those of FIML and hence the procedure loses its appeal for large models. We will discuss these procedures in section 4 again.

## 3. RESCUE EFFORTS ON TWO-STAGE LEAST SQUARES

The case of 2SLS estimation with $T < m$ has received considerable attention in the literature and there have been several efforts to rescue the 2SLS method. In this case there are not enough degrees of freedom to estimate the reduced form. If X is the matrix of observations on the exogenous variables, then the matrix $(X'X)$ is singular. Swamy and Holmes (1971) argue that the 2SLS and 3SLS estimates are still defined in this case and they suggest replacing the generalized inverse of $(X'X)$ where $(X'X)^{-1}$ occurs in the usual 2SLS and 3SLS formulae. However, this is only a mechanical solution to the problem and as noted by Theil (1971, p. 534), when one simplifies the expressions, one notes that the 2SLS estimator is nothing but the OLS estimator. The generalized inverse solution merely conceals the basic issue in a web of algebra.[3] The suggestion of Fisher and Wadycki (1971) is also similar to that of Swamy and Holmes. When $T < m$ their estimator also reduces to the OLS. As Rayner (1972) says, it is better to say that the OLS estimator is being used. "To call it 2SLS might appear to add a lustre to the technique, but this would be misleading since the asymptotic properties usually implied by this name are wholly irrelevant."

Theil has suggested three modifications to the 2SLS method in the case
$T < m$. These are in Theil (1971, p. 535), Theil (1973), and Theil and
Laitinen (1977). None of these procedures seem to have gained any wide
acceptance partly because of the arbitrary restrictions each imposes on
the reduced forms. The logical solution to the undersized sample problem
is to bring in some prior information and usually it is better to bring in
the information pertaining to the restrictions that the rest of the model
imposes on the reduced form. That is why the restricted reduced form
methods outlined in the next section found more empirical acceptance.

The case of $T < m$ is actually an extreme case. Even when $T > m$, if m is
sufficiently large relative to T, it has been found empirically that the
estimated values of the endogenous variables from the reduced form are
very close to the actual values and hence the 2SLS estimates are very
close to the OLS estimates. This is in fact what happens in Liu's model
(1963). In almost all equations the OLS and 2SLS estimates differ only
at the third decimal place. There is a question of how one should interpret
the results. Does this mean we are justified in using the ordinary least
squares method in large econometric models or does it mean that the two-
stage least squares method is not a good method to take account of
simultaneity in such models? Paradoxically, problems seem to occur when
there are too many exogenous variables in the system. As Theil and
Laitinen (1977, p. 3) say: "Our objective is to estimate the structural
equation which may contain only one parameter. It is against intuition
that there are serious problems in estimating such a single parameter
from 20 observations when there are 30 predetermined variables known to
be orthogonal to $\varepsilon_j$, whereas there are no problems when this knowledge
is restricted to only 10 predetermined variables."

Two methods that have received a lot of attention to the empirical work are
the principal component instrumental variable method (PCIV) which goes
back to the work of Kloek and Mennes (1960) and the structurally ordered
instrumental variable (SOIV) method of Fisher (1965 a, b). In the principal component method the first stage consists of using a few principal
components as regressors. The major drawbacks of this method
are that there is no economic principle involved in the method and it is
not necessarily true that the first or second or any high order principal
component is the one that is most highly correlated with the endogenous
variable considered. This latter point, very often ignored, is fairly
obvious because after all, the covariance matrix of the exogenous variables
is all that is considered in computing the principal components. This
implies that one has to consider the entire set of principal components
and start picking up among them by a step-wise procedure. But if this is
to be done, such a search procedure can as well be used with the original
set of predetermined variables and there is no reason to go to principal
components analysis unless, for some obscure reasons, one is interested in
orthogonal components. In spite of these severe limitations, the PCIV
method seems to have attracted a lot of attention from both theoreticians
and those estimating large models.[4]

The SOIV method of Fisher, by contrast, uses the economic theory behind
the model in choosing subsets of predetermined variables as instruments.
The rules for the selection of the order of instrumental variables are
described in Fisher (1965 a, b) and Mitchell and Fisher (1970). Mitchell
(1971) seems to indicate that the SOIV method involves a greater computational expense (in searches) than the PCIV method. He finds that for the

Brookings model with 80 exogenous variables the SOIV method produces coefficient estimates which most closely resemble PCIV with 15 components and have equally small standard errors. These estimates are obtained with fewer than 15 instrumental variables but at greater computational expense. Mitchell argues that the greater simplicity of PCIV might lead us to prefer it to the SOIV method except in block recursive systems where the latter is at an advantage. Given the fact that the SOIV method makes lot more economic sense than the PCIV method, this conclusion is rather disappointing. There has been, however, one major criticism of the SOIV method. Griliches (1968) criticized this method on the grounds that it is the coefficients of the restricted reduced form, not the unrestricted reduced form, that tell us the relative importance of the different exogenous variables on the endogenous variables. Thus the search method involved in SOIV is not the right way of proceeding. This may also account for the fact that the SOIV method did not perform substantially better than the PCIV method in Mitchell's analysis.

## 4.   RESTRICTED REDUCED FORM METHODS

The SOIV method uses the information in the structural system to construct instrumental variables. An alternative and perhaps better approach to use the structural information, as Grilliches (1968) notes, is to use the restricted reduced forms (RRF). There have been many RRF methods suggested in the literature and it is important to elaborate on these and discuss their differences because they are the most important methods that have been suggested for large models, and are likely to be used in at least medium-size models if not the very large models. Dutta and Lyttkens (1974) estimate a medium size model using these methods.

The RRF methods can be classified under the following categories:

(1)   Analogues of the 2SLS and the instrumental variable methods.

(2)   Limited information and full information methods: Here the term limited information has to be used in a sense different from what it is usually used for. Suppose the structural system, in the familiar notation, is

$$BY + \Gamma Z = U \quad \text{with } E(UU') = \Sigma$$

The limited information RRF methods use only the information in the $(B, \Gamma)$ matrix. The full information RRF methods use the information in $(B, \Gamma, \Sigma)$ matrices.

To understand the differences, consider the 2-equation model - commonly called Summers' model:

$$y_1 = b_{12}y_2 + c_{11}z_1 + c_{12}z_2 + u_1$$

$$y_2 = b_{21}y_1 + c_{23}z_3 + c_{24}z_4 + u_2$$

where $y_1$, $y_2$ are the endogenous variables and $z_1$, $z_2$, $z_3$, $z_4$ are the exogenous variables. In 2SLS, we first regress $y_1$ and $y_2$ on all the $z$'s, get the predicted values $\hat{y}_1$ and $\hat{y}_2$ and then regress $y_1$ on $\hat{y}_2$, $z_1$, $z_2$ and $y_2$ on $\hat{y}_1$, $z_3$, $z_4$. One can continue this procedure further by replacing

$\hat{y}_1$ and $\hat{y}_2$ by the predicted values of $y_1$ and $y_2$ obtained from the solved reduced form. This is what is done in iterated 2SLS. Nagar (1959) reports that such iterations on 2SLS met with some trouble with convergence.

In the Iterative Instrumental Variable method, we use the predicted values of the y's as instruments rather than as regressors. Of course in the usual 2SLS method, whether $\hat{y}_1$ and $\hat{y}_2$ are used as regressors or as instrumental variables one gets identical results. However, with further iterations, when $\hat{y}_1$ and $\hat{y}_2$ are replaced by the predictions from the solved reduced forms, it is no longer true that the two methods are equivalent.

Wold's Fix-Point Method (1965) is related to iterated 2SLS but there are essential differences. First, instead of using $\hat{y}_1$ and $\hat{y}_2$ from the unrestricted reduced form to start the iteration, we can use arbitrary values (excluding those that introduce perfect multicollinearity) as starting values. This is what makes it a feasible method in large models where unrestricted reduced forms cannot be estimated. Second, we do not solve the structural system at each stage of iteration. Instead we proceed as follows:

Start with some $y_1^{(0)}$ and $y_2^{(0)}$. Obtain the estimates of the structural parameters of the system by ordinary least squares replacing $y_1$ and $y_1^{(0)}$ and $y_2$ by $y_2^{(0)}$. Let these estimates by $b_{ij}^{(0)}$ and $c_{ij}^{(0)}$. Now, instead of solving the system, define

$$y_1^{(1)} = b_{12}^{(0)} y_2^{(0)} + c_{11}^{(0)} z_1 + c_{12}^{(0)} z_2$$

(2)

and

$$y_2^{(1)} = b_{21}^{(0)} y_1^{(0)} + c_{23}^{(0)} z_3 + c_{24}^{(0)} z_4$$

The $y_1^{(1)}$ and $y_2^{(1)}$ so obtained are used as regressors in the next stage of iteration in place of $y_1^{(0)}$ and $y_2^{(0)}$ and new estimates $b_{ij}^{(1)}$ and $c_{ij}^{(1)}$ are obtained for the structural parameters. The above procedure similar to (2) is repeated to get $y_1^{(2)}$ and $y_2^{(2)}$. This procedure is repeated until convergence is attained. Wold's Fix Point method can be modified so that instead of using the predicted y's as regressors at each stage, one could use them as instrumental variables.

Since the essential feature of all these iterative procedures is that when the iterations converge, the predicted values of the y's in the final stage (used as regressors or instruments) satisfy the restricted reduced forms, Maddala (1971) called these estimators Restricted Reduced-form Two Stage Least Squares (RRF2SLS) and Restricted Reduced Form Instrumental Variable (RRFIV) estimators. Either estimator can be computed by (a) the solved reduced form iteration and (b) Wold's iteration. However, it has been found in practice that except the RRFIV estimator computed by the solved reduced form method of iteration, the other methods either failed to converge or converged to different solutions depending on the starting point, and sometimes even produced oscillatory solutions. (See Maddala (1971) for details on these experiments in iteration.)

The iterative procedures discussed above utilize all the structural information pertaining to the coefficients (B, Γ) in the structural system. However, they are not full-information methods. Another important point to notice is that as in the case of 2SLS the covariances among the endogenous variables are not used in computing the estimates. If we consider the covariance matrix of the endogenous and exogenous variables in the system,

$$\begin{pmatrix} Y'Y & Y'X \\ X'Y & X'X \end{pmatrix}$$

then, like the 2SLS procedure, the above iterative procedures make use of the information on Y'X and X'X only. Thus the maximand or minimand for these procedures should involve only these quantities. However, it is not clear what this function exactly is that these procedures maximize or minimize. Unless this issue is settled the problem of choice between multiple solutions and the problem of non-convergence cannot be solved satisfactorily.

As for asymptotic efficiency, it might be thought that because the iterative least squares methods use more structural information, than 2SLS, that one would gain in efficiency. This, however, is not true. With the restricted reduced form instrumental variable methods, there is no gain in efficiency over those methods that use the unrestricted reduced form, whereas, in those methods where the restricted reduced form predictions of the y's are used as regressors, there can even be a loss in efficiency as a consequence of the fact that the orthogonality between the regressors and the residual that is present in the ordinary 2SLS method is not preserved.

Since the iterative least squares procedures do not result in any gain in efficiency relative to 2SLS and since we do not know what they converge to, Maddala (1971) argues that it would be more fruitful to consider the FIML estimator with a diagonal covariance matrix. It uses precisely the structural information on $(B, \Gamma)$ that the iterative least squares procedures use, is computationally no more cumbersome, is asymptotically more efficient than 2SLS, and finally has a well defined maximand unlike the iterative least squares procedures. If we stop at some stage of the iteration, with the other procedures we have no way of judging whether we are better off or worse off than at the previous stage whereas with the ML method we can compute the value of the likelihood function at each stage of the iteration and know in which direction we are going.[5]

Consider an n equation model with n endogenous and m exogenous variables $By + Cz = u$. The reduced form is $y = -B^{-1}Cz + B^{-1}u$

$$= y* + v \text{ (say)}$$

If the residuals are independent, the ML estimates of the elements of B and C are obtained by maximizing (see Malinvaud (1966), p. 572).

$$\text{Log } |B| - \frac{1}{2}\sum_i \text{ Log } \sum_t [b_{i1}y_{it} + b_{i2}y_{2t} + \cdots + b_{in}y_{nt} + c_{i1}z_{1t} + \cdots + c_{im}z_{mt}]^2 \tag{3}$$

This expression is the concentrated likelihood function after substituting the ML estimate $\hat{\sigma}_i^2$ (i=1,2..n) in the likelihood function. Let $(b^{ij}) = B^{-1}$.

Differentiating (3) with respect to $b_{ij}$ we get

$$b^{ji} - \frac{\sum_t y_{jt} u_{it}}{\sum_t u_{it}^2} = 0$$

i.e.

$$\sum_t [y_{jt} - b^{ji} u_{it}] u_{it} = 0$$

But

$$y_j = y_j^* + v_j = y_j^* + \sum_k b^{jk} u_k$$

Hence the above equation can be written as

$$\sum_t [y_{jt}^* + \sum_{k \neq i} b^{jk} u_{kt}] u_{it} = 0 \tag{4}$$

Also differentiating (3) with respect to $c_{ij}$ we get

$$\sum_t z_{jt} u_{it} = 0 \tag{5}$$

The difference between the ML method and the Iterative Instrumental Variable method is the expression $\sum_{k \neq i} b^{jk} u_{kt}$ in equation (4). This also suggests the appropriate modifications to be made to the IIV method so as to obtain the FIML estimates. The procedure would be as follows:

Start with any consistent estimates, $\tilde{B}, \tilde{C}$ of the structural parameters B and C. Get the solved reduced form $\tilde{B}^{-1}\tilde{C}z = \tilde{y}$. Also get the residuals from the structural equations $\tilde{u}$. Let $[\tilde{b}^{jk}] = [\tilde{B}]^{-1}$. Then for the IIV method we use $\tilde{y}_j$ as the instrumental variables in the next stage. For the ML estimates, we use $(\tilde{y}_j + \sum_{k \neq i} b^{jk} \tilde{u}_k)$ as the instrumental variable if $y_j$ occurs in the ith equation. Note that the additional computational burden in computing the ML estimates is very small. We now get new consistent estimates for B and C. It can be easily verified that there is no further gain in (asymptotic) efficiency by subsequent iterations. However, to obtain the ML estimates, we have to continue the above iteration until convergence is attained.

One might object to the assumption of a diagonal covariance matrix for the residuals. But some such assumption is anyhow implied in the iterative least squares methods considered above. It is better to make the assumption explicit. That this ML estimator is asymptotically more efficient than the 2SLS estimator follows from the results proved in Rothenberg and Leenders (1964). If the covariance matrix of the residuals is diagonal, the 3SLS estimates and 2SLS estimates coincide but 3SLS is known to be less efficient than FIML in this case.

The iterated 2SLS method was first discussed by Nagar (1959, Chapter 8) and was also suggested by Wold (1965) under the name "Fix-Point Method" (though the iteration procedure is, as described earlier, is different). Cooper (1972) used only the first iterate of the iterated 2SLS. Dhrymes and Pandit (1972) show that this first iterate of iterated 2SLS is consistent but as for its asymptotic efficiency compared with 2SLS, no definite conclusions can be drawn. The instrumental variable version of the same procedure is the LIVE estimator suggested by Brundy and Jorgenson (1971) and Dhrymes (1971) and this has been shown to be asymptotically as efficient as 2SLS. The iterated version of this is the IIV estimator considered by Dutta and Lyttkens (1974) and Lyttkens (1974) and this too has the same asymptotic efficiency as 2SLS. Brundy and Jorgenson (1971) and Dhrymes (1971) also consider a system method of constructing instrumental variables that also uses the information on the covariance matrix of the residuals of the structural equations. This estimator called FIVE is asymptotically as efficient as FIML and 3SLS and, in fact, when iterated yields the FIML estimator as shown by Hausman (1975). Brundy and Jorgenson (1974) also suggest that the FIVE estimator is not worth the extra computational effort and suggest using only the LIVE estimator.

Given that the FIVE estimator is not likely to be used in large models and that we know what it converges to when iterated, we have discussed at length the iterated version of the LIVE method. It is important to note that the name 'LIVE' is a misnomer because the estimator is not a limited information estimator in the usual sense. The structural information is incorporated in the restrictions on $(B, \Gamma, \Sigma)$. The LIVE estimator uses all the information in the restrictions on $(B, \Gamma)$ only. Thus, it is somewhere in between a limited information and a full information estimator in the conventional sense. The question is what does it assume about $\Sigma$? We have seen that whereas the FIVE estimator when iterated leads to FIML, and LIVE estimator when iterated i.e., the IIV estimator of Dutta and Lyttkens (1974) does not lead to FIML with a diagonal $\Sigma$. In fact I am not able to show what it converges to.

Brundy and Jorgenson (1971) illustrate the LIVE and FIVE methods with the Lui model (1963) for which, (because they use an extended period) there are 88 quarterly observations (1948-1969), 27 endogenous variables (17 stochastic equations and 10 identities) and 46 predetermined variables. Klein's necessary condition for the existence of the FIML estimates is satisfied in his model. But what if this condition is violated? Even then one could get the FIVE estimates but if one iterates the procedure, sometime during the iteration, the inadequacies of the sample-size will become transparent. With the iteration of the LIVE estimator (as used by Dutta and Lyttkens) or with the Fix-Point method of Wold, we are not sure whether the sample-size inadequacies are ever going to be transparent because we do not know what the method converges to. If the LIVE or IIV procedures are used, it is better to modify them as described earlier in equation (4) so that one can interpret the procedure in terms of the relevant likelihood function and also evaluate successive iterations in terms of likelihood values.[6]

As mentioned earlier, the restricted reduced form methods are intermediate between what we traditionally consider the full-information and limited-information methods. One alternative class of estimators that are also intermediate between the two are the subsystem methods discussed in recent econometric literature under the title: "Incomplete Models". In these incomplete models we consider only part of the structural system. The reason for this could be computational simplicity as in large models or an attempt to quarantine specification errors. We specify only part of the system and as for the rest we are not so sure of its specification. Court (1973) suggests a method wherein we write the structural equations of interest together with any number of reduced form equations and estimate all equations jointly. He uses the 3SLS method. His method has subsequently been generalized by Hendry (1976) to include other estimation methods. Godfrey and Wickens (1976) discuss the subsystem FIML method in detail. All these methods can be implemented with existing computer programs for 3SLS and FIML.  I am not, however, aware of any important empirical applications of these subsystem methods.


## 5.  MULTICOLLINEARITY PROBLEMS IN LARGE MODELS AND UNDERIDENTIFICATION

One argument often made against using simultaneous equations methods in general and maximum-likelihood methods in particular with large models is that these latter methods are very sensitive to multicollinearity.  Klein and Nakamura (1962) argued that 2SLS is more sensitive to multicollinearity than OLS and that LIML is more sensitive than 2SLS.  They give examples from LIML estimation where the estimates 'exploded'.  They also conjecture that FIML would be as sensitive (if not more) as LIML to multicollinearity problems.  Subsequently, Klein (1969) estimated the Klein-Goldberger model by FIML and there were no serious multicollinearity problems.  In any case, in a large model there is no doubt that some particular sets of variables (the set of different price variables, the set of different interest rate variables etc.) will be highly intercorrelated.  So there will be a multi-collinearity problem.  But the solution is perhaps to reduce the number of variables to a smaller number.  Hester (1970), for instance, found that among eleven interest rate variables he considered, two principal components accounted for almost all the variation and he could identify these as "a long-term rate" and "a short-term rate".  The multiplicity of highly related variables in a large model might really mask an underidentification problem.  As an illustration consider a two equation model

$$y_1 = \beta_{12}y_2 + \gamma_1 p_1 + \delta_1 r_1 + u_1$$
$$y_2 = \beta_{21}y_2 + \gamma_2 p_2 + \delta_2 r_2 + u_2$$

where $p_1$, $p_2$ are two price variables and $r_1$, $r_2$ are two interest rate variables.  If $p_1$ and $p_2$ are highly correlated (so that there is indeed only one price variable $p$) and $r_1$ and $r_2$ are highly correlated (so that there is only one interest rate variable $r$) then the above system may be (almost) under-identified, though by a simple counting rule the equations are over-identified.  Klein and Nakamura (1962) give examples of the LIML estimates exploding and seem to suggest that this is a drawback of the LIML method relative to the 2SLS method.  In fact this might well be a good feature of the LIML method and a drawback of the 2SLS method, in the sense that the LIML method gives a warning signal that the equation may be underidentified whereas the 2SLS method does not give any such indication.[7]  We rarely apply any tests for identifiability in our models - much less so in large models.  In this case using the ML method (as opposed to the several stages of least squares) helps in uncovering the underidentification problem.  Koopmans et. al. (1950) mention two possible signals of underidentification:  (i) If maximum likelihood estimation is used, then the convergence of the iterative procedure used to derive the estimates will be slow and (ii) the values of the estimated asymptotic standard errors of estimators of parameters erroneously thought to be identified will be very large.  With the 2SLS, 3SLS, LIVE, IIV etc. methods there are no such warning signals.

One solution to both the multicollinearity problem and the so-called undersize sample problem (which is usually interpreted as a case where the number of predetermined variables m is greater than the number of

observations T) is to use modifications of the ridge regression methods
(see Hoerl and Kennard (1970, a, b)) to the Simultaneous equations models.
As stated earlier in section 3 the undersized sample problem does not
necessarily manifest itself when T < m. Even if T > m, if m is sufficiently
large, it has been found that the 2SLS and OLS estimates are identical.

Extensions of the ridge regression methods to simultaneous equations models
can be found in Lee and Trivedi (1978), Maasoumi (1980), Mehta and Swamy
(1978), Turker (1980), and Zellner and Vandaele (1965).  There are as yet
no empirical applications of these procedures in even medium-size models
and given the wide differences in opinion regarding the choice of the
appropriate "ridge constants" in the usual ridge regression methods, it is
not surprising that these methods have not yet found wide acceptance in
the estimation of simultaneous equation models.[8]  Lee and Trivedi discuss
an extension of the ridge regression method to instrumental variable
estimators and Turker discusses an extension to the 2SLS method.  Turker
(1980, Chapter V) also estimated Tintner's familiar econometric model of
the American meat market, and Klein's Model I of the U. S. economy (both
of which are pegs on which most econometric methods are hung on).  Her
conclusion is that "the 2SLS-Ridge estimator offers an appealing improvement over the 2SLS estimator for the two simple empirical models considered
here.  The mechanical implementation of the 2SLS-Ridge estimator is rather
simple, nearly as simple as the implementation of the 2SLS estimator.
However, more practical guidelines are needed in the choice of the ridge
constants than those used here".

A summary discussion of the currently known results on the choice of the
ridge constants is contained in Maasoumi (1980, pp. 166-168).  It is not
worth repeating here all those results.  Maasoumi suggests the following
class of d scalars:

$$d = \frac{x}{T} = O\left(\frac{1}{T}\right)$$

where x is a non-negative constant and T is the sample size.  In deriving
x, Maasoumi uses the following result: Let $\alpha$ be the vector of unknown
parameters and suppose we have the prior information that $\alpha'\alpha \leq r^2$.  Denote
by $\alpha^*$ any estimator of $\alpha$ that incorporates this prior information.  Then
$(\alpha^*-\alpha)$ will possess finite moments of all orders.  Maasoumi next argues
that given that the optimal (minimum risk) value $x^*$ of x is $\geq \frac{1}{r^2}$, a choice
of $x = \frac{2}{r^2}$ would guarantee some reduction in risk.

All in all the conclusion that emerges from this discussion is that the
ridge methods are worth trying in at least medium-size econometric models,
and there are a few guidelines available on the choice of the ridge
constants, provided we make use of any prior information we have on the
magnitudes of the coefficients we are trying to estimate.  Any justification
for the choice of the ridge constants has to come from such prior information or else the method would be purely arbitrary.

Both the ridge methods discussed in this section as well as the RRF methods
discussed in the previous section use some prior information.  As to the
relative merits of these two procedures, it clearly depends on which
pieces of information we have more confidence in, though nothing prevents
us from using both simultaneously.  It is sometimes argued that the ridge
estimators have finite risk but the RRF estimators (and also the ML
estimators) might have infinite risk because their moments may not exist.

But this conclusion rests on a particular (quadratic) loss function and there is nothing holy about it.  We can use truncated loss functions and compare the risks of the different estimators in cases where higher order moments do not exist.[9]  The issue of existence or non-existence of higher order moments has received far too much attention in the econometrics literature than it deserves and no estimators need be ruled out solely on this criterion.

## 6.  SERIAL CORRELATION PROBLEMS

Cooper (1972) ran several macro-econometric models against an autoregressive rabbit and announced that the rabbit had won.  Though his paper elicited a lot of criticism (see the discussion of his paper by Goldfeld and McCarthy and the paper by Howrey, Klein and McCarthy (1974), there is an important point in his paper and other papers that talk of Box-Jenkins methods vs. Econometric models.  This is that not much attention is paid in the macro models to autoregression and serial correlation.  Notable exceptions are Fair (1973) and Hendry (1974).  The models considered by Fair and Hendry are no doubt small but the results are very interesting.  Fair considers an 8 equation model with three types of estimates:  OLS, 2SLS and FIML, and in each case zero autocorrelation, first order auto-correlation and second order autocorrelation.  His main conclusion is that going to FIML gives considerably better results and also accounting for autocorrelation gives considerably better results.  Hendry (1974) considers the twin problems of simultaneity and autocorrelation.  Even assuming that we cannot tackle both problems simultaneously in the large models, Hendry argues, the usual practice is to dump the problem of autocorrelation and try to concentrate on the simultaneity problem.  However, it is not obvious which of these two is the more serious one.  It is well-known that mis-specification of the error structure in dynamic equations can have serious effect on both estimation and accuracy of forecasting (Malinvaud (1966), Chapter 14).  Hendry's main conclusion is that the autoregressive least squares (ALS) and autoregressive instrumental variable (AIV) methods suggested by Malinvaud (1966) and Sargan (1958, 1964) are very useful in uncovering serious specification errors and hence should be used in all macro-econometric models even if methods like autoregressive maximum likelihood (AML) that take into account both simultaneity and auto-correlation cannot be used.

## 7.  SOME POSITIVE ASPECTS OF ESTIMATION FOR LARGE MODELS

It is not necessarily true that by enlarging the size of the model we get into messy estimation problems.  To start with we should ask why we go to a large model at all.  (This is a question we should have asked at the beginning of the paper but it is never too late.)  The basic idea in enlarging the model is that by doing so we

(a)  Reduce specification errors.  For intance, we can define the relevant explanatory variables (interest rates, price indices, etc.) more finely, we can specify the relationships more accurately.
(b)  Reduce correlations between residuals.  Assuming that these inter-correlations are due to common omitted variables, we can reduce these intercorrelations by including more of the relevant explanatory variables in the different equations.

(c)   Reduce error variances again by virtue of the fact that we have
      accounted for a large number of explanatory variables.

If enough care is used in the formulation stage of the model so that the
above objectives are indeed accomplished then this will also lead to some
simplifications in the estimation.  Objective (a) makes 'full-information'
methods more attractive.  Objective (b) makes the assumption of diagonality
or block-diagonality of the covariance matrix more reasonable.  Objective
(c) gives some justification for the use of OLS by virtue of the proximity
theorem of Wold and Faxer (1957) extended to simultaneous equation by
Fisher (1961).  Objective (c) might also help us get some guidance regarding
the relative merits of the different estimation methods from the small-$\sigma$
literature.  However, I am not sure that many substantive results have
emerged from the small-$\sigma$ work.  The conclusions that have emerged are:

(i)     LIML is better (has smaller mean square error) than 2SLS if the
        degree of over-identification is $> 6$.  This suggests that for really
        large systems one should prefer LIML to 2SLS.  "Monte Carlo results
        for small systems where 2SLS is better, may mislead when applied to
        large systems."  See Kadane (1971, p. 728).
(ii)    OLS dominates 2SLS if the number of observations barely exceeds the
        number of exogenous variables in the system.  More precisely, OLS
        dominates 2SLS if $0 \leq T-m \leq 2(L-1)$ where L is the degree of over-
        identification.  See Kadane (1971, p. 728).
(iii)   Misclassification of endogenous variables as exogenous is typically
        less serious than omission of variables.  See Ramage (1971), Mariano
        and Ramage (1975).
(iv)    For disturbance variance estimation, the residual sum of squares,
        from ordinary least squares estimation divided by T-N+2, where T
        is the number of observations and N the number of structural param-
        eters estimated, is uniformly the best among k-class estimators.
        See Srivastava (1972).  This result is relevant for significant
        tests.

Before deciding what use can be made of these results we have to ask what
the small-$\sigma$ results really are.  As Anderson (1977, p. 514) notes, both
Nagar (1959) and Kadane (1971) "wrote equations stating that the expressions
are asymptotic expansions of the moments instead of interpreting these
expressions as the moments of expansions of distributions.  A careful
analysis of the derivations of the authors shows that the latter is the
case; more precisely, the various steps of the derivations hold for this
interpretation.  On the other hand, that some of the expressions are not
expansions of moments is seen from the fact that exact moments of LIML
are infinite."  Later Brown, Kadane and Ramage (1974, p. 668) wrote that
what is done in the small-$\sigma$ approach is to approximate the estimates by
random variables obtained from Taylor's series and find the moments of
these variables.  They write it is not claimed "that the moments of the
approximating variables are close to the moments of the approximated
variables.  The claim is rather that when $\sigma$ is small, the first two
asymptotic moments will give useful measures of location and dispersion
for the approximated distribution, ....  Small disturbance approximations
will be good or poor depending on whether $\sigma$ is small nor not."

Much depends on whether objective (c) mentioned above is accomplished or
not.  If it is, then we can use the limited results mentioned above from
the small-$\sigma$ work and conclude that it is better to use the LIML than 2SLS
in cases where both are feasible.

Anderson has recently proposed an alternative method of looking at the problem of asymptotic expansions valid for large econometric models. In his paper (1976) he points out that the maximum likelihood estimator of the slope coefficient in a linear functional relationship is mathematically equivalent to the LIML estimator of a coefficient of an endogenous variable in a simultaneous equations system when the variance-covariance matrix is known to within a proportionality constant, and that the OLS estimator in the former model is equivalent to the TSLS estimator in the latter under certain assumptions. He also derived asymptotic expansions of the distributions of the ML estimator and the OLS estimator and compared them by using numerical computations. Anderson also notes that the sample size minus one, N-1, in the linear functional relationship model corresponds to $K_2$, the number of excluded exogenous variables in a structural equation. This correspondence, Anderson says, enables us to consider a third type of asymptotic theory (instead of the large T asymptotic theory and small $\sigma$ asymptotic theory) which seems appropriate for large scale models. We might call this the "large $K_2$ asymptotics". From the distributions calculated by him[10] under this third form of asymptotic theory, it is found that as the number of exogenous variables increases (to about ten) the 2SLS estimator has a probability of almost one of being on a particular side of the true value of the structural parameter. Thus the 2SLS estimator is not consistent in this sense but the LIML estimator is. Both estimators are asymptotically normally distributed and the variance of the LIML is larger than that of the 2SLS estimators.

All these results suggest that in large and medium size models, it is far better to use the LIML method than the 2SLS method.

## 8. SOME NOTES ON SIGNIFICANCE TESTS IN LARGE MODELS

In addition to the problem of choice between estimators, there is the question of how good the usual (asymptotic) tests of significance are in large models. The Nagar expansions are not of much guidance for testing procedures. Kadane (1974) using his small-$\sigma$ approach has derived some alternative tests of significance applicable to k-class estimators.

In addition to the Nagar and Kadane expansions there are two other approaches that try to shed light on small sample distributions. One the pioneering work of Basmann (1963) and the subsequent work of Richardson, Sawa, Mariano, Anderson, Rohr and others. This work has been done for equations with two (or at most three) endogenous variables. The work does not seem to have yielded any insights regarding testing procedures that we can use even in small models, leave alone the large models.[11] The distribution approximation method of Sargan and Mikhail (1971), Anderson and Sawa (1973, Mariano (1973) and Sargan (1976) is useful for improving the usual (asymptotic) significance tests but Sargan (1976, p. 428) notes that we can presently deal with only models consisting of say 4 equations and 10 exogenous variables. In his paper Sargan talks of other methods of improving the significance tests we use in simultaneous equations models but these too are not applicable in large systems.

Hatanaka (1977) discusses hypothesis testing in large macro-economic models. Unfortunately, his discussion is concentrated on a comparison of the usual 'asymptotic test' and Dhrymes test for large models under the conditions Sargan (1975) considered viz. $m \to \infty$, $n \to \infty$ as $T \to \infty$. Hatanaka comes to the conclusion that it is better to use the usual 'asymptotic test' than the Dhrymes test if m and n increase faster than T (otherwise both tests are valid), and that the former test can be easily applied with the efficient instrumental variables method LIVE and FIVE discussed earlier. In view of the earlier criticism of the Dhrymes' test and its demonstrated weaknesses in the papers by Maddala (1974) and Morgan and Vandaele (1974) the conclusions of Hatanaka do not advance our understanding of the hypothesis testing problem in large econometric models. Maddala (1974) shows how the Dhrymes' test does not use any information on the variances of the endogenous variables and hence is expected to be less powerful than the conventional text-book tests of significance.[12]

In summary, we have not made much progress as yet on the issue of hypothesis testing in large macro-economic models. If by appropriate specification we can accomplish objective (c) in the previous section so that we can invoke the small $\sigma$ argument, then I feel that even small values of T would be sufficient to apply large sample asymptotic results. The argument being made here is that the smaller the noise in the model relative to the systematic part, the smaller the sample size necessary to invoke asymptotic results. This argument made in Maddala and Rao (1973) has, however, been questioned by Hendry (1975) who "demonstrates the immense value of asymptotic results in finite sample situations." Sargan (1975, p. 87) also argues that "for a wide variety of simultaneous equations models the results of asymptotic sampling theory are still a good approximation even in very large models".

The results on the distrubution functions tabulated by Anderson et. al. (1980), however, show that using the asymptotic normal distribution would not lead to meaningful inferences in the case of 2SLS if $K_2$, the number of excluded exogenous variables, is large. Anderson and Sawa (1979) study the rate at which the distribution of 2SLS approaches normality. They argue that the speed with which the distribution of 2SLS approaches normality is far slower than might be expected by most econometricians. They study the distribution of the 2SLS estimator for different vales of some key parameters like $K_2$, $\delta^2$ (the "non-centrality parameter") and $\alpha$ (which measures the difference between the structural parameter and a regression coefficient among disturbances). They conclude that typically $K_2 \geq 30$ and $\delta^2$ is around 1000 or 2000. ($\delta^2$ is usually of the order of $TK_2$.) For such values they say that the normal distribution is not a good approximation for the distribution of the 2SLS estimator. It is likely to seriously under-estimate the actual significance. In fact on the basis of the estimates of the key parameters in a number of econometric models compiled by Anderson, Morimune and Sawa (1978), Anderson and Sawa (1979) conclude that the normal approximation is not adequate for most econometric investigations.

The main problem with 2SLS when $K_2$ is large is that the estimates are very badly biased. By contrast the LIML estimate is not but this desirable property is bought only at the expense of increased dispersion. In the case of LIML, the normal approximation is likely to overestimate the actual significance.

On the whole the small sample properties of LIML and 2SLS are substantially different. From the point of view of tests of significance, using the standard asymptotic tests is totally invalid in the case of the large and medium sized models if the estimation is done by the 2SLS method.

As far as the LIML is concerned the bias component is very small. It is the variance that is likely to be underestimated by the normal approximation-thus leading to an overestimation of the actual significance.

Anderson and Sawa (1979, p. 180) argue that one needs really large sample sizes to invoke the asymptotic equivalence of 2SLS and LIML if $K_2$ is large. They say "For instance if $K_2$ is as large as 30, we may need more than 200 observations to guarantee our reliance on asymptotic theory. Such a large sample is never available in macro-economic analysis".

In summary, there is no point in using some alternative tests like the Dhrymes test or the Richardson-Rohr test in large or medium-size models. As for the conventional asymptotic tests, these are also invalid when the estimation is done by the 2SLS method. If the model is estimated by the LIML method, these tests are applicable with the previso that perhaps the significance is over-estimated. Exactly by how much is yet to be studied.


9. LARGE MODELS AND TENDER LOVING CARE

Howrey, Klein and McCarthy (1974), henceforth abbreviated as HKM, criticize Cooper's Study (1972) saying that he did not give the different models he considered the same tender loving care (TLC) that the authors of these models gave them in considering their models. What exactly is meant by "Tender Loving Care(TLC)"?

According to HKM, model building consists of four interrelated activities:

(i)   Specification
(ii)  Sample Selection
(iii) Estimation and
(iv)  Application including prediction, simulation, and cyclical analysis.
Regarding specification, HKM say (p. 379): "Economic Theory and Knowledge of the world around us can suggest a list of variables and some general parametric relationships. It cannot, however, set out in advance what the precise lag structure is nor all the departures from linearity. <u>That is a matter of sample experimentation and not purely a matter of specification.</u>" Regarding estimation, HKM say (p. 380): "Each model should be estimated by a method that will give the best performance for that system. Best performance might be determined by simulation testing within the sample used for fitting. This is all part of TLC." Again (p. 381): "Some parameter estimates may be manifestly unsatisfactory. The system should be re-specified and re-estimated until the investigator is sure that all coefficients are satisfactory. This is estimation with TLC." and "It is simply a fact of life that estimation or re-estimation of models in new or modified samples changes a few parameter estimates from being reasonable to being unreasonable. By re-specifying and re-estimating, these changes can be effectively dealt with. In some cases re-normalization is all that is needed."

In summary, by 'tender loving care' the authors mean changing the specifications and re-estimation till the investigator finds that all co-efficients are "reasonable" (by some criterion that also changes frequently). The immediate reaction of pure statisticians to the 'TLC method' would be that this will invalidate all statistical inference. It will make the tests of significance invalid. But to understand the seriousness of this criticism, we have to ask why we need to apply significance tests in the first place.

Practical statisticians have been long aware, at least since Berkson's
article (1938), that the question of exact "truth" of a sharp hypothesis
is hardly ever appropriate and that almost every model used, particularly
in social sciences, is known to be literally false because the null
hypothesis can be rejected given a large enough sample.  No model we
consider is the 'true model'.  Every model is an approximation.  The
question we have to ask is not whether the model we have is the true model
but whether what we have is a useful approximation.  This will depend on
what use we are going to put the model to.  In this context one has to do
some exploratory data analysis and ever since the papers by Tukey (1962)
and Anscombe (1963), some practical statisticians have viewed tests of
sharp null hypotheses not as ends in themselves but as a means to help
decide upon the Statistical model for the final analysis.  Box and
Jenkins (1970) call these tests, "diagnostic checks."  Anscombe calls
them "confirmatory measures".  However, these people are talking of
systematic procedures designed to turn up new clues when things to wrong
in the initial estimation.  Box and Jenkins' book (1970), Tukey's book
(1976) and Leamer's book (1978) all discuss systematic procedures for
uncovering new hypotheses and discarding old hypotheses and thus changing
the specification of the model for re-estimation.

The TLC procedure, however, does not fall in this category.  Whether it
can be systematized into the above mentioned procedures is yet to be seen.
As things stand now, the systematic specification searches are confined
to single equations and small models.[13]


10.  WHEN IS OLS A DEFENSIBLE TECHNIQUE FOR THE ESTIMATION OF LARGE MODELS?

Intersperced throghout our discussion have been some comments on the
applicability of the OLS method in large models.  We might bring these
together here.

Take first the example of a medium-sized model like that of Liu (1963)
where the often heard undersized sample problem does not arise explicitly
but the OLS and 2SLS estimates are very close.  Does this make OLS a
defensible technique?  The answer is clearly no.  The matter is that
there is something wrong with the 2SLS method.  It is not an appropriate
one to take account of simultaneity (as suggested by the results derived
by Anderson described in sections 7 and 8).  To quote from Anderson and
Sawa (1979, p.180): "Some econometricians argue as follows:  The OLS and
2SLS methods give almost identical values in large scale models because
of the small degrees of freedom in reduced form equations.  On the other
hand, since we usually employ quarterly data over say, twenty years, the
sample size would be large enough to guarantee the asymptotic equivalence
the 2SLS and LIML estimates.  Therefore, it is expected that the three
estimates are virtually identical, and hence the OLS method is preferred
simply because it is the least complicated in computation.  The fallacy of
this paragraph is easily seen on the basis of findings stated in the
above paragraph".

The basic conclusion we can draw is that where the model size is such
that estimation by the 2SLS method is feasible, the model should be
estimated by the LIML method.  The fact that the OLS and 2SLS estimates
are very close does not make the OLS method defensible.  What if the
model is so large that 2SLS and LIML are not feasible?  Even in these

cases the model can often be broken up into a block diagonal one as outlined by Fisher (1965a).  Each block can then be estimated by the LIML method.[14]

The only defense one can give for the OLS method in large models is, as stated in section 7 based on the proximity theorem of Wold and Faxer (1957) extended to simultaneous equations by Fisher (1961).  The validity of this argument depends on the error variances being very small by virtue of the fact that in a large model we can take account of almost all the explanatory variables that should belong in an equation.  This is an empirical issue and some guidance can be provided by the magnitude of the $R^2$'s from the estimated OLS equations.

## 11.  CONCLUSIONS

The present paper discusses the different definitions of size,[15] the estimation problems posed under these different definitions, the different efforts undertaken to rescue the 2SLS method (most of these are mechanical and not too useful), the principal components 2SLS method, the restricted reduced form (RRF) methods, the ridge regression methods etc.  The basic arguments that emerge from this discussion are:

(1)  In large and medium size models it is better to use LIML rather than 2SLS.  The issue of non-existence of moments for LIML is not important.  One can consider truncated loss functions.
(2)  The solution to the undersized sample problem is not to rescue the 2SLS method mechanically but to bring in more prior information.  There are essentially two methods that do this:  the ridge methods that depend on prior information about the ranges of the parameters being estimated, and the restricted reduced form (RRF) methods which use information in the remaining part of the structural system.  There is, in principle, no reason why these two methods cannot be combined.
(3)  Again the superiority claimed for the Ridge estimators that they possess finite sample moments whereas the RRF estimators may not have finite sample moments is an unimportant issue.  The more important issue is which prior information is more reliable.
(4)  The maximum likelihood procedure that is closest in spirit to the RRF methods is the ML estimator for a structural system with a diagonal covariance matrix for the residuals.  Given that the RRF methods essentially use the same sample information as that used by the 2SLS estimation of each equation separately, and given the demonstrated superiority of the LIML method over the 2SLS method in large models, it seems reasonable to expect that the ML estimator for a model with diagonal covariance matrix would perform much better than the RRF estimators in large scale models.  In large models one would have to assume diagonality or block diagonality of the covariance matrix of the errors.  It is better to make this assumption explicit and use the ML method.  Klein (1969) is a useful first step in the ML estimation of a medium sized econometric model.[16]
(5)  Since ridge methods and stein-type methods are all really justifiable as methods of using prior information and since this is best analyzed in a Bayesian framework which itself uses the likelihood function, the ML method should be a reasonable starting point for all these methods.  Thus even for ridge estimators, it is better to consider modifications of the LIML or than the 2SLS method in the case of

large models.  Even the specifications searches implied in "tender
loving care" can be done only with a clearly defined likelihood
function.


FOOTNOTES

*     Financial support from the NSF grant SOC-78-07304 is gratefully
      acknowledged.  The NSF, however, is not responsible for any opinions
      expressed.  I would like to thank Professor T. W. Anderson for
      bringing the papers by Junitomo to my attention.  Also, I would like
      to thank Robert Rasche, T. W. Anderson and Jan Kmenta for helpful
      comments on an earlier draft.  None of them is responsible for any
      possible errors in the paper.

1.    In my paper, Maddala (1971, p. 443) I erroneously said that a two-
      equation model with 40 exogenous variables and 38 observations can be
      estimated by FIML.  Of course, it is possible to estimate this model
      by the full information instrumental variable method FIVE discussed
      by Brundy and Jorgenson (1971) which is asymptotically as efficient
      as the FIML method.

2.    See Maddala   (1971), p. 442.

3.    The 3SLS estimator suggested by Court (1974) for the case of a singular
      covariance matrix is, however, not trivial like the Swamy-Holmes
      suggestion for the singular $(X'X)$.  Court does not use generalized
      inverses about which he says "their automatic use may obscure the
      question of which equations are being solved, and perhaps also obscure
      the most efficient method of solution."  (p. 549).  Picking these
      comments on generalized inverses from a preliminary draft of this paper,
      P.A.V.B. Swamy has vehemently defended the Swamy-Holmes estimator in
      his paper:  "A Comparison of Estimators for Undersized Samples"
      (forthcoming in the Journal of Econometrics).  Since all my statements
      are quoted in Swamy's paper I am leaving everything in this final
      version as it was in the preliminary draft.  In spite of all the tirade
      in Swamy's paper I am not convinced of the practical usefulness of the
      Swamy-Holmes estimator.  If only Swamy works out a simple example
      involving an undersized sample, the readers would understand the use-
      fulness of the Swamy-Holmes estimator.  The readers can also verify
      that the Court example is not as trivial as Swamy says it is, and
      does not rest on the rank conditions that Swamy claims in his paper.

4.    See the dissertation by Taylor (1962), and the discussion in Amemiya
      (1966).  The old Wharton model with 99 endogenous and 39 exogenous
      variables used 2SLS with 12 principal components.  See Evans and
      Klein (1968). Mitchell (1971) used the PCIV method as a leading con-
      tender to compare with the SOIV method for the Brookings model.  See
      also Klein (1969) who considered 2SLS with 4 and 8 principal components.

5.    In his discussion   of LIVE estimators, Hausman (1975, p. 734) says
      "Since the a-priori restrictions are being imposed, FIML or its one
      iteration special case might as well be used to provide fully efficient
      estimates rather than only consistent estimates which the Brundy-
      Jorgenson Procedure gives."  This however, is not correct.  The LIVE

procedure uses all the information in the matrix of structural coefficients but not the covariance matrix of the residuals. The LIVE procedure does not specify anything about the covariance matrix of the residuals and the closest specification is that this matrix is diagonal.

6.  For a discussion of the likelihood principle and the different justi-fication of the ML method see Edwards (1972).

7.  For a similar example and argument see Maddala (1976).

8.  Given the relationship that exists between the principal component method and the ridge method (see, among others, Lee and Trivedi (1978) for this correspondence), we might say that some use has been made of the ridge method in the estimation of simultaneous equation models. However, this use is not systematic and without any choice of the appropriate ridge constants.

9.  This point was emphasized by Carl Christ during the discussion at the conference. It was also supported by William Krasker who pointed out that any reasonable cutoff points will serve the purpose of constructing a usable loss function if the sample is large.

10. The comparison of LIML and 2SLS with known covariance matrix is in Kunitomo (1980). Anderson, Kunitomo and Sawa (1980) relax this assumption of a known covariance matrix and use numerical methods to compare LIML and 2SLS.

11. To my knowledge, there is only one test-statistic that has come out of this work - the Richardson and Rohr test statistic. For a criticism of this, see Maddala (1974).

12. To make things more elementary, consider a regression model with a dependent varaible y and an explanatory variable x. Given cov(x,y) and var(x) we can compute the regression coefficient but we cannot test its significance. For that we need also the variance of y. In 2SLS, denoting by Y the matrix of included endogenous variables and by X the matrix of exogenous variables, we can compute the 2SLS estimates if we are given only Y'X and X'X. But to use the usual tests of significance we also need the covariance matrix of the endogenous variables Y'Y. In Dhrymes' test this is not needed at all! Of course the test can be applied only if the equation is overidentified and what it says is that in this case Y'X contains some information on the residual variance and what Hatanaka shows is that as the degree of overidentification tends to infinity the test is consistent.

13. In the oral discussion Robert Rasche remarked that the tender loving care accorded to a model can be classified as "pre-natal" and "post-natal". There is not much to complain about the former. It is excessive use of the latter that is a problem.

14. At the conference Arnold Zellner commented that this emphasis on ML estimates is too extreme. He referred to Charles Stein's analytical results showing that there exist estimators which uniformly dominate ML estimators in finite samples for regression and other problems. Furthermore ML estimators pose problems in that they often do not possess finite moments and in these cases their mean square error is

infinite. These arguments, however, do not invalidate the demonstrated superiority of LIML over the 2SLS method in large models. The mean square error, and quadratic loss functions are not always the best criteria to use. As remarked earlier, the existence or non-existence of finite sample moments should not be the sole criterion to judge the different estimators.

15. In his discussion Arnold Zellner pointed out that "size" is not simply a question of variables and equations but also of complexity. He referred to contributions by H. Jeffries and H. Gottinger in the literature.

16. Ray Fair pointed out that he estimated his models by the ML method without imposing the assumption of diagonality on the covariance matrix. However, his model is not as large as some other models are. See Table 1.

# REFERENCES

[1]   Amemiya, T. (1966), "on the use of principal components of independent variables in two-stage least squares estimation", International Economic Review, 7, 283-303.

[2]   Anderson, T. W. and T. Sawa (1973), "Distributions of estimates of coefficients of a single equation in a simultaneous system and their asymptotic expansions", Econometrica, 41, 683-714.

[3]   Anderson, T. W. (1977), "Asymptotic expansions of the distributions of estimates in simultaneous equations for alternative parameter sequences", Econometrica, 45, 506-518.

[4]   Anderson, T. W. (1976), "Estimation of linear functional relationships: Approximate distributions and connections with simultaneous equations in econometrics", Journal of the Royal Statistical Society, Series B, Vol. 38, No. 1, pp. 1-36.

[5]   Anderson, T. W., N. Kunitomo and T. Sawa (1980), "Evaluation of the distribution function of the limited information maximum likelihood estimator", Technical report No. 319, Aug. 1980, IMSSS, Stanford Univ.

[6]   Anderson, T. W. and T. Sawa (1979), "Evaluation of the distribution function of the two stage least squares estimate", Econometrica, Vol. 47, No. 1, pp. 163-182.

[7]   Anderson, T. W., K. Morimune and T. Sawa (1978), "The numerical values of some key parameters in econometric models", Technical report No. 270, IMSSS, Stanford University, Sept. 1978.

[8]   Anscombe, F. J. (1963), "Tests of goodness of fit", Journal of the Royal Statistical Society, B. Series, 25, 81-94.

[9]   Basmann,R. L. (1963), "Remarks concerning the application of exact finite sample distribution functions of GCL estimators in econometric statistical inference", J.A.S.A. 58, 943-976.

[10] Berkson, J. (1938), "Some diffilcuties of interpretation encountered in the application of the chi-squared test", J.A.S.A. 33, 526-42.

[11] Box, G.E.P. and G. M. Jenkins (1970, Time series analysis:  forecasting and control, San Francisco, Holden-Day.

[12] Brown, B. W. (1978), "Sample size requirements in full information maximum likelihood estimation", Research memorandum #222, Feb. 1978, Econometric Research Program, Princeton University.

[13] Brown, G. F., Jr., J. B. Kadane, and J. G. Ramage (1974) "The asymptotic bias and mean-squared error of double k-class estimators when the disturbances are small", International Economic Review, 15, 667-679.

[14] Brundy, J.M. and D. W. Jorgenson (1971) "Efficient estimation of simultaneous equations by instrumental variables", The Review of Economics and Statistics, 53, 207-224.

[15] Brundy, J. M. and D. W. Jorgenson (1974), "The relative efficiency of instrumental variables estimators of systems of simultaneous equations", Annals of Economic and Social Measurement, 3, 679-700.

[16] Christ, C. F. (1975), "Judging the performance of econometric models of the U.S. economy", International Economic Review, 16, 54-74.

[17] Cooper, R. L. (1972), "The predictive performance of quarterly econometric models of the United States" in B. G. Hickman (ed.) Econometric models of cyclical behaviour Vol. II, Studies in Income and Wealth No. 36. New York, Columbia University Press.

[18] Court, R. H. (1973), "Efficient estimation of the reduced form from incomplete econometric models", The Review of Economic Studies, 40, 411-417.

[19] Court, R. H. (1974), "Three stage least squares and some extensions where the structural disturbance covariance matrix maybe singular," Econometrica, 42, 547-558.

[20] Dhrymes, P. J. (1971), "A simplified structural estimator for large-scale econometric models," The Australian Journal of Statistics, 13, 168-175.

[21] Dhrymes, P. J. and V. Pandit (1972), "Asymptotic properties of an iterate of the two-stage least squares estimator," J.A.S.A. 67, 444-447.

[22] Dutta, M. and E. Lyttkens (1974), "Iterative instrumental variables method and estimation of a large simultaneous system," Journal of the American Statistical Association, Vol. 69, No. 348,  977-986.

[23] Edwards, A.W.F. (1972), Likelihood, (Cambridge University Press).

[24] Evans, M. K. and L. R. Klein (1968),  The wharton econometric forecasting model, Philadelphia, University of Pennsylvania.

[25] Fair, R. C. (1973), "A comparison of alternative estimators of macro-economic models," International Economic Review, 14, 261-277.

[26] Fisher, F. M. (1961), "The cost of approximate specification in simultaneous equation estimation," Econometrica, 29, 139-170.

[27] Fisher, F. M. (1965a), "Dynamic structure and estimation in economy-wide econometric models," Chapter 15 in J.S. Duesenberry et.al. (eds.) The Brookings Econometric Model of the United States, (Chicago, Rand McNally).

[28] Fisher, F. M. (1965b), "The choice of instrumental variables in the estimation of economy-wide econoemtric models," International economic review, 6, 245-274.

[29] Fisher, W. D. and W. J. Wadycki (1971), "Estimating a structural equation in a large system," Econometrica, 39, 461-465.

[30] Godfrey, L. G. and M. R. Wickens (1976), "The estimation of incomplete econometric models," Working paper no. 36, December 1976, Australian National University.

[31] Griliches, Z. (1968), "The brooking model volume: a review article," The Review of Economics and Statistics, 50, 215-234.

[32] Hatanaka, M. (1977), "Hypothesis testing in the large macro-economic models," International Economic Review, 18, 607-627.

[33] Hausman, J. A. (1974), "Full information instrumental variables estimation of simultaneous equations systems," Annals of Economic and Social Measurement, 3, 641-652.

[34] Hausman, J. A. (1975), "An instrumental variable approach to full information estimators for linear and certain non-linear econometric models," 43, 727-738.

[35] Hendry, D. F. (1974), "Stochastic specification in an aggregate demand model of the united kingdom," Econometrica, 42, 559-578.

[36] Hendry, D. F. (1975), "The limiting distribution of inconsistent instrumental variables estimators in a class of stationary stochastic systems," Cowles Foundation, Discussion paper, September 1975.

[37] Hendry, D. F. (1976), "The structure of simultaneous equations estimators," Journal of Econometrics, 4, 51-88.

[38] Hester, D. D. (1970), "On the dimensionality of market interest rates and price movements," (Abstract) Econometrica, 38, 119.

[39] Hoerl, A. E. and R. W. Kennard (1970a), "Ridge regression: biased estimation of non-orthogonal problems," Technometrics, 12, 55-67.

[40] Hoerl, A. E. and R. W. Kennard (1970b), "Ridge regression: applications to non-orthogonal problems," Technometrics, 12, 69-82.

[41] Howrey, E. P., L. R. Klein and M. D. McCarthy (1974), "Notes on testing the predictive performance of econometric models," International economic Review, 15, 366-383.

[42] Klein, L. R. (1968), An essay on the theory of economic prediction, Yrjo Jahnsson Lectures, Helsinki, Enlarged U.S. edition (Chicago, Markham, 1971).

[43] Klein, L. R. (1969), "Estimation of interdependent systems in macro-economics," 37, 171-192.

[44] Klein, L. R. (1971), "Forecasting and policy evaluation using large econometric models: the state of the art," in M.D. Intrilligator (ed.) Frontiers of Quantitative Economics (Amsterdam, North Holland Publishing).

[45] Klein, L. R. and M. Nakamura (1962), "Singularity in the equation systems of econometrics: some aspects of the problems in multi-collinearity," International Economic Review, 3, 274-299.

[46] Kadane, J. B. (1971), "Comparison of k-class estimators when the disturbances are small," Econometrica, 39, 723-737.

[47] Kadane, J. B. (1974), "Testing a subset of the over-identifying restrictions," Econometrica, 42, 853-867.

[48] Kloek, T. and L. Mennes (1960), "Simultaneous equations estimation based on principal components of predetermined variables," Econometrica, 28, 45-61.

[49] Koopman, T. C., H. Rubin and R. B. Leipnik (1950), "Measuring the equation systems of dynamic economics," in T. C. Koopmans (ed.) Statistical Inference in Dynamic Economic Models (New York, Wiley).

[50] Kunitomo, N. (1980), "Asymptotic expansions of the distributions of estimators in a linear functional relationship and simultaneous equations," Journal of the American Statistical Association, Vol. 75, No. 371, 693-700.

[51] Leamer, E. E. (1978), Specification searches: ad hoc inference with non-experimental data, (New York, Wiley).

[52] Lee, B. M. S. and P. K. Trivedi (1978), "Instrumental variable estimation of structural equations in undersized samples," Working Paper No. 65 (Revised July 1978), Australian National University.

[53] Liu, T. C. (1963), "An exploratory quarterly econometric model of effective demand in the post-war U.S. economy," Econometrica, 31, 301-348.

[54] Lyttkens, E. (1974), "The iterative instrumental variables method and the full information maximum likelihood method for estimating interdependent systems," Journal of Multivariate Analysis, 4, 283-307.

[55] Maddala, G. S. (1971), "Simultaneous estimation methods for large and medium size econometric models," The Review of Economic Studies, 38, 435-445.

[56] Maddala, G. S. (1974), "Some small sample evidence on tests of significance in simultaneous equations models," Econometrica, 42, 841-851.

[57] Maddala, G. S. (1976), "Weak priors and sharp posteriors in simultaneous equations models," Econometrica, 44, 345-351.

[58] Maddala, G. S., and A. S. Rao (1973), "Tests for serial correlation in regression models with lagged dependent variables and serially correlated errors," Econometrica, 41, 761-774.

[59] Malivand, E. (1966), Statistical methods of econometrics (Chicago, Rand McNally).

[60] Mariano, R. S. (1973), "Approximation to the distribution functions of the OLS and 2SLS estimators in the case of two included endogenous variables," Econometrica, 41, 67-77.

[61] Mariano, R. S. and J. G. Ramage (1975), "Finite sample effects of misspecification on structural coefficient estimates," Discussion paper no. 320, University of Pennsylvania.

[62] Maasoumi, E. (1978), "A modified stein-like estimator for the reduced form coefficients of simultaneous equations," Econometrica, 46, 695-703.

[63] Maasoumi, E. (1980), "A ridge-like method for simultaneous estimation of simultaneous equations," Journal of Econometrics, 12, 161-176.

[64] Mehta, J. S. and P.A.V.B. Swamy (1978), "The existence of moments of some simple bayes estimators of coefficients in a simultaneous equation model," Journal of Econometrics, 7, 1-13.

[65] Mitchell, B. M. (1971), "Estimation of large econometric models by principal components and instrumental variable methods," The Review of Economics and Statistics, 53, 140-146.

[66] Mitchell, B. M. and F. M. Fisher (1970), "The choice of instrumental variables in the estimation of economy-wide econometric models:  some further thoughts," International Economic Review, 11, 226-234.

[67] Morgan, A. and W. Vandaele (1974), "On testing hypotheses in simultaneous equation models," Journal of Econometrics, 2, 55-65.

[68] Nagar, A. L. (1959), Statistical estimation of simultaneous economic relationships (paperbound processed dissertation at the Netherlands School of Economics).

[69] Ramage, J. G. (1971), "A Perturbation study of the k-class estimators in the presence of specification error," Unpublished Ph.D. thesis, Yale University.

[70] Rayner, A. C. (1972), "A comment on estimating a structural equation in a large system," Econometrica, 40, 907.

[71] Rothernberg, T. J. and C. T. Leenders (1964), "Efficient estimation of simultaneous equation systems," Econometrica, 32, 57-76.

[72] Sargan, J. D. (1958), "The estimation of economic relationships using instrumental variables," Econometrica, 26, 393-415.

[73] Sargan, J. D. (1964), "Wages and prices in the united kingdom: a study in econometric methodology," in Hart, P. et.al. (Eds.), Econometric Analysis for National Planning, Colston papers 16, (Butterworths Scientific Publications, London).

[74] Sargan, J. D. (1975), "Asymptotic theory and large models," International Economic Review, 16, 75-91.

[75] Sargan, J. D. (1976), "Econometric estimators and the edgeworth approximation," Econometrica, 44, 421-448.

[76] Sargan, J. D. and W. M. Mikhail (1971), "A general approximation to the distribution of instrumental variable estimates," Econometrica, 39, 131-169.

[77] Srivastava, V. K. (1972), "Disturbance-variance estimation in simultaneous equations when disturbances are small," J.A.S.A., 67, 164-168.

[78] Swamy, P.A.V.B. and J. M. Holmes (1971), "The use of undersized samples in the estimation of simultaneous equation systems," Econometrica, 39, 455-458.

[79] Taylor, L. D. (1962), "The principal-component-instrumental-variable approach to the estimation of systems of simultaneous equations," Unpublished Ph.D. dissertation, Harvard University.

[80] Theil, H. (1971), Principles of econometrics, (New York, Wiley).

[81] Theil, H. (1973), "A simple modification of the two-stage least squares procedure for undersized samples," in A.S. Goldberger and O. D. Duncan (Eds.) Structural equation models in the social sciences, (New York, Seminar Press).

[82] Theil, H. and K. Laitinen (1977), "A maximum entropy approach to the problem of under-sized samples in simultaneous-equation estimation," Report #7713, Feb. 1977, Center for Mathematical Studies in Business and Economics, University of Chicago.

[83] Tukey, J. W. (1962), "The future of data analysis," Annals of Mathematical Statistics, 33, 1-67.

[84] Turker, Z. (1977), "A modification of two-stage least squares: 2SLS ridge estimator," Dissertation (under progress), University of Rochester.

[85] Wold, H. (1965), "A fix point method with econometric background I-II," Arkiv for Matematik, 6, 209-240.

[86] Wold, H. and R. Faxer (1957), "On the specification error in regression analysis," Annals of Mathematical Statistics, 28, 265-267.

[87] Zellner, A. and W. Vandaele (1975), "Bayes-stein estimators for k-means, regression and simultaneous equation models," in S. E. Fienberg and A. Zellner (Eds.), Studies in bayesian econometrics and statistics in honor of L. J. Savage (Amsterdam, North Holland Publishing Co.).

LARGE-SCALE MACRO-ECONOMETRIC MODELS
J. Kmenta, J.B. Ramsey (editors)
© North-Holland Publishing Company, 1981

THE MAJOR STREAMS OF ECONOMY-WIDE MODELING:

IS RAPPROCHEMENT POSSIBLE? [1]

Alan A. Powell [2]

IMPACT Project Centre
University of Melbourne
Parkville, Victoria, 3052.   AUSTRALIA.

Three classes of economy-wide models are distinguished: the KK (or Wharton) class, the PB
(continuous-time disequilibrium) class, and the
WJ (applied general equilibrium) class.  Experience gained in the Australian Government's
inter-agency IMPACT Project leads to the following conjectures:

(i)     The integration of small macro models
        in the PB class with large applied
        general equilibrium models in the WJ
        class is feasible.

(ii)    The integration of models in the KK
        class with models in the WJ class does
        not seem feasible.

(iii)   The three major approaches within the
        WJ class  - -  development planning,
        neoclassical general equilibrium models
        solved in the levels, and Johansen
        models  - -  seem likely to be dominated
        by the Johansen models for reasons of
        flexibility, computability and trans-
        parency.

1.  INTRODUCTION

In a recent survey of economy-wide model building, Challen and
Hagger [7] introduced the following nomenclature to describe
the three major classes of ongoing work in Australia :

    (i)      Keynes-Klein (KK) models ;
    (ii)     Phillips-Bergstrom (PB) models ;
    (iii)    Walras-Johansen (WJ) models .

Whilst acknowledging some room for disagreement on the choice
of labels, Challen and Hagger motivate their taxonomy ([7], p. 4)
as follows:

> "The second name in each label is the name of the
> econometrician who produced the model which we regard
> as the prototype  - -  the father of the family, so to
> speak.   The first name belongs to the theoretical
> economist who provided the vision  - -  whose special
> way of looking at the working of the macroeconomy was
> taken over by the second-named and used as the frame-
> work for his prototype model."

For the moment I will assume that each of these terms is
sufficiently suggestive to allow postponement of their definitions.  What I wish to attempt in this paper is to provide a
perspective on the scope for reconciling the three approaches.
In the case of the PB and WJ models, I will draw heavily on my
experience over the last half decade with the Australian Government's inter-agency IMPACT Project. [3]   The project does
not provide direct experience of the KK models;  I will however
attempt to integrate my remarks with the insights on KK models
provided by the other participants in the NSF-NBER Conference
reported in this volume and, in the Australian context, by
Challen and Hagger.

The plan of the paper is as follows.   In Section 2, I define
the three classes of models discussed in the paper.   My discussion is confined to 'econometric' as distinct from 'time
series' models.   Section 3 contains my perspective on why we
bother to model at all, and highlights some of the risks of
overenthusiastic salesmanship and wishful thinking.   In section 4 I try to show how various design features and practices
in model building reflect the purposes for which the models
were built, and the constraints under which the modelers perceive themselves to be working.   In the fifth section I
describe briefly some developments in the IMPACT Project which

seem to indicate that a measure of reconciliation between the
different approaches is possible. The sixth and final section
contains my concluding remarks.

## 2. DEFINITIONS

In the case of the first two categories, the definitions adopted here are in the spirit of Challen and Hagger [7]. The
boundary lines between the three groups are somewhat blurred
and some (but not many) models would fall partly into more
than one of them.

### 2.1 *KK Models*

These models may be identified by their emphasis on behavioral
relations determining the big components of the national
accounts : consumption, investment, government spending, imports and exports. The flavor of the models is decidedly
demand dominated and disequilibrium (especially business cycle)
oriented. KK models are invariably formulated in discrete
time - - lag mechanisms, often of the geometric and/or polynomial families are directly posited and freely used in an
attempt to come to grips with expectations and other frictions
in the system. Finally, relative prices of all sorts play a
minor role by comparison with 'activity variables.' These
five characteristics - - emphasis

|       |     |                                                       |
|-------|-----|-------------------------------------------------------|
| on    | (a) | large aggregates which are largely                    |
|       | (b) | demand determined,                                    |
| on    | (c) | disequilibrium (especially business cycle) dynamics formulated in |
|       | (d) | discrete time,                                        |
| and on| (e) | activity variables to the exclusion of relative prices [4] - - |

are the major distinguishing marks of the KK models.

The prototype KK model recognised by Challen and Hagger is
Klein's 1950 model [31]. From this 16 equation beginning
developed the 200 - 400 equation models in the KK class which
today exist for many OECD countries. In this development large
aggregates were successively broken down into smaller and
smaller components, e.g., consumption was split first into
durables and non-durables, then the former into automobile

purchases and other durables, and so on.    As characteristic
(a) became attenuated under finer and finer disaggregation,
likewise (b) became less prominent as supply side constraints
were added to the models.   In some (but by no means all) of
the KK models equilibrium began to assume a role as consistency constraints were imposed on steady state properties, thus
tending to soften characteristic (c).    Ando puts the point
nicely in his discussion of the design of the MPS (MIT - Pennsylvania - Social Science Research Council) model :

> "the model should exhibit the neoclassical features
> at the steady state, but be Keynesian in its adjust-
> ment process." [4]

Given the considerable falling away from (a), (b) and (c) as
marks of the latter day KK models, will these characteristics
nevertheless still serve to identify them?   I believe the
answer is 'yes.'   Surviving design features of the KK models
(like vestigial gills) point to their origins.  No student of
the MPS model is likely to be in doubt which came first  - -
its short term dynamics or its steady state properties.   Nor
would a student of any of the many models in the Wharton tradition be likely to believe that these models had been built on
a 'bottoms up' rather than a 'tops down' approach to aggregation.

### 2.2  *PB Models*

Challen and Hagger have used formulation in continuous time as
a major distinguishing characteristic of the newer macro models
developed by Bergstrom and Wymer [5], Jonson [28] and his co-
workers [29].   By comparison with the KK class, the steady
state properties of a PB model are much more visible, and critical, elements of its structure.  Behavioral relations are
mainly of two types : functions describing the target (or long
run) values of the endogenous variables, and adjustment rules
describing the time paths by which the endogenous variables
approach these targets.   The adjustment rules are specified
as differential (rather than difference) equations;  conceptually an endogenous variable is capable of *instantaneous*
response to an exogenous stimulus, even in the sense that its

target value can be reached instantly if the value of the estimated adjustment coefficient is high enough. This provision for rapid approach to equilibrium reflects the strong interests of the model builders in monetary and financial markets [5] - - it is not (they argue) unreasonable to suppose that in some international financial markets arbitrageurs are able to close price gaps by telephonic/telegraphic transactions within a matter of hours. Whilst the development of the PB models in the seventies coincided with the resurgence of monetarism, it is not clear that the marriage of monetarism and continuous time modeling was historically inexorable.

The PB modelers have introduced new techniques of econometric inference designed to cope with the continuous time nature of their systems, [6] and have exploited the flexibility of temporal aggregation allowed by such a formulation. Notwithstanding the non-linearity (in the parameters) of the PB models, Wymer's massive contribution to econometric software [50] has made it possible to estimate substantial sub-sectors, or even entire models, by FIML. [7] This is, of course, only possible because the models are (by today's standards) small - - typically less than 30 equations.

What, then, are the principal marks of the PB models? Apart from a monetarist flavor (which may not in the longer run turn out to be an indispensable characteristic), they are

      (A)   formulation in continuous time

with

      (B)   a target or equilibrium value of each
           endogenous variable determined according
           to a function respecting notions of neo-
           classical equilibrium

and

      (C)   differential equations (usually of first
           order, though occasionally of second)
           specifying adjustment paths.

## 2.3  *WJ Models*

Challen and Hagger's taxonomy was designed to cope with the
contemporary thrust of Australian applied work.   This led to
a less than exhaustive classification of applied general equilibrium models.   The more neoclassical of these models are
characterized by non-linear production and consumption relations which recognise various kinds of substitutability
pertaining among factors in production, and among commodities
in consumption.   In the words of Dervis [11],

> [These models]"postulate neoclassical production
> functions and price-responsive demand functions,
> linked around an input-output matrix in a
> Walrasian general equilibrium model that endog-
> enously determines quantities and prices."

The solutions for the endogenously determined quantities and
prices are continuous and differentiable functions of the
exogenous variables.   As used in this paper, the term
*Johansen model* refers to the subset of neoclassical WJ models
which, in the words of Taylor, are solved

> " ... by logarithmically differentiating the
> equations characterising a Walrasian competi-
> tive equilibrium with respect to time in order
> to get a simultaneous set of equations which
> are linear in all growth rates.   A set of
> growth rates is specified exogenously and a
> matrix inversion then suffices to calculate
> the other growth rates in the system." [8]

Examples of neoclassical members of the WJ class are Adelman
and Robinson's model of Korea [1],  and the Australian policy
model ORANI. [9]    Of these, the latter is a Johansen model,
while the former is solved in the levels.   Later in this paper
it will be claimed that suitable extensions of the Johansen
solution method are likely to dominate, and in time replace,
other approaches to the solution of these models.

The less neoclassical models of the WJ class have often been
referred to as 'mathematical programming' and/or 'development

planning' models. Like other members of the WJ class, these models recognise explicit inter-industry relations, and factor constraints. Unlike the neoclassical members of the class, many of the production and consumption relations, and/or constraint sets, are linear. Kuhn-Tucker conditions need to be invoked in specifying the Walrasian general equilibrium solution of such models. The solution itself involves corners, and is not everywhere a differentiable function of the exogenous variables. Such models have usually been solved either as full non-linear programming problems, or by successive approximations based on linear programs. Non-neoclassical WJ models have been built for many countries, including India [44], Israel [6], Mexico [38], Australia [22], [15], [19], and the Ivory Coast [25].

It will be argued later in this paper that the non-neoclassical members of the WJ class do not possess any worthwhile advantages over the neoclassical members, and that the latter will in time replace them. In the remainder of this section, therefore, attention is concentrated on the neoclassical members, which are compared briefly to the KK and PB classes.

Neoclassical WJ models and PB models are, on one scale, much closer to each other than is either to the KK class. Both WJ and PB models have been described at times as 'neoclassical growth models.' In terms of numbers of equations, latter day KK models and WJ models are 'big' relative to the current set of PB models. The KK and WJ models also share an emphasis on the real economy in contradistinction to the monetary emphasis of the existing PB models. Also like KK models, WJ models are usually formulated in discrete time. Unlike either the KK or the PB models, the methodology of the WJ class is strictly comparative static (although the comparative static element, of course, does have an important subsidiary role in all PB, and in some KK, models). The emphasis on relative prices of commodities and of factors is nowhere stronger than among neoclassical members of the WJ class.

## 3.  METHODOLOGY AND MORALS

Before canvassing the scope for reconciliation between the
different approaches to economy-wide modeling, a prior issue
needs at least brief attention.    I believe considerable dis-
enchantment is evident in the U.S., Australia, and elsewhere,
with the performance over the 1970's of models (and modelers). [10]    It is perhaps timely to reflect on why we bother to
build models at all.

First, I take it as self evident that a model is primarily a
device to organize one's thinking.    Second, the potential and
actual performance of any model is only defined relative to the
purpose for which it is constructed.    I shall take up this
theme in the context of forecasting versus policy analysis in
the next section.    Given a clearly defined purpose for which
a model might be constructed, there exist at least the following advantages in proceeding actually to construct it :

(a)  A formal model forces its builder to identify in a
     systematic, precise and *explicit* way the range of
     concepts necessary to address the issue in question.

(b)  Equally important, a formal model identifies the
     factual evidence (i.e., data base) needed to
     support analysis, and often leads to recognition
     of important gaps and inconsistencies in the
     available information.

(c)  Models *improve* communication.    Although some
     effort is usually required to understand the
     language in which any particular model is con-
     structed, of necessity any adequately documented
     model gives a clear statement of every assumption.

(d)  Models form the basis for formally articulated (as
     distinct from intuitive) knowledge, which can be
     taught and learnt.

(e)  Models provide a framework for learning from
     experience.

(f)  Many issues of interest are not amenable to
     analysis in terms of a small number of relation-
     ships.  Formal modeling may be the only
     practical way of handling the information load.

(g)  Finally, the enormous intellectual effort which
     has gone into the theory of measurement over the
     last three decades would be largely lost outside
     the framework of formal models.

It is not usually on these issues that disagreement surfaces.
Whilst attractive, the features listed above would not per-
suade governments or foundations to support model building in
a big way - - a fact of which every model builder is aware.
In attempting to 'sell' models to the clients we have sometimes been trapped by our own wishful thinking.  Economics is
a well developed *non-experimental* science, i.e., a science
which, in spite of its strong analytical traditions, is almost
never able to settle differences of opinion about empirical
magnitudes by recourse to experimentation.  Not only are our
data generated by uncontrolled 'experiments' : they are
generated in limited amounts.  Typically nature presents to
the applied economist an indifferently designed experiment
which she doesn't even have the courtesy to replicate. [11]

It follows that we are confronted by an irreducible core of
ignorance.  If

(1)  $$\hat{E}(y|x) = \hat{\beta}^T x$$

is an optimal conditional forecast (according to some agreed
criterion) of $y$ given $x$ , and $y$ follows the model

(2)  $$y = \beta^T x + \varepsilon , \qquad \text{Var} (\varepsilon) = \sigma^2 ,$$

with $\varepsilon$ classically well behaved, then attempting to reduce
the forecast error by modeling $\varepsilon$ (or even $(\hat{\beta} - \beta)$) is
silly.  Yet a good deal of the 'fine tuning' of quarterly
models (so that they track superlatively *within* sample) is
undoubtedly an attempt to do just this.  This amounts to a
never ending quest for a $\sigma^2$ that is smaller than any reasonable
reading of the evidence would suggest.  If the $\sigma^2$ suggested

by the evidence is 'too large' for the client with the cheque
book, then it is a matter of morals, not of methodology to tell
him so.   Similarly, if a neo-Keynesian theorist and a monetarist hold severely conflicting theories which are, nevertheless,
observationally equivalent with respect to the available historical evidence, no pretence should be made in attempting to
sell either product that its superiority has been *scientifically* (i.e., objectively) demonstrated.   Although it may be
difficult to discuss with a clientele steeped in a naive
belief in the objectivity of scientific method, it is nevertheless encumbent upon us to try to explain to our customers
the role of *a priori* knowledge in our models. [12]

Lipsey also sees self-inflicted wounds in the contemporary
profession.   He puts it this way [35] :

> "Some of the difficulties are of our own making.
> It is common practice for an investigator to try
> many *ad hoc* specifications and to fit them to
> alternative data sets, then to choose to publish
> the specification and data that produce the
> highest *t* statistics, and then in his article
> to use the *t* statistics as if they were valid
> tests of the particular *ad hoc* theory.   This is
> very common practice but if you describe it, as I
> have done to biologists and medical researchers,
> they will usually refuse to believe that a prof-
> ession so highly regarded as economics could
> expect to proceed in so unscientific a fashion.
> Because of this common procedure, we should not be
> too surprised if the literature contains at least
> one *ad hoc* version of many competing high level
> theories, each one of which makes a fair fit to
> existing data.   Of course, the proof of the
> pudding comes when the models are extrapolated to
> new data and here they fail in droves."

We do not yet have widely accepted procedures for calculating
effective loss of degrees of freedom during specification
searches based on a given stock of data. [13]   In cases that

we all know of, effective degrees of freedom must have become
zero well before the selection of the 'preferred' *ad hoc* version of the high level theory.    In these instances the specification search is probably best regarded as nothing more than
an extremely inefficient way of fitting a high order polynomial
in time.

## 4.   THE RELATIONSHIP BETWEEN PURPOSE AND DESIGN OF MODELS

A 'good' model is one which achieves the purpose for which it
was designed.    A tailor's dummy is a good model of the human
body from the viewpoint of displaying a suit;   as a vehicle to
teach anatomy to medical students it leaves something to be
desired.    Economic models are built for a wide variety of
reasons, including pedagogy and pure intellectual curiosity.
But the two purposes most often attracting support from the
government, from business, and from foundations are forecasting
and policy analysis.

### 4.1  *WJ Models and Forecasting*

IMPACT's ORANI model [14] belongs to the WJ class.    It has
never been used to make 'forecasts' in the sense of providing
unconditional projections or best guesses about the likely
levels of its endogenous variables at some sequence of future
dates.    The WJ models lack the temporal disaggregation of the
KK and PB models, so that statements surrounding simulation
results naturally seem somewhat vague from the macroeconomic
perspective.    In typical 'short run' ORANI solutions  - -
solutions in which no net addition to capacity actually in use
is allowed  - -  we have offered the opinion that the simulated
outcome could be expected to occur 'one or two years' after the
initial sustained changes in the chosen exogenous variables.
(To provide some factual evidence for this surmise is a major
methodological problem, which is dealt with below in the discussion of the interface between a PB model and ORANI).    We
have not to date used the ORANI model to project levels of the
endogenous variables, but only those components of changes in
levels due to the postulated changes in the selected exogenous
variables.

The discussion becomes clearer if we think of the final form of
a Johansen model in simulation mode :

(3)                                  $y = Az$ ,

where  $y$  is a vector of growth rates of endogenous variables,
$z$  is a vector of growth rates of exogenous variables, and  $A$
is a rectangular matrix whose coefficients are built up as
(non-linear) functions of the parameters appearing in the
model's structural form (i.e., in its production functions,
demand relations, primary factor constraints, etc.).  Equation
(3) says that if the economy is initially in a state consistent
with the structural model and data base that gave rise to  $A$ ,
and is then subjected to the shock  $z$  in its exogenous
variables, the proportional difference between the initial
levels of the endogenous variables and their levels *after a*
*period long enough for 'full'adjustment to occur* is  $y$ .   In
this sentence the phrase "'full' adjustment" is defined relative to

        (a)   the model structure ,  and
        (b)   the notional adjustment lags underlying
              the values of the parameters used to
              construct  $A$ .

I shall take in turn an example of each of these in the ORANI
context, commencing with (a).  The structural form of this
model includes demand functions for nine categories of labor,
but does not include their supply functions.[15]  Consequently,
simulations with ORANI proceed in one of two basic ways : real
wages are set exogenously on the assumption of excess labor
supply (the actual situation in Australia since 1975), or else
the changes in employment are set exogenously and the real wage
changes which would generate the required changes in labor
demand are projected.   In an ORANI simulation, therefore,
'full adjustment' does *not* mean a period long enough for the
simultaneous interaction of labor supply and demand forces to
lead to an unconditional clearing of the labor market.   I now
turn to (b).   Incorporated within  $A$  are a large number of
behavioral parameters such as capital-labor and labor-labor
substitution elasticities, expenditure elasticities, and

demand-side substitution elasticities between imported and domestically produced commodities at the input-output level of disaggregation.   These parameters have been estimated by a variety of techniques, from a variety of different sources.[16] Associated with each estimate is a time frame and an explicit or implicit lag structure of the particular response involved. Among the successfully estimated parameters lags are often short (less than a year), and rarely exceed two years.  This is one consideration that led us to propose that 'full' adjustment in our short run simulations would correspond to a period of 'one to two years.'   I want now to leave, for the timebeing, the difficult question of timing, the point of the above dis-cussion being that the actual conditions in which the compara-tive static approach must be applied in WJ models rules out statements with the 'precision' common in the idea of forecast-ing as often purveyed by the builders of KK models. [17]

Accepting the inherent limitations with respect to the timing of events of the WJ class, what other considerations are relevant to their ability to produce forecasts?  I will attempt to answer this question again by reference to the Johansen sub-class.

Consider a particular scalar equation belonging to (3) :

$$(4) \qquad\qquad y_i \;=\; \sum_{j=1}^{N} a_{ij}\, z_j \;\;.$$

In ORANI 77, the number of exogenous variables  N  is typically 900.   The number of endogenous variables runs into some millions, the vast majority of which are there for reasons of accounting necessity only.   However the model contains sever-al thousand endogenous variables of policy interest, including activity levels and rates of return in 109 industries, employ-ment demand by industry and occupation, domestic prices, imp-orts and exports, all on a disaggregated basis.   In spite of this vast size (an issue addressed below), the use of the model to make point forecasts clearly presents difficulties.   The first is that although the 900 exogenous variables cover many

of the determinants of the domestic economy - - the list
typically would include items such as foreign prices and domestic tariff levels, and perhaps the *aggregate* level of real
absorption [18] - - there are many other variables of potential
importance which are left out of account.   In ORANI 77, for
instance, industry specific technological change is not recognised. [19]   To forecast on the basis of (4) one would need

> (i)    to extend the set of exogenous variables
>        to include *every* exogenous influence
>        relevant to  $y_i$ ;
>
> (ii)   to prepare forecasts on a very large
>        (>> 900) number of exogenous variables.

If the forecast is required in terms of levels, then the initial level of the  $i^{th}$  endogenous variable must also be known.
In all, this is a formidable information load which it will
rarely be feasible to meet in applied forecasting.

4.2 *Flexibility and Policy Analysis*

I now wish to turn to the strengths of the WJ models, and
especially of the Johansen approach as further developed in the
ORANI model, in the area of policy analysis.   In this field,
flexibility is a key requirement.   In our experience the ability to use different partitions of the variables into endogenous and exogenous sets is a major source of flexibility in
Johansen models. [20]

In estimation, the partition of variables into endogenous and
exogenous sets reflects a maintained hypothesis about the way
the economy worked during the sample period.   Given his view
of how the economy actually operated, there is no further
degree of choice open to the investigator as to how he should
classify the variables.   In *simulation* with a Johansen model
like ORANI, however, no such strictures apply.   The applied
econometrician attempting to supply consistent estimates to
the ORANI parameter file, of course, will have opted for some
view about endogeneity/exogeneity with respect to the particular variables and sample with which he worked. [21]   A variety
of different reduced forms, however, can be derived for

simulation purposes from any given consistent set of estimates of structural form parameters. It is, of course, required that every new partitioning into endogenous and exogenous variables be a maintained hypothesis under which the simulation is mounted. These ideas can be clarified with the use of some simple notation.

In the formulation of the ORANI model of which (3) is a reduced form, an earlier stage involves the structural form of the model (after expression in logarithmic differentials) :

$$(5) \qquad Cx = [\Gamma \ B] \begin{bmatrix} x_1 \\ x_2 \end{bmatrix} = 0 \ ,$$

in which $C$ is a rectangular matrix with row order and rank equal to the number $M$ of endogenous variables in the system (in ORANI, very large) and with column order equal to the total number of variables $(M + N)$ . In the middle term of (5), one feasible partitioning of $C$ is shown. Many such partitionings are possible, the essential requirement being that $\Gamma$ is square of rank and order $M$ . For a given partitioning of $x$ into endogenous variables $x_1$ and exogenous variables $x_2$ , a reduced form is obtained as

$$(6) \qquad x_1 = - \Gamma^{-1} Bx_2 \ .$$

This is equation (3). Provided care has been taken to use consistent methods in the estimation of $C$ , then the consistency of any particular reduced form matrix,

$$(7) \qquad A = - \Gamma^{-1} B \ ,$$

is assured. Because the estimated structural form should transform to a consistent estimate of an arbitrary reduced form which is user determined (and therefore highly variable), emphasis has been placed on consistency in the estimation of the elements of the ORANI parameter file (which undergo transformations to become $C$ ).[22]

Two examples of pairs of variables which have been routinely switched between the endogenous and exogenous lists in ORANI

simulations are (i) real absorption and the balance of trade
and (ii) the real wage vector and the vector of occupational
employment demands. [23]    This flexibility is a design feature
of the ORANI model clearly reflecting the policy analytic purpose for which it was built.    KK models are not usually
designed to accommodate the analysis of hypothetical questions
involving switches of endogenous and exogenous variables.    The
widespread use of single equations techniques for the estimation of KK models clearly works against the possibility of
mounting counter-factual simulations of the type described
above.    Even if it could be established that the single equations estimators are 'optimal' in the context of the tracking
properties of KK models, such a property would not survive a
reallocation of variables into the endogenous and exogenous
sets.    Partly due to their smaller size, and due partly no
doubt to the different methodological orientation of their
builders, the PB models have often been estimated by full-
information techniques. [24]    For this reason the possibility of
switches between the endogenous and exogenous list is real for
simulations with PB models. [25]    Also for this reason the
prospects of interfacing a Johansen model with a PB model are
much better than those for interfacing a Johansen model with a
KK model.

4.3  *Size and Complexity*
In the Conference discussion of Gregory Chow's paper, Zvi
Griliches remarked that 'much of the objection to large models
is motivated by a lack of understanding of the internal mechanisms of large models.' [26]    As Griliches saw it, size was not
the issue, but appropriateness of the model design in relation
to its purpose.    Many concepts of size were discussed by Conference participants, but the distinction drawn by Zellner
between nominal size and complexity is useful and (in my
view) a fundamental one.    Lawrence Klein expressed the consensus view that 'the optimal size of a model is essentially
determined by the use to which the model is to be put.' [27]
What I wish to examine here is the idea of the optimal
*complexity* of models.

Complexity is a many-faceted concept, but I think agreement can be expected on the following :

(a) For a given number of equations in a model, the larger the number of 'families' to which the equations belong, the more complex is the model.[28]

(b) The existence of an interpretable linear-in-the variables representation of the structural form of a model makes for simplicity.   Other things equal, a model with such a linear transform is less complex than one lacking such a transform.

On these criteria the majority of KK models (say, those having more than about 50 equations) are more complex than most in the WJ class.   The ORANI 77 model, which is available for routine use in policy analysis, has some 50 families of equations in the structural form.   In this sense it is not a complex model.   In training courses on the use of the model some 5 formal lecture hours are sufficient for students to develop a basic understanding of what makes the model tick.   Like other members of the Johansen sub-class, ORANI has a linear representation (and it is in this form that the structural form is taught).   In attempting to make transparent to the clientele the mechanisms at work and the prior assumptions incorporated within a large model, this is an enormous advantage : most users, after all, find no difficulty in differentiating a polynomial of the first degree!

The concept of a family of equations is a valuable heuristic. It allows for economies of scale in model design and in the development of computer systems.   With models containing many thousands (or even millions) of endogenous variables, the tailor made equation-by-equation approach would be infeasible. The optimal complexity of a model is determined by asking (a) what is the minimum number of equations having algebraically and economically different structure needed to allow the model to address the questions for which it is to be built; and (b) which among the competing structural formulations (which in other respects are considered adequate) provides the best prospects for an economically interpretable linear-in-the variables representation?

Some constraints on the determination of this optimum need to be recognised.  Management is one such constraint.   In many agencies building large KK models, OLS equation-by-equation is a very attractive proposition to management.   Individual researchers can be assigned individual equations, greatly reducing the amount of co-ordination needed and hence the level of management necessary for team research.

On the basis of these ideas, we can type the *typical* member currently in use of each class of model as follows :

| Model Class | Nominal Size (No. Eqns) | Complexity |
|---|---|---|
| KK | large | high |
| PB | small | low |
| WJ (lacking linear representation) | large | medium |
| WJ (Johansen) | large | low |

If this view is accepted, but it is nonetheless held that only the KK class offers the prospect for "accurate forecasting," then there is a conundrum.   Whilst the mechanisms producing results in a large, but simple, model seem to be capable of explanation to the clientele, those from a large and complex model clearly are not.   The forecasting model is then reduced to the status of a 'black box.'   Having reached this point, it becomes impossible, in my view, to point to advantages *from the user's point of view* of the econometric approach over a purely time series approach with a similar forecasting power - - from the user's viewpoint the black box with the best track record dominates. [29]

4.4  *Validation*

The annual and quarterly econometric models of the KK class

brought about a revolution in the scientific status of economic
models.   It was no longer sufficient for a model to constitute
an internally consistent logical structure, it was necessary
for it to have an identifiable image in the real world.   The
inferential procedures necessary to identify and estimate
relationships in a non-experimental science were produced by
the Cowles Commission [32] well ahead of the availability of
computer hard and software needed to make them a practical
proposition.   But these systems approaches to inference had
their drawbacks.   With the ascendency of within-sample tracking properties as the criterion of a successful econometric
model, builders reverted to OLS in droves.   This was partly
due to the management difficulties mentioned above;  it was
also due to an awareness that a

> "single equation appearing to be reasonable enough
> on every theoretical and statistical criterion
> can destroy the simulation properties of a model" [21].

Under estimation by OLS, such a fractious equation could easily
be 'worked on;' attempts to discipline the offender within a
full information framework however, would be more likely than
not to cause so much trouble elsewhere in the system as to be
self defeating.   The pressure to produce accurate short term
forecasts resulted not only in a decline in the use of the
simultaneous equations methodology, but in the widespread
adoption of a host of *ad hoc* procedures designed to ensure
superb tracking within sample.   These procedures (commented
upon by many of the Conference members and in Section 3 above)
make it difficult indeed to achieve agreement on when a model
has been successfully validated.   Nor was the debate running
through the pages of *Econometrica* for more than a decade able
to settle the issue, or to establish agreed standards for best
practice technique.

While all of this is unsatisfactory, it may merely reflect the
ambitiousness, or perhaps over-ambitiousness, of the young
science of applied econometrics.   The available supplies of

data may very well be incapable of serving both to test hypotheses about an initially maintained prior specification and to
fine tune a model so that its within-sample dynamics and long
run steady state properties will look 'respectable.'

Validation of the PB models presents difficulties which the
builders of KK models have purposely avoided in the choice of
their methodology.   With emphasis on system and on full information estimators, it is not uncommon to find that one or
more key parameters are poorly determined in the sense that, in
the relevant region, the likelihood surface is relatively flat.
'Relevant region' in this context refers to the subset of the
parameter space containing the global maximum of the likelihood
function and one (or more) co-ordinate sets which are much more
amenable to economic interpretation than the MLE's of the parameters.   Within the context of the constraints imposed within
and across equations by the maintained structural specification, one or more uninterpretable parameter estimates can have
disastrous consequences for the interpretability and simulation
properties of the entire system.   An approach to this problem
adopted by  Jonson  and  co-workers on the Australian Reserve
Bank's RBA models is to force troublesome coefficients into an
economically interpretable range by assigning arbitrary (but
sensible) values to them, and re-estimating for the remaining
coefficients using FIML. [30]   It is amazing that this transparent and sensible procedure has been regarded as 'fudging' by
some critics who would think nothing of running tens, or
hundreds of regression equations on the same data until they
'got it right.'

Without wishing to minimize the difficulties  encountered with
PB and KK models, validation of WJ models is a much taller
order again.   In the first place, the data necessary to compare a model solution with its real world image often do not
exist for more than one or two points in time.   In our validation of the (non-neoclassical) SNAPSHOT model, the necessary
input-output and other accounts were available for exactly two
years.   The only question whose answer the available data
would support was the following one : given a knowledge of the

structure of the economy in fiscal 1962-63, and a knowledge of the actual values of SNAPSHOT's exogenous variables in 1971-72, would it have been possible in 1962-63 to have forecast, with any degree of accuracy, the structure of the Australian economy in 1971-72?    The answer turns out to be *yes* [19].   Before congratulating ourselves, however, I should point out that the exogenous information load required by SNAPSHOT is formidable. And of course to obtain a tracking of the economy through a single point a decade distant is a far cry from tracking its quarter-to-quarter movements.

From the viewpoint of Australian policy analysis the greatest drawback of the SNAPSHOT model is the necessity to exogenise international trade (on a disaggregated basis).    IMPACT's WJ model in the Johansen sub-class, ORANI, is much larger than SNAPSHOT, and because of the wide range of substitution mechanisms operating within it, does not produce the corner solutions which led to the exogenisation of international trade in SNAPSHOT.    However, other aspects of the exogenous information load required to mount even a simple 2 year validation of ORANI (covered partially above in Section 4.1) have so far proved too demanding of the available data base and other resources. [31]      How, then, does one present policy simulations convincingly and honestly, given this dearth of available information?

The issue was given some attention by the designers of the ORANI model [18] :

> "... we have relied, in ORANI applications papers, on explaining at length the mechanisms by which the model produces the results.  Ultimately it is up to the user to decide whether these mechanisms capture the crucial elements of the economic phenomena in which he is interested.  Similarly the values of the para- meters used in the simulations and the methods by which they are derived are fully documented and freely available.
>
> Testing the sensitivity of the model's results

to variations in its mechanisms and parameter values
is another element in establishing the plausibility
of simulation results  .... .

   With a model the size of ORANI there is, however,
an almost infinite amount of sensitivity analysis
which could be undertaken for any experiment.  Again,
it is for the user to decide which areas of the model
he wishes to investigate in this way, and given the
scarcity of research resources available to the IMPACT
development team, it is for the user to undertake much
of the analysis.  Completed IMPACT models can be made
available for 'hands on' experiments by outside users."

This approach means that users have to take much more of the
responsibility for many of the inferences drawn on the basis
of simulations, which entails both advantages and disadvantag-
es.   On the credit side, no user is permitted the fantasy
that he can use an economic model in the same way as he might
approach a computerised airline reservation system.   On the
debit side, decision makers are busy people.   There is a limit
to how much time they can, or will, invest in understanding an
economic model.   On many of the relevant critical issues
(e.g., is $\sigma_{KL}$ closer to unity than to zero?), moreover, their
judgments are not likely to be well informed without the back-
up of a first class professional staff.

4.5 *Summary*

Many aspects of design and practice in applied model building
can be seen as natural responses to what is dictated by the
purposes for which the models are designed, to constraints
imposed by the supply of data, and to the expectations of the
model using clientele.   The KK models emphasize validation
and forecasting, but as we have seen above, rigorous inferential procedures in the validation department can be sacrificed
in an attempt to improve the appearance of forecasting power.
The WJ models have not emphasised validation or forecasting to
anything like the same extent, but have concentrated on preser-
ving sufficient simplicity of structure to enable a clear

exposition of the mechanisms generating any simulated result.
They are particularly well suited to policy analysis of periods
long enough to abstract from adjustment dynamics. The PB
models offer a compromise between these two positions; while
forecasting is seen as one role, adherence of the estimated
system to a simple and interpretable economic structure is
high on the builders' list of priorities. Achievement of
the latter objective is facilitated by the comparatively small
size of these models.

## 5. SCOPE FOR RECONCILIATION

It will be evident that the differences in approach between
the builders of KK, PB and WJ models are sufficient to make
reconciliation a formidable task. Nevertheless there are
large potential pay-offs to the science from attempting to
bridge the gaps. In this section again I will be drawing
largely upon experience with the IMPACT Project where we have
been attempting

(a)  to develop a methodology for interfacing a
     quarterly macro model in the PB class with a
     comparative static model of the Johansen
     variety ;

and

(b)  to evaluate the comparative performance of
     the Johansen models and other members of the
     WJ class.

In both cases the work I will be describing is ongoing : it is
too early to claim definitive results.

### 5.1  *Separability of the Macro from the Microeconomy*

In the Conference discussion, Jan Kmenta (and others) emphasised block recursiveness and other separability ideas as
important potential devices for reducing the complexity of
models. [32]   Separability in economic relationships enables
model builders (and users) to localise the features responsible
for some particular type of economic behavior within some well
defined segment of the model.   It makes for order, for tidy

book-keeping.

In the initial design for IMPACT's medium term model, the
paradigm adopted involved the following, strong, maintained
hypothesis : financial and money markets, as well as fiscal
actions, are only important for individual industries and
occupations insofar as they exert a real effect upon the big
components of national income;  namely, private consumption,
private capital formation, and government spending [41].

It was, of course, realised from the outset that such a high
degree of neutrality (with respect to their incidence across
industries) of monetary and financial variables could only
hold as a first approximation.  Particular exceptions sprang
immediately to mind (for example, the specific incidence of
money market conditions on housing starts) [43].

The paradigm was nevertheless particularly attractive for the
following reasons.  The prototype model of ORANI developed by
Peter Dixon before the commencement of the IMPACT Project
lacked macroeconomic closure.  By that I mean that an aggregate consumption function, an aggregate investment function, an
aggregate capital inflow equation, an equation determining the
extent to which changes in the CPI are passed into wages, and
labor supply equations, were needed to close the model.  For
the last-mentioned, a separate economic-demographic model
(BACHUROO) is being constructed.  As far as the components of
absorption are concerned, for many applications of the ORANI
simulation framework it was eminently reasonable to treat them
as exogenous.  A marginal change in the tariff protecting a
relatively small industry, for example, could be expected to
have negligible macro (as distinct from political) feedback.[33]
And with respect to the flow-on of price level changes into
wages, the behavior of Australia's various wage-fixing tribun-
als could be monitored to provide exogenous estimates.  But
in spite of this, it was realised that macro and micro policy
interact, and it was therefore desirable to have a vehicle
capable of addressing both simultaneously.  This progressi-
vely has become more urgent in perceived institutional
priorities as the debates on stabilisation policy and struct-

ural adjustment become intertwined against a background of
continuing high unemployment.

Like other neoclassical applied general equilibrium models,
ORANI concentrates on real variables and on relative prices.
(Unlike the other such models that I know of, ORANI's option
for exogenising selected relative prices is able to induce the
model to produce, if so desired, simulations with more of a
neo-Keynesian than a neoclassical flavour - - see [16],
Section 3.5, pp. 36-40.)    ORANI does not model monetary or
financial markets.    If these variables are to have a role in
determining disaggregated real activity levels and employment
demands, then the natural channel is through those macroeconomic variables which are exogenous to ORANI but endogenous
to a macro model.

In research no less than in other areas of life, luck is
important.    IMPACT's need was for a small model giving a role
to monetary and financial markets and endogenising real   C
and   I  but not too much else.    The model should have a disequilibrium dynamics capable of tracking the business cycle.
Fortunately, such a model entered the research portfolio of
the Reserve Bank of Australia under Peter Jonson at about the
right time from our point of view.    Because of its size (some
22 equations) and emphasis (about half of the endogenous variables are monetary or financial) the Australian Reserve Bank's
RBA model did not present a frighteningly large number of
double endogeneities vis-à-vis ORANI.    Because it also
happened to be a PB model it had two big potential advantages
over KK models from our point of view.    First, being formulated in continuous time, the inevitable problems of temporal
aggregation to be faced at the ORANI interface become much
simpler.    Second, PB models (like Johansen models) may be
approximated as linear equations in logarithmic differentials.
In crudest outline, therefore, the interface could be visual-
ised as augmentation of  C  in equation (5) with additional
rows and columns, and the addition of further variables to  x .

Having conceived our broad lines of attack, we were left with two problems :

    (i)    reconciling the timing in ORANI with that in
           our macro model (hereafter, MACRO) ;

    (ii)   eliminating double endogeneities.

Examples of the latter (in most configurations of ORANI) are
aggregate exports, aggregate imports, and aggregate employment
demand.   Since the timing of the employment consequences of
policy action is, in Australia, an acutely politically sensitive variable, the last of these double endogeneities presented
a particular challenge.

It took some time to see that the double endogeneities also
had advantages.   They present opportunities for a methodology
of interfacing the models which would otherwise be lacking, and
provide an indirect validation framework for at least part of
the ORANI model itself.   To see this, it is necessary first
to define the 'ORANI short run.'

The ORANI short run is defined in conventional text book terms.
It is a period ([16], p. 17)

    " .... short enough to allow one to neglect changes
        in the amount of plant and equipment in use but
        long enough for the investment plans of industries
        (as revised in the light of the ... exogenous
        changes under scrutiny) to affect the demands faced
        by capital goods producing industries."

The ORANI model has been used to analyse the short run effects
on levels of activity and rates of return in 109 industries of
uniform ([16], Ch. 3) and non-uniform ([16], Ch. 5) changes in
in tariff rates, of exogenous changes in real wages ([16],
Ch. 3), of a spontaneous relaxation in the balance of payments
constraint due to the opening up of major mineral exports
([16], Ch. 4), of a move from an artificial to a world parity
pricing structure for oil [49], and of changes in real aggregate demand brought about by the independent use of monetary
and/or fiscal policy ([16], Ch. 3).   In all of this work the
reported changes in the simulated values of the endogenous

variables notionally takes place after a time unit equal to
'one ORANI short run.'    On the definition above the ORANI
short run cannot be longer than the typical gestation lag of
new investment (say 1 or 2 years).    Is it possible to be more
precise than this?

It is here that the double endogeneities are useful.    Consider
a scalar variable  Y  endogenous in both MACRO and (the chosen
configuration of) ORANI.    To keep matters as simple as possible, suppose there is a once-off proportional shock  z  in a
scalar variable  Z  which is exogenous to both MACRO and ORANI.
Further suppose that there exist logarithmic differentials
$x_1, \ldots, x_M$ endogenous to MACRO but exogenous to ORANI, but
that there are no linkages in the other direction.    If  $\eta_{yz}$
is the elasticity of  Y  with respect to  Z  in the chosen
configuration of ORANI, then the ORANI response to the shock
z  comes in two parts : the direct response

$$(8) \qquad y^0_{direct} = \eta_{yz}\, z \quad,$$

and the indirect response induced by  $x_1, \ldots, x_M$ .  Because of
the differences in timing between MACRO and ORANI, the differentials  $x_1, \ldots, x_M$  as output by MACRO are not the appropriate exogenous inputs to ORANI;   the temporal aggregation
problems involved in finding a suitable transform
$f_1(x_1, t), \ldots, f_M(x_M, t)$ [conditional on an assumed value  t
of the ORANI short run] have been solved by Cooper and
McLaren. [34]      Using an obvious notation, the indirect part of
the ORANI response is found as

$$(9) \qquad y^0_{indirect} = \sum_{j=1}^{M} \eta_{yx_j}\, f_j(x_j, t) \quad,$$

and the total as

$$(10) \qquad y^0 = y^0_{direct} + y^0_{indirect} \cdot$$

MACRO, on the other hand, is a continuous time model estimated
from quarterly data and is capable of producing a continuous

time profile of accumulated responses.   After  t  quarters
the accumulated (deviation from control) response in MACRO of
y  can be written

(11)                              $y^M(t) = \phi_t(z)$ .

The value of  t  which equates (10) and (11)  ($t^*$, say) turns
out to be uniquely determined for any pair of doubly endogenous variables and is a measure of the ORANI short run in the
context of the response variables  y  and the shocks  z .
Whilst  $t^*$  will undoubtedly vary between different choices of
(y, z) ,  initial experiments in which  z  represents an
increase in real government spending and  y  is selected to be
total employment and either nominal GDP or aggregate imports,
lead to values of  $t^*$  which fit well with our prior convic-
tions (6 - 8 quarters).   Notice that some groupings of  y's
are more suitable than others.   The particular set of  y's
chosen to estimate  $t^*$  should reflect the prior confidence one
has in the story told by the models for those variables.   If
the  $t^*$  value obtained is plausible, then the double endogeneities have provided an indirect, partial, validation of ORANI
via MACRO.

Given an estimate of the ORANI short run the MACRO model has to
be  temporally  reaggregated to a discrete time representation
based on time intervals of length  $t^*$ .   Even with  $t^*$
estimated to be non-integral, this causes no problem in view of
the continuous time representation of MACRO [10].

Double endogeneities which are consistent with the accepted
value of  $t^*$  lead to no real problem  - -  the ORANI and the
MACRO stories are observationally equivalent for these variables.   In the other cases (fortunately few in number) it will
be necessary to opt either for the ORANI or the MACRO story.
This will obviously depend partly on our conception of the
relative strengths of the models, and partly on simulation
results. [35]

The IMPACT experience has generated clearly hopeful signs for
the integration of one type of quarterly dynamic model (in the

PB class) with a Johansen type model.    It is difficult, however, to see how similar progress can be made for interfacing
KK models with members of the WJ class.    In the first place,
KK models are not only macro models in the sense used above,
but have their own procedures for disaggregating the economy.
Moreover, the number of variables endogenised both in the KK
and simultaneously in the WJ model would be far too large for
comfort.    It might nevertheless be possible to extract a
closed subset of equations from a KK model designed to track
the big aggregates in the macroeconomy.    Given a guess (to
the nearest number of quarters) of the length of the ORANI
short run, the reduced form of the KK subset could be aggregated to this number of quarters.    The resultant system could
then be approximated at or near the initial conditions of the
control path by a set of elasticities like the matrix  A  in
(3).    Interfacing such a system with a model like ORANI would
be possible at least in the mechanical sense.

5.2 *Likely Developments Within the WJ Class*

I wish now to consider the scope for convergence in the three
major sub-classes of applied general equilibrium models;
namely :

(i)     Development planning models ,
(ii)    Neoclassical models formulated and solved
        in the levels ,
(iii)   Johansen models.

The IMPACT Project has had direct experience in departments (i)
(with the SNAPSHOT model [15], [19]) and (iii)(with the ORANI
model [14], [20]).

Models in the development planning sub-class (including SNAP-
SHOT) are the least neoclassical of the models in the WJ class.
Their tendency to produce corner solutions (which has been
remarked on above) is a major drawback.    In the ORANI model
liberal provision is made for price induced changes in factor
and consumption mixes.    In particular, substitution elasticities (which are not necessarily zero or infinity) are specified
to allow substitution between the primary factors land, labor

and capital, between import competing and domestically
produced products in the same input-output category, and
between the different products consumed by the household
sector.    No substitution, however, is allowed between different types of materials used as intermediate products.    In the
case of labor, nine occupations are recognised and substitution
among them is possible.    Seven different types of agricultural
land are recognised. [36]    Substitution among these different
classes of land is not allowed;  on the other hand the production technology in agriculture is specified as multi-product
[17], [48], so that the output mixes of different agricultural
industries can change in response to changing relative product
prices.    While the small country assumption is maintained on
the import side, export demand functions are allowed to be
downward sloping.    Aggregate investment is exogenous in most
applications of ORANI, but the model contains allocation equations which distribute the aggregate investment bundle across
industries in line with their relative general equilibrium
rates of return.    Thus relative prices can affect the composition of investment and consumption.

Like all Johansen models, ORANI is solved in logarithmic
differentials. We do not believe that it would have been
possible, either in terms of available human talents or in
terms of computer feasibility, to have incorporated all of the
substitution mechanisms listed above into a model which was
(a) to be solved in the levels,  and (b) to maintain user
flexibility about the choice of endogenous and exogenous
variables in the simulations.    The SNAPSHOT model (for
instance), like the majority of WJ models solved in the levels,
for feasibility required the design of an efficient special
purpose algorithm [13].    SNAPSHOT lacks most of the substitution possibilities mentioned above, as well as many other
attractive features of ORANI.    In spite of the development of
highly efficient special software for the solution of SNAPSHOT,
it is much more costly than ORANI to run.    There would be no
chance of using a model like SNAPSHOT on a routine basis in the
flexible way available to users of ORANI.    This is because

minor changes in the structure of non-linear mathematical programming problems require re-design (and often major re-design) of packages to compute their solutions within available computer budgets. This remark applies to all members of the WJ class solved in the levels. [37]

Johansen models have the enormous advantage of being solvable by matrix inversion. The unpleasant, non-linear, mathematics is all relatively simple, and is over with once the matrices Γ and B in equation (6) have been computed. There are, however, two objections to the Johansen procedure :

(i)    The method only applies for small changes in the exogenous variables ;

and

(ii)   Solutions are given only as percentage changes relative to the initial conditions. It is a maintained hypothesis under the Johansen technique that the model correctly describes the levels of the endogenous variables in the notional base period from which any particular simulation is mounted.

We have carried out research at IMPACT ([12]; [14] Ch. 5) into the potential seriousness of the linearisation errors (i). In many straightforward applications these errors can be neglected. In others it may be necessary to divide the exogenous shocks into a series of smaller components and to integrate numerically. The striking feature of our results to date is that the numerical integration (that is, a full non-linear solution) can be achieved at a computer cost of only approximately double what is involved in an ordinary Johansen solution.

If the ORANI reduced form in levels could be shown to be globally translog then it can be shown that only two iterations of the solution (3) are necessary to be able to predict exactly the result of an experiment in which the number of iterations is allowed to become indefinitely large. [38]   Of course, ORANI is not translog in the levels, and the question is, to what extent does its functional form approximate

translog?    Our methodology for answering this question is
to compute the predicted full non-linear solution for percentage changes in the endogenous variables on the assumption that
ORANI <u>is</u> sufficiently translogarithmic in the levels, and to
compare that approximate solution with one obtained by taking
a very large number of iterations so that the changes in the
exogenous variables proceed (for all practical purposes) in
arbitrarily small steps.    Our preliminary results indicate
that the final non-linear solution can be predicted with high
accuracy from the first two iterations only. [39]

If these results turn out to be robust after the accumulation
of sufficient experience (and we have confidence that they
will), then it will be very difficult to identify the advantages associated with solving WJ models in the levels.    There
is, of course, the question of whether the structural form of
the model corresponds to the actual state of the world at a
notional base period.    It is true, of course, that (3) would
be consistent with a variety of structural forms expressed in
the levels, the differences being due to different choices of
integration constants.    The parameter file of ORANI, however,
is generated largely from data for an actual base year;    in
particular, the cost and sales shares of different industries
come from an historical input-output table.    With the choice
of the obvious integration constants, therefore, ORANI fits
its base year identically in the levels, *by construction*.

If these judgments are accepted then we can expect to see
Johansen models gradually come to dominate the WJ class.    They
may be of the order of twice as expensive to solve as their
prototypes in which linearisation errors were ignored.    If the
ORANI model is any guide, these solutions will be obtainable
on quite large models (more than 100 industries) for figures
measured in hundreds rather than thousands of dollars.    This
fact, coupled with their very flexible nature, makes the
Johansen models very attractive by comparison with other
members of the WJ class.

6. CONCLUDING REMARKS

In this paper I have given a personal reaction to the issues raised at the 1978 NBER-NSF Conference on econometric modeling. This reaction has been highly colored by my experience as leader of the Australian government's inter-agency IMPACT Project. The thrust of the Project has been policy analytical rather than oriented towards forecasting, and this is clearly evident in the design of our models and the emphasis given to different issues.

From this experience it is possible to discern some scope for rapprochement between the different schools of modeling. Early results indicate that it may be possible to develop a methodology to interface a small dynamic macroeconometric model with a large general equilibrium model. This possibility is highly contingent on the design features of the two models. Within the applied general equilibrium class of models, I have speculated that members of the Johansen family will become dominant. This is because of

    (a)   the practicability of building large, flexible, models of this type recognising a wide range of price responsive phenomena

which

    (b)   nevertheless are highly feasible within computer budgets,

and in which

    (c)   linearisation errors have been eliminated.

FOOTNOTES

1.   Paper written in response to the discussion of issues in
     modeling at the NBER-NSF Conference on Macroeconometric
     Models, Ann Arbor, Michigan, October 26-27th, 1978.

2.   I wish especially to thank Peter B. Dixon for feedback on
     the first draft.    Others who kindly commented on drafts
     include Don Challen, Ken Clements, Russel Cooper, Bill
     Evans, Alf Hagger, Peter Jonson, Jan Kmenta, Warwick
     McKibbin, Keith McLaren, Ian McDonald, Bill Norton, John
     Taylor and Rob Trevor.    To all of these, my sincere
     thanks.    The errors are my own.

3.   IMPACT is an inter-agency project of the Australian
     federal government in co-operation with the University of
     Melbourne.    Its purpose is to facilitate the analysis of
     the impact of economic, demographic, and social changes
     on the structure of the Australian economy.    For a brief
     description of the institutional history and the flavor
     of the project, see Powell and Parmenter [42].    For a
     comprehensive non-technical description of the Project,
     see Powell [41].    For technical details of the largest
     of the Project's models, ORANI, see Dixon, Parmenter,
     Ryland and Sutton [20], or Dixon, Parmenter, Vincent and
     Sutton [14].    Since July 1975, the Project has produced
     about one hundred working papers, most of which are
     available on request.    For a catalog, write to :
     Mr  Mike Kenderes, IMPACT Information Officer, Industries
     Assistance Commission, P.O. Box 80, Belconnen, A.C.T.,
     Australia,   2616.

4.   A reader has pointed out that the KK models blossomed
     during a period of relatively stable relative prices.
     The minor role accorded the latter may therefore have
     reflected the times rather than the proclivities of the
     KK model builders.

5.   In Wymer's 1971 model [51], all but 9 of 37 variables in
     the system are holdings of assets or the yields on these
     assets.    In Jonson's minimal macro model of the Austra-

lian economy [29], about half of the two dozen endogenous variables in the system are financial or monetary variables.

6.  See the papers in A. R. Bergstrom (ed.) cited in [5] above.

7.  For an example of a discrete time general equilibrium model estimated *as a complete model* by FIML using Wymer's software, see Clements [8] and [9] .

8.  See Taylor [46] .   The seminal study by Johansen is [27].

9.  Dixon *et al.* [14], [20].

10. Thus Ando [4] feels compelled to defend the  KK class of models against the charge of 'spectacular recent failures,' while from within its central bank two of Australia's best known model builders take a somewhat agnostic stance concerning the likely future influence and utility of further modeling effort.   See Norton and Jonson [40].

11. This distinction between the design of experiment and number of replicates is important.  Except in extreme pathological cases, it is possible to compensate for poor design by multiplication of replicates.

12. This view has been put forcefully by Christopher Sims in his review [45] of Leamer's *Specification Searches*.

13. It is to be hoped that in time Leamer's work [34] will lead to a more systematic, and honest, approach to specification searches.

14. The version of ORANI that I will refer to most often is ORANI 77, as documented in [20].   Occasionally I will also refer to ORANI 78, documented in [14].

15. Labor supply functions are handled in a separate model called BACHUROO.  It is planned at a later date to interface the latter model with ORANI.   See Powell [41], Ch. 3, Section 3 , and [43a].

16. Given the state of collection of official statistics in many countries (including Australia), for large WJ models

like ORANI, typically there will not exist an integrated
data base giving quarterly (or even annual) time series
for any but a small subset of the variables.   Researchers are necessarily inventive and opportunistic in their
attempts to mobilise data to support parameter estimation.
In the case of the ORANI model the largest and most important deficiency lay in the area of the trade statistics
needed to support reliable estimates of demand side substitution elasticities between imported and domestic
products at the 109  industry level of disaggregation.
This deficiency was made good by a special purpose data
mobilisation exercise [39].   The creation of this data
base paid off handsomely in the precision of the estimates
subsequently obtained (Alaouze, Marsden and Zeitsch [3]).
The only parallel I am aware of is the data mobilised by
the CIA's trade flow project (see Goodman [24]), of which
at least some have been published (see McMenamin and
Pinard [37]).

17.  I have already indicated above in Section 3 that insofar
     as claims to accuracy of timing are based on within-sample
     tracking performance, I believe that the appearance of
     precision may be an illusion.   And as E. Phillip Howrey
     and others pointed out in discussion at the NBER-NSF Con-
     ference, our present economic theory has little to say
     about short run dynamics.   A framework for developing a
     dynamics based on prior theory, but which has not yet
     filtered down to practical procedures in model building,
     is given by McLaren [36].

18.  Absorption is defined as gross domestic product minus the
     balance of trade, and therefore equals consumption plus
     investment plus government spending.

19.  ORANI 78 (Dixon *et al.* [14]) includes provision for an
     extremely flexible treatment of technological change.
     The cost is a major explosion in the size of the model.

20.  There is no reason in principle preventing the same
     flexibility being exploited in the use of KK or PB models

in simulation work.    The targets/instruments allocation
problem in the theory of economic policy (Tinbergen [47])
is, after all, a manifestation of this flexibility.
Practical difficulties mitigating against simulations which
reallocate variables between the endogenous-exogenous list
include   (i) the widespread practice of estimating the
coefficients of the system by OLS or other estimators with
no known invariance properties under the transformation
involved in repartitioning, and   (ii) non-linearities.

21.   The rational expectations debate has led applied workers
to the view that 'policy variables' may sometimes be
endogenous and sometimes exogenous.    If prior evidence
is available to identify in which period a particular
variable is endogenous and in which exogenous, no particular problem arises.    If there is uncertainty about the
status of a policy variable at different points in the
sample, then our inferential (viz., likelihood) framework
breaks down.    Hillier and Giles have recently addressed
this problem and suggested methods for its solution [26].

22.   For a fuller account of the procedures involved in moving
from the structural form of ORANI to any chosen reduced
form, see Section 17 of [20].

23.   See, e.g., Dixon, Powell and Parmenter [16].

24.   Jonson *et al.* [29], [30].

25.   This possibility so far remains unexploited, to the best
of my knowledge.

26.   Circulated report of discussion on Chow's paper.

27.   Circulated report of the discussion on the paper by Fromm
and Klein.

28.   A 'family' of equations is here defined as a set of equations each of whose members is conveniently represented
by the same algebraic formulation.    The basic economic
interpretation of this formulation must be the same for
every member of the set.

29.  And, of course, Zellner and Palm [52] have demonstrated
     the *formal* equivalence of the time series and simultan-
     eous equations approaches.

30.  Jonson *et al.* [30].   Within the strict sampling-
     theoretical frame of inference associated with the use of
     maximum likelihood, the above procedure is only valid if
     the likelihood at the preferred point in the parameter
     space is not significantly lower than its global maximum.
     Unfortunately, the available $\chi^2$ test is only asymptoti-
     cally valid.   Moreover, experience in the demand systems
     area [33] has detected a serious small sample bias in this
     context towards accepting significant differences in like-
     lihood when in fact none exists.

31.  This is one of the considerations leading to the proposals
     for indirect validation of ORANI through its interface
     with a smaller model, described below in Section 5.

32.  Circulated report of Conference discussion.

33.  In any event, the assumption that real aggregate absorp-
     tion remains fixed under a change in commercial policy
     leaves room for the independent exercise of monetary and
     fiscal instruments in the determination of real absorp-
     tion.

34.  The above discussion is highly stylized and abstracts
     from all of the more difficult aspects of the problem.
     These are thoroughly dealt with by Russel J. Cooper and
     Keith R. McLaren in [10].

35.  While the approach described above is showing promising
     preliminary results, it is not difficult to think of
     shocks  z  for which difficulties could arise.   This is
     particularly likely to be the case if expectational lags
     and/or other frictions are long, but differ among differ-
     ent variables.   A version of ORANI introducing adjustment
     lags has been specified algebraically, but so far has not
     been implemented [23].

36.  This statement refers to ORANI 78 [14].   The earlier

version of ORANI [20] only recognised one type of
agricultural land.

37. With the advent of a much more powerful generation of
computers, the cost of computing solutions to WJ models
expressed in levels may decline so rapidly as to make
design of efficient algorithms redundant. At this point
(not discernable given the current outlook for development of computer hardware) it may be possible to use
general purpose algorithms to solve medium sized (or even
large) WJ models in the levels.

38. This statement remains true if the phrase 'represented by
a quadratic form in the levels of the variables, or in
simple monotonic transformations of them,' is substituted
for 'translog.'

39. For some variables, and some circumstances involving very
large non-uniform changes, it may be necessary to enter-
tain further iterations. We suspect that even here it
may be possible to predict the full non-linear solution
from relatively few iterations.

[1]    Adelman, I., and S. Robinson, *Income Distribution Policy
       in Developing Countries : A Case Study of Korea*
       (Stanford University Press, Stanford, 1977).

[2]    Alaouze, C. M., Estimates of the Elasticity of Substi-
       tution Between Imported and Domestically Produced
       Goods Classified at the Input-Output Level of
       Aggregation, IMPACT Working Paper No. O-13, Indust-
       ries Assistance Commission, Melbourne, October 1977.

[3]    Alaouze, C. M., J. S. Marsden, and J. Zeitsch, Estimates
       of the Elasticity of Substitution Between Imported
       and Domestically Produced Goods at the Four-Digit
       ASIC Level, IMPACT Working Paper No. O-11, Industries
       Assistance Commission, Melbourne, July 1977.

[4]    Ando, A., On a Theoretical and Empirical Basis of Macro-
       econometric Models, Paper presented to the NBER-NSF
       Conference on Macroeconometric Models, Ann Arbor,
       Michigan, October 26-27, 1978, this volume.

[5]    Bergstrom, A. R., and C. R. Wymer, A Model of Disequili-
       brium Neoclassical Growth and its Application to the
       United Kingdom, in A. R. Bargstrom (ed.), *Statistical
       Inference in Continuous Time Econometric Models*
       (North-Holland, Amsterdam, 1976).

[6]    Bruno, M. A Programming Model for Israel, Chapter 12 in
       I. Adelman and E. Thorbecke (eds), *The Theory and
       Design of Economic Development* (Johns Hopkins,
       Baltimore, 1966), 327-352.

[7]    Challen, D. W., and A. J. Hagger, Economy Wide Modelling
       with Special Reference to Australia, Economic Society
       of Australia and New Zealand, Eighth Conference of
       Economists, La Trobe University, Melbourne, Australia,
       August 1979;  paper available from Department of
       Economics, University of Tasmania, Hobart, Tasmania,
       Australia, 7000.

[8]    Clements, K. W., *The Trade Balance in Monetary General
       Equilibrium* (Garland Publishing Company, New York,

forthcoming).

[9]     Clements, K. W., A General Equilibrium Econometric
        Model of the Open Economy, *International Economic
        Review* (forthcoming).

[10]    Cooper, R. J., and K. R. McLaren, The ORANI-MACRO Inter-
        face, IMPACT Preliminary Working Paper No. IP-10,
        University of Melbourne, May 1980.

[11]    Dervis, K., Planning Capital-Labour Substitution and
        Intertemporal Equilibrium with a Non-linear Multi-
        sector Growth Model, *European Economic Review* 6
        (1975), 77-96.

[12]    Dixon, P. B., A Skeletal Version of ORANI 78 : Theory,
        Data, Computations and Results, IMPACT Preliminary
        Working Paper No. OP-24, Industries Assistance
        Commission, Melbourne, June 1979.

[13]    Dixon, P. B., A Jointmax Algorithm for the Solution of
        SNAPSHOT, IMPACT Preliminary Working Paper No. SP-03,
        Industries Assistance Commission, Melbourne, April
        1976.

[14]    Dixon, P. B., B. R. Parmenter, J. Sutton and D. P.
        Vincent, *ORANI, A Multi-Sectoral Model of the
        Australian Economy* (North-Holland, Amsterdam, forth-
        coming).

[15]    Dixon, P. B., and D. P. Vincent, The SNAPSHOT Model :
        Underlying Theory and an Application to the Study of
        the Implications of Technical Change in Australia to
        1990, IMPACT Preliminary Working Paper No. SP-14,
        Industries Assistance Commission, Melbourne, October
        1979, forthcoming in *Economic Record*.

[16]    Dixon, P. B., A. A. Powell, and B. R. Parmenter, *Struct-
        ural Adaptation in an Ailing Macroeconomy* (Melbourne
        University Press, Melbourne, 1979).

[17]    Dixon, P. B., B. R. Parmenter, A. A. Powell and D. P.
        Vincent, The Agricultural Sector of ORANI 78 :

Theory, Data and Application, IMPACT Preliminary Working Paper No. OP-25, Industries Assistance Commission,
Melbourne, June 1979.

[18]   Dixon, P. B., and B. R. Parmenter, A Reply to Burley, 201-
214 in C. J. Aislabie and C. A. Tisdell (eds) *The Economics of Structural Change and Adjustment*, No. 5 in the
Conference Series of the Institute of Industrial Economics, University of Newcastle, N.S.W., Australia,
May 1979.

[19]   Dixon, P. B., J. D. Harrower, and D. P. Vincent, Valida-
tion of the SNAPSHOT Model, IMPACT Preliminary Working
Paper No. SP-12, Industries Assistance Commission,
Melbourne, July 1978.

[20]   Dixon, P. B., B. R. Parmenter, G. J. Ryland, and J. Sutton,
*ORANI, A General Equilibrium Model of the
Australian Economy : Current Specification and Illustra-
tions of Use for Policy Analysis*, First Progress Report
of the IMPACT Project, Volume 2 (Canberra, Australian
Government Publishing Service, 1977).

[21]   Eckstein, O., Economic Theory and Econometric Models,
Paper presented to the NBER-NSF Conference on Macro-
econometric Models, Ann Arbor, Michigan, October 26-
27, 1978, this volume.

[22]   Evans, H. D., *A General Equilibrium Analysis of Protection : The Effects of Protection in Australia* (North-
Holland, Amsterdam, 1972).

[23]   FitzGerald, V. W., A Variant of the ORANI Model for the
Analysis of Short-Period Responses, IMPACT Preliminary
Working Paper No. OP-23, Industries Assistance Commis-
sion, Melbourne, April 1979.

[24]   Goodman, S. H., Overview of the CIA Trade Flow Model
Project, Office of Economic Research, Central Intell-
igence Agency, Washington, D.C., April 1974; Paper
presented to the Winter Meeting of the Econometric
Society, December 1973.

[25] Goreux, L. M., *Interdependence in Planning : Multilevel Programming Studies of the Ivory Coast* (Johns Hopkins for the World Bank, Baltimore, 1977).

[26] Hillier, G. H., and D. E. A. Giles, Estimation in Equilibrium Models Involving Discretionary Instruments Choice : An Application to the Australian Monetary Sector; Paper presented to Section 24 of the 49th Congress of the Australian and New Zealand Association for the Advancement of Science, Auckland, New Zealand, January 1979 (available from the Department of Econometrics and Operations Research, Monash University, Clayton, Victoria, Australia, 3168).

[27] Johansen, L., *A Multisectoral Study of Economic Growth* (North-Holland, Amsterdam, 1960).

[28] Jonson, P. D., Money and Economic Activity in the Open Economy : The United Kingdom, 1880-1970, *Journal of Political Economy* 84 (1976), 979-1012.

[29] Jonson, P. D., E. R. Moses, and C. R. Wymer, The RBA 76 Model of the Australian Economy, in *Conference in Applied Economic Research, December 1977* (Reserve Bank of Australia, Sydney, 1978), 9-36.

[30] Jonson, P. D., J. C. Taylor, M. W. Butlin, J. K. Eberhardt, and R. W. Rankin, Development and Use of RBA 76, in *Conference in Applied Economic Research, December 1977* (Reserve Bank of Australia, Sydney, 1978), 37-114.

[31] Klein, L. R., *Economic Fluctuations in the United States 1921-1941* (Wiley, New York, 1950).

[32] Koopmans, Tj. C. (ed.), *Statistical Inference in Dynamic Economic Models*, Cowles Commission Monograph 10 (Wiley, New York, 1950).

[33] Laitinen, K., Why is Demand Homogeneity So Often Rejected? *Economic Letters* 1 (1978), 187-191.

[34]  Leamer, E. C., *Specification Searches : Ad Hod Inference with Non-experimental Data* (Wiley, New York, 1978).

[35]  Lipsey, R. G., World Inflation, Charles Joseph La Trobe Memorial Lecture, La Trobe University, Melbourne, Australia, 1979 2;  Reprinted in *Economic Record* 55 (1979), 283-296.

[36]  McLaren, K. R., The Optimality of Rational Distributed Lags, *International Economic Review* 20 (1979), 183-192.

[37]  McMenamin, J. S., and J. P. Pinard, Specification and Estimation of Dynamic Demand Systems Incorporating Polynomial Price Response Functions : An Application to US Clothing Imports, *Journal of Econometrics* 7 (1978), 147-162.

[38]  Manne, A. S., Key Sectors of the Mexican Economy 1960-70, Chapter 16 in A. S. Manne and H. M. Markowitz (eds) *Studies in Process Analysis* (Wiley, New York, 1963), 379-400.

[39]  Marsden, J. S., and L. F. Milkovits, The Construction of Price and Quantity Indexes for Australian Trade Flows, IMPACT Preliminary Working Paper No. IP-03, Industries Assistance Commission, Melbourne, October 1977.

[40]  Norton, W. E., and P. D. Jonson, Macroeconomic Modelling : the RBA Experience,  Paper read to the Eighth Conference of Economists of the Economic Society of Australia and New Zealand, La Trobe University, August 1979 (available from Research Department, Reserve Bank of Australia, Sydney, N.S.W., Australia, 2000).

[41]  Powell, A. A., *The IMPACT Project : An Overview, March 1977*, First Progress Report of the IMPACT Project, Volume 1 (Canberra, Australian Government Publishing Service, 1977).

[42]  Powell, A. A., and B. R. Parmenter, The IMPACT Project as a Tool of Policy Analysis, *Australian Quarterly* 51 (1979), 62-74.

[43]  Powell, A. A., P. B. Dixon, and M. McAleer, Durables in

the Consumption Function : A Systems Approach to Employment Effects, IMPACT Preliminary Working Paper No. MP-02, Industries Assistance Commission, Melbourne, February 1977.

[43a] Powell, A. A., *Aspects of the Design of BACHUROO, An Economic-Demographic Model of Labour Supply*, Paper presented to the Taskforce on General Equilibrium Modeling, International Institute for Applied Systems Analysis, Laxenburg, Austria, November 1980.

[44] Sandee, J., *A Long Term Planning Model for India* (Asia Publishing House, New York, and Statistical Publishing Company, Calcutta, 1960).

[45] Sims, C., Review of E. Leamer's *Specification Searches*, in *Journal of Economic Literature* 17 (1979), 566-568.

[46] Taylor, L., Theoretical Foundations and Technical Implications, Chapter III in C. R. Blitzer, P. B. Clark and L. Taylor (eds), *Economy Wide Models and Development Planning* (Oxford University Press for the World Bank, New York, 1975), 100.

[47] Tinbergen, J., *On the Theory of Economic Policy* (North-Holland, Amsterdam, 1952).

[48] Vincent, D. P., P. B. Dixon, and A. A. Powell, The Estimation of Supply Response in Australian Agriculture : the CRESH/CRETH Production System, *International Economic Review* 21 (1980), 221-242.

[49] Vincent, D. P., P. B. Dixon, B. R. Parmenter, and D. C. Sams, The Short Term Effect of Oil Price Increases on the Australian Economy with Special Reference to the Agricultural Sector, *Australian Journal of Agricultural Economics* 23 (1979), 79-101.

[50] Wymer, C. R., *Computer Programs* (International Monetary Fund, Washington, D.C., 1977) (mimeo).

[51] Wymer, C. R., A Continuous Disequilibrium Model of United Kingdom Financial Markets, in A. A. Powell and

R. A. Williams (eds), *Econometric Studies of Macro and Monetary Relations* (North-Holland, Amsterdam, 1973), 301-334.

[52]    Zellner, A., and F. Palm, Time Series Analysis and Simultaneous Equation Econometric Models, *Journal of Econometrics* 2 (1974), 17-53.

LARGE-SCALE MACRO-ECONOMETRIC MODELS
J. Kmenta, J.B. Ramsey (editors)
© North-Holland Publishing Company, 1981

COMMENTS ON THE SIZE OF MACROECONOMIC MODELS

Robert H. Rasche

Economics Department
Michigan State University
East Lansing, Michigan
U.S.A.

My instructions were to concentrate my comments on the
Eckstein [2] paper to insure that all of the papers receive
some attention. Much of the Eckstein paper is devoted to a
discussion of the implications of the output of the DRI model
for current controversies such as 'crowding out', rational
expectations and sources of expectational errors. Since all of
these results are conditional on the structure of a particular
econometric model, a structure whose details are not revealed
in this paper, I have chosen largely to ignore them, and
address my comments to the procedures through which the structure of the model evolves and the evolution of that structure.
As an introduction to some conjectures about the procedures
discussed by Eckstein, I would like to direct a few remarks
toward the Maddala [5] paper, since it arrived first and to
some extent it conditioned my reaction to the Eckstein paper.

Maddala proposes four measures of model size, all defined in terms of some number of equations or number of variables relative to the total sample size. It seems to me that
there is an additional dimension to the problem of defining
the size of an econometric model, which involves comparing the
number of independent parameters that are estimated with the
size of the information set that is available for the estimation. Maddala seems to suggest this in his example of two
single equation regression models, both with 50 explanatory
variables (and correspondingly 50 parameters to be estimated),
but with 100,000 and 60 observations respectively. He, as
would I, intuitively characterizes the latter as the 'larger'
model. In terms of this characteristic of size, I would define
a model as becoming 'large' for purposes of estimation as the

ratio of p, the number of independent parameters, to $(m+n_1)*T$, the total number of independent pieces of information available approaches 1, where m is the number of exogenous variables, $n_1$ is the number of stochastic equations, and T is the sample size. Conversely, a model in this sense becomes 'small' as this ratio approaches 0.0. The ultimate in 'small' models from this perspective is one in which all of the coefficients are assigned values by the model manufacturer based on apriori information. If model size is measured by the ratio of p to $(n_1+m)*T$, then the problem of expanding the model by adding identities or definitional relationships that do not involve any new exogenous variables is handled in a fashion that seems intuitively correct and also meets with prevailing practice. Two models that have the same number of stochastic equations and the same number of independent parameters, regardless of differences in the number of identities or definitions of the above type are the same size on this measure.

With this definition of model size, consider the estimation problem proposed by Maddala. Assume that a model is sufficiently large on Maddala's definition (4), so that FIML estimation is not feasible. Under such circumstances, Maddala advocates FIML with a diagonal covariance matrix as an appropriate, indeed it is his preferred estimation technique, and suggests that it is not only feasible, but computationally no more burdensome than some alternative iterative estimation techniques. Why should this latter estimator be feasible when FIML is not, yet on any of Maddala's four definitions of size there has been no change? Clearly it is appropriate to view the Maddala proposal as a respecification of the model structure such that the number of independent parameters to be estimated have been reduced. In the pure diagonal case, the reduction is $n_1(n_1-1)/2$ parameters. The reductions in 'size' associated with such constraints can be appreciable. Consider a model with 60 stochastic equations and an average of 10 independently estimated parameters per equation. Without constraints, the dimensionality of the parameter vector is in excess of 2400; with the Maddala constraints it is 660. Thus the 'size' of the constrained model is only about 1/4 of the unconstrained model:  the model is much 'smaller'.

With this lengthy introduction, I would like to direct my comments on the Eckstein paper to the section devoted to model validation.  Eckstein describes a series of exercises that are applied to each reestimation of the DRI model, before the final set of parameter estimates are accepted.  This process has been characterized by Howrey, Klein and McCarthy [3] as Tender Loving Care.  TLC would appear to be one of the most controversial aspects of current econometric practice; being adamently defended by the model manufacturers and strongly criticized by the statisticians.  What is TLC and why should it be offered?

Consider the list of DRI TLC (validation) exercises elaborated by Eckstein.  These include computing the value of important policy multipliers, examining the implied values and elasticities of income shares, computing implied Engel curves, determining the behavior of the model under conditions of balanced growth, and exposing the model the 'destructive' tests. My conjecture is that most, if not all of these TLC exercises are checks on apriori constraints on the parameters of the model.  The problem is that specific constraints that the model manufacturer has in mind are not easily specified in terms of the structural parameters, but rather are specified in terms of some set of derived reduced form parameters, or even some set of derived final form parameters.  If this interpretation is correct, then the TLC process consists of an iterative estimation procedure that procedes until the estimated parameters satisfy the implicit constraint.  At least to the extent that the implicit constraints are equality constraints, the TLC process can be viewed as reducing the 'size' of the model in the sense suggested above, since the application of the constraint (as an equality) reduces the number of independent parameters.  Viewed this way, Eckstein's validation procedures are analogous to the procedures advocated by Maddala to reduce the FIML model to a feasible 'size' for estimation.  Consequently, the DRI model is probably a much 'smaller' model than is conventionally believed.  Given the multiplicity of the validation checks, it may possibly be a 'very small' model.

If this conjecture is a proper view of TLC, then several questions are raised.  The first is whether or not there is an objective basis for the implicit constraints on the structural coefficients, or are they purely subjective?  I think that it is possible to identify two sources of objective apriori contraints of this form.  This first is economic theory. Howrey-Klein and McCarthy [3] argue 'Economic theory ... cannot, however, set out in advance what the precise lag structure is nor all the departures from linearity'.  What economic theory does suggest is equilibrium constraints responses of various endogenous variables to sustained changes in exogenous variables. In the case of linear structural models, this translates into constraints on the derived final form coefficients.

The second source of objective apriori constraints is information that is not included in the sample on which the model is estimated.  Most econometric models use only a small fraction of the data that is available on even one economy. Typically, in the case of popular U.S. models this involves quarterly time series data over a period of 20-25 years, although in some cases they may be annual or even monthly time series.  Certainly other information generated by the economy exists, and even though it may not be convenient to explicitly incorporate it into the model structure, there is no reason why such data should not be used to establish apriori standards for the behavior of the model.  It seems to me that Eckstein's examples of checking the Engel curve implications and the range of fluctuation of income shares are examples of the use of this type of information to impose apriori constraints on the structure of the model.

The second question raised by this view of TLC is really a challenge to the econometrics theoreticians.  Can estimators be developed that can explicitly introduce the type of con- straints discussed above in terms of constraints on structural parameters.  In principle, the answer to this question is probably that such an estimator exists.  All that has to be done is to state explicitly the constraints in terms of the structural parameters of the model and apply FIML subject to the (nonlinear) constraints on the structural parameters.  In practice, it seems to me that it will be difficult, if not impossible to state the constraint in this form. Thus for practical purposes it would seem that we need to know if there are any systematic and convergent techniques for iterating an estimator until such constraints are achieved?

The third question is probably the most important and is directed toward the model manufacturer. If the conjecture about the nature of TLC is correct, then isn't an explicit statement of all such prior constraints that have been applied an integral part of the definition of the model. Without such a list it is impossible for an independent researcher to replicate the estimation and the conventionally reported test statistics are meaningless. Current practice does not include such a statement, but I suspect that most model manufacturers are capable of constructing such a list, if not expost for existing models, at least exante during the course of the reestimation of such models.

If as econometric modelers, we seek recognition as scientists rather than association by innuendo with crystal ball gazers or witch doctors, then it would be prudent for us to provide adequate information for independent analysts to assess the 'size' and statistical properties of the models. Without such information, it is impossible to determine if a given economic property of the model is an assumption or a conclusion. The implication of Eckstein's description of the DRI modeling process is that we have a long way to go before such a standard is the generally accepted research procedure.

A second aspect of Eckstein's paper that warrants attention is his response to the Lucas [4] critique. As Eckstein appropriately notes, changes in policy regimes are merely a subset of the events that could render the structure of an econometric model inadequate for forecasting and/or policy analysis. Eckstein suggests that historical changes in policy regimes or other shocks have not proved troublesome in this respect.

A retrospective analysis of the DRI model (or models) suggests that such a conclusion may be unduly optimistic. In Table 1, selected dynamic fiscal policy multipliers under

TABLE 1

D.R.I. MODEL:  SELECTED FISCAL POLICY MULTIPLIERS

1974 VINTAGE[3]

| With Accomodating Monetary Policy[1] | 10 quarters 3.1[p] | 9 quarters 2.3[p] |
|---|---|---|
| | 24 quarters 2.1 | 32 quarters 0.0 |
| | 40 quarters 1.0 | |

| With Non Accomodating Monetary Policy[2] | 10 quarters 2.3[p] | 5 quarters 1.9[p] |
|---|---|---|
| | 40 quarters 2.0 | 20 quarters  .5 |

[1]Unchanged federal funds rate.

[2]Unchanged unborrowed reserves.

[3]Five billion real dollar shock to federal government purchases of goods and services.

[4]10 billion real dollar shock to federal government purchases of goods and services.

p = Peak multiplier.

Sources:  D.R.I. 1974 VINTAGE:  Eckstein, O., Green, E. W., and Sanai, A., The Data Resources Model: Uses, Structure and Analysis of the U.S. Economy, in:  Klein, L. R., and Burmeister, E., (eds.), Econometric Model Performance, (Pennsylvania, Philadelphia, 1976) p. 228.

D.R.I. 1978 VINTAGE:  Eckstein, O., Economic Theory and Econometric Models, this volume, Chart 2.

conditions of accomodating and nonaccomodating monetary policies are compared for two vintages of the DRI model.  My evaluation of these multipliers is that there has been a substantial shift in the implications of the DRI model over a four year period. The fiscal policy multipliers now peak earlier and are different in the long run.  If, as Eckstein suggests, the DRI model is 'closer to the monetarist than to the fiscalist position', then the model suffers from the same credability problems as those that likely plagued Benedict Arnold after 1778. If the DRI researchers have concluded 'that the potential expected benefit [of short-term demand management policy] is modest but it's variance is great', under the assumption of a stochastically stationary model structure, then I cannot help but suspect that such policies may have a negative expected value when one allows for the nonstationary of the structure. Perhaps DRI and other model proprietors should be subjected to truth in packaging regulations before they are allowed to market their wares to firms, policy makers, and/or government agencies such as the CBO. In the meantime, Caveat Emptor!

## REFERENCES

[1]  Eckstein, O., Green, E. W., and Sanai, A., The Data Resources Model: Uses, Structure and Analysis of the U.S. Economy, in: Klein, L. R., and Burmeister, E., (eds.), Econometric Model Performance, (Pennsylvania, Philadelphia, 1976).

[2]  Eckstein, O. "Economic Theory and Econometric Models," this volume.

[3]  Howrey, E. P., Klein, L. R., and McCarthy, M. D., Notes on Testing the Predictive Performance of Econometric Models, in: Klein, L. R., and Burmeister, E., (eds.), Econometric Model Performance, (Pennsylvania, Philadelphia, 1976).

[4]  Lucas, R. E., Econometric Policy Evaluation: A Critique, in: Brunner, K., and Meltzer, A. H., (eds.), The Phillips Curve and Labor Markets, (North Holland, Amsterdam, 1976).

[5]  Maddala, G. S., (1981) "Statistical Inference in Relation to the Size of the Model", this volume.

LARGE-SCALE MACRO-ECONOMETRIC MODELS
J. Kmenta, J.B. Ramsey (editors)
© North-Holland Publishing Company, 1981

ECONOMIC THEORY, MODEL SIZE AND MODEL PURPOSE: REMARKS

Edward C. Prescott

Department of Economics
University of Minnesota
Minneapolis, Minnesota

In these comments, the term equilibrium will be substituded for economic theory. Some substitution was necessary for the expression   Keynesian theory is also used, and I did not want to imply that Keynesian theory is not economics.  The Keynesian and equilibrium approaches are fundamentally different methods of reasoning and have radically different econometric implications.  The implication of equilibrium theory for the size of equilibrium macroeconometric models will be briefly explored in these remarks.  I will not comment on the implications of equilibrium theory for the size of Keynesian macroeconometric models nor the implications of Keynesian theory for the size of equilibrium macroeconometric models, except to say there are none.

It is not surprising then that John B. Taylor (1980) dodged the issue of equilibrium theory and Keynesian model size.  There is nothing to be said.  Instead, he contributed to aggregation theory.  His example demonstrates that within the Keynesian framework that the appropriate disaggregation, and therefore number of stochastic equations, depends upon the purpose to which the model is put as well as the theory underlying these equations.  The aggregation principle developed may also be applicable to equilibrium models.

In these comments, I will summarize some views most of which have been expressed elsewhere, but, not by others at this conference.  Throughout, the Lucas and Sargent (1979) view that equilibrium and Keynesian macro models are fundamentally different is adopted.  The objective is neither to evaluate the approaches nor to convince anyone that one is better than the other.  Rather the goal is to clarify the differences with particular emphasis on their differing econometric implications.

My definition of equilibrium is close to the one adopted by John B. Taylor. It is more general in that it does not assume market clearing though, of course, competitive equilibrium models are equilibrium models.  My definition of the equilibrium approach is the method of reasoning based on consistent maximizing behavior of agents given their preferences, the technology, the information structure, legal constraints and processes governing exogenous variables.  An econometric implication of this approach is that the Cowles simultaneous equation model, which is the econometric discipline of Keynesian theory, is inappropriate for studying macroeconomic phenomena. This point has been made by Lucas (1976) in his critique of the Keynesian approach. Sargent (1980) explains why the restrictions of the Cowles Commission variety, particularly exclusionary restrictions, are of little use in identifying dynamic equilibrium models and why error terms can not be added to the equations subsequent to the theorizing.

Dynamic equilibrium theory when there is uncertainty, which is needed if one is applying the full discipline of equilibrium theory to analyses of economic fluctuations, is a relatively recent development. This explains why only recently there was an equilibrium model of the business cycle. The econometric analysis needed for the construction of equilibrium econometric models is still at an embryotic stage (see Sargent (1979) for a review of the current state of this development). Resources allocated to its development have been modest when compared to those allocated to the Cowles simultaneous structural model. The task of developing the econometrics for the equilibrium approach is even more intellectually challenging than the task that the Cowles group faced.

There are a class of abstractions which have been labelled disequilibrium models. Some of these just assume the rate of change of prices is some function of the excess demand. Such efforts are truly disequilibrium structures. Other of these abstractions are attempts at developing a deeper understanding of the price setting phenomena. I would call these latter attempts equilibrium theories for consistent maximizing behavior is assumed. It is too early to judge whether any one of these many attempts has been successful. I am certain that ultimately these efforts will result in abstracts that will prove useful in developing testable theories of significant economic phenomena. My prediction is that some equilibrium theory will supersede the competitive theory in a way analogous to relativity superseding Newtonian mechanics. To carry the analogy further, I suspect competitive rather than the more general theory will be used for most applied problems in economics as Newtonian economics is used in most engineering applications. These generalizations will justify the use of the simpler theory as an adequate approximation.

There is a macroeconometric model which clearly is not Keynesian. It is the model of John B. Taylor (1979). It is a forward looking model based upon the staggered long term nominal wage contracts. Whether this model should be categorized as an equilibrium model is ambiguous for there is no explicit derivation of some of the assumed relationships based upon the problems facing the agents. If all the relationships followed from some more micro set of assumptions, and they very well could, the model is an equilibrium model. The econometric tools that Taylor employs are closely related to those meeded for equilibrium analyses and not those needed for Keynesian analyses.

One non issue is whether Keynesian macro models are scientific. The procedures for constructing and using such models are reasonably well defined. It is true that the process is not so well defined that we can automate the procedures using computers. Necessarily, judgment enters into the construction and use of the Keynesian macro models, but then, judgment enters into the construction and use of equilibrium macro models as well. Klein and McCarthy (1979) provide an excellent blueprint describing how to construct and use Keynesian macro models.

A second non issue is whether one approach is or is not realistic. Both the Keynesian and the equilibrium approaches require highly abstract models and necessarily neither is realistic. The world is complex and the art of scientific discovery is to provide a simplification that can be used to rationalize some set of observations and to answer certain questions such as predicting the effect of policy interventions.

This raises the issue of model purpose. For purposes of short run unconditional forecasting the equilibrium approach is dominated not only by Keynesian macro forecasting models but also by both a theoretic time series methods and the leading indicator approach. The survival and pre-eminence of the Keynesian macro models in the forecasting business suggest that they contribute to improved short-run forecasts. If so, the benefits of this activity far exceed its costs, for improved forecasts contribute to economic efficiency. An implication of equilibrium theory is not that these models are not useful in making short run forecasts. The implication is that the implied tradeoffs, except possibly in the very short run, are not the true ones and that anticipations of attempts to exploit short run tradeoffs alter these tradeoffs. It has been shown that the solution that ignores the effect of changes in the policy rule upon behavioral equations can be very inferior to some other policy rule within the context of equilibrium models capturing some of the elements of the economy.[1]

Taylor defines a model size to be the number of endogenous variables. This definition may be appropriate for Keynesian models but not for equilibrium models. As Sargent (1979) points out, there are no stochastic equations for equilibrium models just exogenous variables that affect the decisions of the economic agents and that are not observed by the econometrician. With the equilibrium approach one does not just tack stochastic disturbance terms onto equations. Therefore, some criterion other than the number of stochastic equations is needed to indicate the size of equilibrium models.

The size of equilibrium models is probably best indicated by the number of free parameters. Computational consideration necessitates small models in this parametric sense, for imposing the cross equation restrictions needed to identify the model is costly. With the equilibrium approach, a fixed point problem must be solved to determine the equilibrium process for each parameter point for which the likelihood function is evaluated.

Besides the cross equation restrictions, an added discipline of the equilibrium approach is that the estimated parameters of preference and technology must be consistent with findings in other applied areas. For example, the degree of risk aversion should be consistent with risk premia found in financial markets. The elasticity of substitution of leisure for consumption should be consistent with findings in labor economics. The estimated parameters of production relationships should be in line with micro production function studies. Just meeting this discipline has proven difficult.

FOOTNOTE:

1. See Kydland and Prescott (1977) for such an analysis within the framework of time being required to build new capital and an investment tax credit policy. See Prescott (1977) for a similar analysis within the framework of Fischer's (1977) long term nominal wage contract model.

REFERENCES:

1. Fischer, S., Long-term contracts, rational expectations and the optimal money supply rule, Journal of Political Economy 85 (1977) 191-206.

2. Klein, L.R. and McCarthy, M.D., A Blueprint for the Validation of an Econometric Model and its Forecasts, or How to Build an Econometric Model and use it to Produce Good Forecasts, University of Pennsylvania Research Report (Revised November 1979).

3. Kydland, F.E. and Prescott, E.C., Rules rather than discretion: the inconsistency of optimal plans, Journal of Political Economy 85 (1977) 473-93.

4. Lucas, R.E.,Jr., Econometric policy evaluation: a critique, in: Brunner, K. and Meltzer, A.H. (eds.), The Phillips Curve and Labor Markets, (North Holland, Amsterdam, 1977).

5. Lucas, R.E., Jr., and Sargent, T.J., After keynesian macro economics, Federal Reserve Bank of Minneapolis Quarterly Review 3 (spring 1979) 1-16.

6. Prescott, E.C., Should control theory be used for economic stabilization, in: Brunner, K. and Meltzer, A.H. (eds.), Optimal Policies, Control and Technology Export (North Holland, Amsterdam, 1977).

7. Sargent, T.J., Interpreting economic time series, Journal of Political Economy 88 (1980).

8.  Taylor, J.B., Estimation and control of a macroeconomic
    model with rational expectations, Econometrica 47 (1979)
    1267-86.

9.  Taylor, J.B., Economic theory, model size and model
    purpose, in:  Kmenta, J. and Ramsey, J.B. (eds.), Large
    Scale Macro-Econometric Models: Theory and Practice,
    (North-Holland, Amsterdam, 1981).

LARGE-SCALE MACRO-ECONOMETRIC MODELS
J. Kmenta, J.B. Ramsey (editors)
© North-Holland Publishing Company, 1981

Discussion by T. W. Anderson of

"STATISTICAL INFERENCE IN RELATION TO THE SIZE OF THE MODEL"

by

G. S. Maddala

This paper is a comprehensive and instructive survey of features of statistical inference arising when the number of equations and number of endogenous variables is large compared to the number of observations.  I am
flattered that in this written version the author quotes my coauthors and
me extensively on the comparison of LIML and 2SLS estimators in large
models.  In addition to including material from our technical reports, some
issued since the conference, much of my discussion of the paper as presented verbally has been incorporated into the current presentation.  Hence,
I am left with the opportunity of writing new comments on this paper.  In
fact, I shall amplify some of the remarks of the author comparing LIML,
2SLS, and OLS (single-equation) methods for large models.

We now know a great deal about the sampling distributions of the various
single-equation estimators, particularly the estimators of the coefficient
of one endogenous variable when the disturbances are normally distributed.
The expressions for the exact densities are too complicated to yield any
insight into properties of the estimators (except that the moments of the
LIML estimator are not finite).  However, Anderson and Sawa (1979) and
Anderson, Kunitomo, and Sawa (1980) have given tables of the distributions
of the 2SLS and LIML estimators, respectively, for $K_2$ = 2, 10, and 30  and
various values of the standardized structural coefficient and the non-
centrality parameter.  ($K_2$ is the number of exogenous variables in the
system that are not included in the particular equation.)  For typical
values of the standardized coefficient (Anderson, Morimune, and Sawa (1978))
the distributions of the 2SLS estimator are badly distorted when $K_2$ is
substantial, such $K_2$ = 10; the distortion increases with $K_2$.  (The
distribution of the OLS estimator is that of the 2SLS estimator with $K_2$
replaced by $K_2$ + T - m.)  The analysis from these tables leads to the
author's conclusion that the LIML estimator is preferred to the 2SLS estimator when there are many excluded predetermined variables--which is the
case in medium-sized and large models.  (Anderson, Kunitomo, and Sawa
(1980a) have presented a series of figures that show the comparison between
the 2SLS estimator and a slight modification of the LIML estimator.)

A strong reason that has been given for using the SSLS estimator instead of
the LIML estimator is that it is easier to compute while having the same
asymptotic distribution.  Here "asymptotic" may mean $\sigma \to 0$  or  $\delta^2 \to \infty$.
($T \to \infty$  is assumed to imply  $\delta^2 \to \infty$.)  Our results show that if  $K_2$  is
large the asymptotic theory holds poorly for the 2SLS estimator at reason-
able values of  $\sigma$, $\delta^2$, or  T.  The reason is again that the distribution is
distorted; the center (the median, say) is far from the parameter value.
This also implies that in large models the meaning of computed standard
errors in the 2SLS analysis is suspect as is the hypothesis testing of

279

coefficients.

The asymptotic approach has been developed with expansions of the Edgeworth type. The properties of these approximate distributions are consistent with those obtained from small samples. The comparisons also apply to the estimators of coefficients of several endogenous and exogenous variables. (See Fujikoshi, Morimune, Kunitomo, and Taniguchi (1979), for example.)

Another approach is to develop asymptotic theory, including Edgeworth-type expansions, under the condition that $K_2 \to \infty$ as well as $\delta^2 \to \infty$. (Patefield (1976), Kunitomo (1980) and unpublished work of Kunitomo and Morimune). In this theory the 2SLS estimator is not consistent, while the LIML estimator is consistent. They are both asymptotically normal, but the distribution of the 2SLS estimator is centered at a value different from the parameter (and has a smaller standard deviation). Intuitively we expect that this asymptotic theory will give better approximations to the exact distributions than the other asymptotic theories, and a study is under way to verify this conjecture.

Small sample distribution theory and asymptotic expansions of distributions have not been developed as much for full information estimators. However, one can expect that comparisons of FIML and 3SLS estimators will correspond to those of LIML and 2SLS estimators.

## REFERENCES

[1]  Anderson, T. W., Kunitomo, N., and Sawa, T. (1980a), Comparison of the densities of the TSLS and LIMLK Estimators for Simultaneous Equations, Technical Report No. 323, Economics Series, Institute for Mathematical Studies in the Social Sciences, Stanford University.

[2]  Fujikoshi, Y., Morimune, K., Kunitomo, and Taniguchi, M. (1979), Asymptotic expansions of the Distributions of the Estimates of coefficients in a Simultaneous Equation System, Technical Report No. 287, Economics Series, Institute for Mathematical Studies in the Social Science, Stanford University.

[3]  Patefield, W. M. (1976), On the Validity of Approximate Distributions Arising in Fitting a Linear Functional Relation, The Journal of Statistical Computation and Simulation, 5, 43-70.

IV.    CONSTRUCTION OF MACRO-ECONOMETRIC MODELS

LARGE-SCALE MACRO-ECONOMETRIC MODELS
J. Kmenta, J.B. Ramsey (editors)
© North-Holland Publishing Company, 1981

AN AUTOREGRESSIVE INDEX MODEL FOR THE U.S.,
1948-1975

Christopher A. Sims

Department of Economics
University of Minnesota
Minneapolis, Minnesota
U.S.A.

Innovation accounting, a scheme for analyzing the behavior
of a vector-valued time series based on the moving average representation, is described. The connection of the natural
structural interpretation of the scheme to Wold's ideas on the
causal interpretation of multiple-equation time series models
is laid out. A nine-variable model of the U.S. is discussed
as an example. The model is treated as a restricted vector
autoregression, imposing the "index model" form, and technical aspects of specifying and estimating such models are
discussed in an appendix.

## Introduction

In an earlier paper [1977b] I criticized large-scale macroeconometric
models constructed by the usual methods, suggested alternative methods,
and applied them to analysis of the German and U.S. economies. In interpreting any econometric model, one is implicitly or explicitly "identifying" the model, in the usual econometric sense of that word. That is, one
is assuming some connection between the estimated parameters of the model
and the behavior patterns of the people in the economy being modeled.
While the earlier paper was quite explicit about what is wrong with the
usual rules of identification as used in building standard models, it left
the rules of identification underlying my interpretation of loosely
structured models largely implicit. Because this makes it hard to discuss
the limitations of the methods, and because certain aspects of these
methods are being applied by other economists, this paper begins with a
discussion of the assumptions underlying the most direct interpretation of
what I call "innovation accounting."

As will become clear in the methodological discussion, it is critical
to the reliability of some of the conclusions obtained in the earlier paper
that the list of variables included in the model be rich enough. The
latter part of the paper discusses empirical results obtained with a model
for the U.S. similar in spirit to that of the earlier paper, but with a
longer list of variables. Many of the most important conclusions persist
despite the increase in number of variables: Unpredictable movements in
the money supply still are the dominant source of variation in the price
level; a "monetarist Phillips curve", in which relatively short-lived (2-
year) rises in real GNP and real wage follow a money shock again emerges;
and the real quantity variables as a block cannot be taken exogenous,
despite the fact that two of the three additional variables are components
of GNP. On the other hand, the larger model is in some respects more

hospitable to what might be labeled "Keynesian" views.  In the larger
model a slightly larger proportion of variance of real quantity variables
is accounted for by innovations in real quantities, which focuses attention on an aspect of the earlier paper's results which received little comment in the text of the paper: Most variance in real GNP and unemployment is
not accounted for by variables associated with monetary policy.  The view
that the main source of instability in the U.S. economy has been unpredictable policy shifts of the Federal Reserve looks implausible in the
light of these results.  Also, the "monetarist Phillips curve" is mediated
by interest rates movements, with money supply movements which are not
associated with interest movements having very different effects on real
quantity variables.

## Innovation Accounting

        We begin by assuming we are dealing with an mx1 vector time series
$y(t)$.  Denote by $\hat{y}(t)$  the best linear forecast of  $y(t)$ based on $y(s)$,
$s < t$.[1]  The innovation in  $y(t)$  is then defined as  $y(t) - \hat{y}(t)$.  Because the innovation in  $y(t)$,  $e(t)$, is itself a linear combination of
current and past values of  $y(t)$  for each t,  $e(t)$  is serially uncorrelated.  Under rather general conditions,  $y(t)$  can be expressed as a
linear combination of current and past innovations.  Under slightly more
restrictive conditions, the coefficients on  $e(t-s)$  in the formula ex-
pressing  $y(t)$ as a linear combination of  $e(t-s)$  for  $s \geq 0$ depends only
on  s, not on  t.[2]  The representation of  $y(t)$  as a linear combination
of current and past innovations, i.e. as a distributed lag on  $e(t)$, is
called the moving average representation (MAR) of  y.  We will assume
further that  $y(t)$  can be approximated well by a finite linear combination of past  y's, with the weight on  $y(t-s)$  dependent on  s  but not
t.[3]  This leads us to a linear regression equation of the form

1)      $y(t) = \Sigma^q_{s=1} A(s)y(t-s) + e(t).$

If the equation is exact, i.e. if  $\hat{y}$  is an exact function of  q  past
y's, then the usual distribution theory applies to least-squares estimation of the A's in this equation asymptotically, if we assume  $e(t)$  has
constant finite variance and that  y  is the conditional expectation of
y  given past  y.[4]

        Once we have estimated the  A's  (the coefficients of what is called
the autoregressive representation or AR) it is a straightforward exercise
to compute the coefficients of the moving average representation.  Suppose
the MAR is written

2)      $y(t) = \Sigma^\infty_{s=1} B(s)e(t-s).$

Then it is not too hard to see that the  i,j'th component of  $B(s)$,
$b_{ij}(s)$, when treated as a function of  s,  traces out the response of  $y_i$
over time to an initial condition in which all past values of all variables
are zero except for  $y_j(0)$, which is unity.  Thus while the coefficients
$A(s)$  in the AR are the coefficients of the reduced form of a standard
econometric model, the coefficients in  $B(s)$  can be thought of as obtained
from simulations of the model.

There is a common-sense rule which states that it is dangerous to simulate a model's response to conditions widely different from what occurred in the sample period. Since $e(t)$ is serially uncorrelated, a unit shock of the type "simulated" in the $B(s)$ coefficients is not unlike the sample behavior of $e$ as regards serial correlation. However, the components of $e$ may be contemporaneously correlated. If these correlations are high, simulation of a shock to $y_j(0)$ while all other components of $y$ are held at zero, may be misleading. E.g., if GNP and unemployment have negatively correlated innovations, simulation of the economy's response to a unit shock to GNP while unemployment remains fixed may imply a pattern of movement in $y$ which is unlike anything which has occurred historically and is likely therefore to be unreliable.

Furthermore, because of the contemporaneous correlation among components of $e$, it is not possible to partition the variance of $y$ into pieces accounted for by each innovation. For these two reasons it is appealing to apply an orthogonalizing transformation to $e$, to obtain $v(t) = Ge(t)$, where $G$ is a matrix chosen to make the covariance matrix of $v(t)$ the identity. There are many ways one could choose $G$, but for reasons we will discuss below it is natural to consider first $G$'s of triangular form. The triangular form preserves the connection of the elements of $v$ with the corresponding variables in $y$, in the sense that, if $G$ is lower triangular, $v_j(t)$ is the normalized error in forecasting $y_j(t)$ from past values of the $y$ vector and current values of $y_i(t)$ for $i < j$. We can represent $y$ as

3) $\quad y(t) = \sum_{s-1}^{\infty} B(s)G^{-1}v(t-s).$

The components of the matrix function $B(s)G^{-1}$ thus are still interprable as responses to "shocks" in particular variables, but now the shocks are of a more typical sort and, because the components of $v$ are uncorrelated, we can allocate the variance of each element in $y$ to "sources" in elements of $v$. In particular, the sum of squares from $s = 0$ to $s = T$ of the $i,j$'th component of $B(s)G^{-1}$ represents the component of error variance in the $T + 1$ step-ahead forecast of $y_i$ which is accounted for by innovations in $y_j$.

The moving average representation and the allocation of forecast error variance to innovations summarize the average behavior of the system over the sample period. One can also analyze particular historical episodes by locating the dates of unusually large innovations and using the MAR to determine what aspects of the subsequent evolution of the system the large innovations account for. My own work [1977b] and joint work with Sargent [1977] has concentrated on displaying the "average" characteristics of systems, while Robert J. Gordon [1977], and Gordon and J.A. Wilcox [1978], using closely related methods, has emphasized historical analysis of particular episodes.

As an example of how these methods get fleshed out with economic interpretation, suppose we were interested in whether an inflationary period beginning at date $t$ can in fact be largely attributed to "wage push". A natural procedure would be to fit a vector AR system to a set

of variables including wages, prices, and other relevant variables.[5] One
then asks if there were large wage-innovations near date  t.  If not, it
would not seem reasonable to attribute the inflation to "wage-push",
since even if wage changes were large near  t,  they were explainable by
reactions according to the usual pattern to past values of other variables
in the system.  If there was a large wage-innovation near  t,  one can
then use the MAR to determine whether it had substantial influence on
subsequent developments in prices.  If not, it seems reasonable to claim
that the wage "shock" at  t  does not explain the subsequent general inflation.  We can even see a natural policy implication of such analysis:
if it turned out that large wage-innovations account for most of inflation, historically, we might conclude that government intervention in
the wage-bargaining process would be the most effective method of controlling general inflation.  R.J. Gordon's [1977] international analysis
inflation is in part in the spirit of this example.

As another example, we might interpret the proportion of inflation
accounted for by innovations in the money stock (either in a historical
simulation or in a partition of variance) as a measure of how much of
inflation is accounted for by surprise shifts in monetary policy.[6] If a
great deal of inflation were accounted for this way, we might then conclude that the case for rigidly specified money-supply rule (e.g. a
fixed percentage growth rate) was strengthened.

Using a model to generate policy conclusions is by definition the
process of identifying a structure for the model, in the sense of, e.g.,
Hurwicz [1960].  In the next section the rules of identification underlying the foregoing examples are made explicit and compared with the
usual rules of identification in econometrics.

## Wold-Causal Identification

Interpretation of MAR's along the lines of the foregoing example
rests on an assumed connection between innovations in a variable (or more
generally in a block of variables) and events originating in a behavior-
ally distinct sector.  Thus in the example we assume that wage-innovations
arise in the wage-bargaining mechanism and that policy measures exist
which might affect such events without changing the behavior of other
"sectors" of the economy.[7]  As has already been mentioned, the AR is a
conventional "reduced form" if a model has no exogenous variables.  When
there are exogenous variables, we can obtain an AR by appending to the
conventional reduced form an AR for the exogenous variables.  Thus the
style of interpretation we are discussing involves making a connection
between reduced form residuals (the innovations) and sectors.  In the conventional style of econometric identification  there is no such connection.
In the conventional style sectors are connected to equations of the
"structural form" of the model.  Residuals from structural form equations
might then be interpreted as shocks originating in the corresponding
sector, but in general structural-form residuals are related to reduced-
form residuals by an arbitrary linear transformation.  Each reduced-form
residual is an unrestricted mixture of shocks to all sectors.  From this
point of view there is no sense in the innovation-accounting scheme,
since the innovation in a particular variable has no structural interpretation.

In practice, however, it is quite reasonable to make connections between variables and sectors, as reflected in the usual names of equations in macro-economic models: "investment", "consumption", "price", "wage", etc. One names equations for the most part according to the variable appearing on the left-hand side, though from the point of view of statistical theory the left-hand-side variable could be any endogenous variable in the equation. The equation corresponding to a sector must have on the left a variable which we are sure enters the equation with a non-zero coefficient on the current value. Generally there are only a small number of variables, or even only one, for which we can be sure of this. In other words, generally there are only a few variables which we are sure reflect immediately disturbances originating in a given sector. If it should in fact be true that only a few variables reflect immediately disturbances in the sector, then only those few variables appear contemporaneously in the structural form equations for that sector. In the conventional notation, the structural system

4)     $\Gamma y(t) + \beta X(t) = u(t)$.

where $X(t)$ is the vector of predetermined variables, has a block diagonal $\Gamma$ matrix. Under these conditions, the reduced form residuals for a block are linear combinations of the structural equation residuals for the block; the innovations in the block's variables are determined by shocks originating in that sector. This situation justifies the interpretation of innovation accounting along the lines of the examples.

While this argument does not require any assumptions on correlations among innovations, if in fact innovations show strong correlations across sectors, identification along these lines is strained. We might suppose, for example that wage innovations pertain to a "wage-bargaining" sector and money innovations to a "monetary policy" sector; but if these two innovations are strongly correlated our assumption that these two sectors are in fact distinct becomes questionable. Thus it seems reasonable to append to the assumption that only a few variables react immediately to shocks in a given sector the assumption that shocks from distinct sectors should be only weakly correlated.

With this additional specification, the connection of innovations to sectors becomes testable. Most directly, we can simply check to see whether correlations of innovations in different sectors are "large". In a model with many variables, however, it may not be clear how to decide what is a "large" set of correlations. An operational criterion can be provided by making the triangular decomposition of the covariance matrix which we discussed as part of the innovation accounting scheme. If our connection of variables to sectors is correct and if correlations of shocks across sectors are small, conclusions based on the innovation-accounting scheme should not change much when the ordering of the sectors is varied before the triangular orthogonalization.

In practice, it turns out that some conclusions are robust to the ordering of variables and some are not. When conclusions shift according to the ordering of variables, we need not necessarily abandon efforts at interpretation. For example, one can imagine correlations between money innovations and investment innovations arising from attempts by the monetary authority to stabilize interest rates. It could even happen that the main source of "surprises" in the money stock was shifts in investment demand. It is natural to check for this possibility by observing how the system responds to a money innovation -- if a money innovation results in a drop in interest rates, it is not likely that it is mainly a passive response to an increase in investment demand. In making this kind of interpretation, we begin to use detailed a priori hypotheses about the form of the equations in the various sectors. While in the paper's empirical work we do not do so, one can extend this method of interpreting innovations according to a priori notions of what the structure looks like, until in the limit one is testing the fit of a model which is a fully identified structure -- that is, a model in which the parameters of the AR are one-to-one functions of the parameters of a structural model, as in conventional econometric work.

Recapitulating the preceding paragraphs, it is suggested that one begin by fitting an unstructured AR, attempting an interpretation of it via the MAR and the "natural" interpretation of the innovations. In doing this one tries various triangular orthogonalizations of the innovations, which amounts to trying various Wold causal chain forms for the model. When results are sensitive to the ordering of variables in the orthogonalization, one may make some progress by using a priori hypotheses about the structure. At this final stage one might end up doing something quite similar to estimating overidentified structural models by usual econometric models.

One might ask where the main difference between this and standard methodology lie -- even whether there are important differences. There are two main differences. The first is that the unstructured MAR is estimated first, and used as a standard. The conventional approach (in principle) treats the unrestricted reduced form as a corresponding standard. The "unrestricted" reduced form in fact embodies restrictions excluding lagged values of some endogenous variables from the system, and is likely to include strictly exogenous variables whose strict exogeneity is not subject to test. Also, if residuals from the unrestricted reduced form are serially correlated the conventional approach is to "correct" for the serial correlation, rather than to insist that all the serial correlation be explained by the model. The second main difference is that the approach suggested here does not presume that a unique, unambiguous structural interpretation exists. Even if, at the final stage of the analysis, an overidentified model is estimated, it is to be expected that more than one such model may be tried, their relative merits in capturing the form of the unrestricted MAR to be compared.

Besides the work already cited by Gordon, there is recent work by Hall [1978], Sargent [1977], and Taylor [1978], which proceeds somewhat in the spirit I am suggesting. None of these three experiments with Wold chain interpretations as Gordon and I do, but all three insist that their models account for a complete multivariate serial correlation structure. Sargent and Taylor make direct comparisons of their overidentified models with unrestricted AR alternatives. Hall entertains multiple structural interpretations of the same estimated pattern of serial correlations.

## Innovation-accounting, Granger Causality, and their Pitfalls

Each element of the innovation vector  e  is by construction causally prior in Granger's sense[8]  to all the variables in the estimated AR. The natural, direct, interpretation of the innovation-accounting scheme amounts to giving the natural interpretation to a Granger causal ordering. All the debate and confusion in the econometric literature about interpretation of Granger orderings is thus relevant to innovation accounting as well. I will summarize here some of the main pitfalls of interpreting Granger orderings which I laid out in an earlier paper [1976].

Prices for durable goods set in auction markets are likely to appear causally prior to all other variables. This is an implication of the "perfect market" hypothesis. Thus in a system with, say, a stock-price index included, we should expect that when the innovations are orthogonalized with stock-prices low in the ordering, innovations in other variables will explain little of stock prices. We should not interpret this to mean that stock prices do not depend on the rest of the economy, unless the result persists when other orderings of the variables are used in the triangular orthogonalization.

If one variable in a system of closely related variables is much more heavily affected by measurement error than other variables in the system, it will tend to appear passive. That is, innovations in a variable measured with great error, since they will consist largely of measurement error, will not explain much of the subsequent evolution of other variables. Also, in a system which, with correctly measured variables, would show sharp causal orderings, measurement error will tend to obscure those orderings.

Optimal control of a policy variable to minimize variance in a target variable may lead the policy variable to appear passive. This is not in itself misleading in the context of innovation accounting, except that in this situation the target variable innovations will in general be contaminated by any uncontrollable shocks in policy which may occur.

In all these three examples -- perfect markets, measurement error, and optimal control -- possibilities for error are somewhat more serious in innovation accounting than in testing formally for a causal ordering. As explained in the earlier paper, these three mechanisms cannot produce a Granger ordering without special, rather restrictive assumptions. It is a special form of optimal control, an extreme version of the perfect markets hypothesis, a special pattern of measurement error contamination, which leads to a causal ordering. Thus though these mechanisms could easily obscure a causal ordering which otherwise would be apparent, they cannot easily do the reverse -- make an ordering appear where there otherwise would be none. Sometimes in innovation-accounting we do reach conclusions about Granger-orderings -- e.g., "price and wage innovations have negligible effects on the real sector". But more often we are discussing less absolute conclusions -- "e.g., only 21% of the variance of GNP is accounted for by wage innovations". To get a spurious conclusion that wage-innovations account for no GNP variance would take an extreme pattern of measurement errors. To get a substantial downward bias in the percentage of variance in GNP accounted for in those innovations would take a less extreme pattern.

Omitted variables can easily obscure a Granger ordering. It is easy to verify that if $x_1$ and $x_2$ are jointly Granger-prior to $x_3$, $x_1$ is not likely to be Granger-prior to $x_3$ in the bivariate system consisting of $x_1$ and $x_3$ unless $x_1$ and $x_2$ are unrelated. This amounts to saying that, whereas in a trivariate system $x_3$ - innovations would explain no  $x_1$ - variance, in a bivariate system they might explain quite a bit.

Thus, e.g., if money responds passively to investment and government expenditure for the most part, a system including only money and aggregate GNP might nonetheless show money innovations accounting for a considerable fraction of GNP variance. This could happen if money reflected investment demand with a shorter delay than the delay between investment and its multiplier effects on other components of expenditure. A Keynesian who believes that the business cycle originates in autonomous shifts in demand, not in monetary policy, can rightly object to conclusions that much of the variance of GNP is accounted for by monetary policy shifts if it is based on innovation accounting for a system without measures of the most volatile components of expenditure.

## Nine-Variable Innovation Accounting

In the earlier paper [1977b] I showed results for an innovation-accounting for the U.S. and Germany of six variables:  Money (M), Real GNP (Y), Unemployment rate (U), Wage (W), Price (P), and Import Price (PM).[9]  These variables were chosen to allow a comparison of simple monetarist and simple Keynesian Phillips-curve analyses of inflation. The Keynesian Phillips curve view[10] that money has no effect on inflation except through its effect on real variables like labor market tightness or capacity utilization does not seem compatible with the data for either country. A "monetarist Phillips curve" -- money shocks generating temporary inflation, output increases, and unemployment decrease -- emerges in both countries in roughly similar form. Since these conclusions have a monetarist ring, the additional work reported here has expanded the list of variables in the direction of better articulating "autonomous expenditure" and including the interest rate. To the earlier list of variables has been added government expenditures (G), investment (I), and the interest rate (r).

Each country has one "target" variable (GNP for the US, P for Germany) whose variance is accounted for largely by its own innovation. Since the 6-variable model provides no explanation for such a variable, it was hoped that an expansion of the variable list might provide more insight into the sources of variance in these unexplained variables.

In the earlier paper, the AR was estimated as an unrestricted fourth-order autoregression. Each equation could therefore be consistently estimated by OLS; each contained 24 free coefficients (6 variables, 4 lags on each). The 9 variable system has 36 free coefficients in each equation in unconstrained form, and the same number of observations (about 108) per equation. While estimating 24 coefficients without constraints proved (to my surprise) to give reasonable results, estimating 36 per equation did not give reasonable results. The AR's in this paper are, therefore, estimated using what I have called observable "index models". These models limit the number of parameters in the AR by requiring that all cross-variable relations in the AR be expressible as common dependence of the  m  variables on  k  "indexes", which are themselves linear combinations of past values of the variables in the system.

The use of index models here raises questions concerning the extent to which the index restrictions fit and the extent to which results are affected by the index restrictions. In part because my efforts along

these lines are still rather limited, and in part because discussing how
well the index models perform would change the focus and extend the length
of this paper, these issues are treated only in an appendix. The discussion proceeds from here on the maintained hypothesis that the index-
model form, like the lag length chosen, is flexible enough not to distort
the prominent relationships which appear in the data.

The index models must be fit by iterative methods, as they are nonlinear. While the methods used in preparing this paper did achieve
"reasonable" fits, in the sense that individual equations residual sums of
squares were close to those emerging from smaller linear models, there
remains some question whether they produced fully converged parameter estimates. All the substantive conclusions in the paper ought therefore to
be treated as tentative, subject to confirmation with improved iterative
maximization methods.

Table 1 reproduces from Sims [1977b] the allocation of forecast
error variance to innovations from the U.S. 6-variable MAR, and Table 3
reproduces the corresponding accounting from the 9-variable MAR. Both
tables refer to triangularly orthogonalized innovations, with the order
of the variables as given in the tables. Tables 1 and 3 are in many important respects similar. Wages, prices, and import prices all have most
of their variance explained by money innovations over intermediate to long
horizons. This result emerges even more strongly in the 9-variable system.
Over intermediate horizons, much of GNP and unemployment variance is accounted for by GNP innovations. Money variance is largely accounted for
by money innovations. Looking at Charts 1-9, one can see that the nature
of the response to money innovations is broadly similar to that found in
the earlier paper: wages and prices respond, after a lag, roughly proportionately to money, which itself moves to a new level and persists there.
Price of imports also responds positively to the money innovation, though
more than proportionately as before. A monetarist Phillips curve is still
present, with output rising, unemployment falling, and the real wage rising
temporarily after a money innovation. The Keynesian Phillips curve hypothesis that quantity variables as a block are exogenous relative to money
and price variables is again rejected (with I and G added to the list
of quantity variables), with a $\chi^2$ (24) = 47.7, corresponding to a marginal significance level of about .002 and an F of 1.99.[11]

There are important differences, however, and they point for the most
part in the same direction: This larger system is less compatible with
the naive monetarist view that money is a powerful policy instrument and
that erratic monetary policy is a major source of instability in the
economy. Most obviously, the proportion of variance in GNP and unemployment accounted for in the long run by money innovations drops from .28 to
.12 and from .34 to .15, respectively. It is true that a substantial proportion of variance in these variables is now attributed to interest rate
innovations (.20 and .10, respectively), but when we examine the nature of
the system's response to money and interest innovations, it appears unreasonable to treat money and interest innovations as dominated by shifts
in monetary policy.

The GNP (Chart 2) and unemployment (Chart 3) response to a money innovation is smaller in magnitude than in the 6-variable system initially,
and then reverses sign to produce a negative movement in output as large
or larger than the initial positive movement. (In these respects the

response to a money innovation in this larger system is closer to what
was observed for the German data in the smaller system, though the duration of the positive effects on output is shorter in the 9-variable U.S.
system than in the 6-variable German system.) This pattern of oscillating
response to a money shock could be rationalized by a rational expectations
theory along the lines of the Lucas supply curve[12] -- when producers are
fooled into temporary expansions of monetary policy surprises, the resulting inefficiency reduces future output by as much as the initial gain
in output -- but the required degree of intertemporal substitutability
seems somewhat implausible to me.[13]

If interest-rate innovations are to be attributed to monetary policy
shocks to bring the total proportion of variance accounted for by monetary policy shocks up to a level comparable with that in the smaller system, more serious difficulties arise for a monetarist interpretation. If
injections of reserves affect deposits only with a delay, or if shifts in
policy-makers' notions of the appropriate size of the money stock are anticipated by investors, we might find monetary policy shocks showing up
first in the interest rate. A surprise rise in the interest rate would
then be expected to be followed by a contraction in the money supply, de-
flation, and a fall in output. As can be seen from Chart 2, surprise
rises in the interest rate not associated with contemporaneous surprises
in the money supply do, after considerable delay, result in declines in
output -- larger declines in output than those following negative innovations in the money supply. However, as can be seen from Chart 1, they
are not followed by any substantial drop in the money supply; as can be
seen from Chart 3 unemployment decreases in the first year following a
positive interest rate innovation; and as can be seen from Charts 4, 5 and
6 inflation follows an interest rate innovation, for more than a year.

These patterns themselves may simply reflect sampling error or dis-
tortions due to the index-model form. It might be best therefore to stop
here, having asserted that these patterns clearly are not characteristic
of a shift in money-supply behavior. Nonetheless, I offer some further
speculation. One way to rationalize the signs of the responses is by
comparative statics analysis in a textbook IS-LM framework, with the disturbing element in a downward shift in the full-employment level of output, money stock held constant. This should, in the usual framework,
lead to a new equilibrium with higher interest rate, lower output, and
higher price level. The difficulty with this explanation is that it
leaves the timing a puzzle -- the interest rate movement comes first, with
the drop in output much delayed. To explain the timing we might suppose
that the initial shock is a reduction in supply of durable raw materials.
The initial shock would then first push up the prices of these goods without a sudden effect on production because of the existence of inventories
and costs of rapidly adjusting employment and output. The speculative
activity associated with the rise in raw materials prices would drive up
interest rates immediately. Later, the volatile raw materials prices feed
their way into general price indices and wages, and the higher input
prices reduce output. The s-shaped response of unemployment to such a
shock might be explained as the combined effect of complementarity of raw
materials and labor, combined with speculative demand for labor in the
short run when it becomes apparent that labor costs will be rising.

This highly speculative explanation makes the U.S. results more compatible with the 6-variable German results. In Germany, substantial

feedback from prices to money appeared, and this does not show up in the U.S. Since the German economy is more open, its general price index might be more sensitive to raw materials prices. Also, the fact that the U.S. price index is the deflator for non-farm business product, while the German deflator is that for all of GNP, might be important. Since farm prices are highly volatile, they might contribute substantially to innovations in the GNP deflator and make its innovations more sensitive indicators of raw materials supply shocks. This explanation is also compatible with some of my own ongoing research on use of index-models for forecasting the U.S. economy. In this work, models with a roughly similar list of 9 variables, but with the GNP deflator replacing the business product deflator, show much more feedback of prices into real variables than appears in the U.S. 9-variable system of this paper.

These speculations point to an agenda for further research. An index of raw materials prices should be added to the system; and if it behaves according to these speculations, a check should be made to see whether the effect arises entirely from the 1973-74 commodity price boom or whether instead it fits other postwar episodes as well.

Regardless of how plausible one thinks the foregoing interpretation is, it remains true that most of variance in output is accounted for by output innovation. The conclusion that monetary policy disturbances do not account for much variance in output seems clear.

This does not mean that monetary policy is necessarily a weak instrument. Indeed, if one accepts the idea that some of the observed interest rate innovations are due to supply shocks, it appears likely that the effects of money innovations estimated in this system yield underestimates of the expansionary effects of monetary policy shocks. Money innovations are negatively correlated with interest rate innovations in this system. If in this system money innovations are mixtures of policy shocks, which would have negatively associated movements in M and r, with supply shocks, which would yield positively associated movements in M and r, we would expect that if we could isolate the effects of monetary policy shocks we would find them more expansionary than is the response to a money innovation in this system.

Another difference between the 9 and 6 variable systems which deserves comment is the absence of forecasting power for unemployment innovations in the larger system. In the smaller system, a positive unemployment innovation was followed by an expansion of the money supply and a rise in output and the real wage, with some inflation eventually. This looked like use of money for demand management. If this interpretation were correct, as pointed out in the earlier paper, it would conflict with the view that anticipated movements in the money supply should have no effects on real variables. In the smaller system feedback from unemployment to money supply was statistically significant, so that the null hypothesis that money is exogenous was rejected at the .05 level -- though this hypothesis was rejected less strongly than any of the others tested and rejected in that paper. In the larger system, the hypothesis that money is exogenous yields a $\chi^2(6) = 4.7$, so exogeneity is easily accepted. A policy variable which did not contribute much to explaining variance in GNP might still be used in an important way as a stabilizing tool. Its low explanatory power could simply reflect its not being used in an erratic way. The fact that in this system no patterns appear which suggest stabilizing responses of monetary policy to shocks thus further weakens the case for the importance of monetary policy as a determinant of the behavior of real variables.

Is there any indication from this larger system that a Keynesian view of the economy makes sense? By "Keynesian view" here I mean the notion that variations in output and employment originate in the private sector, probably mostly in autonomous shifts in investment demand, and that government policy measures, fiscal as well as monetary, have an important role to play in moderating the fluctuations arising this way. In the monetarist ordering of variables, Table 3 makes it clear that investment can easily be taken as passive. The only variable to which investment innovations contribute noticeable variance is government expenditure. The test for the hypothesis that investment is completely passive yields a $\chi^2(6) = 13.7$, significant at between .05 and .02 levels with an F of 2.28, but this is obviously due to investment's tendency to induce decreases (see Chart 8) in goverment expenditures. Government expenditure innovations also contribute little to variance in other variables.

This result requires qualification, however, because investment and GNP innovations are very strongly correlated. Charts 10-18 and Table 4 present the MAR and decomposition of variance which emerge when the triangular orthogonalization is done in the more Keynesian order listed. Here the contemporaneous correlation of GNP and investment innovations is allocated to investment, and investment innovations become extremely important sources of variation in GNP and unemployment. Government expenditure still has no substantial explanatory power, however, despite being placed first in the ordering.

The nature of the response to an investment innovation as displayed in the second line of Charts 10-18 is consistent with these innovations representing shifts in investment demand: money and interest rate rise, wages rises, output rises, unemployment falls. However, the implied multiplier-accelerator mechanism is of modest power. The peak response of output occurs in the first quarter after innovation in investment, coincident with the peak response of investment. At this point, the absolute deviation of investment from trend is roughly equal to the absolute deviation in GNP, so by this measure the multiplier is about one. (The log deviation of investment at the peak is .053, and of GNP is .0088. Their ratio, .17, is about the ratio of investment to GNP in the sample period.) Since the duration of investment's deviation from trend is short, and shorter than the duration of GNP's deviation from trend, a more reasonable measure is the ratio of the integral of GNP's deviation from trend to the integral of output's deviation from trend. Integrating over the first 8 quarters, which is the period in which the output deviation remains positive, yields a multiplier of about 1.6. Thus a Keynesian interpretation does not find bursts of investment demand generating demand increases in other sectors even larger than the burst in investment demand, but it does find short bursts of investment demand increasing GNP without decreasing other components of demand, and the increase is found to persist for a few quarters after the investment increase has dissipated. While this is not a picture of an inherently unstable multiplier-accelerator stabilized only by countercyclical policy, it does leave the view that much of macroeconomic fluctuation originates in shifts in investment demand a more respectable one that the view that much of such fluctuations originate in fluctuations in monetary policy.

The Keynesian policy variable in this system, government expenditure, shows little evidence of effectiveness. The lack of explanatory power for its innovations could be due to the absence of erratic elements in expenditure policy -- were it not that 40% of variance in  G  is accounted for by its own innovations (Table 4). It responds positively to investment and output innovations, so is not apparently playing a strong stabilizing role.

It is interesting to note that, while the interest rate innovation generates a response in this orthogonalization similar to that in the Table 3 orthogonalization, the money innovation in this orthogonalization no longer has any expansionary effect on output. Despite this, it still accounts for the majority of variance in all the price level variables -- W, PM, and P. This result can be interpreted in the same way as, earlier in this paper, we interpreted interest rate innovations. In this orthogonalization, money innovations are not accompanied by corresponding interest rate movements, and it is therefore plausible to interpret them as passive responses, generated by the attempt to maintain constant interest rates in the face of an unforeseen speculative demand for credit as raw materials prices jump. If this interpretation is correct, then reducing variance in the price level is not a matter of reducing erratic shifts in monetary policy but rather of reducing the extent of accomodating response to supply shocks. It is clearly more problematical whether the latter change in monetary policy would be desirable.

As a final interpretive exercise, we will consider "wage-push". Wage innovations account for little variance in quantity variables in either orthogonalization, but in both they account for a small but non-negligible proportion of price variance over horizons of about two years. This is consistent with the existence of some wage-push effect. However, there is strong contemporaneous correlation of wage and price innovations, and all the responses of wages and prices to wage and price innovations are approximately flat. This can be shown with a little algebra to imply that if we were to invert the ordering of wages and prices in the orthogonalization, price innovations would appear to have about the same explanatory power for wage variance which wage innovations have for price variance in this orthogonalization. Thus, though there is some variation in prices and wages which originates within the wage-price pair, this system provides no evidence that one or the other of the wage-price pair has causal priority.

## Conclusion

To the extent that monetarism is identified with the notion that instability is mainly generated by misguided attempts at policy intervention, the expansion of the U.S. model from 6 to 9 variables has made this position look less plausible. To the extent that Keynesianism is identified with the notion that instability originates in the private sector, especially in investment, the expansion has made Keynesianism look more plausible. On the other hand, the real quantity variables in the system do not behave in an unstable way, and there is little evidence of counter-cyclical movement in policy variables. Government expenditure plays a minor role in the system. Thus a sophisticated modern laissez-faire position along the lines of Sargent's recent work [1977] appears consistent with the results in this system. In fact, the one aspect of the smaller system which seemed to contradict that position (the response to unemployment innovations) fails to persist in the larger system.

Obviously a great deal remains to be done before these conclusions are firmly established. Some of the speculations I have introduced could be checked by expansions or modifications of the model. The system is complicated enough that other economists may well develop interpretations of the results which have not occurred to me. The robustness of results to the index-model constraints, to changes in the iterative maximization algorithm, to small changes in the variable definitions, and to variations in time period or country needs to be checked.

I hope pursuit of this additional work proves to be as useful as it is interesting.

## Appendix

### The Index-Model Form

Sargent and I [1977] introduced two related classes of models for multivariate stochastic processes which have the property that the number of parameters in them grows linearly with the length of variable list, instead of quadratically as in an unrestricted vector AR. We called the models "observable index" and "unobservable index" models. Since the latter class of models has come to be called (for good heuristic reasons) "frequency domain factor analysis", I will call the former class simply "index models" henceforth in this appendix. Index models have an AR which can be written as

A1)      $y(t) = D*y(t) + a*c*y(t) + u(t),$

where "*" indicates convolution (i.e. $a*c(t) = \sum_{s=-\infty}^{\infty} a(s)c(t-s)$),

$D(s)$ is an $m \times m$ matrix-valued function which is non-zero only on the main diagonal and has $D(s) = 0$, $s < 1$, $a$ is $m \times k$, $c$ is $k \times m$, $a(s) = 0$ for $s \leq 0$, $c(s) = 0$ for $s < 0$. To keep the number of parameters in this system substantially smaller than the number in an unrestricted AR, one takes $k \ll m$.[A1] In my own work to this point $Var(u(t))$ has been left unrestricted.[A2] This specification has the interpretation that all cross-variable effects in the AR are accounted for by common dependence of the $y$'s on the $k$ "indexes" defined by $z(t) = c*y(t)$. Block Granger causal orderings can be imposed on an index model by linear constraints on the parameters. The earlier joint paper with Sargent [1977] discusses how index structure could arise from a number of simple theoretical macro-models.

In estimation, one must eliminate a redundancy in the parameterization. Obviously we can take any $k \times k$ matrix-valued function $b$ such that $b(s) = 0$ for $s < 0$ ($b$ is one-sided) and such that $b$ has a one-sided inverse under convolution, and we can replace $a*c$ by $a*b^{-1}*b*c$ without changing the AR.[A3] If $a$ or $c$ has a $k \times k$ submatrix with a one-sided inverse under convolution, we can normalize that submatrix at the identity, and eliminate the redundancy. However not every $k \times k$

submatrix will in general be invertible -- in fact none need be -- and in practice it seems to turn out that only a few of the possible normalizations give good results.[A4]

Estimation is carried out by maximum likelihood conditional on the initial observations. The log likelihood is $-.5T$ log det Var(u), where Var (u) is the estimated variance matrix of u and T is sample size. In carrying out tests based on likelihood ratios, I have replaced T by $T-(Q/m)$, where Q is the total number of free parameters in D, a and c and m is the number of variables. This gives results a little more closely comparable to F ratios in small samples.

The starting point of estimation is important, because initial points with many zeroes in a and c can inadvertently introduce singularities in the second derivative matrix. In fact, if a and c are initially set at zero, the gradient of the likelihood is zero with respect to both a and c, so that most estimation routines will simply find the best-fitting array of univariate autoregressions, holding a and c both at zero.

A starting routine which works more often than not is to begin by holding a at zero until good D values are reached. This takes little time since the AR is linear in D. Then c is fixed at some plausible value, usually just ones and zeroes in various locations (though a singularity arises due to exact collinearity of a's with some D's if each c is given only one non-zero element) and the likelihood maximized with respect to a and D. This again takes little time because the AR is linear in these parameters. Finally, all constraints except the normalizations are released.

In this paper, all results reported are for a 9-variable (m=9), 2-index (k=2) system in which a, c, and D are all of length 3. This yields $3[2km + m] = 135$ parameters subject to 12 normalizing restrictions. The maximum lag length is 5.

It has happened often in my work that the highest function values are achieved not from direct maximization of the unconstrained likelihood, but from releasing the parameters after imposition of shrewdly chosen constraints. E.g., in the 9-variable 2-index U.S. system of this paper a substantial improvement in fit was obtained in releasing the system after imposition of the "investment passive" constraints, even though those constraints were rejected.

Assuming the normalization has been chosen well and one is otherwise lucky enough not to hit a bad patch in the likelihood surface, a "converged solution for a $9 \times 2$ model starting from scratch took about 300 seconds of CDC Cyber 74 time, costing (at the University of Minnesota subsidized rates) about $45, though bad luck and experimentation obviously make the costs of fitting a system of variables with which one has no previous experience many times this figure. The program used for this paper estimated the second derivative matrix from the cross products of the gradients, so the 300 seconds comprises some 15 iterations on the 123 free parameters.

The program uses frequency-domain approximations to compute convolutions, leading to an estimate of the cross-product-of-gradients matrix which assumes $\sum_{1}^{T-1} x(t)x(t-1) = \sum_{2}^{T} x(t)x(t-1)$. This approximation may

lead to the routine's ceasing to converge rapidly once a likelihood value
reasonably close to a local maximum has been found. In testing constraints,
likelihood was maximized subject to the constraints. As a check, a few
iterations of the unconstrained maximization routine were run starting
from the constrained maximum. That the highest likelihood emerged from
one of these restarts, not the initial, apparently converged, unconstrained
maximization, suggests that results might differ with a different convergence criterion or maximization algorithm.

## Measures of Fit

In smaller systems it is practical to compare the likelihood for an
unconstrained AR to that for the estimated index model, using the asymptotic $\chi^2$ distribution for the log likelihood ratio. In larger systems
fitting the unconstrained system may be impossible, and in any case a more
powerful test is likely to be a comparison of an index model with low k
against one with higher k. Unfortunately such a test cannot be executed
mechanically, because on the null hypothesis that the low - k model is
correct, the second derivative matrix of the likelihood is singular for
the high - k model.[A5] The singularity is easily avoided, by fixing the
coefficients in the components of c with subscript higher than k --
i.e. by fixing the form of the indexes to be added to the model. One can
of course make an asymptotically valid test by starting at the converged
estimate for the smaller model and taking one Gauss-Newton step. This,
together with the need to fix c, makes testing a k-index model against
a k+1 index model much easier computationally than fitting a k+1 index
model. On the other hand, the power of such a test of fit depends on the
researcher's shrewdness and intellectual honesty in picking the form for
the additional indexes.

Only one test of it has been tried with this paper's model. It consisted
of fitting a 3-index model in which the third index was the interest rate.
(This required constraining the component of D corresponding to the interest rate at its 2-index converged value, to avoid singularity.) The
choice was based on the important role played by interest rates in some
smaller, unconstrained estimated forecasting models. The test results
in a $\chi^2(18) = 30.7$, which corresponds to a marginal significance level of
between .05 and .02 and an F of 1.71. The variances of innovations in
M, Y, and I are all reduced by about 10% by the addition of the third
index. For each of these variables, there is a negative coefficient on
the first lagged value of the interest rate in the corresponding AR
equation.

Though this rejection of the 2-index model is not as strong as that
for some other restrictions we have examined, it is strong enough that
some follow-up action is clearly required.

We can also ask whether the expansion to nine variables improves the
fit to the original six variables. The unconstrained six-variable AR is
not nested in the 9-variable index model or vice versa, so the likelihood
ratio cannot be interpreted in the usual way. The difference in log
determinants of residual covariance matrices between an unconstrained
third order 6-variable system and the 9-variable 2-index system's corres-

ponding 6 × 6 submatrix is, however, about 29. Since the difference in numbers of parameters is about 26, this difference does not appear large.[A6] It does not seem that the additional three variables are helping much in predicting the first six.

It is worth commenting on the philosophy of tests of fit for systems like these -- with many degrees of freedom and many parameters. As Schwarz [1978] and Leamer [1978] have pointed out, mechanical use of significance tests does not lead to consistent decisions as sample size increases. A Bayesian approach to model selection leads to a criterion which compares the asymptotic $\chi^2(n)$ statistic to $n \log T$ (where $T$ is sample size) instead of to the .05 level of the $\chi^2(n)$ distribution. This criterion is only asymptotically correct, however, and because $\log T$ grows slowly with $T$, a complete Bayesian analysis will probably give results quite different from the $n \log T$ criterion in samples of the size we are considering in this paper. Further, in contrast to the .05 significance level, which rejects most restrictions, the $n \log T$ criterion accepts most restrictions. This brings out an important characteristic of the criterion: it aims at providing a good rule for comparing nested hypotheses, or at best hypotheses of different dimension. In this work it is probably more interesting to compare the relative plausibility of various restrictions of roughly similar dimension. A criterion which accepts or rejects them all is of little help.

For these purposes we might just rely on the marginal significance level of the $\chi^2$ statistic, distinguishing very strongly rejected from weakly rejected hypotheses. Even this idea has difficulties, however. The relevant distribution theory is asymptotic only, and requires that the number of degrees of freedom in the $\chi^2$ statistic be small relative to the number of degrees of freedom in the data (total data points minus number of parameters). It is known, for example, (see Miller [1968]), that when there are many degrees of freedom in both numerator and denominator of an $F$ statistic and normality assumptions are violated in the direction of fat tails, then the $F$ distribution will lead to rejection of the null hypothesis more often than indicated by the nominal significance level. This kind of effect might apply here, since we are in effect testing with many degrees of freedom in the numerator.

The conclusion should be that "$\chi^2$-tests" like those reported in this paper ought to be regarded as descriptive statistics, helping to characterize the form of the likelihood function, rather than as yielding decisions about the correct form of the model. To this end, the paper reports not only acceptances and rejections, but also the approximate marginal significance level and, to aid in comparison to the $n \log T$ criterion, the ratio of the chi-squared statistic to its degrees of freecom (a pseudo-F-statistic which we call simply $F$). For the sample size we are considering, the $n \log T$ criterion would call for rejecting only hypotheses for which $F$ exceeds 4.55.[A7]

## References

Fuller, W.A. (1976), Introduction to Statistical Time Series, (New York: Wiley).

Geweke, J. and K. Singleton (1978), "Interpreting the Likelihood Ratio Statistic when Sample Size is Small," processed, University of Wisconsin.

Gordon, R.J. (1977), "World Inflation and Monetary Accomodation in Eight Countries," Brookings Papers on Economic Activity, 1977:2.

Gordon, R.J. and J.A. Wilcox (1978), "Monetarist Interpretations of the Great Depression: An Evaluation and Critique," processed, Northwestern University.

Granger, C.W.J. (1969), "Investigating Causal Relations by Econometric Models and Cross-Spectral Methods," Econometrica, Vol. 37, No. 3.

Hall, R.E. (1978), "Some Evidence on the Sources of Economic Fluctuations," paper presented at the NBER International Seminar on Macroeconomics, Paris.

Hurwicz, L. (1960), "On the Structural Form of Interdependent Systems," in Logic, Methodology and Philosophy of Science, E. Nagel et. al., ed., Stanford University Press.

Leamer, E. (1978), Specification Searches (New York: Wiley), p. 112-113 especially.

Lucas, E. Jr. (1973), "Some International Evidence on Output-Inflation Tradeoffs," American Economic Review, Vol. 63, No. 3.

Miller, R.G. (1968), "Jackknifing Variances," Annals of Mathematical Statistics, Vol. 39.

Sargent, J. (1976), "A Classical Macroeconometric Model for the United States," Journal of Political Economy, Vol. 84, No. 2.

Sargent, T.J. (1977), "Aspects of the New Classical Macroeconomics," processed.

Sargent, T.J. and C.A. Sims (1977), "Business Cycle Modeling without Pretending to Have Too Much A Priori Economic Theory," in New Methods of Business Cycle Research, Minneapolis Federal Reserve Bank.

Schwarz, G. (1978), "Estimating the Dimension of a Model," Annals of Statistics, Vol. 6, No. 2.

Sims, C.A. (1977), "Exogeneity and Causal Orderings in Macroeconomic Models," in New Methods of Business Cycle Research, Minneapolis Federal Reserve Bank.

_____, (1980), "Macroeconomics and Reality," Econometrica 48, 1-48.

_____, (1978), "Least Squares Estimation of Autoregressions with Some Unit Roots," University of Minnesota Center for Economic Research Discussion Paper No. /8-95.

Taylor, J.B. (1978), "Output and Price Stability: An International Comparison," processed, Columbia University.

Data Notes

Money:          This is M1, seasonally adjusted, as prepared by the Board
                of Governors of the Federal Reserve System and published in
                Business Statistics and the Survey of Current Business by
                the Department of Commerce.

Real GNP:       This is the series published in the same sources listed
                above for M1 and prepared by the Department of Commerce.  It
                is seasonally adjusted.

Unemployment rate:  This is the rate for all civilian workers, seasonally
                adjusted, prepared by the Bureau of Labor Statistics and
                published in the sources already cited for the U.S.

Wages:          This is a seasonally adjusted index of average hourly com-
                pensation of all private nonfarm employees, prepared by the
                Bureau of Labor Statistics and published in Business Con-
                ditions Digest by the Department of Commerce.

Prices:         This is a seasonally adjusted price deflator of Gross Na-
                tional Product of the non-farm business sector, as prepared
                by the Department of Commerce and published in the Survey of
                Current Business.

Import Prices:  This is the Unit Value of General Imports as published by
                the Department of Commerce in the Survey of Current Business.

Investment:     This is seasonally adjusted Gross Private Domestic Investment
                from the National income accounts as published in Business
                Statistics and Survey of Current Business.

Government Expenditures:  This is seasonally adjusted federal government
                expenditures on goods and services from the national income
                accounts.

Interest Rate:  This is the rate on 90-day Treasury bills, as published in
                the Survey of Current Business and Business Statistics.

    The data series were all originally for the period 1948-1975,
quarterly.  All were logged, then detrended by linear regression, before
the index model was fit.  Because the index model generated a 5th order
AR, five periods at the beginning of the sample were dropped to yield a
period of fit of 1949.2-1975.4.

## Table 1

PROPORTIONS OF FORECAST ERROR  k  QUARTERS AHEAD
PRODUCED BY EACH INNOVATION:  U.S. 1949-1975

Triangularized innovation in:

| Forecast error in: | k | M | Y/P | U | W | P | PM |
|---|---|---|---|---|---|---|---|
| M | 1 | 1.00 | 0 | 0 | 0 | 0 | 0 |
|  | 3 | .96 | 0 | .03 | 0 | 0 | 0 |
|  | 9 | .73 | 0 | .24 | .02 | 0 | 0 |
|  | 33 | .54 | 0 | .27 | .09 | 0 | .09 |
| Y/P | 1 | .15 | .85 | 0 | 0 | 0 | 0 |
|  | 3 | .35 | .59 | .04 | .01 | .01 | 0 |
|  | 9 | .30 | .18 | .37 | .13 | .00 | .02 |
|  | 33 | .28 | .15 | .33 | .16 | .02 | .06 |
| U | 1 | .02 | .35 | .63 | 0 | 0 | 0 |
|  | 3 | .14 | .49 | .32 | 0 | .03 | 0 |
|  | 9 | .26 | .20 | .41 | .09 | .02 | .02 |
|  | 33 | .34 | .14 | .34 | .13 | .03 | .03 |
| W | 1 | .08 | .05 | .04 | .84 | 0 | 0 |
|  | 3 | .17 | .06 | .07 | .55 | .09 | .06 |
|  | 9 | .45 | .02 | .05 | .25 | .08 | .16 |
|  | 33 | .64 | .02 | .19 | .07 | .02 | .07 |
| P | 1 | .0 | .04 | .15 | .24 | .56 | 0 |
|  | 3 | .04 | .01 | .14 | .36 | .33 | .12 |
|  | 9 | .14 | .02 | .12 | .25 | .11 | .36 |
|  | 33 | .60 | .02 | .20 | .07 | .02 | .09 |
| PM | 1 | 0 | 0 | .06 | .05 | .08 | .81 |
|  | 3 | .01 | .01 | .02 | .13 | .10 | .75 |
|  | 9 | .06 | .02 | .13 | .08 | .03 | .68 |
|  | 33 | .54 | .03 | .20 | .04 | .01 | .18 |

Table 2


PERCENTAGES OF FORECAST ERROR   k   QUARTERS AHEAD
PRODUCED BY EACH INNOVATION:   WEST GERMANY 1958-1976

Triangularized innovation in:

| Forecast error in: | k | M | Y/P | U | W | P | PM |
|---|---|---|---|---|---|---|---|
| M | 1 | 1.00 | 0 | 0 | 0 | 0 | 0 |
|   | 3 | .84 | .04 | .05 | .01 | .04 | .02 |
|   | 9 | .53 | .04 | .14 | .08 | .20 | .01 |
|   | 33 | .39 | .05 | .13 | .07 | .27 | .09 |
| Y/P | 1 | .07 | .93 | 0 | 0 | 0 | 0 |
|   | 3 | .14 | .79 | .01 | .05 | 0 | 0 |
|   | 9 | .15 | .47 | .03 | .06 | .03 | .25 |
|   | 33 | .13 | .22 | .05 | .04 | .42 | .14 |
| U | 1 | 0 | .03 | .97 | 0 | 0 | 0 |
|   | 3 | .19 | .09 | .67 | .03 | .02 | 0 |
|   | 9 | .15 | .10 | .37 | .02 | .08 | .29 |
|   | 33 | .09 | .11 | .15 | .02 | .50 | .14 |
| W | 1 | 0 | .03 | .01 | .96 | 0 | 0 |
|   | 3 | .11 | .18 | .01 | .59 | .03 | .09 |
|   | 9 | .23 | .23 | .02 | .23 | .24 | .05 |
|   | 33 | .21 | .13 | .08 | .15 | .31 | .12 |
| P | 1 | .02 | .02 | 0 | .10 | .86 | 0 |
|   | 3 | .03 | .06 | .05 | .09 | .76 | 0 |
|   | 9 | .05 | .13 | .03 | .05 | .68 | .06 |
|   | 33 | .08 | .10 | .04 | .05 | .67 | .06 |
| PM | 1 | .06 | 0 | .02 | 0 | .02 | .89 |
|   | 3 | .04 | 0 | .02 | .01 | .08 | .85 |
|   | 9 | .10 | .04 | .09 | 0 | .16 | .61 |
|   | 33 | .06 | .08 | .04 | .02 | .57 | .23 |

## Table 3

PROPORTIONS OF FORECAST ERROR VARIANCE  k  QUARTERS
AHEAD PRODUCED BY EACH INNOVATION:

U.S., 1949.2-75.4, 9 Variables, "Monetarist" Ordering.

| Forecast error in: | k | M | Y | U | W | P | PM | I | G | r |
|---|---|---|---|---|---|---|---|---|---|---|
| M | 1 | 1.00 | 0 | 0 | 0 | 0 | 0 | 0 | 0 | 0 |
|   | 3 | .98 | .01 | 0 | 0 | 0 | 0 | 0 | 0 | .01 |
|   | 9 | .97 | .01 | 0 | 0 | 0 | 0 | 0 | 0 | .01 |
|   | 33 | .96 | .02 | 0 | 0 | 0 | 0 | 0 | 0 | .02 |
| Y | 1 | .13 | .87 | 0 | 0 | 0 | 0 | 0 | 0 | 0 |
|   | 3 | .13 | .86 | 0 | 0 | 0 | 0 | 0 | 0 | 0 |
|   | 9 | .09 | .69 | 0 | .01 | .02 | 0 | 0 | .01 | .18 |
|   | 33 | .12 | .56 | .01 | .05 | .02 | .01 | .01 | .01 | .20 |
| U | 1 | .06 | .39 | .55 | 0 | 0 | 0 | 0 | 0 | 0 |
|   | 3 | .05 | .62 | .28 | 0 | .01 | 0 | 0 | 0 | .04 |
|   | 9 | .04 | .75 | .13 | 0 | .01 | .01 | 0 | 0 | .06 |
|   | 33 | .15 | .59 | .10 | .01 | .02 | .01 | 0 | .01 | .10 |
| W | 1 | .14 | .08 | 0 | .78 | 0 | 0 | 0 | 0 | 0 |
|   | 3 | .20 | .11 | .01 | .59 | .01 | .01 | 0 | .01 | .07 |
|   | 9 | .52 | .03 | 0 | .20 | .01 | .03 | 0 | .01 | .19 |
|   | 33 | .85 | .02 | 0 | .05 | 0 | .01 | 0 | 0 | .05 |
| P | 1 | 0 | .12 | .10 | .12 | .67 | 0 | 0 | 0 | 0 |
|   | 3 | .10 | .06 | .02 | .15 | .48 | .04 | 0 | .02 | .14 |
|   | 9 | .44 | .16 | 0 | .03 | .09 | .04 | 0 | .01 | .23 |
|   | 33 | .75 | .09 | 0 | .01 | .03 | .02 | 0 | .01 | .08 |
| PM | 1 | .02 | 0 | .03 | .01 | .06 | .88 | 0 | 0 | 0 |
|   | 3 | .07 | 0 | .01 | .03 | .09 | .76 | 0 | .01 | .04 |
|   | 9 | .36 | .08 | .01 | .02 | .04 | .33 | 0 | .01 | .16 |
|   | 33 | .70 | .08 | 0 | .01 | .02 | .12 | 0 | .01 | .07 |
| I | 1 | .06 | .56 | 0 | 0 | .01 | .01 | .36 | 0 | 0 |
|   | 3 | .08 | .55 | 0 | .01 | .03 | .01 | .28 | 0 | .03 |
|   | 9 | .11 | .49 | .01 | .02 | .03 | .02 | .25 | 0 | .07 |
|   | 33 | .15 | .42 | .01 | .02 | .03 | .03 | .22 | .01 | .11 |
| G | 1 | 0 | .03 | .01 | 0 | .08 | .04 | .18 | .65 | 0 |
|   | 3 | .01 | .16 | .02 | .01 | .07 | .07 | .15 | .52 | 0 |
|   | 9 | .01 | .46 | .01 | .01 | .04 | .05 | .08 | .34 | 0 |
|   | 33 | .02 | .46 | .01 | .01 | .04 | .05 | .08 | .32 | .01 |
| r | 1 | .02 | .15 | .03 | .03 | .05 | .02 | 0 | .08 | .61 |
|   | 3 | .02 | .20 | .03 | .02 | .05 | .03 | .01 | .07 | .56 |
|   | 9 | .02 | .26 | .03 | .02 | .05 | .03 | .01 | .06 | .52 |
|   | 33 | .07 | .25 | .03 | .02 | .05 | .03 | .01 | .06 | .49 |

*C.A. Sims*

## Table 4

PROPORTIONS OF FORECAST ERROR VARIANCE   k   QUARTERS
AHEAD PRODUCED BY EACH INNOVATION:

U.S., 1949.2-75.4, 9 Variables, "Keynesian" Ordering

| Forecast error in: | k | G | I | W | PM | U | Y | r | M | P |
|---|---|---|---|---|---|---|---|---|---|---|
| G | 1 | 1.00 | 0 | 0 | 0 | 0 | 0 | 0 | 0 | 0 |
|   | 3 | .91 | .03 | .01 | .01 | .01 | 0 | 0 | .02 | 0 |
|   | 9 | .64 | .19 | 0 | .02 | .02 | .04 | 0 | .08 | 0 |
|   | 33 | .60 | .20 | .01 | .02 | .02 | .05 | 0 | .10 | 0 |
| I | 1 | .01 | .99 | 0 | 0 | 0 | 0 | 0 | 0 | 0 |
|   | 3 | .01 | .95 | 0 | 0 | 0 | 0 | .02 | .01 | 0 |
|   | 9 | .01 | .84 | .01 | .02 | .01 | 0 | .06 | .04 | .01 |
|   | 33 | .01 | .73 | .01 | .03 | .02 | .01 | .09 | .09 | .01 |
| W | 1 | 0 | .13 | .87 | 0 | 0 | 0 | 0 | 0 | 0 |
|   | 3 | .01 | .19 | .69 | .01 | .01 | .01 | .05 | .03 | .01 |
|   | 9 | 0 | .07 | .35 | .06 | 0 | 0 | .05 | .44 | .02 |
|   | 33 | 0 | .08 | .20 | .02 | .01 | .04 | .07 | .57 | .01 |
| PM | 1 | .01 | .02 | .01 | .97 | .0 | 0 | 0 | 0 | 0 |
|   | 3 | 0 | .04 | .04 | .86 | .01 | 0 | .02 | .03 | 0 |
|   | 9 | 0 | .02 | .06 | .43 | 0 | 0 | .04 | .43 | .02 |
|   | 33 | 0 | .05 | .09 | .15 | .01 | .03 | .07 | .59 | .01 |
| U | 1 | .04 | .28 | .01 | .01 | .67 | 0 | 0 | 0 | 0 |
|   | 3 | .05 | .47 | .01 | 0 | .40 | .02 | .05 | 0 | 0 |
|   | 9 | .04 | .51 | 0 | .02 | .23 | .09 | .04 | .07 | 0 |
|   | 33 | .03 | .39 | .03 | .03 | .17 | .08 | .06 | .21 | .01 |
| Y | 1 | .02 | .65 | .01 | 0 | .06 | .24 | 0 | 0 | 0 |
|   | 3 | .03 | .64 | .01 | 0 | .07 | .25 | 0 | 0 | 0 |
|   | 9 | .01 | .45 | .01 | .02 | .07 | .24 | .12 | .07 | .02 |
|   | 33 | .01 | .36 | .05 | .03 | .06 | .19 | .13 | .13 | .03 |
| r | 1 | .01 | .10 | .01 | .01 | .06 | 0 | .82 | 0 | 0 |
|   | 3 | 0 | .13 | .01 | .02 | .07 | 0 | .77 | 0 | 0 |
|   | 9 | 0 | .18 | .01 | .02 | .07 | .01 | .70 | .01 | 0 |
|   | 33 | .01 | .18 | .01 | .03 | .07 | .01 | .63 | .06 | 0 |
| M | 1 | 0 | .06 | .09 | 0 | .01 | .05 | .08 | .70 | 0 |
|   | 3 | 0 | .03 | .08 | 0 | .02 | .04 | .14 | .69 | 0 |
|   | 9 | 0 | .03 | .08 | 0 | .01 | .05 | .15 | .68 | 0 |
|   | 33 | 0 | .09 | .08 | 0 | .02 | .08 | .15 | .58 | 0 |
| P | 1 | .04 | .01 | .08 | .09 | 0 | .27 | .06 | .03 | .42 |
|   | 3 | .05 | .01 | .16 | .15 | .03 | .11 | .17 | .17 | .15 |
|   | 9 | 0 | .01 | .09 | .13 | .01 | .02 | .07 | .65 | .02 |
|   | 33 | 0 | .06 | .10 | .04 | .02 | .04 | .09 | .65 | .01 |

## FOOTNOTES

1.  To be more precise, $\hat{y}(t)$ is the projection of $y(t)$ on the Hilbert space spanned by past $y(s)$ under the covariance inner product.

2.  Sufficient conditions are that $y$ be a linearly regular covariance stationary process, in the terminology of Rozanov [1967]. However many types of non-stationary processes will also meet the conditions specified here.

3.  This condition, again, will hold for all covariance-stationary linearly regular processes, but in addition for some non-stationary processes.

4.  If (1) without the error term would be an unstable difference equation, then the usual distribution theory has an asymptotic justification, but in a special sense. See Sims [1978] and Fuller [1976].

5.  The question of how one decides what the "other relevant variables" are and what happens if some are omitted will be taken up below.

6.  Specifications in which this connection of money innovations to monetary policy is assumed play a major part in work by T.J. Sargent [1976].

7.  This conclusion about possible policies might appear in a negative form: if most inflation originates in wage-innovations and we suppose that policy cannot effectively influence wage-bargaining, then we might conclude that policy cannot affect inflation.

8.  Granger [1969] did not use the term "causally prior". I use that term to summarize a situation where the "prior" variable causes the other variable and is not caused by it. In Granger's sense of the verb "cause".

9.  Y, I, and G are all deflated by P.

10. Keynes certainly never put forth views of this sort. I use the adjective "Keynesian" here only to distinguish this view from the monetarist Phillips curve.

11. The latter part of the appendix on methodology discusses the interpretation of these statistics.

12. As sketched out in Lucas [1973].

13. I do not claim, however, that any of the arguments given here refute the view that, because markets clear, prices are flexible, and expectations rational, the business cycle is an equilibrium phenomenon on which monetary policy can have no good effect. What is being argued against is the view, sometimes held by the same people, that monetary policy is the source of most of, or much of, macroeconomic instability.

A1. There is no need to require that $a^* c(0) = 0$ as we do here, but a model with $a^* c(0) \neq 0$ leads to a complicated likelihood function and has in practice proven very difficult to fit.

A2.   However to make the number of parameters keep on growing linearly, one
      must start restricting this covariance matrix as size increases.  A
      natural procedure would be to impose a factor analytic structure.  This
      could be done without greatly affecting computation time.

A3.   In a model with a finite number of lags in  a  and  c, we would have
      to have  $b(s) = 0$  for $s \neq 0$  if the change from  a,c  to $ab^{-1}$, bc,
      were not to change lag lengths.  Since lag lengths are in fact not
      known a priori, it is best to fix an entire  $k \times k$  submatrix of  a
      or  c  rather than (say) only a  $k \times k$  matrix of  a(0)  or  c(0).
      This means, of course, that with lag length fixed such a constraint
      does affect the model's structure slightly - it is a pure normaliza-
      tion only in the context of the model which recognizes that lag
      length is in fact estimated.

A4.   As a guide to practice, it should be noted that one should not nor-
      malize on a submatrix of  c  corresponding to variables which do not
      affect other variables or which do so only with substantial delay.
      One should not normalize on a submatrix of  a  corresponding to vari-
      ables which do not respond to other variables or which do so only
      with a substantial delay.

A5.   John Geweke and Kenneth Singleton have pointed out [1978] that a
      similar problem arises in frequency-domain factor analysis, invalida-
      ting some of the tests of fit appearing in my joint paper with Sar-
      gent [1977].

A6.   There are  $6 \times 6 \times 3 = 108$  parameters in the 6-variable unconstrained
      system.  In the 9-variable system there are 123 free.  Allocating 6/9
      of these to the first six variables yields 82 parameters to fit the
      first six variables.  If the models were nested we could use an
      asymptotic  $\chi^2(26)$  distribution for the difference in log deter-
      minants of 29, and by this standard the difference is not "signifi-
      cant".  However, this is obviously only a crude rule of thumb for
      deciding what is a big difference in a log likelihood.

A7.   Note that the Akaike criterion (which is described by Schwarz [1978])
      can be expressed as calling for rejecting restrictions for which the
      F  exceeds 2.0.  The Akaike criterion has at best a heuristic justi-
      fication, apparently, and it is, like mechanical hypothesis testing,
      not consistent as sample size increases.

## NOTES TO THE CHARTS

Each of the following charts displays the response of one variable to one-standard-error shocks in the innovations in each of the other variables in the system. More precisely, each displays one row of the function $B(s)G^{-1}$ in (3). The labels along the left margin identify the variables whose innovations produce the responses plotted along the corresponding horizontal axis. $G$ has in each case been chosen to be upper triangular, with the variables ordered as they are down the left margin of the graph. That is, in the first nine charts, e.g., money shocks are allowed to have contemporaneous impact on all other variables, while $R$ shocks are constrained to have no contemporaneous effect on other variables. The time unit is quarters, along the horizontal axis. The distance between adjacent horizontal axes differs across charts and is given as the "Vertical Unit" in the upper right corner of each chart.

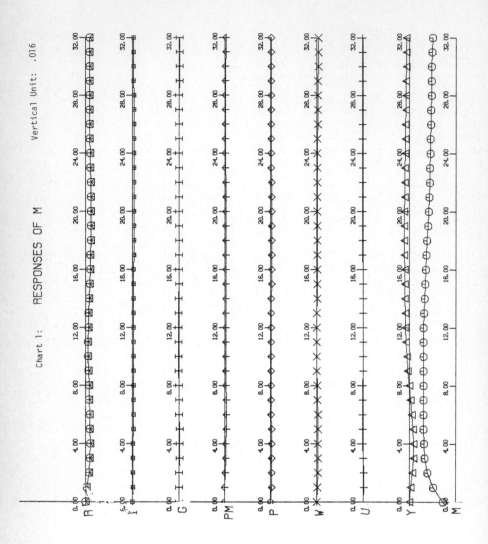

Chart 1: RESPONSES OF M

Vertical Unit: .016

Chart 2: RESPONSES OF Y          Vertical Unit: .01600

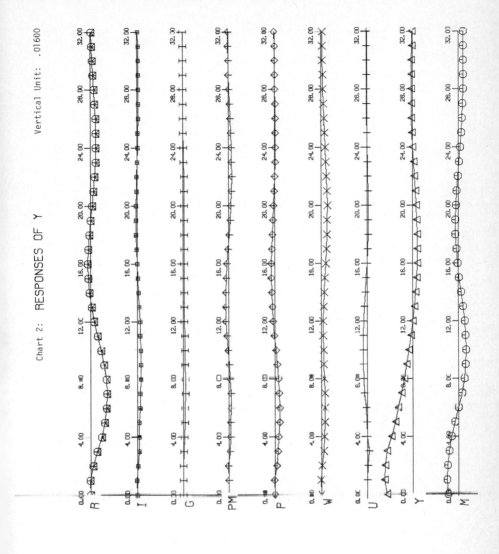

Vertical Unit:   .06400

Chart 3:     RESPONSES OF U

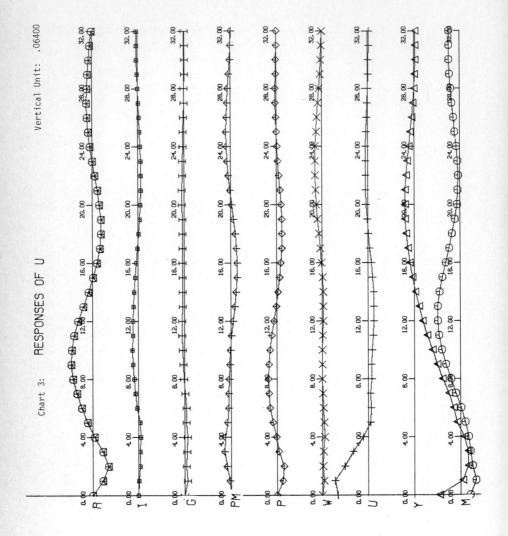

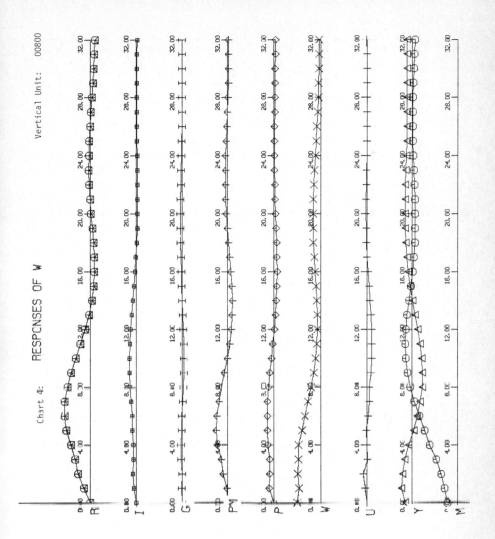

Chart 4: RESPONSES OF W

Vertical Unit: .00800

Chart 5:    RESPONSES OF P                    Vertical Unit:  .01600

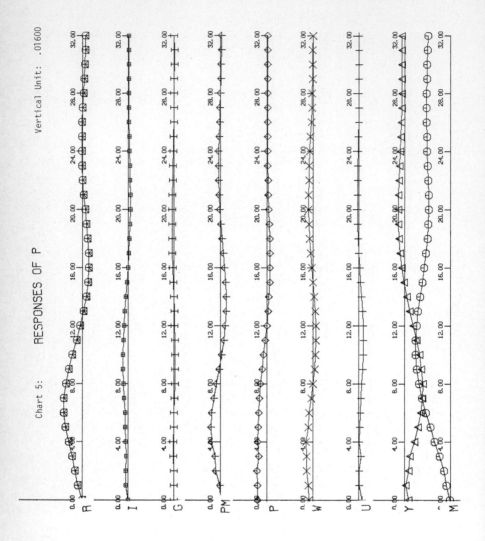

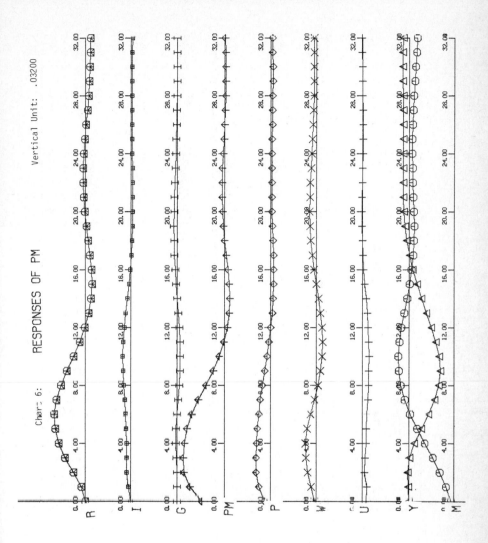

Chart 6:    RESPONSES OF PM      Vertical Unit: .03200

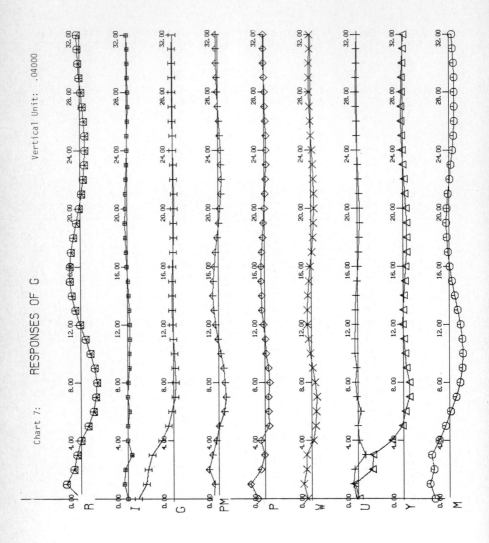

Chart 7:   RESPONSES OF G          Vertical Unit:   .04000

Vertical Unit:   .04000

Chart 8:   RESPONSES OF I

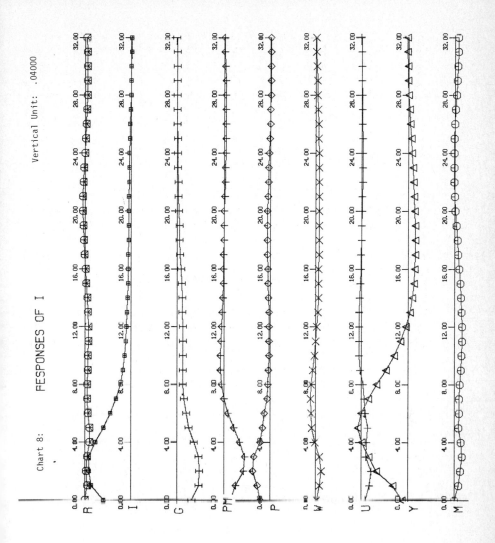

*C.A. Sims*

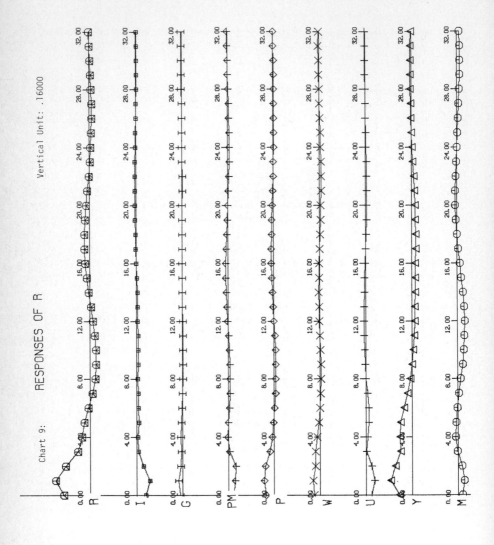

Chart 9: RESPONSES OF R

Vertical Unit: .16000

Chart 10:  RESPONSES OF G  Vertical Unit: .06400

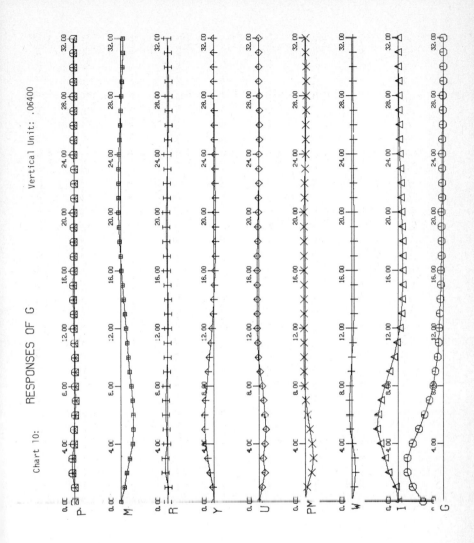

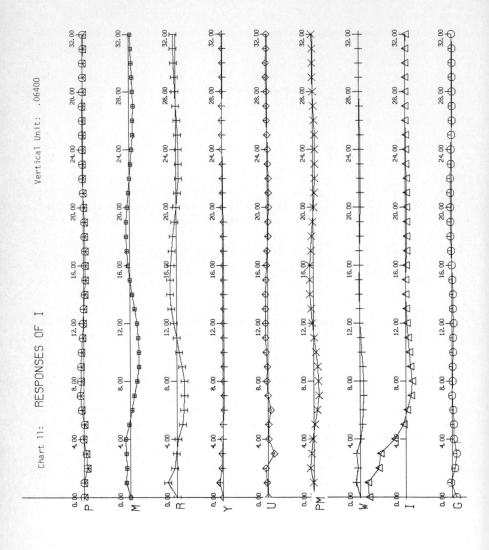

Chart 11:  RESPONSES OF I          Vertical Unit:  .06400

Chart 12:   RESPONSES OF W

Vertical Unit:   .00800

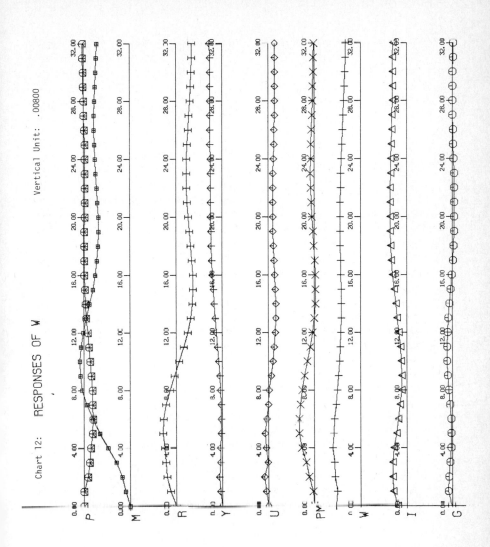

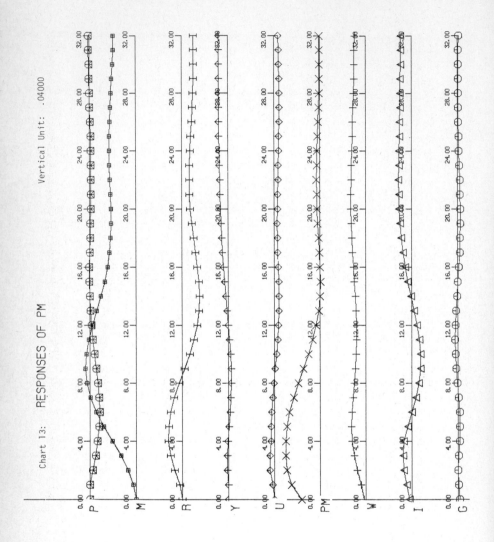

Chart 13:   RESPONSES OF PM

Vertical Unit:  .04000

Vertical Unit: .06400

Chart 14: RESPONSES OF U

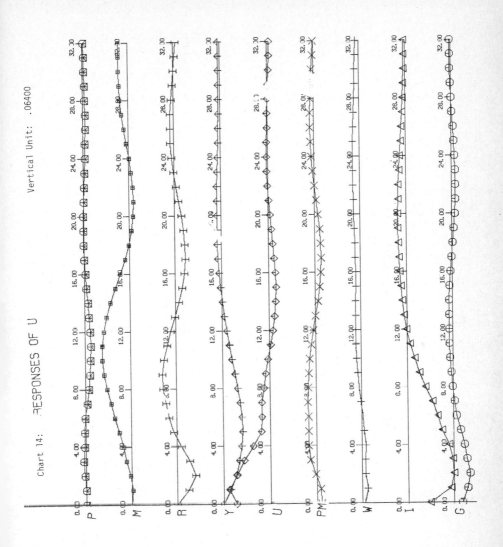

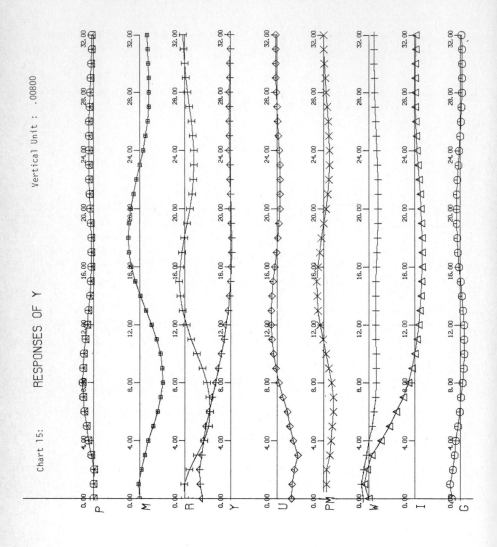

Chart 15:    RESPONSES OF Y                Vertical Unit :    .00800

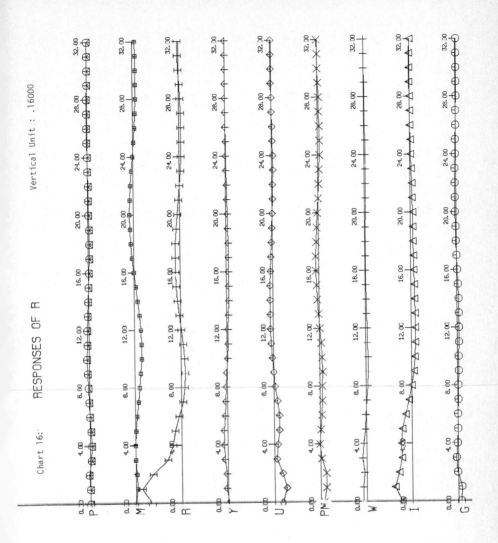

Chart 16: RESPONSES OF R

Vertical Unit : .16000

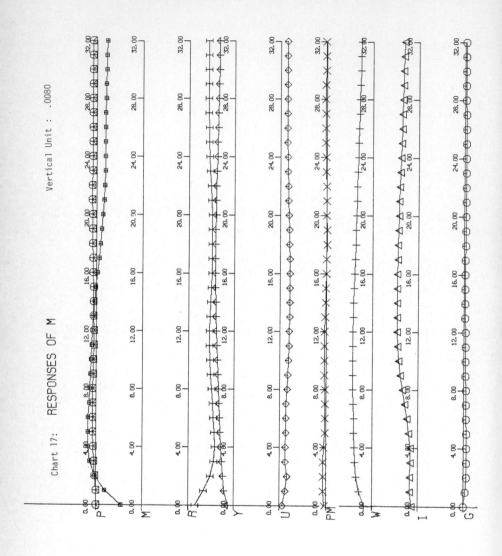

Chart 17:   RESPONSES OF M

Vertical Unit :   .0080

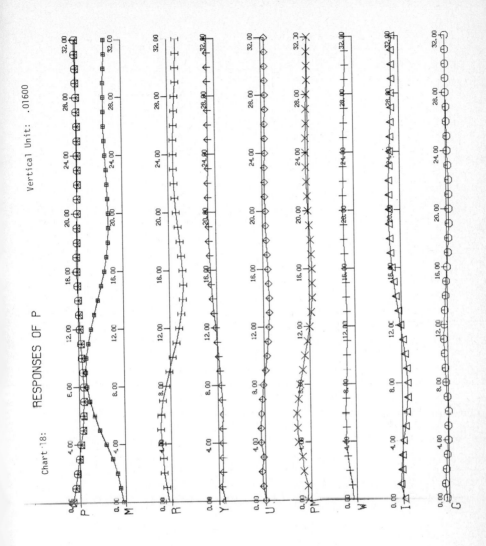

Chart 18:   RESPONSES OF P

Vertical Unit:   .01600

ON A THEORETICAL AND EMPIRICAL BASIS
OF MACROECONOMETRIC MODELS

Albert Ando *

University of Pennsylvania

This essay attempts to assess, from an admittedly biased
point of view, some aspects of recent literature on a
theoretical and empirical basis of macroeconometric
models. Assumptions that must underly the monetarist
and classical equilibrium models of aggregative economy
are also reviewed. A brief discussion of the statistical
tests of causality proposed by Granger as applied to
macroeconomic context is presented, and it is asserted
that this procedure makes the identification conditions
implicit rather than unnecessary. The essay ends by
recalling the well known defect of the statistical
theory when it is used to discriminate among alternative
scientific theories.

## I. INTRODUCTION

When I accepted an invitation to prepare a paper for this conference,
I intended to prepare a paper quite different from the one I am presenting
today. For practicing econometricians, extracting propositions from existing economic theory that are usable for specifying and identifying
estimatable equations is an excruciatingly difficult task. I believe that
this is partly because most of economic theory consists of comparative
static propositions, while historical data are generated by a dynamic
economy and do not directly bear evidence on comparative static propositions of economic theory. My own strategy in dealing with this problem
has been to make sure that all equations, or system of equations, which I
use as the basis for empirical studies, have associated with them proper
steady state solutions to which comparative static propositions do apply,
unless there is some persuasive reason to deviate from this principle. I

*The research on which this paper is based has been supported by NSF
Grant #SOC 77-08994. A part of the paper was begun when I was awarded
the Senior American Scientist Award by the Alexander von Humboldt
Foundation of West Germany, and was continued while I was a visitor at
the Institute for International Economic Studies, University of Stockholm.

planned to discuss today how far this strategy helps in identification, estimation, and uses of econometric models.

As I have studied the literature on macroeconomics of the past four or five years, I have become persuaded that I should take this opportunity to review a somewhat wider range of topics, even though my discussion becomes less substantive by doing so.  I refer in particular to the paper by Professors Lucas and Sargent entitled "After Keynesian Macroeconomics", [1]/ and the whole series of papers leading to it.  In that paper, the authors state that "existing Keynesian macroeconometric models are incapable of providing reliable guidance in formulating monetary, fiscal and other types of policy.  This conclusion is based in part on the spectacular recent failures of these models, and in part on their lack of a sound theoretical or econometric basis.  On the latter ground, there is no hope that minor or even major modifications of these models will lead to significant improvement in their reliability".

Had this been an isolated assertion, even by such prominent macroeconomic theorists as Professors Lucas and Sargent, I would not have taken it seriously enough to shift the emphasis of my present paper radically at the last moment.  Judging from papers published in journals and my discussions with some of my colleagues from many institutions, however, the Lucas-Sargent position appears to be more and more accepted.  Their main conclusion, namely, that monetary and fiscal stabilization policies as we have understood them in the past are totally ineffective at best and likely to be positively destabilizing, has already had some impact on actual public policy making.  As I have devoted more than 10 years of my life to the construction and operation of one of standard macroeconometric models and I bear a large share of the responsibility for the way in which this model is structured, estimated, analyzed and utilized for forecasting and for policy analysis, it seems incumbent upon me to express my reactions to the assertions by Lucas and Sargent, and to related discussions in the recent literature.  Since the question is closely related to the question of the reliability of macroeconometric models, the discussion of this topic seems appropriate for this conference.

I shall begin by reviewing historical facts leading to the so called "spectacular recent failures" of macroeconometric models, and argue that this observation cannot be sustained universally under close examination of records.  Secondly, I will indicate that at least some of the existing macroeconometric models share a more common theoretical basis with what

Lucas and Sargent call "equilibrium models" of the business cycle than advocates of these models recognize. Thirdly, I shall attempt to define precisely where the most critical theoretical differences between the traditional Keynesian models and the equilibrium models arise, and to argue that the basic difference is how the short-run, dynamic adjustment processes are modeled and analyzed. The principle of optimization, when it is applied to the description of dynamic adjustment processes, is by no means unambiguous.

Finally, I will review rather informally some statistical procedures that are used to "test" various models in the recent literature. I will argue that most of these tests using macro time series alone are much weaker than they appear. In particular, I present a very simple example in which the Granger-Sims test of causality gives a completely misleading result, and argue that such a result, rather than being an exception, would be the rule when this procedure is applied to a pair of macro time series.

I will end this essay by recalling the fundamental defect of the existing statistical theory for the purposes of building an ever larger body of usable knowledge in sciences like economics. This point was clearly understood and stated by statisticians like L.J. Savage, J.W. Tukey, and F.J. Anscombe, and social scientists like Herbert Simon some 25 years ago, [2]/ but we have not paid as much attention to them as we should have. "A sound basis" of economic theory cannot be anything but all the past accumulated empirical evidence from whatever the source, organized depending on the purpose for which the theory is to be applied. When the statistical theory is adjusted to remedy this fundamental defect and interaction between economic theorists and econometricians becomes much more explicit and routine, only then will we be able to begin accumulating our knowledge about the economy more formally and systematically.

## II. PAST PERFORMANCES OF MACROECONOMETRIC MODELS

I believe we can dispose of one question very quickly. It seems to have become a cliche to say that the Keynesian economics appeared to have "worked" during the Kennedy-Johnson years. It is often added that this seeming success of the Keynesian economics led most economists to believe that they knew enough about the macro structure of the U.S. economy to design a set of stabilization policies to maintain reasonable price stability and full employment, and the only remaining questions are a matter of detail.

The second of these propositions is certainly a false generalization, though some economists, particularly those who were then in the government or associated with other interested organizations, may have made over-confident statements from time to time.

The first of these statements, I believe, has an element of truth that is specific to a particular issue.  In the late 1950's and early 60's, the federal policy was becoming increasingly deflationary (as measured, say, by the full employment surplus) due to, among other things, progressive tax rates that remained virtually unchanged since 1954 in the face of increasing income.  Most economists judged that this was one of the more important causes for the very sluggish performance of the economy in that period, and the tax reform and reduction of 1964 was undertaken after a long public debate on the issue.  Most of us are prepared to accept the evidence indicating that these tax reforms and reductions had the expected effects on the economy, and to the extent that the analysis leading to the 1964 tax reform was typically Keynesian, the Keynesian economics was "successful".

In the period 1966-68, the attempt by the Johnson administration to carry on both the Vietnam war and the ambitious social program without substantial increases in taxes resulted in overly expansionary fiscal policy accompanied by a rather permissive monetary policy.  The conclusion that the federal fiscal policy in this period was too expansionary was again based on a Keynesian analysis, and eventually led to the tax surcharge of 1968, roughly two years too late.  But the tax cut of 1964 was also too late, perhaps three or four years.  Both delays were not so much due to the failure of economic analysis but rather due to the economists' failure to communicate and convince, and to other political considerations.  But very few of us realized how radically important were asymmetric consequences of delays in correcting too deflationary and too expansionary policies.  This was a part of the fatal ignorance on our part at that time, and contributed to the poorer performance of the U.S. economy during the first half of the 1970's.  Thus, the record of the 1960's was not much different from that in most other periods.  Some success, some failures, and some new information added to the fund of our knowledge about the American economy.

I now come to the question of "spectacular recent failures" of existing macroeconometric models.  I am not sure exactly what is meant by this

reference, but Lucas and Sargent appear to take this as a well established
fact, and indeed there appears to be some vague feeling among many economists that econometric models have failed miserably in recent years.   I
suppose this refers, more than anything else, to simultaneous increases in
the rate of inflation and the rate of unemployment that took place in the
first half of the 1970's, contrary to the characteristics of simple versions of the Phillips curve that are presumed to be incorporated into all
macroeconometric models.

That this evidence does not imply anything definitive about the reliability of the model must be obvious to everyone.   Quite aside from the
theoretical and empirical soundness or validity of the Phillips curve relationship, the shape of the Phillips curve alone tells us nothing about the
correlation between the rate of inflation and the rate of unemployment over
time generated by the whole economic system.   This is because both of these
variables are endogenous and there are other variables besides these two
variables in the Phillips curve.   $\underline{3/}$   The presence of complex distributed
lags further complicate the question.

It is easy to outline what the analysis of the 1974-76 period in the
Keynesian macroeconometric model framework should have qualitatively suggested.   First of all, the inflationary expectations resulting from the
excess demand conditions of the late 1960's were still very much with us
in 1973, and this condition was, more or less, captured as initial conditions for operating econometric models in early 1974.   Second, two of the
big shocks that were administered to the U.S. economy just prior to 1974,
namely, the oil price increases and the devaluation of the dollar, were
very much in the nature of the imposition of very large excise taxes on
the economy.   In the case of the oil price rise, this is obvious to the
extent that OPEC countries did not turn around and spend the increased
revenues immediately in oil importing countries.   In the case of devaluation of the dollar, one can think of it as a removal of import subsidies
and export taxes, and therefore as a removal of a negative excise tax.
In the case of price rises in other raw materials including agricultural
commodities, the interpretation is a little more complicated because one
might argue that these prices are endogenous, and that some of the recipi-
ents of higher prices are U.S. residents who would in turn spend their
income.   One can make a rough estimate of the order of magnitudes of these
shocks interpreted as net excise tax changes, and depending on assumptions,
one comes up with figures between $30 billion and $60 billion in current

dollars.  In the Keynesian framework, that shocks of this type and magnitude will produce a substantial reduction in effective demand and simultaneously considerable increases in prices is beyond dispute.  The only
question is how well a particular econometric model is specified in the
particular detail that is needed to handle this type of analysis, and how
quantitatively accurate is the prediction of consequences generated by
the model.

My own records on this point are less than complete, because, by
chance, I began a series of experiments in forecasting using the MPS model
in the spring of 1974, a half year too late.  But for whatever it is worth,
I present below in Table I a brief summary of my forecasting records of
the spring and summer of 1974.  Various qualifications are given in the
footnotes to Table I.  One important point is that, when one is preparing
a forecast, one does not know the fiscal and monetary policies that would
eventually materialize -- indeed, policy makers themselves probably do
not know.  Therefore, I never prepared the forecast, but several alternative forecasts conditional on a plausible alternative set of policies.  In
the spring and summer of 1974, policies that were likely to be followed
were especially difficult to guess, so I do not have forecasts that correspond to a set of policies reasonably similar to the one that actually
materialized.

The following monetary and fiscal policies underlie the one shown in
Table I:

(1)  I assmued that the monetary policy was to let the money
     supply grow at a rigid 6% per year.  At the time, this
     was a caricature of the announced Fed policy, and I thought
     it was the most restrictive of policy options.  It turned
     out, however, that the money supply grew substantially less
     than 6% for the following two years.  Thus, the monetary
     policy was formally more restrictive in reality than that
     assumed in this forecast in the summer and early fall of
     1974.  However, monetary policy turned out in effect to
     have been less restrictive than that assumed in this forecast
     beginning in the later fall of 1974.  We shall come back
     to this point later.

(2)  Fiscal policy was assumed to be that in the books as of the
     summer of 1974, and no stimulative or restrictive new policy
     was introduced.  In reality, of course, a substantial stimu-
     lative policy was undertaken in the spring of 1975; for
     this reason, the forecast shown in Table I should be substan-
     tially biased downwards for the movement of GNP in 1975.

In any case, comparison of the forecast and the realization shown

TABLE I

PRIVATE AND CONDITIONAL FORECASTS OF AN ECONOMETRICIAN
FOR 1974 – 75 PERIOD, A SUMMARY a/

| ANNUAL RATE OF CHANGE | | GNP IN CONSTANT PRICES | GNP DEFLATOR |
|---|---|---|---|
| From 4th quarter, 1973 | Actual | -3.5 | 11.0 |
| to | Forecasts prepared b/ in spring, 1974 | -2.3 | 9.3 |
| 4th quarter, 1974 | Forecasts prepared b/ in summer, 1974 | -3.8 | 10.6 |
| From 4th quarter, 1974 | Actual | 2.4 | 7.4 |
| to | Forecasts prepared b/ in spring, 1974 | -.4 | 6.4 |
| 4th quarter, 1975 | Forecasts prepared b/ in summer, 1974 | -1.1 | 7.8 |

a/ Actual values are computed from NIA data after 1976 revision, while forecasts prepared in 1974 were based on data before the revision. Converting them into rates of change reduces difficulties due to revisions including some conceptual changes, but some serious problems remain for purposes of comparing actual figures with forecasts.

b/ I have picked the forecasts corresponding to monetary and fiscal policy assumptions that turned out to be closest to the ones actually adopted. The monetary policy assumption, by and large, were not too far from the actual, but fiscal policies used did not anticipate the stimulative package adopted in the spring of 1975. Therefore, our forecasts for 1975 should be biased down reflecting the absence of these stimulative fiscal policies of 1975.

in Table I suggests no spectacular failures.  The forecasts are not as good as one wishes, but they are no worse than in other periods.  Actually, these forecasts were somewhat worse in their detail than their summary shown in Table I.  But there were some specific reasons for these failures in certain parts of the model, and the experience helped us understand and correct the offending features of the model.

## III.  A THEORETICAL BASIS OF ECONOMETRIC MODELS

Until the recent group of papers on macroeconomics sharing a distinct point of view succinctly expressed by Lucas and Sargent, we tended to think of general equilibrium models of Debreu, Arrow and others as a reference point with which an attempt to describe a real economy might begin.  Most of us, including most writers in this literature, however, did not think of them as direct descriptions of the American economy, even with the modifications introduced by stochastic components and rationally formed expectations.

I have preferred, in formulating structures of models that I have used as a basis of my past empirical work, to think of classical general equilibrium models as descriptions of an idealized steady state of the economy, while interpreting some version of the Keynesian system as a short-run, conditional description, given the initial conditions.  The differences between the two arise because both volumes and prices do not adjust to new conditions instantaneously, and individuals and organizations are not capable of understanding, computing, and adjusting to the changes in environment instantaneously.  I shall return to this point in some detail a little later.

When I became involved with the MPS model, I attempted to formulate the model in this spirit, namely, that the model should exhibit the neo-classical features in the steady state, but be Keynesian in its adjustment process.  As soon as one attempts to implement such an idea, however, the difficulties with classical formulation becomes immediately glaring.  It is just not true that most firms take their output prices given and maxi-mize profits by adjusting quantities of output and inputs.  To impose an interpretation that there is no monopoly rent in national income accounts seems to me to be not only arbitrary but against our everyday experience. Yet, if we allow monopoly rent to exist in transition, I can think of no sensible limiting process which makes monopoly rent vanish in the steady

state.  Furthermore, there is the well known difficulty in  reconciling the
perfectly competitive, profit maximizing model with the observed distribution of firm sizes. [4]/

Once we admit the possibility that at least some industries have oligopolistic market structure, however, we must also admit that in such a
market the supply function is not well defined, and therefore it is not
helpful to talk about market clearance without a much more careful definition of this term than it ordinarily receives.  In the case of the MPS
model, we have resorted to the following set of assumptions to describe the
behavior of firms in the steady state equilibrium:

(1) Firms in an industry all share a same production function
    with constant returns to scale (except for the initial
    entry cost) and they are aware of this fact.

(2) They are oligopolists, and they set the price of output as
    a mark-up on the minimized average total cost, where the
    range of mark-up is limited to being between zero and the
    level above which the profit propsects would be attractive
    to new entrants to industry.

(3) At this level of price, the industry expects to sell that
    amount of output that is consistent with the demand curve
    for the industry as a whole.

(4) Since we are confining our attention at the moment to the
    steady state, it is not difficult to make sure that expecta-
    tions of managers for relevant variables, such as future
    sales, future real required rate of return, and the future
    real wage rate, are self-fulfilling.  This is because, when
    these assumptions about the behavior of the firm are combined
    with the household behavior discussed below, the resulting
    steady state is a proportional growth path in which all
    real extensive variables, properly defined, will grow at the
    same rate, while all relative prices, including the real
    rate of return, will remain constant.

The behavior of households is assumed to conform with basic features of
the life cycle hypothesis of consumption.  It is well known that, under a
reasonable set of assumptions, this hypothesis implies an aggregate form
of consumption that is linear homogeneous in expected labor income (after
taxes) and net worth of households, in which coefficients are themselves
functions of the population structure and the real rate of return.  While
the definition of the expected labor income and the measurement of net
worth are troublesome problems in reality, when we confine our attention
to the steady state path, they are perfectly straight forward.  This aggregate function in turn implies the equilibrium asset-income ratio as a

function of the parameters of the consumption function, the real rate of return, and the rate of growth of aggregate real income. The supply of savings specified by this behavior of households and the physical capital accumulated by firms, given the technology and the expectations of future output and prices, together determine the value of firms, which in turn must be equal to the reproduction cost of capital and the present value of oligopoly profits in the steady state.

This way of looking at the characteristics of the steady state equilibrium of the economy was the starting point of the real sectors of the MPS model. In adjusting this framework to accommodate the real conditions of the U.S. economy, we must recognize many annoying complications, such as the existence of government in the economy with its expenditures and taxes, external sectors, different types of capital goods such as producers' durables, residential structures, and consumer durables, and the putty-clay characteristics of some capital goods. In doing so, we have tried to preserve the modified neo-classical features of the steady state solution of the model, namely, that all behavioral equations should be derivable as implications of the assumptions that economic agents are rational, except when I had specific reasons to deviate from this guideline. I have also made sure to preserve homogeneity of various functions when the rationality assumption implies it, and to retain the possibility that the model has a steady state growth path, and not to contradict the comparative static propositions of neo-classical analysis when we are comparing one steady state growth path relative to another, again except when I believe I have explicit reasons to violate this rule.

To retain these features even at the steady state while at the same time making sure that the model does not deviate too far from realistic description of the economy, we had to rely on a number of fairly complex devices, and to make presumptions concerning some institutional arrangements such as long run evolutions of the tax system. Some of the requirements are fairly difficult to implement, involving estimations with constraints across equations as well as some non-linear ones. In the end, how well we have succeeded in this task must be checked by numerical analysis. Some of my colleagues and I have undertaken very extensive numerical analysis of this point, and the results seem conclusive that the approximation involved is quite close.

It should also be noted that most of the classical propositions about comparative static analysis of the economy are indeed valid when we are comparing two steady state paths generated by the MPS model: money is neutral in the sense that the size of its supply will have no effect on any of the real variables in the economy, and the price level is proportional to its size. It may or may not be "superneutral" in that its rate of growth will have no effect on real variables. This depends on whether or not the Phillips curve equation becomes vertical in the long run. I consider this question empirical, and the MPS model can accommodate either alternative. Government expenditure and taxes affect output of the economy only through the accumulation or decumulation of government debt, which tends to replace private, productive capital. In this sense, as far as the steady state solution is concerned, neither monetary policy nor fiscal policy has any effect on total output in the economy except through the long process of government debt accumulation. The stabilization policy is not even well defined in this context.

The reason for outlining at length the basic structure of the MPS model on its steady state paths is to dispute the impression recently created in the literature that specifications of macroeconometric models are almost entirely ad hoc, and they bear little relation to traditional economic theory. In this model, it is true that even the steady state system is not entirely consistent with the model of competitive general equilibrium, but the deviations from the general competitive equilibrium are results of deliberate decisions, like allowance for some elements of oligopolistic markets as indicated above, as the empirical necessity. I believe the only major behavioral equation which is not derived from some optimization principle is the supply of labor, which, of course, is the critical element in the new classical revival in macroeconomics.

One additional point may be mentioned briefly. Although the MPS model defines a steady state solution for any appropriate choice of exogenous variables, there is no mechanism in the model to move the system to some optimum solution, say, to the golden-rule path. I have thought about this point, and I have so far concluded that there is no such mechanism in the real economy either. It is my impression that this conclusion is shared by, for instance, Professors Lucas and Sargent, for none of their models have such an internal mechanism, either. But I am prepared to be persuaded to change my mind on this point.

The basic point of the disagreement between Keynesian macroeconomists and those who are leading the recent classical revival centers around

the question of how to move from a model describing the steady state to one
incorporating adjustment processes, or on how to model the short-run dynamic behavior of the economy.            The term "short-run" is a little misleading, because how much and how long the dynamic adjustment mechanisms
rather than the steady state characteristics would dominate the behavior
of the economy must depend on the stability of the dynamic adjustment
mechanism itself.  If it is very stable, the economy will be near a steady
state path except in the most extreme conditions, and our knowledge of the
dynamic adjustment mechanism is not very critical.  If, on the other hand,
the adjustment mechanism is unstable or very weak in its tendency to return the system to its steady state, then the behavior of the economy can
be dominated by the characteristics of the adjustment mechanism most of
the time.  One can interpret Keynes to have begun his departure from the
classical tradition with the conviction that the latter of these two alternatives is closer to reality. [5]

It should be admitted that the specifications of the dynamic adjustment process in macroeconometric models are often not well formulated.  I
believe that, in most cases, the macroeconometrician begins with a set of
ideas.  He is aware that delay in adjustments is due to a number of different causes.  First, many decisions are dependent on expectations rather
than the current values of the relevant variables, and expectations may
respond to changes in relevant variables slowly.  Second, the availability
of information to decision makers may be delayed.  Third, under uncertainty, economic agents may feel they will have to take time to interpret any
signal given to them.  Fourth, it may be difficult, physically and organi-
zationally, to make rapid changes.  Fifth, there may be many long term
contractual commitments that would not allow rapid changes.  The list can
be extended a good deal longer without any difficulty.  I am sure that the
intention of most econometricians is to model these complex processes as
close to reality as possible, while at the same time keeping the formulation simple enough so that it can be integrated with the steady state
characteristics and still remain estimatable.  The problem is that this is
an exceedingly difficult task, and some formulations adopted by econometricians turned out to be too simplistic and unsatisfactory as approximations to reality.

If all economic agents have unlimited power to comprehend, analyze,
and react, except that they cannot see the future with certainty, then the
new classical economists and most of us can agree on the following descrip-

tion of the economic system. First, all economic agents have a complete joint distribution of all future values of exogenous variables and errors, conditional on past observations. They also know in complete detail all behavioral equations for all economic agents other than themselves, and therefore they are capable of transforming the joint distribution of future values of exogenous variables and errors into the joint distribution of all future values of exogenous variables and of endogeous variables, again conditional on past observations. Each economic agent has a well-defined criteria, in which all such considerations as the difficulties of rapid changes are incorporated, and he maximizes the expectation of this criteria function over the joint distribution of all variables just described. He then updates the distribution as new observations become available in the Bayesian manner.

No one will take this description seriously, for the simple reason that we do not know even how to begin to write down such a description, nor do we expect any economic agent to be able to handle such a problem as he is described handling in the preceding paragraph. Therefore any model of the macroeconomic system is necessarily a simplification and an approximation, and the typical classical equilibrium model involves the following series of assumptions, among others. First, it is assumed that behavior of all economic agents in the economy, and distribution among them, are such that their aggregate behavior can be described as a constrained maximization process by two or three agents, say, one called the household, another denoted as the firm, and the third called the government. Second, the adjustment costs and other reasons for delay are such that the consequences of their presence at the micro level will result in no more than the introduction of some past values of aggregate variables into the aggregated behavioral equations in linear form, leaving the basic forms of aggregate functions unchanged. Third, it is assumed that all relevant information about the distribution of future values of all variables is contained in the first moments of the aggregate variables, and that behavior of individual agents are such that all future values of variables appearing in aggregate equations must be generated consistently with the rational expectations hypothesis in the narrow sense applied to aggregate variables. Fourth, excepting for the time trend, all exogenous variables and all errors are generated by stationary stochastic processes. Fifth, all aggregate behavioral equations constitute a stable (linear) dynamic system, so that all endogenous variables can be viewed as a transformation of exogenous variables and errors that retain stationarity.

These are formidable sets of assumptions, but they are formulated in such abstract terms that it would be difficult to check the empirical validity of any of them.  But they do possess internal consistency in one important respect.  Because the economy is defined to be in the stationary state, even though a stochastic one, economic agents are by assumption facing the same environment indefinitely.  Therefore it is logical that they will eventually understand their environment, and behave as though they are maximizing some criterion function, just as I suggested earlier that we can assume on a steady state growth path.  They will therefore have stable decision rules, and all agents will know everyone else's rule and act accordingly.

Before proceeding, I would like to register one remark.  In this theorizing, all economic agents are maximizing the expected values of their criterion functions over the joint probability distribution of future values of all variables, taking account, among other things of (presumed) decision rules (or strategies) of all other agents.  Therefore, the set-up is very much like that of N-person, non-zero sum game situations.  For this reason, I do not believe the uniqueness or the efficiency characteristics of the solution for the system is assured, not even the existence and the stability of the solution can be taken for granted.  Under the circumstances, the linearity of the system and the problems of aggregation of individual behavior into some aggregate relationship cannot be pushed aside, even though virtually all writers in the classical equilibrium macroeconomics apparently wish to do so.  The important characteristics, even the existence, of the solution depend on such details of specifications in this formulation.

Once we understand that the classical equilibrium theory is essentially the theory of an economic stationary state, then most of us will not find conclusions that are derived from this theory particularly startling. The most important conclusion from this type of theory is that there does not exist a monetary and fiscal policy rule that is stabilizing.  But I have already indicated that on steady-states of macroeconometric models, too, monetary and fiscal policy cannot affect output (and employment in the usual sense) except through the long-run effect of government debt on the accumulation of productive capital, and conclusions of the classical equilibrium theory are simply a generalization of this proposition to a suitable stochastic case.

Lucas and Sargent refer to two principles of classical equilibrium models, namely, that economic agents be assumed to act in their own self interest, and that markets be assumed to clear. But in practice, they must adopt the set of assumptions enumerated above or ones similar to it in order to arrive at very simple models which they and their colleagues have analyzed so far. Since these assumptions are not acceptable to most of us as good approximations to reality without strong empirical support, their acceptability is an empirical question, not a matter of principle or of the soundness of the underlying theory. Their work is full of suggestive ideas and ingenious analysis, from which we can all learn. But their model is not based on some higher principle. It must be judged on the same basis as other models. This is true even if their two principles should be accepted as basic to all "sound" economic analysis without any empirical support.

This leads us to two immediate questions: Is there some reason for accepting the two principles of Lucas and Sargent as not subject to empirical validation? What constitutes good empirical support for a theory and, in particular, how should we interpret the test of causality and exogeneity proposed by Granger and Sims and utilized extensively by advocates of new classical economics?

There probably are many economists who would object strongously to ma croeconomic models proposed by new classical economists, and at the same time feel very much tempted to accept two principles of Lucas and Sargent. This distinction between the general principles and the concrete model advocated by new classical economists is a meaningful one, as I have tried to indicate above. One could say that the Lucas-Sargent principle is vacuous, because given any decision, one can almost always construct an optimization problem for which the observed decision is the optimal solution. At the most, their principle of the best self interest as they state it seems to imply no more than that decisions of economic agents be consistent over time. Note, however, that the consistency of decisions of individual agents does not imply that their aggregate behavior in terms of aggregate variables over time would also be consistent.

The second principle, that markets clear, too, can be made true by simply defining the observed quantity transacted to be the demand as well as supply for that market. I believe Lucas and Sargent mean a little more by this principle, namely, that the model must have well defined demand and supply functions such that any observed quantity is on both of these functions.  In some sense, this requirement puts a certain type of discipline on our thinking about macromodels.  It forces an economist to think carefully about both the demand and supply functions, and helps him to avoid the situation in which some behavior is implicitly defined as a residual.

I believe that such a discipline is useful to keep in mind in any economic analysis, but that the formulation by Lucas and Sargent is much too extreme and capable of doing more damage than good.  In the case of commodities, the differences between the demand and supply for any finite time period would be a change in inventory of that commodity.  It is possible to define the demand and supply in such a way that the change in inventory is included in one or the other, and therefore the demand and the supply is always equal.  Normally, however, it is much more fruitful explicitly to model the behavior of inventory, both intended and unintended, and the feed-back of changes in inventory back to the demand and supply conditions.  Similarly, in labor market, we can certainly make a case that it is better to allow for the difference between the demand for and the supply of labor as unemployment, and to model explicitly the impact of unemployment on the demand and supply of labor as well as on other variables in the economy so long as the demand and supply functions of labor are both carefully considered in the process.  In addition to reasons from a purely economic analytical point of view that can be raised in support of this position, there is at least a possibility that such a procedure is more helpful from the statistical point of view by providing additional identification conditions, as Wold argued many years ago. ⁶⁄

The maximizing models have served as the principal source of behavioral hypotheses in economics for many years.  In so far as the purpose of economic investigation is to describe how the economic systems work in reality as accurately as possible, however, the maximizing model cannot be regarded as a teleological principle, but it must be thought of as a working hypothesis, an approximation to reality, and it must be specific enough to have strong empirical content.  It cannot be defined so broadly that it approaches a tautology.

There are many plausible reasons why economic agents do not necessarily maximize in the formal sense of this term.  Perhaps the most important reason is the one cogently argued by Herbert Simon, namely, that the environment which a human agent faces is so complex relative to his ability to comprehend, analyze, and react, that it is often the limit of his ability rather than the detailed nature of the change in his environment that is decisive in determining the behavior of the agent. [7/] Note that, when this argument holds true, we cannot salvage the maximization model by adding the so-called adjustment costs to the original criteria. For, the whole point of the argument is that the original problem was too difficult for the economic agent to formulate and solve quickly. The augmented problem, by definition, must be even more complex and difficult, and therefore, how can we expect the agent who could not solve the original problem to resolve the difficulty by formulating and solving a more difficult problem? We would then have to consider the cost of solving the augmented problem, thus leading to an infinite regression or to a situation akin to the ancient logical problem of self-referential paradoxes.

Experiences in such applied fields as operations research and financial management of firms suggest that, when we set up a constrained maximization problem for a solution, it is inevitably a grossly simplified, approximate formulation of the problem because the exact problem cannot be formulated, let alone be solved. Therefore, it always carries the important proviso that someone will have to make the judgment, outside the formal formulation of the problem, as to when and under what conditions the manager should suspend the rule and substitute his judgment. The higher the level of management, the more difficult it becomes to formalize its decision problem. It is particularly difficult to formalize the crucial decision problem of whether or not the environment has changed sufficiently and hence the decision rule should be reformulated.

For an economist attempting to describe behavior of economic agents at various levels of aggregation, the question is not whether or not the hypothesis of maximizing behavior is absolutely true, but rather, whether or not it is an acceptable approximation for the purpose at hand, in our case, to be used as a basis for constructing an aggregative econometric model for an industry or for a country as a whole on which we can base our forecasts and policy analysis. The fact that the hypothesis of maximizing behavior is contradicted more or less in many cases at the micro level is important to remember and take into account in order that we can judge whether or not the deviations from the hypothesis at the micro level become averaged out (through a process like the central limit theorem) and less significant in the process of aggregation, or they become more significant at the aggregate level through a variety of interactions. Advocates of classical equilibrium models of business cycles appear to presume that the

former of these two alternatives is the only possibility.  I do not see
how such a presumption can be justified.  8/

It should be acknowledged that in most cases, behavioral equations of
Keynesian macroeconometric models have also been formulated with scant
attention to the aggregation process.  9/  In addition, it should also be
admitted that the detailed specifications of dynamic adjustment processes
appearing in most Keynesian econometric models are often not carefully
thought out and all the behavioral and other hypotheses necessary to arrive
at the formulation utilized are not completely spelled out.  In this sense,
the criticisms of Lucas and Sargent that they "lack a sound theoretical
and econometric basis" is justified.  But in this same sense, classical
equilibrium models they advocate are also subject to the same criticisms.
I am surprised to realize that Lucas and Sargent appear to think otherwise.

"A sound theoretical and econometric basis" of any econometric model
cannot be anything like the maximization principle and the market clearance.  I suggest here a tentative definition for this phrase:

(1) All behavioral and other assumptions for deriving the equation to
be estimated must be explicitly spelled out.

(2) All available empirical evidence from whatever the source, formal
or informal, should be marshalled to check the goodness of approximation of all hypotheses at all levels.

(3) When the basic hypotheses are formulated at the micro level and
then aggregated over individuals, commodities, and/or time, hypotheses should be checked at micro level against micro data, and
when some approximations are found to be unsatisfactory, one must
determine whether such poor approximations are likely to become
less important in the process of aggregation, or they become more
significant.  10/

A hypothesis with a sound theoretical basis is a composite hypothesis
most of whose components have been thoroughly checked, leaving one simple,
new hypothesis to be checked against a new set of data.

In the next section, I would like to speculate why it is so difficult
to follow this simple principle in building and improving macroeconometric
models.

## IV.  EMPIRICAL BASIS OF MACROECONOMETRIC MODELS

Any macroeconometric model is a complex composite of many hypotheses
because it is meant to describe a complex interaction among many economic
agents faced with very complex environments.  The smallness and simplicity

of some models do not alter this fact, since it requires very complex and strong assumptions to reduce the description of complex economic systems down to a few simple equations.  These assumptions, which are usually extremely difficult to check against empirical evidence, are crucial for the possibility that such a simple and small model would remain as a good approximation of the macroeconomic system over any length of time.

In these circumstances, it is usually not possible to "test" the whole model against the time series alone.  What is normally possible is to check conditional hypotheses. [11/]  The process of determining identification conditions in a simultaneous equations systems is a part, but not all, of separating those assumptions we shall accept a priori from the remaining ones that are to be checked against data.  The matching of particular time series with a particular theoretical concept in the model, the detailed specifications of distribution of residual errors, and sometimes even the choice of estimation procedures all contribute to this conditioning process.

The problem with such a situation, of course, is that anyone who finds results of the final statistical tests distasteful can raise questions about the a priori choice of conditions.  Not only that, in the absence of some evidence from sources other than the time series with which the final system is estimated, the critic has just as much right to the choice of a priori conditions as the econometrician doing the estimation, and therefore the dispute between them can never be settled.

Serious statisticians, including Sims, have become very disturbed by this situation, and explored the possibility of opening up somewhat different avenues of attack.  They wished to formulate a procedure for testing at least some economic propositions with as little and weak a priori conditions as possible.  One of the proposals that came out of this effort is the so-called Granger-Sims test of causality (or exogeneity).  The basic idea in this test is that, if x is caused by y, then the movement of y can precede the movement of x but the movement of x can never precede the movement of y.  This notion can be generalized to cases in which x and y are both vectors of variables.  The fundamental a priori assumption that must be satisfied in order to construct a statistical test based on this notion is that after moving average and autoregressive processes for x and y are allowed for, the true residual of the relationship between x and y must be strictly white noise.

It may be said that this assumption is not an assumption, but a normalization just as in the case of the lack of correlation between X and
the remaining residual after Y is regressed on X. [12/] This proposition is
certainly true when it is applied to the relationship between the independent variables of a regression and the observed, sample residual. Similarly, it is true that the observed residual of the Granger-Sims causality
test will always turn out to be white noise. [13/] The basic question in
both cases is whether the true residual possessed the necessary properties
and therefore the estimates of the coefficients involved are unbiased, or
the true residual did not possess these properties and therefore, by using
procedures that force the estimated residuals to possess these properties,
resulting estimates of coefficients becomes biased.

When the question is asked in this way, I believe that this fundamental assumption can seldom be satisfied if x and y are a pair of variables
which are generated as a part of a large system, and not independent of
other variables. Let us consider a special case that may help to clarify
my point. Suppose that the true system is very large but strictly linear
so that we can write the reduced form equations. In a situation of this
sort, it is most unlikely that, for any reduced form equation, the independent variables on the right hand side are strictly limited to current and
past values of one exogenous variable, and past values of the endogenous
variable in question. If, in this situation, we applied the bivariate
version of the Granger-Sims test, then we are in effect running a regression omitting any number of independent variables that should have been
included, compounding all omitted variables into the residual term. In
this situation, we can say nothing about the lack of correlation between
the included independent variable and the excluded variables, nor about
the serial correlation characteristics of omitted variables. Hence, the
Granger-Sims procedure applied to this type of situation is more likely to
produce biased results than not, unless the investigator had very solid
reasons to believe that the set of variables which he is considering is
indeed the correct set, and that there is no significant omitted variable
in the equation being analyzed.

The Granger-Sims procedure can be generalized so that it can be applied to a group of variables relative to another group of variables,
rather than to a pair of scalar variables. [14/] But the same problem remains. By what criteria can an investigator decide which variables are to

be included in the test and the rest excluded? I suggest that we need the same set of a priori restrictions as that required for identifying the system under consideration for estimating parameters by one of the standard simultaneous equations estimation procedures. The difference is that, at least in theory, we can test the validity of identification conditions provided that the system is over-identified. I believe a test for the equivalent characteristics of residuals in the Granger-Sims procedure is much harder to devise and carry out.

Of course, like all scientific hypotheses, this fundamental assumption too, is an approximation, and the question is not whether it is strictly true or not, but whether it is a good enough approximation; that is, do data generated by the actual economy deviate from the fundamental assumption enough to generate seriously misleading results when the test is applied to such a set of data? If the answer to this question is negative, my objections to the fundamental assumption of the Granger-Sims test of causality is irrelevant.

Since the direct test of the question posed above is next to impossible, I have resorted to a simple quasi-Monte Carlo experiment. Using the full MPS model, I have generated an artificial time series, the critical feature of which is that (i) the short-term interest rate was taken as exogenous and determined as a time trend; (ii) the money stock was generated as an endogenous variable by the demand function for money in the system; (iii) the supply function of money was reversed and used to generate unborrowed reserves.

The structure of the MPS model is such that the only equations in which the quantity of money supply appears explicitly are the demand and the supply equations for money. Both the level of real GNP and the price deflator are influenced by many variables including many financial variables, but the channels of influence from the quantity of money supply to both the real GNP and the level of its deflator goes through the short term interest rate almost exclusively. To put it another way, when the short term interest rate is taken as exogenous in this model, the reduced form equations for both real GNP and its deflator will not contain the quantity of money supply, although they will contain dozens of other predetermined variables including the short term interest rate. 15/ In other words, when the short term interest is taken as exogenous and the quantity of money supplied and the unborrowed reserves of the monetary authority is taken as endogenous, then the MPS model may be thought of as

being block triangular, so that the causality goes from GNP, prices, and
the rate of interest to the quantity of money, but not the other way around.

If we now generate a set of artificial time series data by simulating
the MPS model in this mode, and run regressions using this set of artificial data with nominal GNP and the quantity of money as dependent variables
we should observe the following:

(1)  In the regression with nominal GNP as the dependent variable,
     if we select all predetermined variables which were included
     in the reduced form equation for nominal GNP, the fit should
     be perfect (except for the nonlinearities) and the current
     and past values of money supply should have coefficients
     equal to zero.

(2)  In the regression with the quantity of money supplied as the
     dependent variable, the inclusion of real GNP, its deflator,
     and the short rate of interest, together with the lagged
     values of the dependent variable should give us fairly close
     fit.  The residual error should reflect the non-linearity
     and a few additional variables that were present in the
     equivalent equation in the model used to generate the data --
     the latter effect is not very great, while the former is
     quite important.

Given this construction, it seems clear that the Granger-Sims test,
when it is slightly generalized to include all relevant variables and
applied to this artificial data, must result in the conclusion that
income causes money supply but money does not cause income.  In practical
situations, however, we do not know exactly which variable should or should
not be included in the testing procedure, and suppose that we have procee-
ded by considering the pair, money supply and nominal income, by themselves.
We are then excluding all variables, among them the short term rate of
interest, that we have discussed in the preceding paragraph.  The critical
question is whether the Granger-Sims procedure applied to the pair of variables can nonetheless tell us something about the structure of the system
generating the time series. [16/]

In Table II below, I report the result of this experiment using the
artificial data described above.  We have followed Sims' procedure exactly,
and added the Granger version of the same test.  Part A of the table repeats
the Sims test with the historical data for our sample period, and it con-
firms Sims' result that the money stock is not caused by the nominal GNP,
that is, money stock is clearly exogenous according to this test.  The
Granger version of the test gives us the same result.  Part B reports the
result of the same test, applied to the artificial data just described.

Quite surprisingly, very small values of the F-ratios between hypotheses $H_1$ and $H_0$ in Part B, as in Part A, make it quite decisive that additional variables introduced in $H_1$ relative to $H_0$ have very little explanatory power, which in these tests must be interpreted as providing strong support for the proposition that the quantity of money is not caused by income. But this result, of course, is contrary to the structure of the model generating the data, as described in preceding paragraphs. Evidently, the omission of additional variables that should have been included in the analysis is sufficient to cause biases in the test procedure to generate this seriously misleading result.

I should probably add an obvious point. If our aim is not to learn about the structure generating data but to forecast the value of the next observation, then the result of the Granger-Sims test is clearly relevant. The numerical results reported above then says that, if we are interested in forecasting the next observation of the quantity of money supplied, if we take account of past values of money supply optimally, then any past observation that we have on nominal GNP will not be useful for reducing the variance of error of our forecast of money supply, if the only data we have are limited to money supply and nominal GNP. This does not exclude the possibility that, when GNP is used together with a third variable, for instance, the nominal short term rate of interest, then these two variables together will materially contribute to our forecasting ability.

I do not believe that the result of my experiment should be particularly surprising to econometricians who have struggled with the problem of estimating structural models from time series data for many years. As I indicated a while ago, the basic problem has always been that we needed a great deal of maintained hypotheses, including identification conditions, in order to estimate or test only a small part of macroeconometric models. We are on shaky ground for at least some of these maintained hypotheses, and this is obviously a serious obstacle for progress of econometric research. Sims is certainly right in insisting that this is a serious problem, though some of his judgements may be a bit extreme. However, I do not believe that his suggested solution is a promising one. It is essentially a proposal to lump all maintained hypotheses, good and bad, together into one catch-all assumption that the residual errors of his test equation is pure white noise. This is particularly unfortunate because such an assumption can never be evaluated against data, while at least some of the

maintained hypotheses in their original forms could be checked against empirical evidence provided that we broaden our source of empirical information beyond aggregate time series data.

This brings me to a   point which has been neglected in recent discussion of macroeconometric models and economic time series analysis.  The
ultimate source for all those maintained hypotheses necessary to use the
time series data effectively in estimating econometric models must be
sources of information other than time series data themselves.  These other
sources must include cross-section data, data for other countries, time
series data for earlier periods, and even informal insights one may have
obtained by observing and talking with critical decision-making agents in
the economy.  If we can effectively and systematically exploit all the
information available from these other sources and relate it to specific
maintained hypotheses including identification conditions, we would begin
to make more systematic progress in the accumulation of our knowledge about
the functioning of the economy.

I must digress at this point and comment on one obvious but neglected
aspect of these maintained hypotheses.  It is not necessary that all of
these maintained hypotheses be exactly true, but they should be approximately satisfactory.  Some twenty years ago, T.C. Liu, in a series of papers
one of which is cited by Sims at the beginning of his 1977 Fisher-Schulz
Lecture  |1979|, advanced the very pessimistic thesis that estimation of
structural equations is impossible because many of the maintained hypotheses, such as the exclusion assumptions needed for identification, classification of variables into exogenous and endogenous variables, and the complete exclusion of some variables and hence some equations from the system,
can never in reality be strictly true.  This was a very disturbing thesis
at the time, and we felt rather relieved when Franklin Fisher was able to
show that the properties of estimators are continuous with respect to the
deviation of these maintained hypotheses from their exact satisfaction so
that if they are only slightly violated, then the properties of estimators
are only slightly disturbed.[17/]

The same argument applies to the famous proposition put forward by
Lucas on the near-impossibility of estimating structural equations in macroeconometric models in the face of changing government policy rules.  He
argues that behavioral equations in any econometric model reflect, in principle, optimal responses of economic agents to a given government policy

rule. Therefore, these equations must change when the government abandons one policy rule in favor of another, because economic agents presumably must respond to the new rule. Therefore, unless all behavior equations in the model are so designed to be capable of reflecting automatically the changing optimal responses of economic agents to government policy rule changes, the structure of behavioral equations of the econometric model will be unstable whenever government policy rules change. If we then nevertheless go ahead and estimate an econometric model without explicit attention to this problem, such a model will be worthless for the purposes of economic policy analysis.

This argument of Lucas is true as far as it goes. But the crucial question is again how quantitatively serious this problem is. If the structure of behavioral equations are only very slightly affected by changes in government policy rules, the assumption that they are unaffected would be nearly correct, and for most purposes econometric models using such an assumption would be good enough, because both the estimates of parameters and behavior of the model would then be nearly correct.

In practice, when major government policy changes occur, it is not too difficult to identify a small number of behavioral equations that are likely to be affected, and isolate them from the remaining equations on which the impact of the policy changes would be minimal. Once this identifica-tion is made, it is usually possible to handle the difficulty stressed by Lucas in some reasonable manner. This does not mean that the problem pointed out by Lucas is trivial or easy to deal with. This reasoning does, however, bring it down from the level of some higher teleological principle where Lucas placed it, and makes it another difficult empirical problem like many others that we face in econometric studies.

We have thus come to the conclusion that the basic problem of macro-econometric models, and more generally, of all econometric studies, is to ascertain how approximately accurate are the maintained hypotheses that are needed to confront the results of the study being undertaken. The crucial point is that these maintained hypotheses are neither exactly true nor false, but rather a continuum of approximations to reality. The more accurate the maintained hypotheses, the more precise the additional information one can obtain from the data concerning the hypotheses studied. Our objective must then be to improve the accuracy of the approximation of these maintained hypotheses as well as that of the hypotheses being tested

by accumulating more and more information over time, bearing in mind that
the accuracy of some hypotheses are much more important than the accuracy
of some other hypotheses for the particular purpose at hand.

Let us restate our proposition a little differently.  The collection
of hypotheses that we use to describe the world is a simplified, abbreviated description, because our ability as economists to comprehend, describe
and analyze is limited just as the abilities of economic agents.  We are
continually attempting to improve the degree of approximation of such a
collection of hypotheses to reality.  Our procedure normally involves sing-
ling out one or two hypotheses at a time and studying them against a set
of data, assuming for this purpose that the approximation of the remaining
hypotheses are good enough.  But we must always watch out for the possibility that the degree of approximation attained by the maintained hypotheses may turn out to be unsatisfactory.  When this turns out to be the case,
our task is to identify which of the maintained hypotheses are the offenders
and to strive to improve the formulation of defective hypotheses.  This
often involves appealing to a data source other than the one utilized for
studying the original set of hypotheses, or reinterpreting studies undertaken in a very different context.

There are two very serious difficulties when one attempts to proceed
in this manner.  The first is the obvious one of pooling information from
two or more data sources, although the situation is not quite the same as
the one with which statisticians are familiar.  In the standard problem of
pooling samples, we are dealing with the question of how to combine two
samples that may be generated by two somewhat different processes, and use
the total information contained in both of them to test one specific hypothesis.  In the situation that I have been describing, we wish to strength-
en one hypothesis with one set of information in order more effectively to
test another hypothesis with a separate set of sample information.  Our
problem is how to formalize this problem in such a way so that the whole
collection of hypotheses will become improved in the end.

This brings me to the final and most difficult point I wish to raise
in this paper.  For many of us, most of our time as economists is spent on
checking our understanding of how the economy functions against information
generated by the economy itself, finding that some aspect of our understanding is particularly defective, and then attempting to improve that particular aspect of our knowledge.

The formal apparatus that we use in carrying out this task is the testing procedure that we have all learned from any textbook on statistical theory. We single out a particular hypothesis or a small group of hypotheses, assume that whatever other hypotheses that are necessary for testing the hypotheses in question are true, and then carry out the statistical test of the hypothesis against whatever data is available to us. What is in fact being done is to define when the discrepancy between the data and the hypothesis is no longer likely to have arisen by chance. (The larger the sample size, the more critically dependent the answer to. this question on the accuracy of the maintained hypothesis.) Such a determination is not at all the same as settling the question of whether or not the hypothesis is a tolerable approximation to the reality. [18]/

No statistical theory that enables us to treat the latter problem of judging the adequacy of approximation in a general way exists. In principle, the Bayesian philosophy is sympathetic to this formulation of the problem, and indeed in some very simple cases where prior-posterior analysis can be carried out easily and completely, we can formulate our problem in the Bayesian framework. But in general, the technical difficulties of carrying out Bayesian analysis becomes so formidable that the appeal to the Bayesian framework cannot be considered promising, at least at the present time.

Because there is no generally acceptable formal procedure for checking and improving approximations systematically, scientists, including economists, tend to carry out this task informally and implicitly. One unfortunate consequence of this situation is that there sometimes arises methodological controversies that are due to some misunderstanding of the nature and the structure of theories about empirical phenomena. In particular, when some researcher feels especially strongly about some maintained hypothesis, either positively or negatively, he can be easily trapped into forgetting that these hypotheses are all empirical approximations, and believing that some of these hypotheses are absolutely false or absolutely true. More subtly, how badly a minor violation of the maintained hypotheses will invalidate our inference concerning the hypothesis being tested will depend on the structure of the testing procedure, and nothing definite can be said without analyzing the detailed structure of the testing procedure. The consequence of ignoring this last dependence can be quite devastating.

Many observations by new classical economists and time series analysts are well-taken, and all of us who work in applied econometrics are grateful for their contribution. There is no doubt that we have benefited from their observations and analysis, and all econometric models are changing for the better because of them. I believe, however, that some of their positions become untenable when they take an absolutist position in some of their propositions, as I have tried to demonstrate above. Thus, when Lucas points out that, in some cases, the rational expectations hypothesis may be a good approximation to reality, that behavior of some economic agents could be affected by government policy rule changes and therefore these induced behavioral changes must be allowed for in econometric models in some cases; when Granger and Sims point out that some of maintained hypotheses in estimating econometric models may be poorer approximations than builders of models supposed; we must take them seriously, and I for one believe that their points are often well taken. But when Lucas makes the final jump and says that any econometric model that does not rigidly adhere to his assumptions is inferior to his in principle independent of direct empirical evidence on his assumption, or when Sims advocates that all structural and identifying assumptions in econometric models be abandoned in favor of his catch-all assumption that the residual errors of his test equations are pure white noise, which can not be directly verified, they have gone much too far.

Before I end this essay, I would like to present a brief observation on the major defect of current statistical theory as a tool of empirical science described in the preceding few paragraphs. As I indicated earlier, the awareness of this difficulty is nothing new to statistical theorists and empirical scientists. Many of us felt in the 1950s and 60s that some form of Bayesian formulations would provide a flexible enough framework to remedy this situation, but technical difficulties involved proved to be so formidable that we have made little progress in this direction, and I am afraid it will be some time before we will be able to resolve this issue satisfactorily.

In the meanwhile, economics and other empirical sciences must go on, and one must answer the question of how best to cope with this difficulty. In practice, an econometrician usually has in his head and in his files a collection of evidences accumulated over many years concerning a particular empirical phenomenon. These are often results of his own studies, reading of works of others, of conversations with his colleagues and many other sources. These evidences are probably not compatible with each other for a number of complex reasons, and some of them may even be too informal to be used in any statistical analysis. Nonetheless, the econometrician is likely to have built up some well defined ideas on the general form of a model that would probably approximate relevant aspects of the behavior of agents which are expressed in formal and informal data from all these sources. Thus, when he then formulates his specific hypothesis and confronts it against a new set of data, and this new set of data in some way does not conform to the prediction of his hypothesis, he would not necessarily abandon his hypothesis or one of the maintained assumptions immediately, though his confidence in them would be somewhat weakened. He would instead look for causes of failures, scrutinize the characteristics of data carefully, and attempt to modify gradually his hypothesis and perhaps some of the maintained assumptions to improve the approximations involved. [19]/

This situation is very unfortunate because it appears to involve so much subjective judgement by the econometrician in question, and it takes so much time to develop a concensus among economists. But until a major development in statistical theory will enable us to formalize this process, we have no alternative, and the best we can do is to make the process as transparent as possible so that interested outsiders can accurately judge the reliability of results obtained by econometricians. For this purpose, I believe it is much more fruitful to stress the credibility of each of small components of econometric models one at a time, relative to over-all performances of the model, including however the contribution of the components to the overall dynamic characteristics of the system.

In this difficult task, we need all the help we can get from classical economists, time series analysts, and anyone else who brings either additional information about the behavior of economic agents, or fresh approaches on how most effectively to approximate their behavior. If some of them sometimes get carried away by enthusiasm for their own ideas, we would not be able to accept them in their extreme versions, but we are still grateful for the fresh ideas themselves.

*A. Ando*

TABLE II

CHECK ON GRANGER–SIMS TEST OF CAUSALITY:    TEST

<u>THAT THE STOCK OF MONEY IS EXOGENOUS RELATIVE TO NOMINAL GNP</u>

PART A:   HISTORICAL DATA
(Total Number of Observations = 43)

| | Number of Variables | SSR | F |
|---|---|---|---|
| Granger $H_0$ [b/] | 9 | 7.7392 | |
| Granger $H_1$ [c/] | 13 | 6.8144 | 1.0178 [f/] |
| Sims $H_0$ [d/] | 14 | 8.5034 | |
| Sims $H_1$ [e/] | 18 | 6.9617 | 1.3841 [g/] |

PART B:   ARTIFICIAL DATA IN WHICH THE STOCK
OF MONEY IS ENDOGENOUS [a/]
(Total Number of Observations = 43)

| | Number of Variables | SSR | F |
|---|---|---|---|
| Granger $H_0$ [b/] | 9 | 3.0845 | |
| Granger $H_1$ [c/] | 13 | 2.6641 | 1.1835 [f/] |
| Sims $H_0$ [d/] | 14 | 14.4464 | |
| Sims $H_1$ [e/] | 18 | 12.7985 | 0.8647 [g/] |

a/ For a brief description of the simulation run that generated the data for this purpose, see the text of this paper.

b/ The dependent variable of this regression is the logarithm of M1, and independent variables are constant, time, three seasonal dummy variables, and the logarithm of M1 lagged 1 to 4 periods, inclusive.

c/ This is the same regression as for Granger $H_0$, except the logarithms of the nominal GNP lagged 1 to 4 periods, inclusive, were included as additional independent variables.

d/ The dependent variable of this regression is the logarithm of the nominal GNP, and independent variables are constant, time, three seasonal dummies, and current and lagged vaules of the logarithm of M1, 1 to 8 periods.

e/ This is the same regression as for Sims $H_0$, except values of the logarithm of M1, led 1 to 4 periods, were included as additional independent variables.

f/ F was calculated as $30(SSR_0-SSR_1)/4SSR_1$. $F(4, 30) = 2.69$ for 5%.

g/ F was calculated as $25(SSR_0-SSR_1)/4SSR_1$. $F(4, 25) = 2.76$ for 5%.

NOTE Nominal GNP and M1 were filtered through the same filter used by Sims in his original article.

## FOOTNOTES

1/ Lucas and Sargent [1978].

2/ Savage [1954], and Simon [1968].

3/ It should be remembered, in particular, that the Phillips curve relationship normally refers to the wage rate or the price index of value added in the country. Prices of final goods must depend, among other things, in addition to the factors considered in the Phillips curve, on the costs of imported goods and of some raw materials. Some changes in these external prices are clearly exogenous, such as the oil price increases of 1973-4, and such changes must affect final good prices unless the prices of value added in the country (and therefore most likely the wage rate) declines just enough to offset them exactly. The particular wage equation in the MPS model is a version of the Phillips curve with some modifications exhibiting parameter value which implies the existence of the natural rate in a very long run. This equation performs extremely well in terms of fits against the historical data and in forecast performance from the late 1960s to the present. This puts me in a quandary because I have some serious doubts about the behavioral hypothesis underlying this equation.

4/ If the production functions for all firms are strictly homogeneous of degree one, then the size distribution of firms in each industry should be completely arbitrary. Therefore, at least in some cases, there must develop firms that are much larger than others, controlling more than a significant portion of the market for its output. If the entry cost into the industry is exactly zero, even in this situation, the price may be equal to the minimized average cost, and therefore it may be possible to define an unambiguous supply function for the industry. In most industries however, the entry cost is not zero, and hence the market must be oligopolistic if there are some dominant firms in the industry. It is well known that the size distribution of firms is very skewed, and there are some plausible theories explaining why they are almost always skewed. Simon and Ijiri [1977].

5/ For examples of the type of interpretation of the Keynesian models, see Tobin [1975] and Ando [1974].

6/ Wold and Juréen [1953].

7/ For example, Simon [1969] and [1978].

8/ Some advocates of classical models may conciously or unconsciously be relying on the famous methodological principle of Milton Friedman: "Truly important and significant hypotheses will be found to have 'assumptions' that are wildly inaccurate descriptive representation of reality, and, in general, the more significant the theory, the more unrealistic the assumptions." Sometimes, this proposition is interpreted to imply that it does not matter how much direct evidence there is against the maximization hypothesis so long as its "market implications" are not rejected by aggregative data. The difficulties of this methodological position has been thoroughly discussed in the literature, for instance, by Samuelson and Simon. In the present case, the situation is particularly troublesome because the macro implications of the maximization principle cannot be isolated from those of many other assumptions such as the ones enumerated earlier. Indeed, it is not clear that the isolation is possible, even in principle, when the empirical evidence for them is confined to aggregate time series data. Friedman [1953], Samuelson [1962].

9/ The derivation of an aggregate consumption function from the life cycle hypothesis may be considered an exception. I have also prepared a note on one aspect of the aggregation problem that occurs frequently in the context of building macroeconometric models, and this note served as one of the methodological guidelines for those who worked on the MPS model. Ando [1971].

10/ Of course, from a purely logical point of view, there is no reason why some macro relationship among aggregate variables, such as nominal GNP and money supply, should not be taken as the basic hypothesis, assumed to hold true unconditionally except for purely white noise disturbances. Milton Friedman sometimes takes a position that is very close to this. But the problem, then, is that any such relation, like all scientific hypotheses about reality, is an approximation and we have no basis deciding whether the observed degree of approximation is "good enough" or not. Furthermore, if someone disagrees with this point of view, and asserts that the strong correlation between nominal GNP and money supply is a result of more basic, behavioral relationships plus the processes of aggregation, there is no possibility at all of settling such a disagreement by appeal to time series data alone. We would then find ourselves inquiring into

the details of behavioral hypotheses that could serve as the foundation
for the macro relation in question in the effort to shed some light on such
a dispute.

11/ Take, for example, the work of Bischoff in the investment function.  If
we are prepared to accept all of his other assumptions, then it is possible
in his framework to test whether the nature of producers' equipment is
putty-putty or putty-clay, and the result appears quite conclusive.  Alternatively, if we add the putty-clay nature of producers equipment to all
other assumptions to be accepted without tests, then we can test the
Jorgenson-Bischoff view of flexible production function against the possibility that the labor-capital ratio is fixed independent of the cost of
capital.  Under the best of conditions, we may be able to test two or three
hypotheses together, but certainly not much more than that at a time using
time series data.  Bischoff [1971].

12/ Sims made this point to me on several occasions.  I hope the following
discussion will clarify the nature of the remaining disagreements between
us.

13/ This proposition follows from the well-known proposition that, under
fairly general conditions, a regular full rank stationary process possesses
a unique one-sided moving average representation as well as an autoregressive representation, whose innovations are white noise.  See, for example,
Rosanov [1961], and Masani [1966].

14/ However, for complications that may arise in interpreting results when
more than two variables are involved, see, for example, Hsiao [1980].

15/ It should be noted at once that we cannot actually write such a reduced
form equation explicitly, because of the non-linearity of the system.

16/ The "residual" of the relationship between the money supply and the
nominal income, then, is the sum of all omitted variables times their true
coefficients.  Strictly speaking, I should have generated all relevant exogenous variables and the initial conditions by some well defined stochastic
process, and used them as input to the simulation generating the artificial
data.  I should also have repeated such an experiment many times, and only
then would I have had a well-defined Monte Carlo experiment.  Instead, I
used the historical values of exogenous variables and performed the experiment only once.  While my procedure seems crude, I believe it provides some
indication of how misleading this set of tests can be in actual applied

situations.

17/ At about the same time, Herbert Simon and I analyzed the dynamic behavior of nearly, but not exactly, decomposable systems. We were able to show that, within a certain time interval, the nearly decomposable system behaved like the corresponding perfectly decomposable system, while for another, longer time interval, we can define an aggregate system in terms of aggregate variables, each of which would represent a non-decomposable subsystem. This analysis enabled us to generalize the original definition of the causality by Simon, and it also turned out that the mathematical characteristics of the problem we have solved are equivalent to that of Fisher's referred to in the text. See Simon [1953], Fisher [1961], Simon and Ando [1961] and Ando and Fisher [1963].

18/ This formulation of the problem is due to Herbert Simon. The main reference is a series of his essays collected in his Models of Discovery [1977]. See also L.J. Savage, The Foundations of Statistics [1954], pp. 254-256. The point of distinction made in this paragraph may be seen more clearly through the following consideration. Suppose that we have a hypothesis (including the specification of stochastic characteristics) that is an extremely good description of some phenomenon. The hypothesis is an approximation in that it does not take account of some very small effects of a few variables. But errors due to this approximation are extremely small, and it is of no importance to anyone for any purpose.

Nevertheless, there will always be a large enough interger such that, if the sample size is greater than that number, the standard statistical test will reject this hypothesis. It does not help the matter to set a very high level of significance, because it will be nullified by a larger sample size. This point is well understood by statisticians, but to my knowledge, no one has yet reformulated the statistical procedure to deal with this kind of decision problem adequately.

19/ Take, for example, my own experience with the aggregate consumption function. I believe that an aggregate version of the life cycle model that is now in the MPS model is a good approximation, not because it fits well with the quarterly time series data of the U.S. on which it is estimated, not even because it has predicted consumption reasonably accurately during the past several years, although these facts are encouraging. I believe in it because I have applied the theory to the cross section data on several occasions, and I have worked through the aggregation problem using

the U.S. population structure as weights and observed that parameter
values of the aggregate function predicted by this process are roughly
confirmed by direct estimates of these values from time series data, and
that the aggregate behavior of the asset-income ratio of consumers predicted by the model is roughly confirmed by the data.  I have also learned
about application of this model to many other countries as well as to
international data, and finally, we have been watching the shift in saving
behavior as the U.S. population structure shifts over time to see if we
are qualitatively on the right track.  Thus, while I am unable formally to
attach any probabilities for the accuracies of the maintained assumption
of this aggregate equation, I am prepared to defend my estimates with some
confidence.  As I survey all equations in the model, my confidence in this
sense varies from quite strong to almost non-existent; this variation in
my confidence has only very vague relation to the standard statistical
measures of the reliability of these equations.

## ACKNOWLEDGEMENTS

I have benefited from comments on an earlier draft of the paper from
B.M. Friedman, R.J. Gordon, E.J. Hannan, L.R. Klein, C.A. Sims,
R.J. Shiller, R.M. Solow and J. Tobin.

The computation presented in Table 2 was carried out by Mr. Edward
Hendricks, for which I am grateful.

REFERENCES

1   Ando, A. [1971] "On a Problem of Aggregation," International Economic
    Review, 1971, pp. 306-311.

2   Ando, A. |1974| "Some Aspects of Stabilization Policies, The Monetarist
    Controversy, and the MPS Model," International Economic Review, 15,
    pp. 541-571.

3   Ando, A. and F.M. Fisher [1963] "Near-Decomposability Partition and
    Aggregation and Relevance of Stability Discussions," International
    Economic Review, Jan. 1963.

4   Anscombe, F.J. [1963] "Test of Goodness of Fit," Journal of the Royal
    Statistical Society, Series B, 25, pp. 81-94.

5   Bischoff, C.W. [1971| "The Effects of Alternative Lag Distribution,"
    in Tax Structures and Capital Spending, ed. by G. Fromm, The Brookings
    Institution, Washington, D.C.

6   Fisher, F.M. [1961| "On the Cost of Approximate Specifications in
    Simultaneous Equation Estimation," Econometrica, April 1961.

7   Friedman, B.M. |1977| Optimal Expectations and the Extreme Information
    Assumptions of "Rational Expectations" Macromodels, unpublished.

8   Friedman, M. |1953| "The Methodology of Positive Economics" in his
    Essays in Positive Economics, The University of Chicago Press, Chicago
    Illinois.

9   Gemeke, J. [1978| "Testing the Exogeneity Specification in the Complete
    Dynamic Simultaneous Equation Model," Journal of Econometrics, pp. 163-
    183.

10  Granger, C.W.J. and P. Newbold [1977| Forecasting Economic Time Series,
    Academic Press, New York, NY.

11  Hendry, D.F. [1977] "Comments on Granger-Newbold's 'Time Series Approach
    to Econometric Model Building' and Sargent-Sims' 'Business Cycle Model-

ling Without Pretending to Have Too Much A Priori Economic Theory,"
in New Methods in Business Cycle Research, edited by C.A. Sims,
Federal Reserve Bank of Minneapolis.

12   Hsiao, C. [1980] A Characterization of Multivariate Granger Causality
Using Time Series Data, Institute for Policy Analysis, University of
Toronto, unpublished.

13   Lucas, R.F. and T.J. Sargnet [1978| "After Keynesian Macroeconomics"
Proceedings of the Conference in After the Phillips Curve, Federal
Reserve Bank of Boston Conference Series No. 19, Federal Reserve Bank
of Boston, Boston, Massachusetts.  See also discussions by B. Friedman
and R.M. Solow in the same volume.

14   Masai, P. [1966| "Recent Trends in Multivariate Prediction Theory,"
Multivariate Analysis I, ed. by P.R. Krishnaiah, Academic Press, New
York, NY.

15   Razanov, Yu A. [1967] Stationary Random Process, Holden-Day, San
Francisco.

16   Samuelson, P.A. [1962| "Comment" presented at the Session on Problems
of Methodology, American Economic Association Papers and Proceedings,
May 1962.

17   Savage, L.J. [1954| Foundations of Statistics, John Wiley & Sons, Inc.
New York, NY.

18   Simon, H.A. [1953] "Causal Ordering and Identifiability," in Studies
in Econometric Methods, ed. by W.C. Hood and T.C. Koopmans, John Wiley
and Sons, Inc., New York, NY.

19   Simon, H.A. [1977] Models of Discovery, D. Reidel Publishing Co.,
Boston, Mass.

20   Simon, H.A. [1968| "On Judging the Plausibility of Theories" in Logic,
Methodology, and Philosophy of Sciences III, ed. by Van Roostelaar and

Staal, North-Holland Publishing Co., Amsterdam, The Netherlands.

21   Simon, H.A. [1978] "Rationality as Process and as Product of Thought," Richard T. Ely Lecture, American Economic Review, March 1978.

22   Simon, H.A. [1969] The Science of the Artificial, MIT Press, Cambridge, Mass.

23   Simon, H.A. and A. Ando [1961] "Aggregation of Variables in Dynamic Systems," Econometrica, April 1961.

24   Simon, H.A. and Y. Ijiri [1977] Skew Distributions and the Sizes of Business Firms, North-Holland Publishing Co., Amsterdam, The Netherlands.

25   Sims, C.A. [1980] "Macroeconomics and Reality," Econometrica, January 1980, pp. 1-48.

26   Sims, C.A. [1972] "Money, Income and Causality," American Economic Review, pp. 540-555.

27   Tobin, J. [1975] "Keynesian Models of Recession and Depression," American Economic Review Papers and Proceedings, 65, 195-202.

28   Tukey, J.W. [1962] "The Future of Data Analysis," Annals of Mathematical Statistics, 33, pp. 1-67.

29   Wold, H. and L. Juréen [1953] Demand Analysis: A Study in Econometrics John Wiley and Sons, Inc., New York  NY.

LARGE-SCALE MACRO-ECONOMETRIC MODELS
J. Kmenta, J.B. Ramsey (editors)
© North-Holland Publishing Company, 1981

SCALE OF MACRO-ECONOMETRIC MODELS AND ACCURACY OF FORECASTING[*]

Gary Fromm
Center for Economic Policy Research
SRI International
1611 North Kent Street
Arlington, Virginia  22209


Lawrence R. Klein
Department of Economics
University of Pennsylvania
Philadelphia, Pennsylvania
U.S.A.

Appropriate scale for economic models has been a
subject of controversy.  Reasons for scale differences
and foreasting accuracy of 12 U.S. economy models are
examined, as well as questions of manageability and
criteria for selecting optimum scale. The controversy
seems to stem more from subjective perceptions and
attitudes toward preferences for models of given scale
than can be justified by evidence on usefulness, costs,
and other characteristics.  In sum, neither big nor
small is beautiful; it is the quality of a model that
truly matters and not its size.

1.   WHY HAVE MODELS BECOME LARGE IN SCALE?

Tinbergen's model of the United States, constructed at the League of
Nations in the 1930's, appeared to be large by standards of the times.
Haavelmo's critique of Tinbergen's statistical procedures was based on a
small 2-equation example, and the Cowles Commission models, intended to
update Tinbergen's efforts, deliberately were limited in scale in order to
deal with statistical problems of interdependence.  Also, the compact
mathematical formulations of the Keynesian system were exploited from the
side of economic theory so as to limit model scale.

At the time (1940's) the small 3-equation system known as Klein-Model
I was used as a prototype to test statistical methods.  A larger model was
intended for more serious application; it would be considered very small
today, and was smaller than Tinbergen's original U.S. system.

There were two serious limitations to model size in the early years of
macro-econometric model building.  One was sample size, or the larger
consideration of data availability.  The other was lack of facilities,
principally computers.  There were not enough degrees of freedom, not
enough statistical materials for construction of many individual variables,

and not enough facilities for handling large amounts of data. Use of desktop electro-mechanical calculators manned by numerous clerical workers imposed size limitations and accurate results were difficult and expensive to obtain and reproduce.

Calculating solutions of relatively small simultaneous systems, say of fewer than twenty equations, was an oppressive task. It required a day or more to solve a 20-equation simultaneous system and the possibility of repeated dynamic simulations under alternative conditions was simply out of the question.

Partial exceptions to these rules were the early input-output systems. These, too, were limited in scope, but had dimensions that were much larger than counterpart macro systems. However, there also were severe computational limitations to use of input-output systems and their linkage with macro models of final demand-income generation as known today, was not feasible.

As data and computational facilities became more available, models grew correspondingly in size. This growth was in natural response for investigation into detail. When the first postwar consumption function failed in the aggregate, it was natural to look into the possibility of explanation of the failure through separate analysis of durables, nondurables, and services expenditures. There will always be a quest for detail to see if more can be learned about any micro process by examining its components.

Not only were specific aggregate problems investigated in component parts, but it became obvious that there was a need for general purpose analysis. The economic system continuously goes through periods of "rolling readjustments." At one time, consumer spending is a predominant factor, then it becomes inventory change, or net exports, or net capital formation. Price and wage behavior may come next. Or, the leading disturbance or growth factors may be in particular markets or sectors at one point in time while shifting focus at another moment of time. To have a system to enable ready analysis of different and shifting readjustments, it is necessary to build large models that incorporate the different main areas of change at all time points. The general purpose model, serving many users at once, will necessarily have to be large. It is inexpensive to manage small models, but there is enormous cover-up of economic action, at one time or another, in such highly aggregative systems.

A system may be big, but consisting of many decomposable subsectors. Simple treatments of small subsector equation systems can be part of a larger model which, when analyzed by themselves, can appear to be quite manageable. But partial, as opposed to general, equilibrium analysis can be very misleading. Partial treatments are inadequate to account for many known feedback effects. Simultaneity is at least as important as recursiveness. A partial model will undoubtedly miss many feedback effects and tend to be biased, as will small "self-contained" systems.

An econometrician is a technician who serves many masters. It is impractical, especially in today's world of fast turnaround, to have new sectors tailor-made as needs arise. It is better to have available the most general system that can be constructed. Then the econometrician is potentially ready to analyze the effect of recent crop harvests, of a longshoremen's strike, of the oil shortage, of new tax legislation, or of federal spending shortfalls. It is never known where the next request for model information is coming from or what will be asked. To be ready for any contingency, it is important to be able to serve many masters. That is a principal reason today for the large size of many models.

Nothing has brought home more forcefully the need for a large detailed model than have two recent events--significant agricultural failures (1972, 1975, 1977) and the energy crisis. As each of these issues came to the fore some simple calculations were made in order to study their macroeconomic impacts. But, it became apparent without much delay that these problems were so large and pervasive that they had to be studied within a general equilibrium rather than a partial or small macro system context.

In the first place, both food and energy are intermediate goods; therefore, they are best analyzed in the framework of an input-output system (although not necessarily one of the fixed proportions Leontief type). When such a system is fully linked to a final demand/factor income model, the resulting system must necessarily be large. It is no exaggeration or stretching of reasoning to ague that complex subsectors such as food and energy fit best in 1,000-equation systems, just to give an order of magnitude. Food demand is part of the comsumption sector but, in order to be met, also requires current factor inputs and fixed capital formation. In addition, it is a major aspect of imports and exports. It is too large a component of the consumer price index, the consumer spending total, or foreign trade to be treated in a decomposable partial system, apart from its role in the economy as a whole. Similarly, energy is used so widely throughout the production system, has such a big impact on foreign trade accounts, and figures so importantly in price level determination, not to mention automobile demand, that it, too, must be studied, if it is to be done properly, in the framework of a complete general equilibrium system of the economy as a whole. By such a system, we mean a model that integrates I-O accounts with the NIA system in one complete unit. This was pioneered in the Brookings Model and carried to fruition in the Wharton Annual Model, both large scale systems by any method of reckoning. The Brookings model looked large at the time it was first built--some 300 equations--but that would be moderate in size now if compared with today's largest models.

It is instructive to consider the presently popular KLEM production function. That is a concept of great importance in contemporary analysis, not in any particular parametric form, but in general specification as to the variables included.

Econometricians retained a high degree of simplicity in model structure by working with the production concept:

$V = F(L,K),$

where

$V$ = real value-added output

$L$ = labor input

$K$ = capital input.

Value added is an awkward concept except as a nominal magnitude. Its price
has little natural meaning. Agricultural economists had consistently been
more sophisticated in developing production functions with feed, seed,
fertilizer, irrigation and other intermediate inputs. To account for these
fully, and to make allowance for similar inputs simultaneously being used
in other sectors, requires use of an I-O system.

The generalization of production anaysis to:

$$X = G(K,L,E,M)$$

where

$X$ = real gross output

$L$ = labor input

$K$ = capital input

$E$ = energy input

$M$ = materials input.

provides a great deal more information. At the macro level for the economy
as a whole, this production function requires price, supply, and demand
equations for $E$ and $M$. This immediately increases the number of variables.
Once these are introduced on an interrelated sector basis, it can
immediately be seen that use of I-O analysis and large systems are
entailed.

Food and fuel are the most notable examples of foci of recent economic
problems. Similar considerations pertain for environmental protection and
general exhaustible resources. Even KLEM is much too restrictive a concept
for macro analysis. However such problems are perceived, it seems
necessary to analyze them in the context of large-scale systems. The I-O
framework is convenient and suggestive, but is not the only way of
proceeding. In any event, much greater detail and more sophistication are
needed than that embodied in the standard small macro model consisting of a
mere handful of equations.

If models were decomposable, large systems may be capable of being
split into several small components. Small model approaches could then be
used for each component. Triangularity of the Jacobian:

$$J = \frac{\partial(f_1 \ldots f_n)}{\partial(y_{1t} \ldots y_{nt})}$$

and diagonality of the covariance matrix of error

$$\Sigma = \underset{e_{it}e_{jt}}{E}$$

where $f_i$ are the structural equations, $i = 1, 2, \ldots, n$, $y_{it}$ are the dependent variables, $e_{it}$ are the random disturbances, would provide complete recursiveness and enable one to treat each separate equation as a complete system. Block recursiveness would be a generalization that would permit the system to be broken up into many small blocks, each block being treated as though it were a complete system.

There is little basis in economic theory or from other sources of a priori information to justify an assumption about complete or block diagonality of . As for the triangularity of J, that is plausible if the unit of time accounting is very short. Data limitations usually preclude the use of data more frequent than quarterly intervals for macroeconometric model construction. There is, of course, one well known attempt to create a monthly model.[1] Although use of such models might spread and be important in the future, that system is not presently in operation and the predominant mode is quarterly.

With months or weeks as basic time units, there is great possibility of triangularity of J, although not diagonality of . In that case, model application can proceed recursively but estimation would not necessarily be optimal according to methods of single equation OLS calculation. Quarterly data cover unit time spans that are long enough to permit much simultaneity; therefore, the mainstream model is highly interdependent and requires general rather than partial analysis.

## 2. EVIDENCE

Over the last 30 years, and especially the last 10, a wide variety of models have been seen, some large and some small. What can be said about their performance? How do their comparative performances throw light on the size issue?

In econometric modeling statistical evidence is rarely conclusive, yet it motivates researchers in their quest towards certain objectives that are being followed. Available evidence shows that small models largely have not survived the rigors of forecast tests.

Consider, first, the St. Louis Model. As so often happens in economic analysis, the discoverers of high multiple correlations tend to become prematurely convinced that they have found an empirical regularity, only to learn, n extrapolations later in the rough field of economic forecasting, that it breaks down. The St. Louis version of the quantity equation looked very impressive in the late 1960's on the basis of good fits to historical samples, but it was no later than August 15, 1971 that breakdown became apparent. Benjamin Friedman found that even the estimate of relative contributions of fiscal and monetary variables in the sample period would not hold up under the impact of data revision.[2]

A telling point, as far as we are concerned, is the remark by Leonall Andersen and Keith Carlson that the St. Louis Model was not suitable for short run forecasting.[3] Andersen and Carlson said that "... the model was not designed for exact quarter-to-quarter forecasting." They also noted that the model:

"Failed to capture short-run movements in velocity"

"Failed to shed light on price developments during periods of government controls and world-wide inflation"

"Failed to cope successfully with large variations in government spending and in the money stock and to anticipate revisions in the money stock data."

Our position is that these recognized failures occurred because of smallness of the model, and undoubtedly of some other factors, too.

A small model tends to rely on very limited pieces of input information. If the St. Louis Model is so small that it has no entry point for exchange rates, raw material prices, energy prices, and government controls how can it contribute to understanding of an economy that was hit by the General Motors strike of 1970, the Nixon NEP program, the Smithsonian Agreement, Soviet crop failures, the oil embargo, OPEC pricing, and similar major stochastic events, that are bound to keep occurring every few years.

Consider the issue of fluctuations in velocity. The simplicity of the quantity theory and the ability to rely on it for estimating movements in nominal income or price levels, in a small system mode, depend on stability of velocity as a parameter or as a systematic time distribution of parameters. The alternative view which is, of course, our position, is that velocity is a variable--a ratio of two variables to be more precise--and is not a parameter. It is precisely because velocity is a variable and needs to be modeled together with a number of other variables that one is led down the route of constructing large systems, as large as a combined flow-of-funds and final demand/factor income model. Here, the issue of largeness vs. smallness in econometric system design is only partly involved because there are also other issues asssociated witih doctrinaire aspects of the St. Louis Model. We would contend, however, that highly doctrinaire systems often are small, and that the two issues cannot be fully separated.

A second piece of empirical evidence concerns the findings of Stephen McNees on the relative forecasting performance of the Fair and St. Louis models versus large scale models. The evidence is clear on the point; the forecasting performance of the large scale models is superior. An issue to be disentangled is the mechanical use of the small models in comparison with the constant (term) adjustment made to the large models.

While it is true that adjustment of large scale econometric models improves their forecasting accuracy, no model, large or small, is going to perform well in ex ante forecasting without regular adjustment of the sort practiced by large-scale model managers. That is, the size and detail of large-scale models permits efficient use of adjustment procedures, and pure judgmental procedures without models will not perform as well in forecast tests as models with judgment. Further, the practice of some small model operators in re-estimating parameters with the receipt of every new data point--possibly a good feature of small models--is, in fact, an adjustment process and fails to bring small models up to the standards of performance of the large models.

The St. Louis Model depends in a doctrinaire way on the money supply. But, also, the original small-scale Fair Model had its doctrinaire aspect, namely that expectations variables, as measured in sample surveys, are good predetermined predictors (instrumental variables) in econometric systems. There are many provocative arguments in favor of use of expectations variables, but they have, like leading indicators, occasionally given false signals and, what is more important, are hard to predict. It often happens that some hard-to-predict variables are used in econometric models.[5] They frequently give impressive sample-period correlations, but they leave the econometrician stranded when it comes to ex ante extrapolation. The expectations variables in the Fair Model were subject to a great deal of error, but they also had a very short future time horizon. This seriously limited their usefulness. One might try to generate expectations in order to project more than six months or so ahead, but then the problems of hard-to-predict input variables arise.

Rather than because of lack of "subjective" adjustments, small models performed poorly mainly because they did not contain much information and thus were not able to cope with strikes, controls, shortages, and many other factors that are important for understanding the economy but that find no entry point in small models.

Error statistics for large models are interesting. In comparisons of different models in the CEME seminar group (see Table 1), superior results are not found for large versus small models nor is there dominance among the large models themselves.[6] These are all within-sample and ex post exrapolation experiments. It is primarily in ex ante forecasting, under all the pressures of doing the real thing, that the advantage of largemodels become evidence. In the tabulations of Stephen McNees, the following properties of large model forecast errors can be observed:[7]

(i)    Errors of levels of economic magnitudes generally grow as the length of the forecast horizon grows.

(ii)   Errors of percentage change (or Theil statistics) grow between very short-run and medium term forecasts but do not appear to grow significantly after one year.

As far as GNP forecasting is concerned, large-scale models are not demonstrably superior, especially in the short run, to some small scale models or to the ASA consensus forecasts. But, it was never contended that large-scale models did a better job of forecasting the main aggregate. The point is:    There is no loss of comparative accuracy in using large-scale models for forecasting main economic magnitudes. The contribution of the large-scale models is in the detail. They are no worse than the ASA and at least as good as the small-scale models forecasts, but they provide much more information. They are to be preferred to pure "judgmental" forecasts because they premit forecasts to be prepared quickly under alternative assumptions and because they are reproducible by independent investigators.

The size debate has been seriously misguided and has paid far too much attention to pure GNP forecasting. Total GNP is becoming a less

Table 1

SIMULATION OF GNP IN TWELVE MODELS, ROOT--MEAN--SQUARE--ERROR
(Billions of Dollars)

| | Scale | | Periods ahead--Within sample | | | | | Periods ahead--Extrapolation | | | |
|---|---|---|---|---|---|---|---|---|---|---|---|
| | | | 1 | 2 | 3 | 4 | Long run | 1 | 2 | 3 | 4 |
| BEA | medium | nominal GNP | 2.39 | 4.68 | 6.57 | 7.81 | 13.65 | 4.30 | 12.47 | 18.21 | 20.78 |
| | | real GNP | 1.97 | 3.99 | 5.68 | 6.94 | 9.53 | 3.51 | 9.05 | 11.54 | 11.02 |
| Brookings | very large | nominal GNP | 4.08 | 5.38 | 5.83 | 5.85 | | 6.74 | 11.36 | 16.08 | 20.94 |
| | | real GNP | 3.70 | 4.66 | 5.01 | 5.13 | | 5.86 | 9.64 | 13.40 | 16.41 |
| MQEM | small | nominal GNP | 3.25 | 4.72 | 7.11 | 8.15 | 6.51 | 6.04 | 9.88 | 12.45 | 16.49 |
| | | real GNP | 2.97 | 4.83 | 7.11 | 8.27 | 9.48 | 5.16 | 8.38 | 9.95 | 12.09 |
| DRI '74 | very large | nominal GNP | 4.73 | 5.82 | 6.02 | 6.29 | 5.24 | | | | |
| | | real GNP | 3.97 | 4.91 | 4.78 | 4.60 | 6.30 | | | | |
| Fair | small | nominal GNP | 2.80 | 4.12 | 4.49 | 4.50 | | 2.91 | 4.35 | 4.52 | 6.77 |
| | | real GNP | 2.81 | 4.14 | 4.32 | 4.22 | | 3.12 | 4.74 | 4.71 | 5.40 |
| St. Louis | very small | nominal GNP | 3.16 | 4.51 | 5.52 | 6.34 | 19.41 | 10.29 | 14.88 | 13.83 | 11.69 |
| | | real GNP | 2.88 | 4.09 | 4.77 | 4.98 | 4.34 | 6.81 | 8.54 | 8.36 | 10.25 |
| MPS | large | nominal GNP | 2.65 | 3.73 | 5.31 | 5.27 | 10.60 | | | | |
| | | real GNP | 2.76 | 3.60 | 4.11 | 4.23 | 8.20 | | | | |
| Wharton (Mark III) | large | nominal GNP | 2.89 | 4.60 | 6.14 | 6.81 | 10.01 | 5.71 | 17.04 | 25.09 | 27.25 |
| | | real GNP | 3.21 | 4.23 | 4.65 | 4.64 | 11.93 | 5.02 | 12.93 | 17.96 | 19.35 |
| Wharton Anticipations | large | nominal GNP | 2.82 | 4.11 | 5.49 | 6.18 | 12.14 | 7.07 | 17.66 | 23.16 | 23.49 |
| | | real GNP | 2.98 | 3.65 | 3.89 | 3.96 | 12.83 | 5.80 | 13.00 | 16.14 | 16.07 |
| H-C Annual | Medium | nominal GNP | 13.54 | 13.11 | 12.74 | 17.65 | 9.57 | | | | |
| | | real GNP | 9.20 | 12.77 | 12.31 | 13.09 | 10.00 | | | | |
| Wharton Annual | very large | nominal GNP | 4.96 | 5.74 | 10.33 | 14.32 | 21.76 | | | | |
| | | real GNP | 6.20 | 7.08 | 6.37 | 8.84 | 7.21 | | | | |
| Liu-Hwa (monthly) | medium | nominal GNP | 2.53 | 2.67 | 2.95 | 3.43 | 11.66 | 5.94 | 5.44 | 5.92 | 6.28 |
| | | real GNP | 2.23 | 2.54 | 2.83 | 3.31 | 11.47 | 5.29 | 6.19 | 6.19 | 7.88 |

Note: Sample periods generally are within the 1960s and post sample extrapolation periods are the early 1970s.

Source: Gary Fromm and Lawrence R. Klein, "The NBER/NSF Model Comparison Seminar: An Analysis of Results," Annals of Economic and Social Measurement, 5/1, 1976, pp. 8-9.

interesting magnitude as understanding and knowledge about the economy increases. Not only do large models provide more detail over a wide spectrum of variables, but they also provide valuable information about the economy when it is really needed. They are better than other tools for forecasting at turning points. The last two major downturns, 1969 and 1973, were associated with marked changes in exogenous variables and disturbances in specific sectors of the economy. The Wharton Model group, for example, was able accurately to predict effects of the fiscal/monetary shifts of 1969 and factor-in the General Electric strike, forecasting a downturn by August, 1969. Many other operators of large-scale models missed this turn but, together with the Wharton Model group, predicted that the policy induced slowdown of 1973 combined with the oil embargo would produce a recession. This forecast was made by early November 1973.

These turning points were recognized in advance because of the ability of model operators explicitly to enter information about disturbances and policies at specific points in their systems. Closer examination of procedures used to forecast the downturn of Autumn, 1973, associated with the oil embargo,is instructive in showing how bigness and detail are beneficial for prediction purposes. The crucial thing was to ascertain how petroleum use affects the economy. Many analysts used rule-of-thumb calculations showing that the ratio of GNP originating in the oil sector to total GNP is small and, therefore, concluded that the OPEC embargo and price increases should not cause a recession. These were serious misjudgments and demonstrate the advantage of using a detailed model.

The oil disturbance was, in good measure, a supply side phenomenon; thus, an input-output cum macro model appeared to be the appropriate tool for analyzing this situation. This approach required the use of a very large system that had a great deal of inter-industrial detail.

The effect of the embargo was to limit import supplies of crude oil into the United States. The Wharton Model group guessed that the reduction would be about 2.0 million barrels per day, and this proved to be an excellent assumption. From the standard equations of input-output analysis

$$(I-A) \ X=F$$
$$X = (I-A)^{-1} \ F,$$

two equations were selected for special treatment:

$$X_i = \sum_{k=1}^{m} \alpha^{ik} F_k + \delta_i \qquad\qquad i = \text{crude oil production}$$

$$X_j = \sum_{k=1}^{m} \alpha^{jk} F_k + \delta_j \qquad\qquad j = \text{refined petroleum products}$$

where

$$\alpha^{ik} \text{ is the } i,k \text{ element of } (I-A)^{-1}$$

$F_k$ is the $k_{th}$ element of final demand.

The problem was to find values for $\delta_i$ and $\delta_j$ such that solutions for $X_i$ and $X_j$ in the complete model would be lower than values obtained from a no-embargo solution by the equivalent of 2.0 million barrels per day. There was no possibility of substituting domestic for imported fuel because the domestic industry was operating at full capacity. Also, as part of the solution process, fuel and refined petroleum imports and appropriate domestic final demand components were reduced by amounts consistent with the embargo.

These adjustments to the model, when combined with fiscal/monetary restraints that were otherwise being imposed, enabled prediction of a recession. How could a result like this have been achieved with a small model? This was a critical model application, pinpointing a turning point just in advance of the event. It was obtained in a large model solution, with a great deal of supply-side detail. Some of the supply side solution results were translated into inventory, imports, and final demand shifts for use in the somewhat smaller short-term model. But, this latter model was also large (about 300 equations) and not at all in the small system category. This example illustrates one of the best uses of large scale models, one that is much too complicated for analysis by small systems.

The criterion for judging the value of models should not be that of simple GNP forecasting under conditions of prolonged upswings or downswings in the economy, but that of accurate prediction and analysis when interpretation of events involving intricate detail really matters. The record of large model performance under these difficult circumstances is well documented in published releases and generally is good.

The technical adjustments to a large-scale model occurred in many places in connection with interpretation of the embargo. Adjustments had to be made to imports, consumer spending on gasoline and oil, consumer spending on household operation, and to selected elements of production. The total effect was composed of several moderate size components. That is typical of large system operation; the whole is built from many parts.

In the ordinary course of events, the estimation of GNP, among other magnitudes, is from identities such as:

$$GNP = \sum_i C_i + \sum_j I_j + \sum_k G_k + \sum_l E_l - \sum_m M_m,$$

in which components of consumption, investment, government spending, and exports less imports range over many categories that are summed to obtain a total of GNP. Small errors in components are likely to have some offsets, and it is generally the case that risks are spread in estimating totals from many parts. In large model solutions, rather than rely on the movement of one or two exogenous indicators or instruments, there is a reliance on many--possibly 50 or more--in order to obtain final aggregates. Errors in isolated components need not be disastrous. It is possible that errors in one part of the system could cascade through other parts; that is a charge often leveled against use of large systems. But, experience does not show this to be the case. In general, there are positive benefits from spreading prediction risks across an increasing number of equations.

Unfortunately, little direct testing has been done on effects of scale of econometric models on their predictive performance within and outside of sample periods and of scale effects on their policy and exogenous shock response properties. The question as to whether large or small models are more accurate in good measure is empirical and cannot readily be answered solely on theoretical grounds. This can be illustrated as follows.

Assume two hypothetical systems A and B for which it is possible to derive, at least in principle, their corresponding restricted reduced forms. These systems, eliminating both current and lagged right-hand side explanatory variables, may be written as:

System A: $y_1 = g_1 (Z_A) + V_1$

System B: $y_1 = y_2 + y_3 = g_1' (Z_A, Z_B) + V_1'$

$\qquad y_2 = g_2 (Z_A, Z_B) + V_2$

$\qquad y_3 = g_3 (Z_A, Z_B) + V_3$

where the $V_i$ are additive random disturbances and $\hat{g}_1' = g_2 + g_3$. If there are nonlinear specifications in the structural forms of Systems A and B, it is highly unlikely that the random error terms would be strictly additive in both the structural and restricted reduced forms. The assumption of additive residuals is made for the sake of expositional simplicity and does not affect the conclusions.

Assuming that the first two small sample moments of forecast error disturbance exist and are finite, the predictive ablity of the two systems may be compared via use of mean squared errors (MSE), which are the sum of variance (VAR) and squared bias components. Thus,

$$MSE(y_1 - \hat{g}_1) = VAR (y_1 - \hat{g}_1) + \bar{V}_1^2$$

$$MSE(y_1 - \hat{g}_1') = VAR (y_1 - \hat{g}_1') + \bar{V}_1'^2$$

where $\bar{V}_1$ and $\bar{V}_1'$ are the means of $y_1 - \hat{g}_1$ and $y_1 - \hat{g}_1'$, respectively, and hats denotes estimates. The variance of $y_1' - \hat{g}_1'$ can be expanded as:

$$VAR(y_1 - \hat{g}_1') = VAR (y_2 - \hat{g}_2) + VAR (y_3 - \hat{g}_3)$$
$$+ 2COVAR [(y_2 - \hat{g}_2)(y_3 - \hat{g}_3)]$$
$$= S_2^2 + S_3^2 + 2S_{23}$$

where COV is the covariance operator.

Often undue attention is given to the sign of the covariance term, $S_{23}$. The argument made is that this sign normally is positive and that, therefore, more disaggregated models, such as System B, will generate greater forecast errors than smaller scale models such as System A. Implicit in this argument is that the sum of the variances of the disaggregated equations $(S_2^2 + S_3^2)$ is equal to or greater than the variance of the condensed model. Obviously, this need not be true.

Proponents of disaggregated models often argue that much more efficient individual equation estimates can be obtained if behavioral specifications are more detailed. If so, then $S_2^2 + S_3^2$ would be substantially less than VAR($y_1 - \hat{g}_1$) and $S_{23}$ could still be positive and VAR($y_1 - \hat{g}_1$) could be greater than VAR($y_1 \hat{g}_1$).

Whether overall forecast error of larger is greater than that of smaller systems depends, too, on the squared bias components of MSE. Again, there is no necessary condition that biases of larger systems exceed those of smaller systems.

Similar to variance characteristics, biases arise from a variety of sources, including equation specifications, imperfections in data, estimation techniques, small sample estimation of parameters, and aggregation. Predictive accuracy is affected by the interaction of many elements and is not, except in special and unusual circumstances, a function only of scale.

Therefore, comparisons of scale and accuracy across models can only validly be made if proper account has been taken of the influence of factors other than scale. Such standardization can more readily be accomplished for a given model wherein the degree of endogeneity, data, sample period, and estimation technique can be fixed. Then effects on accuracy of changing the degree of disaggregation can be determined under more or less ceteris paribus conditions.

A test of this nature was run on the Brookings Model by Fromm and Schink. A larger version of the model with 230 endogenous variables was condensed to 167 equations by collapsing the number of endogenous production sectors from six to two and by some reduction in final expenditure equation detail. The principal problem that arose from the condensation was in equations that relate implicit deflators for GNP demand components to industrial final demand prices. The lack of detail of the latter caused GNP prices to perform poorly on an individual equation basis and adversely affected complete system solutions. To compensate for these effects and make condensed and full system solutions more nearly comparable, Koyck adjustments were added to the condensed model's price sector.

Comparisons of the predictive abilities of the condensed and large versions of the model were based on two types of forecasting experiments: (1) long-term dynamic simulations over a 36-quarter span and (2) six-quarter simulations around sample turning points. The longer term dynamic simulations enable assessment of average predictive abilities while minimizing the impact of initial conditions. The turning point simulations test predictive ability under adverse and difficult forecasting circumstances.

Two variants of the condensed model were compared with the large version. These variants differ only in the formulation of equations for GNP expenditure implicit deflators. The price sector in the first variant, labeled "Standard" contains specifications which are like those in the larger model; in the second condensed variant, Koyck adjustment processes were introduced into these equations. Results of long-term predictive proprties are presented in Table 2, in which root mean square errors (RMSE) and mean bias (MB) are shown for 17 variables.

TABLE 2

BROOKINGS MODEL PREDICTION ERRORS FOR SELECTED VARIABLES: DYNAMIC SIMULATIONS FROM 1957 : 1–1965 : 4

| Variables Description[a] | Symbols | ROOT MEAN SQUARE ERRORS | | | MEAN BIASES | | |
|---|---|---|---|---|---|---|---|
| | | Large Model | Condensed Model | | Large Model | Condensed Model | |
| | | | Standard | Koyck | | Standard | Koyck |
| Nominal gross national product | GNP | 5.84 | 6.86 | 6.09 | 1.40 | 0.31 | -0.37 |
| Real gross national product | GNP58 | 5.00 | 7.20 | 5.89 | 1.38 | -2.16 | -2.15 |
| Deflator for GNP (index, 1958 = 1.00) | PGNP | 0.0072 | 0.0119 | 0.0071 | -0.0005 | 0.0041 | 0.0029 |
| Real consumption | C58 | 2.43 | 3.59 | 3.17 | 0.34 | -1.20 | -1.37 |
| Real net exports | EX58-M58 | 1.35 | 1.22 | 1.24 | 0.06 | 0.03 | 0.10 |
| Real nonfarm fixed investment | IBLSEA58 | 0.95 | 1.88 | 1.41 | 0.32 | -1.13 | -1.09 |
| Real nonfarm residential construction | ICNFR58 | 1.01 | 1.30 | 1.09 | 0.49 | 0.20 | 0.24 |
| Real nonfarm inventory investment | ΔINVEAF58 | 2.65 | 2.90 | 2.82 | 0.17 | -0.02 | 0.04 |
| Real unfilled orders | OUM58 | 4.16 | 7.66 | 6.63 | -0.94 | -5.48 | -5.56 |
| Personal income | YP | 3.38 | 2.89 | 2.56 | 1.31 | -0.28 | -0.45 |
| Corporate profits before taxes | ZB | 3.65 | 4.12 | 3.70 | -1.95 | 0.67 | -0.08 |
| Employment (millions of persons) | EHH | 0.534 | 0.503 | 0.541 | 0.324 | 0.109 | 0.170 |
| Average weekly hours | H | 0.15 | 0.132 | 0.142 | -0.006 | -0.024 | -0.015 |
| Unemployment rate (proportion) | RU | 0.0062 | 0.0061 | 0.0070 | -0.0020 | -0.0004 | -0.0008 |
| Money wage rate ($ per hour) | RWSS | 0.021 | 0.019 | 0.016 | 0.007 | 0.001 | 0.004 |
| Treasury bill rate—90 day (percent) | RMGBS2NS | 0.226 | 0.222 | 0.234 | 0.039 | 0.029 | 0.028 |
| Long-term Treasury bond yield (percent) | RMGBLNS | 0.177 | 0.237 | 0.229 | 0.113 | 0.171 | 0.169 |
| Components of Real Consumption | | | | | | | |
| Automobiles | CDA58 | 1.30 | 1.39 | 1.48 | 0.56 | 0.03 | 0.09 |
| Durables excluding automobiles | CDEA58 | 0.75 | 0.85 | 0.72 | 0.15 | -0.13 | -0.09 |
| Nondurables | CN58 | 1.25 | 1.77 | 1.34 | 0.01 | -0.35 | -0.21 |
| Services | CS58 | 0.53 | 0.90 | 1.20 | -0.37 | -0.70 | -1.11 |
| Components of Real Nonfarm Fixed Investment | | | | | | | |
| Manufacturing | IBLSEM58 | 0.56 | 1.14 | 1.06 | 0.18 | -0.85 | -0.89 |
| Nonmanufacturing | IBLSR—0.258 | 0.55 | 0.88 | 0.53 | 0.14 | -0.29 | -0.20 |

[a] All variables except interest rates are seasonally adjusted. Expenditures and income flows are measured in billions of dollars (or billions of 1958 dollars for variables in real terms) at annual rates. Units of other variables are as noted in the table.

Source: Gary Fromm and George R. Schink, "Aggregation and Econometric Models," *International Economic Review*, Vol. 14, No. 1, February 1973.

The RMSE estimates for the large model are, for a majority of the variables, significantly lower than those for either condensed variant. In most instances where the estimated RMSE for either condensed variant is lower, the differences in RMSE are extremely small. While the larger model generally outperforms either condensed variant on the basis of RMSE, the performance of both condensed variants is still quite good in relation to other models, as can be seen by comparing results in Table 2 with those in Table 1.

The conjecture that aggregation increases bias is supported to some extent by estimated mean bias (MB) values for real GNP and most of its expenditure components. The condensed versions of the model generally have higher absolute mean biases for aggregates of expenditure, income, and other components than the larger model.

Tests of turning-point performance were run around peaks and troughs of the 1954-61 recessions and recoveries. Simulations were started one, two, and three quarters before each turn to ascertain leads and lags and predictive accuracy. As measured by RMSE, predictions around turning points were not much worse, on average, than over the longer-run period. However, swings were damped and peak values generally were underpredicted and trough values were overpredicted. The turning-point simulations were not as uniformly favorable to the larger model. It was superior at peaks of cycles and for price predictions at peaks and troughs. But, notwithstanding its extremely poor long-run predictions, the Standard (although not the Koyck) variant of the condensed model had lower RMSE for real GNP at troughs.

These results do not prove that disaggregation necessarily leads to greater forecasting efficiency. Many observations from a large universe of possible models and alternative scales for each model would be needed to support that conclusion. Nevertheless, the evidence is at least suggestive that even more complex systems of even greater scale than are now available need not lead to deterioration in predictive performance. An indication that this is likely also follows from the many sector studies (for investment, production, prices, and so forth) that have reported significant aggregation errors and from the growing size of existing and new complete econometric systems.[10]

## 3.  MANAGEABILITY

A principle for selecting the scale of a model is to aim for the largest system for which adequate data can be obtained and can be managed efficiently, without loss of accuracy in estimation of main aggregates than would be generated from a small system solution. Is such a large system a "black box?"

Many outsiders claim that they lose patience in attempting to understand the workings of large models or that they otherwise fail to be able to discern the meaningful underlying structure of large complete systems. But, surely this is just a matter of taking sufficient time and effort to acquire the desired knowledge. Those who build and operate large models do understand them and develop abilities to anticipate most principal results of standard multipliers, sensitivity, or scenario analyses. After a model has been estimated, it should be put through a series of regular tests to develop its response characteristics to numerous types of disturbances. Proficient model builders know these characteristics, but they cannot usually be depicted as curve shifts on two-dimensional diagrams.

The economy is a complicated mechanism and there is little reason to presuppose that it can be modeled sensibly in a simple aggregative way. If it is inherently difficult to approximate the economy by sets of statistical equations, it should not be surprising that those systems are large and seemingly complicated. In well-run modeling projects all equations are fully explained and documented so that results can be replicated by other, independent investigators. This has been done for systems whose results are used by many organizations or that are employed by third-party scholars to explore questions of technical interest. Large models are not "black boxes," but they do require extensive careful study and training in use.

Nowadays, most large models are managed by teams. The mode of a lone researcher pursuing construction of a large model is not completely obsolete, but is quite unusual. The typical large-model team consists of data resource specialists, computer programmers, research assistants, and senior theorists and econometricians. Each has specific duties both in model construction and operation. One or more senior econometricians can efficiently manage the enterprise so that many questions can be answered within fractions of a day. With use of efficient data, programming, and computer systems, large models can be fully updated, re-estimated and re-simulated within a few days. Complete re-estimation with respecifications of mainstream models, however, may take weeks or months depending upon the extent of changes undertaken.

The entire operation can be done efficiently with a moderate size team. There is no question that 500, 1,000 or 2,000 equation systems are not too large to manage efficiently. There surely is an upper limit even with modern facilities, but it is doubtful that maximum efficient scale has been reached or closely approached at the present time. Data availability probably constitutes one of the most significant obstacles, at the present time, to attaining the highly detailed Walrasian ideal.

In textbooks, small, hypothetical static or noncomplex dynamic models are exercised in very simple ways in order to illustrate economic principles and effects. But, it is misleading to have students think that models actually are used in that manner for policy purposes. Policy rarely is neat and simple in practice. Government spending does not change in one lump sum in actual budget planning. Tax changes almost always are made multi-faceted and complex when lawyers draft legislation. Single exogenous variable shifts at a time rarely occur. Policymakers usually alter several things at once, some positively and some negatively. Changes normally are phased-in over months or years, each component according to its own schedule. The detail of a large system which includes many tax-transfer parameters, expenditure categories, monetary reserve parameters, and foreign commercial credit rates is needed in order to interpret policy in full, as it is ultimately formulated. Moreover, the detailed approach to policymaking, which seems inevitable and probably desirable, most likely would benefit from use of large systems for policy formulation and evaluation.

When Milton Friedman and David Meiselman compared the multiplier equation's performance with that of the quantity equation,

$$y = m_0 + m_1 I \qquad \text{(multiplier)}$$

$$py = v M \qquad \text{(quantity equation)}$$

they were testing vulgar Keynesianism against vulgar monetarism. Both systems were too simple to be realistically useful, and neither should survive a careful and demanding assessment. We find that bit of testing to be irrelevant.

When at first advanced, Keynesian doctrine was attractive because it was so simple. In the hands of Sir John Hicks and Oskar Lange it became readily understandable in terms of their elementary small equation systems. The large scale systems embodied in today's mainstream models are elaborations of the IS-LM framework of Hicks. But lags, institutional detail, numerous exogenous variables, openness, and disaggregation tend to obscure the relation to the parent model.[11] In the realm of pedagogy, the IS-LM system will surely survive, but in the real world of policymaking and application, the multiequation elaboration will have to be used. Possibly if the monetarist model were sufficiently disaggregated it, too, would become more useful.

The idea of moving towards greater detail and model size is not new, born of sudden fascination with capabiilities of modern computers. At the time of formulation of the Klein-Goldberger Model, in 1950, detail was already being sought in connection with savings estimates.[12] A critique of this viewpoint was made by Alvin Hansen, who represented the macro Keynesian school. But in order to understand savings processes, detail is needed, as it is, as well, for flow-of-funds modeling, a current emphasis in much present research. When a detailed flow-of-funds model is combined with an already large model of income and expenditure accounts, a very large model of the whole economy results. It is therefore evident that the trend towards models that will be even greater in scale than today's systems had roots in early efforts and ideas of some 25 years ago.

Some reasons for wanting small models are quickness in comprehension, elegance, and impatience with detail. Appeal to the rule of parsimony could lead one in a direction opposite to modern tendencies. The simplest possible explanation of a given body of data or information normally would be desired. But application of that rule would indicate excessive preoccupation with rudiimentary techniques and findings of the past. Samples of economic time-series data generally are small and limited in content. It is usually possible to find a good fit to a stretch of historical data, as did the monetarists in the late 1960's. It already has been noted that these impressive correlations did not hold when new situations arose in which factors that were not very important in their fitting period suddenly emerged. Such is likely to be the fate of any mechanical atempt to justify simplistic theory on the basis of the rule of parsimony.

The economic systems of nations are complicated and cannot be approximated well with any small model, monetarist or otherwise. Small models, by their nature fail to include significant variables that are quiescent in sample periods but are bound to become prominent on future occasions, variables that are needed for application outside the sample period. Large systems are required to cope with emergence of quiescent factors.

Models also become large for a variety of other reasons reflecting desires more accurately to depict underlying structural processes. For example, constrained estimation, as applied in analysis of consumer expenditures, is needed in order to capture cross effects from a wide spectrum of prices and market yields. Input-output sub-systems provide for arrays of intersectoral reactions and impacts. Both should be built into macro models. This is what is needed to implement empirically a Walrasian view of the economy and entails that the rule of parsimony be rejected in principle for use of understanding the econometric structures of actual economic systems.


4.  WHAT IS AN OPTIMUM SCALE?

Critics of large models often have focused on scale as the most debilatating characteristic of econometric systems. Somehow, if models were smaller, it is averred, they would be better. The thought corresponds well with the "small is beautiful" syndrome so popular within the last decade.

But even proponents of small models are confronted with needs to determine the best scale for these systems. Is it one, or 4, or 10, or 50, or many more equations? After emotion is stripped away and rational attention is given to the issue, it becomes clear that there are numreous tradeoffs and considerations to be taken into account.

The optimum scale for a model truly depends on many elements. Some of these are listed in Table 3.

If, for instance, a model is to be used primarily for pedagogical purposes, desires for rapid and ease of understanding would lead to specification of a smaller system than would be the case if a model were to be employed for realistic applications and actual decisionmaking. Similarly, if a model is to be used only to provide broad indications of possible unconditional or conditional outcomes, then it would probably be made smaller than if precise point estimates are needed. The reason for this is that supporting detail is desired in order to be better able to judge the reasonableness and internal consistency of highly specific predictions.

The presumed normal, partial effects on optimum scale of other factors could also be described and justified at length. Surely, some would argue about the direction of a number of the indicated effects in Table 3. There are cases in which the reverse impact of that shown might apply. For present purposes this should not be of concern. The list is illustrative of a host of considerations.

Now, suppose that the utility of a model is a function of its ease of understanding, prediction accuracy, detail, cost, and other arguments. Suppose, too, that magnitudes of some of these arguments are affected by model scale, with positive effects for some arguments and negative effects

Table 3

FACTORS INFLUENCING OPTIMUM SCALE OF MODELS

|  | Effect on Scale | |
|---|---|---|
| Factor | Smaller | Larger |
| Purpose | Pedagogical | Realistic applications |
| Nature of Use | Indicative | Precise decision formulation or evaluation |
| Number of users | Few | Many |
| Frequency of use | Low | High |
| Need for detail | Low | High |
| Complexity of underlying structure | Low | High |
| Need for structural understanding | Low | High |
| Sensitivity of decisions to model solutions | Low | High |
| Decision error losses | Low | High |
| Data availability | Sparse | Abundant |
| Data quality | Low | High |
| Computer and staff availability | Limited | Abundant |
| Adequacy of theory | Low | High |
| Aggregation bias | Low | High |
| Error covariances | High | Low |
| Adequacy of alternative tools | High | Low |
| Prediction accuracy | Low | High |
| Stability of underlying structure | High | Low |
| Frequency of stochastic shocks | Low | High |
| Size of stochastic shocks | Small | Large |
| Cost of model construction | High | Low |
| Cost of model operation | High | Low |
| Frequency of required re-estimation | High | Low |
| Time required for re-estimation | Long | Short |
| Time required for validation | Long | Short |

for others. Then it would not be unreasonable to posit, at least for a given set of intended uses and other conditions which are to hold over a particular period (starting at a given point in time so that data and computer availabilities are known), that utility and scale might have a relationship like that shown in Figure 1.

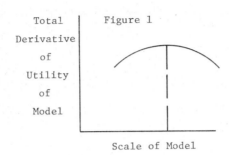

Total
Derivative
of
Utility
of
Model

Figure 1

Scale of Model

The curve therein has a point at which the total derivative of utility with respect to scale of a model is at a maximum, which thereby defines the optimum scale. This preferred scale obviously depends on a variety of influences, such as those listed in Table 3, and need not be identical for model builders, reviewers, students, users, or sponsors. Reviewers, for example, would most certainly place a higher weight on ease of understanding than would model builders. Because scale and ease of understanding are inversely correlated, especially for systems nonlinear in variables and parameters, it can readily be supposed that reviewers and students would be critical of large and complex systems and would prefer smaller, simpler models.

## 5. CONCLUSION

That "beauty is in the eye of the beholder" has become a cliche but is very applicable to discussions about model scale and accuracy. Much of the controversy seems to stem more from subjective perceptions and attitudes than it does from careful examination of evidence on prediction errors. Comparison of ex ante an ex post solutions shows that larger models are at least as accurate, on average, as their smaller counterparts. Larger systems are more dependable for analysis of impacts of fine-grained policy changes, structural shifts, and large stochastic shocks. Yet, they are more costly to construct and operate and harder to understand. Preferred scales for models are functions of these and other characteristics. There are many criticisms that can be leveled at models. To concentrate much attention on scale, large or small, is to misplace emphasis that deserve to be devoted elsewhere. Being critical of scale is an easy point to make, but a hard one to sustain. Neither big nor small is beautiful; it is the quality of a model that really matters and not its size.

\*

The support of the National Science Foundations, which helped to make this research possible, is gratefully acknowledged.

1

See T.C. Liu and E.C. Hwa, "A Monthly Econometric Model of the U.S. Economy," Econometric Model Performance, ed. by L.R. Klein and E. Burmeister, (Philadelphia: University of Pennsylvania Press, 1976), 70-107.

2

Benjamin Friedman, "Even the St. Louis Model Now Believes in Fiscal Policy," The Journal of Money, Credit, and Banking, IX (May, 1977) 365-369.

3

Leonall C. Andersen and Keith M. Carlson, "St. Louis Model Revisited," Econometric Model Performance, ed. by L.R. Klein and E. Burmeister, (Philadelphia: University of Pennsylvania Press, 1976), 47-69.

4

Stephen McNees, "A Comparison of the GNP Forecasting Accuracy of the Fair and St. Louis Econometric Models," New England Economic Review, (Sept/Oct. 1973), 29-34.

5

See the paper by Howrey, Klein, McCarthy, and Schink, in which this issue is explored by the model builders in their questionnaire responses.

6

Gary Fromm and L.R. Klein, "The NBER/NSF Model Comparison Seminar: An Analysis of Results," Econometric Model Performance, ed. by L.R. Klein and E. Burmeister, (Philadelphia: University of Pennsylvania Press, 1976), 380-407.

7

Stephen K. McNees, "An Evaluation of Economic Forecasts," New England Economic Review, November/December 1975, pp. 31-39; "The Forecasting Performance in the 1970's" New England Economic Review, July/August 1976, pp. 1-13; and "The Accuracy of Macroeconometric Models and Forecasts of the U.S. Economy," Economic Modeling, ed. Paul Ormerod, (London: Heinemann, 1979), 245-64.

8

Some aggregative magnitudes, such as real GNP, will be constrained by capacity limitations; consequently, there may be negative covariance between components, giving rise to smaller forecast error.

9

Gary Fromm and George R. Schink, "Aggregation and Econometric Models," International Economic Review, Vol. 14, No. 1, February 1973.

10

For example, Dale Jorgenson and J.W. Stephenson obtained significant gains in efficiency for equation estimates when investment for total manufacturing was disaggregated into durable and nondurable components. See the "Investment Behavior in U.S. Manufacturing: 1947-1960," Econometrica, XXXV (April 1967), 169-220.

11

For the IS-LM interpretation of the Wharton Model, see Vijaya Duggal, Lawrence R. Klein and Michael D. McCarthy, "The Wharton Model Mark III; A Modern IS-LM Construct," Econometric Model Performance, ed. by L.R. Klein and E. Burmeister (Philadelphia: University of Pennsylvania Press, 1976), 180-210.

12

L.R. Klein, "Savings Concepts and Data: The Needs of Economic Analysis and Policy," Savings in the Modern Economy, ed. by W.W. Heller, F.M. Boddy and C.L. Nelson, (Minneapolis: University of Minnesota Press, 1953), 104-107.

LARGE-SCALE MACRO-ECONOMETRIC MODELS
J. Kmenta, J.B. Ramsey (editors)
© North-Holland Publishing Company, 1981

## COMMENTS ON SIMS AND McNEES

Ray C. Fair

Cowles Foundation, Department of Economics
Yale University
New Haven, Connecticut
U.S.A.

Although Sims's methodological position regarding macroeconomic modeling
is quite different from mine, it is difficult to argue about this directly.
I can shout "I trust economic theory to impose many prior constraints on a
model!" and Sims can shout back "I don't!" Arguing at this level is similar to arguing over moral questions; there is in many cases no obvious way
to settle the debate. Sims is, of course, right in pointing out that
structural models are not identified without the imposition of a number of
prior constraints, but to argue, as Sims does in [3], that models are not
likely to be identified requires the added premise that economic theory
cannot be trusted to impose prior constraints.

The question, then, is how can this debate be resolved? My view is that
in the long run it may be resolved by using methods like the one that I
have recently proposed [1] to compare alternative models. As discussed in
Sims's paper in this volume, he is in the process of constructing models
with few prior constraints imposed on the specification. Call one of
these models, Model A, and call a model based on many prior constraints,
Model B. (Models like B are usually nonlinear, at least in variables,
whereas Sims's models have so far been linear.) My method allows one to
estimate forecast-error variances for both models, where for each model
the four main sources of uncertainty are accounted for. The models can be
nonlinear in both variables and coefficients. Given the assumptions behind the method, it puts all models on an equal footing and thus allows
estimated variances to be compared across models. Say that one used the
method on Models A and B and consistently found the estimated variances for
Model B to be smaller than the estimated variances for Model A. This would
seem to be evidence in favor of the proposition that Model B is a better
approximation to the structure of the economy than is Model A and thus
that the economy theory used for Model B has imposed reasonable prior
constraints.

In [2] I have used the method to compare the six-equation model in Sims
[3] to my model and two others. Although the results are very tentative,
they are not encouraging regarding Sims's model. If one were forced to
choose on the basis of these results between my model and Sims's model, it
is clear that my model would be chosen. This conclusion would, however,
be premature, since Sims has only recently begun working on the less constrained models. The main point here is not that one of Sims's model is
currently dominated by others, but that the method does allow a way in the
long run to decide whether Sims's methodological position is valid.

I have two comments on McNees's paper. First, one need not use, as McNees's
discussion of my method seems to imply, the same constancy assumption for

389

each model in order to compare the estimated variances across models.  One should choose for each model the constancy assumption that seems to approximate the truth best, just as one should choose for each model the assumption about exogenous-variable uncertainty that seems to be the best approximation.  If for each model one has accounted in the best possible way for the four sources of uncertainty, then the estimated variances across models are on an equal footing and so can be compared.

Second, I do not find McNees's argument that "ex ante evidence should be considered as one, albeit imperfect, indicator of relative model validity" at all convincing.  There is just too much subjectivity involved in most ex ante forecasting to allow ex ante results to be used to compare models qua models.  It does seem to me, however, that information regarding ex ante exogenous-variable errors is useful for estimating exogenous-variable uncertainty and thus is useful in applications of my method.  McNees mentions this in his discussion of the method, but he seems to dismiss it because it does not take into account learning.  In many applications the learning problem may not be all that serious or may be subject to being modeled itself.  It seems to me that the idea of using past ex ante exogenous-variable forecast errors to estimate exogenous-variable uncertainty is a very good one.  One advantage of my method is that once the exogenous-variable uncertainty is estimated, by whatever procedure, this information can be used in a straightforward way in the estimation of total endogenous-variable uncertainty.

[1]    Fair, Ray C., "Estimating the Expected Predictive Accuracy of
            Econometric Models," International Economic Review, 21
            (June 1980), 355-378.

[2]    ____, "An Analysis of the Accuracy of Four Macroeconometric Models,"
            Journal of Political Economy, 87 (August 1979), 701-718.

[3]    Sims, Christopher A., "Macroeconomics and Reality," Econometrica,
            48 (January 1980), 1-48.

LARGE-SCALE MACRO-ECONOMETRIC MODELS
J. Kmenta, J.B. Ramsey (editors)
© North-Holland Publishing Company, 1981

COMMENT ON ALBERT ANDO
"ON A THEORETICAL AND EMPIRICAL BASIS OF MACROECONOMETRIC MODELS"

James Tobin
Yale University

Albert Ando's paper is a stalwart defense of structural macroeconometric
models as they have developed over the last thirty years. I agree with almost every word, and I am grateful that he has spoken out so forcefully. I
would stress particularly the following points:

1. The stubborn stagflation of the 1970s is not a decisive prima facie
reason to discard the economic theory and econometric methodology of existing models in favor of the continuous-equilibrium approach of the new
classical macroeconomics. We have not done well in modeling the inflation
process, it is true. But it is not true history to interpret the record as
the failure of a deliberate policy to ride up the Phillips curve and purchase higher employment at the cost of higher inflation. An equally
plausible interpretation, also only partially accurate, is that the record
displays the costly failure of anti-inflationary monetary and macroeconomic
policies.

2. Assuming the economy to be composed of competitive markets continuously
and simultaneously cleared by prices is not a promising foundation for
econometric modeling or for policy analysis. Not only is this premise contradicted by microeconomic facts of every-day observation; it cannot be
justified by "the methodology of positive economics" by congruence of its
macroeconomic implications with available data. At this date the ancient
view of both Keynesian and old classical or neoclassical economists--that,
whatever its long-run steady-state properties, the economy spends most of
its time in disequilibrium adjustment--remains the better hypothesis.

3. Disequilibrium adjustment and aggregation make for messy specifications,
in which ad hoc empiricism plays a disturbingly large role. It is a noble
enterprise to extend to this range of economic behavior the paradigms of
optimization with which we are trained to feel more comfortable. But it is
a very difficult enterprise, far from fruition; and the paradigms may not
apply in any more than a tautological sense. Note that equilibrium models
explain commonly recognized regularities of macroeconomic fluctuations only
by auxiliary assumptions, for example informational imperfections and
asymmetries, which are no less ad hoc and arbitrary than the elements of
rigidity, stickiness, and slow adaptation in conventional models.

4. While I recognize that exogeneity should be tested and not simply assumed, I share Ando's skepticism of nonstructural tests, especially when
applied only to two variables or to a small set. I do not understand why
we should assume that autoregressions of simple variables or vectors take
explanatory priority over contemporaneous structural interdependence.

5.  Macro-econometricians were too slow to incorporate policy reaction
functions in their models.  Although their inclusion magnifies problems of
identification, it does not introduce any new issues of principle and
should aid both in the explanation of historical data and in the estimation
of effects of policy shifts.  However, the specification of policy reaction
functions should pay careful attention to what policy-makers were doing,
and thought they were doing, at various times.  In particular the monetary
authorities have, fairly explicitly, followed different procedures and
aimed at different objectives in various periods; pre-Accord 1946-1951,
leaning against the wind 1953-1961 and 1966-1970, lowest bill rate consistent with foreign rates 1961-1965, monetary aggregate targets since 1971.
It is foolish and misleading to assume they were always doing the same
thing, or that they were always aiming at targets expressed in terms of
endogenous monetary aggregates.

6.  Lucas's famous "critique" is a valid point; surely private behavior
will adapt to perceived changes of government policy rules.  The policy-
makers will adapt in turn, and I am not aware that the new classical
theorists have worked out the fully extended game except in simple illustrative cases.  Anyway the critique is not so devastating that macro-
econometric model-builders should immediately close shop.  The public's
perception of policy régimes is not so precise as to exclude considerable
room for discretionary policy moves that the public would see neither as
surprises nor as signals of a systematic change of régime.  Moreover, behavioral "rules of thumb," though not permanent, may persist long enough
for the horizons of macroeconomic policy-makers.

7.  Finally, pragmatic economists and econometricians must always have
recognized that the structure of any empirical model reflects the historical experience and environment of the period for which it is estimated.
Changes in the environment--including not only government policy but many
other conditioning factors, demographic, technological, institutional,
international, cultural--are bound to alter structural behavioral equations.
Thus models become obsolete and must be revised or replaced.  The quest
for timeless and permanent regularities in social science is important.
But any "laws" thus discovered, other than identities, are likely to be
qualitative and general, of little value in forecasting and policy evaluation.

8.  Revolutionaries and counter-revolutionaries generally exaggerate their
criticisms of prevailing orthodoxies, and overstate the novelties and
virtues of the alternatives they propose.  Keynes and the Keynesians did
that, and it is no surprise that Lucas, Sargent, et al. fall into this
mode.  But scientific debate and inquiry lead to synthesis, and I already
detect this process at work.  As theorists and econometricians work with
the new and fruitful tools of rational expectations conditional on information, adding implicit or explicit contracts, imperfect competition, and
costs of adjusting both prices and quantities, the sharp distinctions
between disequilibrium adjustment and equilibrium market-clearing is giving
way.  In time there is likely to be a convergence, in which mainstream
theory and econometric modeling are improved and the new ideas have less
revolutionary implications for methodology and policy than now appears.

LARGE-SCALE MACRO-ECONOMETRIC MODELS
J. Kmenta, J.B. Ramsey (editors)
© North-Holland Publishing Company, 1981

COMMENT ON G. FROMM and L.R. KLEIN'S PAPER,
SCALE OF MACRO-ECONOMETRIC MODELS AND ACCURACY OF FORECASTING

Franco Modigliani

Sloan School of Management
Massachusetts Institute of Technology
Cambridge, Massachusetts   USA

I am in basic agreement with Klein and Fromm's view about the
relative merits of large versus small models.  The choice between large and small is not a matter of theoretical principle
but rather a purely pragmatic one.  There is no a priori reason
to believe nor any systematic empirical evidence to suggest
that size is per se a major determinant of forecasting accuracy,
at least beyond some minimum size and complexity.  As their
Table 3 helps to bring out, it is also true that, for given accuracy, one would generally prefer a smaller to a bigger model
for reasons such as cost of estimation, maintenance and use,
and easiness of understanding the working of the model.

Why then have models grown so big?  There are basically two
reasons that push for bigger, less aggregated models.  The
first and most important may be labelled disaggregation for
its own sake.  It arises because the users or customers of the
econometric models are interested in forecasts of subaggre-
gates of subsectors of the economy.  Disaggregation is thus
induced by customer demand rather than by the view that a less
aggregated model will yield a better forecast of the broad
aggregates.

The second motivation is the model builder's conviction that a
certain level of disaggregation is useful to account for the behavior of the economy, not as a matter of principle, but in
terms of the particular way he is modeling the economy.  Also,
disaggregation may sometimes appear like the most suitable way
of examining the effect of unusual disturbances or innovations
and of new types of economic policies.

In addition, the ever present temptation toward enlarging the
model has become easier to gratify thanks to great strides in
computer technology.  And for this reason I am inclined to
share the authors' prediction that average size is likely to
continue to rise in the near future.

Concerning the various models' simulations in Table 1, one
should recognize a serious limitation:  the extrapolations,
which provide in principle the most meaningful comparison, are
based on the actual value of the exogenous variables (so-called
ex-post forecasts) and these variables can be quite different
from model to model.  One can try to remedy this shortcoming by
replacing the actual value of the exogenous variables by a forecast based (usually) on some mechanical extrapolative formula.
This procedure too, however, is objectionable insofar as the exogenous variables include variables which the model takes as
policy variables.  In this case, the model is basically intended
to provide a forecast conditional on the actual value of the
policy variables.  One might suggest therefore that in the simulation of each model, any bona fide policy variables should be
assigned their historical value.  The comparability would be enhanced if the policy variables could be standardized across
models, though this may prove quite difficult.

# V.  EVALUATION OF MACRO-ECONOMETRIC MODELS

LARGE-SCALE MACRO-ECONOMETRIC MODELS
J. Kmenta, J.B. Ramsey (editors)
© North-Holland Publishing Company, 1981

# THE METHODOLOGY OF MACROECONOMETRIC MODEL COMPARISONS

Stephen K. McNees

Vice President and Economist
Federal Reserve Bank of Boston
Boston, Massachusetts
U.S.A.

The divergence of opinion about how best
to model the economy reflects, in part,
limitations of existing methods of model
evaluation. Comparisons between
structural econometric models and time
series equations, when interpreted
properly, provide little useful
information for establishing model
validity. The application of formal
statistical tests of model validity rest
on assumptions that do not permit
statistical comparisons across models and
need not reflect model reliability in
specific applications. Even though
forecasting ability and model validity
are distinct concepts, ex ante evidence
bears on model validity if it is assumed
that more valid models can be used to
generate more accurate forecasts. As
current evidence reflects substantial
interaction between model and forecaster,
a framework is proposed for collecting
evidence which might help disentangle the
roles of model and forecaster.

Macroeconometric models are widely used in government,
academe, research institutes and private businesses for
forecasting and decision-making. This seems to indicate
that macroeconometric model building has achieved some
success. Concurrently, severe criticisms of existing
macroeconometric models have appeared frequently in the
professional literature. Questions have been raised about
the economic theories on which the models are based, the
econometric procedures with which they are estimated, and
the ways models are brought to bear on particular problems.
However useful macroeconometric models have been found to
be, there appears to be increasing disagreement about how
best to represent a nation's economy with a macroeconometric
model, and thus sharp disagreement about how successfully
this task has been accomplished. As a result of this
divergence of professional opinion and perhaps also in
response to the increasing use of macroeconometric models,

the number of models has proliferated and shows signs of
continuing to do so.

In light of these circumstances, it would be highly
desirable to establish methods for narrowing the divergent
trends in academic thought and guiding users to the model(s)
most helpful for their applications.  Progress on model
evaluation has, in fact, been extremely limited.  Numerous
methods of evaluating econometric models have been offered
and new methods are frequently proposed, with no clear
consensus emerging on which method is the more informative
for particular purposes.  In addition, existing methods
either have not been widely applied or have been applied
very imperfectly.  Finally, there have been surprisingly few
attempts to summarize, synthesize, and interpret the bodies
of evidence which have been generated by applying each
method.

This paper examines three of the methods of model evaluation
which have been pursued recently.  The discussion is guided
by previous empirical results but no attempt is made to
provide a comprehensive survey of the evidence or to offer
new evidence.  The object of the paper is to contribute to a
greater appreciation of the problems of model evaluation and
of the reasons why our knowledge on this subject is so
incomplete.


THE DILEMMA OF MODEL COMPARISONS

An econometric model is contingent on a set of information
external to the model itself.  This external or exogenous
information is a critical feature of the model because the
exogenous variables are the factors underlying the model's
outcome or solution.  An econometric model's solution is
conditional upon the assumed values of its exogenous
variables.  This simple fact poses the following dilemma:

(1)  If any other than the actual values of the exogenous
variables are used to solve a model, any errors in the
solution may be attributable either to the model or to the
incorrect values of the exogenous variables used.  The
model's performance can only be isolated when actual values
of the exogenous variables are used, i.e., an ex post
simulation is conducted.  For this reason, the vast majority
of evidence on macroeconometric models comes from ex post
simulations.

(2)  When different models contain different sets of
exogenous variables (as they will so long as alternative
models differ significantly), ex post simulations cannot be
used to obtain informative comparisons of alternative
models.  How, for example, might one compare the ex post GNP
predictions of a model that took inventory investment (or
the money stock) as exogenous with one that treated it as

endogenous? In the current state of macroeconometric modeling, there are nontrivial disagreements about the size and composition of the appropriate set of exogenous variables. So long as (or to the extent that) significant differences of opinion exist, ex post simulations will not provide fruitful comparisons of alternative models.

This paper analyzes three alternative responses to this dilemma: (1) a model can be evaluated by comparing it with an alternative method, such as purely statistical time series equations, that contains no external information; (2) models can be evaluated by devising procedures to control for differences in exogenous variables across different models; and (3) models can be evaluated by examining how well they perform in the particular application of prediction in which all models are on an equal footing with respect to information on the future values of exogenous variables.

## TIME SERIES EQUATIONS AS A STANDARD OF COMPARISON

Economic forecasts traditionally have been evaluated by comparing their accuracy with that of a "naive" statistical rule-of-thumb such as a no-change, a same-as-last-period change, or average-change rule. Most recently, the "naive" standard of comparison has often taken the statistically more sophisticated form of time series equations. Using time series equations (TSE) as a standard of comparison for structural econometric models (SEM) is a natural response to the difficulties of comparing models. If differences in exogeneity impede cross-model comparisons, why not compare SEM with a common standard that requires no exogenous information? This approach appeared so attractive that a voluminous literature has developed contrasting the summary error measures of TSE with those from ex post simulations of SEM.

The early studies (Cooper, 1972), (Nelson, 1972), (Cooper and Nelson, 1975), and (Ibrahim and Otsuki, 1976) all found the summary error measures of the TSE were smaller than those of SEM for a majority of the variables examined.[1] (See Table 1.) This is, of course, prima facie evidence that these SEM did not fully capture the time series properties of several variables and, therefore, casts some doubt on the validity of these models.

However, a well-constructed model should capture the dynamics of the economy. More precisely, a tendency toward error accumulation (or offsetting) over time is an important characteristic of a model. All of these early studies concentrated exclusively on one-quarter-ahead predictions even though it was acknowledged that "predictions of longer horizons are available... and are of considerable practical interest" (Nelson, 1972, p. 906). This omission was

TABLE 1

EX POST POST-SAMPLE MODEL COMPARISONS

Ratio model RMSE to time series
RMSE for forecast horizon

| Variable | 1 | 2 | 3 | 4 | 5 | 6 |
|---|---|---|---|---|---|---|
| (Nelson, 1972) FMP Model 1967:1-1969:1 | | | | | | |
| GNP | 1.45 | -- | -- | -- | -- | -- |
| Consumers' Expenditures on Nondurables | 1.48 | -- | -- | -- | -- | -- |
| Consumers' Expenditures on Durables | 1.64 | -- | -- | -- | -- | -- |
| Nonfarm Inventory Investment | .47 | -- | -- | -- | -- | -- |
| Expenditures on Producers' Durables | 1.89 | -- | -- | -- | -- | -- |
| Expenditures on Producers' Structures | .48 | -- | -- | -- | -- | -- |
| State and Local Government Expenditures | 3.24 | -- | -- | -- | -- | -- |
| Housing Expenditures | .86 | -- | -- | -- | -- | -- |
| Unemployment Rate | 2.26 | -- | -- | -- | -- | -- |
| GNP Deflator-Price Index | .75 | -- | -- | -- | -- | -- |
| Consumer Goods Price Index | .70 | -- | -- | -- | -- | -- |
| Yield on U.S. Treasury Bills | 1.18 | -- | -- | -- | -- | -- |
| Yield on Commercial Paper | 1.12 | -- | -- | -- | -- | -- |
| Yield on Corporate Bonds | 1.10 | -- | -- | -- | -- | -- |
| (Cooper and Nelson, 1975) St. Louis Model 1967:1-1968:4 | | | | | | |
| GNP | .62 | -- | -- | -- | -- | -- |
| GNP Deflator | .90 | -- | -- | -- | -- | -- |
| Real GNP | 1.25 | -- | -- | -- | -- | -- |
| Unemployment Rate | .81 | -- | -- | -- | -- | -- |
| Long-Term Interest Rate | 2.46 | -- | -- | -- | -- | -- |
| Short-Term Interest Rate | 2.05 | -- | -- | -- | -- | -- |

Table 1 (continued)

| | | | Ratio model RMSE to time series | | | |
| | | | RMSE for forecast horizon | | | |
| Variable | 1 | 2 | 3 | 4 | 5 | 6 |
|---|---|---|---|---|---|---|
| **(Cooper and Nelson, 1975) FMP Model 1967:1-1968:4** | | | | | | |
| GNP | .93 | — | — | — | — | — |
| GNP Deflator | .87 | — | — | — | — | — |
| Real GNP | 1.28 | — | — | — | — | — |
| Unemployment Rate | 2.53 | — | — | — | — | — |
| Long-Term Interest Rate | 1.04 | — | — | — | — | — |
| Short-Term Interest Rate | 1.24 | — | — | — | — | — |
| **(Ibrahim and Otsuki, 1976) OBE Quarterly Model 1966:1-1969:3** | | | | | | |
| GNP | 1.63 | — | — | — | — | — |
| Total Consumption | 1.33 | — | — | — | — | — |
| Domestic Investment | .92 | — | — | — | — | — |
| Consumer Services | 4.78 | — | — | — | — | — |
| Consumer Nondurables | 1.75 | — | — | — | — | — |
| Residential Structures | 1.10 | — | — | — | — | — |
| Imports | .93 | — | — | — | — | — |
| **(Hirsch, Grimm and Narasimham, 1976) BEA Model 1970:3-1973:2** | | | | | | |
| GNP | .81 | .68 | .47 | .33 | .36 | .34 |
| Real GNP | .90 | .83 | .63 | .49 | .51 | .46 |
| Real Personal Consumption Expenditures | .73 | .70 | .68 | .67 | .65 | .59 |
| Real Nonresidential Fixed Investment | .95 | .93 | .84 | .62 | 1.05 | 1.08 |
| Real Changes in Business Inventories | 2.77 | 2.72 | 3.96 | 2.09 | 1.90 | 1.79 |
| Corporate Profits and Inventory Valuation Adjustment | 1.38 | 1.36 | 1.21 | 1.08 | 1.25 | 1.16 |
| GNP Deflator (1958=100) | .79 | .46 | .27 | .24 | .34 | .37 |
| Unemployment Rate | 1.48 | .82 | .62 | .56 | .61 | .72 |

Table 1 (continued)

| Variable | Ratio model RMSE to time series RMSE for forecast horizon | | | | | | | |
|---|---|---|---|---|---|---|---|---|
| | 1 | 2 | 3 | 4 | 5 | 6 | 7 | 8 |
| (Fair, 1978b) Fair Model 1968:4-1977:4 | | | | | | | | |
| Real GNP | .71 | .64 | .59 | .60 | .63 | .67 | .69 | .72 |
| GNP Deflator | 1.06 | .95 | .90 | .83 | .76 | .70 | .64 | .59 |
| Unemployment Rate | 1.00 | .80 | .66 | .54 | .46 | .42 | .38 | .36 |
| Money Supply | .95 | 1.24 | 1.40 | 1.51 | 1.64 | 1.77 | 1.87 | 1.95 |
| Wage Rate | 1.16 | 1.33 | 1.41 | 1.57 | 1.69 | 1.74 | 1.69 | 1.64 |
| (Fair, 1978b) Sims Model 1968:4-1977:4 | | | | | | | | |
| Real GNP | 1.28 | 1.30 | 1.28 | 1.36 | 1.55 | 1.76 | 1.99 | 2.24 |
| GNP Deflator | 1.15 | .92 | .96 | 1.01 | 1.03 | 1.08 | 1.10 | 1.14 |
| Unemployment Rate | 1.31 | 1.21 | 1.15 | .98 | .95 | 1.00 | 1.14 | 1.28 |
| Money Supply | 1.04 | 1.14 | 1.45 | 1.75 | 2.01 | 2.29 | 2.48 | 2.65 |
| Wage Rate | 1.99 | 2.52 | 2.74 | 2.82 | 2.87 | 2.79 | 2.65 | 2.60 |
| (Fair, 1978b) Sargent Model 1968:4-1977:4 | | | | | | | | |
| Real GNP | 1.18 | 1.15 | 1.10 | 1.07 | 1.04 | 1.04 | 1.04 | 1.02 |
| GNP Deflator | 6.15 | 5.03 | 4.42 | 3.73 | 3.25 | 2.89 | 2.63 | 2.43 |
| Unemployment Rate | 1.22 | 1.16 | 1.15 | 1.11 | 1.08 | 1.03 | .99 | .93 |

remedied in more recent studies that examined longer horizons (Hirsch, Grimm, and Narasimham, 1976), (Fair, 1978), and (McNees, 1978b). This later evidence, which pertains to more recent specifications of SEM and covers substantially longer post-sample periods, presents an impression far different from that of the early studies. The principal findings can be summarized as follows: (1) ex post simulations of SEM produce smaller summary error measures for a majority, though not all, of the variables, and (2) the margin of superiority typically increases over longer horizons.

While these conclusions generally contradict those of the early, single-period studies, they provide very weak confirmation of SEM. The ex post simulations of SEM obviously benefit greatly from information in the actual, future values of their exogenous variables, while TSE extrapolations contain no information which was not available at the start of the projection period. This advantage takes on increasing importance as the horizon extends into the future. In addition, it is disturbing to note that even with full information on the future values of the exogenous variables, the SEM do not fully capture the time series properties of some variables. Although, as suggested below, this may not be sufficient grounds for rejecting an SEM even as a predictive technique, it does cast doubt on the proposition that the SEM examined has succeeded in representing the "true" structure.

Cooper and Nelson (1975) conducted a stricter test in which SEM do not benefit from information on the actual, future values of the exogenous variables. Under the assumption that all exogenous variables in the SEM are generated by covariance stationary processes, an SEM can be simulated with exogenous variable values obtained from dynamic extrapolations of TSE of those variables. Under this assumption, Zellner and Palm (1974) have shown that any linear structural model can be transformed into "final equations" in time series equation form. In other words, there is some set of TSE that implicitly incorporates the complete structure of any linear SEM (or the linear approximation of a nonlinear SEM). Since these TSE and the corresponding SEM are the same, their error characteristics would be identical. If a linear SEM outperformed a TSE, this would only indicate, under these assumptions, that the appropriate TSE had not been found.[2]

Most existing large-scale macroeconometric models contain many elements of nonlinearity and thus have no stable time series counterparts. If a nonlinear SEM outperforms a "well-chosen" TSE in this test, this could be interpreted as evidence that the SEM captures nonlinearities in the true structure that are important enough to offset any misspecification. Viewing TSE as representations of linearized versions of the nonlinear SEM, a close similarity

could be expected over very short horizons where the linear
approximation is likely to hold fairly closely. If the
nonlinear specification is valid, however, this similarity
will diminish as the prediction horizon is extended and the
TSE linear approximation becomes less exact. The advantage
of the nonlinear specification, if it is warranted, will be
reflected primarily in multiperiod comparisons.

Even if a TSE dominated an SEM over all horizons under this
test, this would not be sufficient grounds for rejecting the
SEM. This test is based on the strong assumption that all
exogenous variables in the SEM are generated by covariance
stationary processes. That assumption, which amounts to
positing a new model in which all variables are endogenous,
violates a critical feature of the specification of the
SEM--its separation of the variables into exogenous and
endogenous categories in which only the latter are modeled.
It is easy to think of exogenous variables, particularly
policy instruments, whose future values can be anticipated
or controlled with complete certainty. Even if the
historical movements of these variables can be represented
by covariance stationary processes, to do so overstates
their uncertainty and introduces superfluous errors into the
model solution. If some of the exogenous variables cannot
be represented adequately by covariance stationary
processes, the attempt to do so may alter the predictive
performance of the SEM adversely relative to a TSE which is
fit directly to the variable of interest.

These considerations suggest an additional test, a hybrid
between ex post simulations and those based on time series
extrapolations of the exogenous variables. Model
simulations could be conducted with actual values of those
exogenous variables which cannot be reasonably represented
by covariance stationary processes and time series
extrapolations of all other exogenous variables.[3]
Admittedly, this distinction may be difficult to make and
need not be the same for all models or all applications.

The interpretation of all comparisons between TSE and SEM is
hampered by major differences inherent in the two
approaches. Construction of an SEM is inherently a
substantially more ambitious task than fitting a TSE,
requiring significantly more information with
correspondingly greater opportunities for incompleteness or
"error." This point emerges most clearly from contrasting
the steps involved in estimating a linear SEM with those
involved in fitting the time series "final equations" of the
same model. (See, for example, Zellner and Palm (1974)
Table I, p. 22.) In general, construction of an SEM
requires separating variables into endogenous and exogenous
categories, arriving at identifying information, and
specifying the exact forms of equations in a way that
fitting a TSE does not. A well constructed SEM must reflect
the model builder's economic theory and the associated

accounting identities. Empirical proxies must be found for theoretically important concepts such as "expectations," "capacity," "wealth," and "permanent income." In some cases, it may be inefficient to attempt to incorporate factors "known" to be important because they are too difficult to model or because the size and frequency of their impact are expected on average to be small.

By not attempting to incorporate explicitly such a full body of information, routines for fitting TSE "short-circuit" these demanding tasks, focusing directly on the time series properties of the variable of interest. To be sure, fitting a TSE is not so straightforward in all cases that it can be done mechanically without the exercise of judgment but the relative simplicity and lack of informational requirements are acknowledged to be the main advantage of the time series approach to prediction. Ideally, the additional requirements of constructing an SEM should improve its predictive accuracy and perhaps enable it to be used for more tasks than prediction. In practice, for any model other than the "true" model in which all of these requirements have been fulfilled completely, it should not be surprising to find that an SEM does not fully capture the time series properties of all variables over all prediction horizons.

It is also worth stressing the differences in dimensionality between a TSE and an SEM. Most macroeconometric models consist of systems of dozens (or hundreds) of interdependent relationships. It is important to recognize that each TSE is not being compared with a single equation from an SEM but with the model solution, which reflects the interaction among all the variables in the model. This point can best be illustrated by a specific example based on the Fair model (Fair, 1978a and 1978b). Fair presents evidence that his model is more accurate than a "naive" autoregressive equation in predictions of real GNP, the GNP deflator, the unemployment rate, and the bill rate, but less accurate in predicting the wage rate and the money supply.[4] Fair's model does not capture the time series properties of the wage rate and the money supply as fully as a time series equation fit directly to each of those variables. Simply to replace the wage rate (or money supply) equation with its time series counterpart would obviously destroy potentially important interactions within the model. Even an alternative structural equation that captured the time series properties of this variable as fully as a time series equation need not be compatible with the rest of the model. A model's predictive performance for any specific variable does not simply reflect the corresponding structural equation for that variable in isolation. Its shortcomings may stem from other parts of the model.

Even solely in terms of predictive accuracy for these particular variables, it is not clear that the Fair model is

an "inferior" technique.  The Fair model predictions are
consistent with both his economic theory and accounting
identities as a set of TSE need not be.  The TSE predictions
of these particular variables need not be consistent with
the Fair model's predictions of other variables for which
its predictive accuracy is greater.  Without a clear
statement of the relative "losses" associated with errors in
predictions of different variables over different horizons,
no sweeping generalizations about the superiority of one
predictive technique can be made.


STATISTICAL TESTS OF MODEL VALIDITY

A comprehensive survey of "Criteria for Evaluation of
Econometric Models" by Dhrymes et al. (1972) was motivated
by the observation

> that, aside from the simplest single-equation
> cases we suffer the lack of a clear and accepted
> analytical basis for the selection of proper
> criteria for model evaluation.  This is true with
> respect to the criteria by which a single model
> should be evaluated and holds a-fortiori in the case
> of cross-model evaluations.  This state of affairs
> ... [reflects] the fact that we have not yet
> succeeded in identifying a uniquely proper way to
> evaluate a matrix of dynamically generated time
> series forecasts of all the endogenous variables in
> a macroeconomic model.  Nor do we fully understand
> the stochastic properties of such a matrix, a
> necessary first step in the generation of any
> statistically valid inference procedure.  (pp.
> 292-93)


Since that observation was made, Fair (1978a) has proposed a
method for estimating the expected predictive accuracy of an
econometric model.  The method is ingenious in that it
allows for the fact that the variances of total forecast
errors are not constant across time and that it decomposes
the total variance of the forecast error for each forecasted
variable and horizon into the uncertainty due to (1) the
coefficient estimates, (2) the error terms, (3) the
exogenous-variable forecasts, and (4) the possible
misspecification of the model.  A full description of Fair's
method for calculating the total variance of forecast error
is beyond the scope of this paper.  This section is devoted
to a discussion of the assumption used to estimate the
uncertainty from the possible misspecification of a model
and the particular assumption about the uncertainty of the
exogenous variables that Fair used to implement his method.

Some unverifiable assumption that the future will resemble
the past is necessary to make any statement about the

probable future performance of an econometric model.  A
virtue of the Fair method is that it requires this
"constancy assumption" to be made explicit.  In implementing
his method, Fair adopted a quite restrictive "constancy"
assumption:  it is assumed that the model is misspecified in
such a way that for each variable and length of forecast,
the expected value of the difference between the estimated
variance computed by means of stochastic simulation and the
estimated variance computed from outside-sample forecasts is
constant across time.  Fair presents an example to show
"that the assumption that the expected value of the
difference is constant across time is quite strong and is at
best likely to be only a rough approximation to the truth."
Nevertheless, this or some alternative constancy assumption
is necessary and may be fruitful for analyzing the accuracy
of a particular model.  It is doubtful, however, that any
one constancy assumption could hold simultaneously for
different models with differing types and degrees of
misspecification.  The particular constancy that is a
reasonably close "approximation to the truth" for one model
would be likely to be violated for other models, with
different explanatory variables or functional forms, for
essentially the same reasons that the variance of the total
forecast error is not constant across time.  The estimated
variances of total forecast errors for other models will be
contingent upon the constancy assumption that holds for the
original model but that assumption could not be expected to
hold also for different specifications.  It would be
possible to estimate variances of forecast errors for
different models based on different constancy assumptions
suited to each model, but it is not clear how to interpret
comparisons of estimated variances based on differing
assumptions.

Even if it were possible to find suitable, consistent
constancy assumptions for different models, the Fair method,
like other methods, cannot test the hypothesis that the
differences between the estimated variances are
statistically significant because it does not provide
estimates of the standard errors of the estimated
variances.  Even if the Fair method is used to rank models
on the basis of the estimated forecast variances, it does
not permit statistical comparisons of the validity of
different models.

In order to implement the Fair method, some assumption must
also be made about the uncertainty of the exogenous
variable.  As stressed above, this assumption is critically
important for comparing models with different degrees of
exogeneity and especially crucial for evaluating the
predictive accuracy of models for forecasting purposes.  It
is easy to imagine a model (defined as a system of equations
conditional upon the values of a set of external
information) which would exhibit smaller errors than
alternative models in an ex post simulation (or smaller

total forecast variance using the Fair method with the
assumption of no exogenous variable uncertainty) but which
could not forecast well because it was highly sensitive to
some volatile, hard-to-predict external variables such as
changes in the stock market or in "consumer sentiment."

In implementing his method, Fair adopted the particular
assumption that the uncertainty attached to forecasting the
change in each exogenous variable each quarter can be
estimated by the standard error of an eighth-order
autoregressive equation for each exogenous variable. This
assumption is arbitrary and unlikely to provide a realistic
estimate of the actual uncertainty attached to selecting
future values of exogenous variables in a practical
application such as forecasting. It does not reflect the
covariations among exogenous variable values and would be
unlikely to measure the uncertainties that would accompany
changes in "policy regimes." For example, estimates of
future values of exogenous variables are likely to depend
both on the predicted values of the other exogenous
variables (e.g., future corporate income tax rates are
likely to depend upon future personal income tax rates and
the future investment tax credits) and upon forecasted
values of the endogenous variable (e.g., the future behavior
of the monetary instrument variable will depend upon future
rates of inflation and real growth). It would be impossible
to account for the interdependencies in a systematic way
without expanding the original model until all exogenous
variables were endogenous.

An alternative, perhaps more natural, assumption would be to
examine the previous ex ante forecasts of the exogenous
variables to estimate their uncertainty. This procedure
would reflect past, imperfect attempts to take account of
these interdependencies but, like Fair's assumption, would
not adequately account for learning on the part of the
exogenous variable forecaster.

Finally, it should be noted that the Fair method is
relatively expensive to implement since it requires
successive reestimation and simulation of the model. When
applied to the Fair model, the estimates of total variances
of forecast errors correspond fairly closely to the
outside-sample root-mean-squared errors (RMSEs) based on ex
post model simulations.[5] If this result were general,
outside-sample RMSEs might serve as a low-cost approximation
to Fair's estimated total variance of forecast error.

Fair has developed an innovative technique for estimating
the total variance of the forecast error of an econometric
model, accounting for the four main sources of uncertainty.
A valuable feature of this technique is that it lays bare
the assumptions which must be made to address the problem of
model evaluation. Like any other approach, the method is
only as strong as the assumptions required to implement it.

Strong assumptions are required to estimate error due to
misspecification and to exogenous variable uncertainty. To
one who regards these assumptions as questionable, the Fair
method vividly illustrates the difficulty, if not the
impossibility, of statistical comparisons of the "validity"
of different models. To those willing to accept its
assumptions, Fair's method provides the analytical basis for
the evaluation of a single model. Unless its assumptions
become widely accepted, the Fair method does not provide a
basis for comparing the validity of different models. That
problem appears to be analytically intractable.


THE RELATION BETWEEN EX ANTE EVIDENCE AND MODEL VALIDITY

The traditional approach to model validation dismisses ex
ante evidence because it reflects both the quality of the
model and a forecaster's subjective estimate of the future
values of the exogenous variables in the model. The
traditional approach, in other words, is based on the
distinction between a model as a conditional statement
relating the values of endogenous variables to the assumed
values of exogenous variables and a model solution or
"prediction" which reflects both the model qua model and the
exogenous variable values used to solve the model. An
expert forecaster, skilled at choosing future values of
exogenous variables, might be able to generate an accurate
forecast with a poor model while a poor forecaster might
generate an inferior forecast with a model that best
represents the structure of the economy. Consider, for
example, a "true" model that uses wealth as an exogenous
variable and a "forecasting model" that relies only on
policy instruments as exogenous variables. It is easy to
imagine that the "true" model would be the more valid in
that it exhibits smaller errors but would also produce less
accurate ex ante forecasts because future changes in wealth,
which includes the value of common stocks, are so difficult
to predict.

This distinction, however, implies that model validity can
only be established by ex post simulation, using actual
values of the exogenous variables used to solve the model.
If any other than the actual values of exogenous variables
are used to solve the model, the resulting errors would be
partly attributable to the incorrect values of the exogenous
variables--which are not part of the model qua model--and
not solely to the deficiencies of the model as a conditional
statement.

Strict adherence to this distinction, in other words,
renders it impossible to compare models, one horn of the
"dilemma of model comparison." Whenever there is more than
one candidate for the "true" model, or, more precisely,
whenever there are nontrivial disagreements about the size
and composition of the appropriate set of exogenous

variables, ex post simulations of alternative models are not
strictly comparable because they reflect both the quality of
the models and the quantity of external information supplied
to each model in the form of actual values of exogenous
variables.  In order to compare models, the strict
distinction between model and model solution must somehow be
relaxed.  Allowance must be made for the fact that the
models' solutions require different amounts of external
information.

It was argued above that there is no obvious, mechanical
procedure for allowing for differences in exogenous variable
uncertainty in alternative models.  It is doubtful that a
specific procedure could be agreed upon because any
procedure is open to the criticism that it may either over
or understate the exogenous variable error that would be
encountered in a particular application of the models.

Generating an ex ante forecast with an econometric model is
one way of standardizing for different degrees of exogeneity
among models.  In contrast to solving the model with the
actual, ex post values, using a forecaster/model
proprietor's subjective ex ante estimates of future values
of exogenous variables confines all model solutions to
information available at the start of the forecast period.
Unlike various mechanical procedures for selecting exogenous
variable values, these estimates account for the relative
uncertainty of different exogenous variables by reflecting
historical patterns of interaction among exogenous variables
and between exogenous and endogenous variables as well as
any external information that can be brought to bear on
expected deviations from historical patterns.  They thus
allow for any learning that has occurred but, like most
methods, do not incorporate any future learning that may
occur.

The accuracy of ex ante forecasts is clearly the best
evidence for judging the past performances of
model/forecaster combinations but, because it reflects the
skills of the forecaster, it has traditionally been regarded
as irrelevant to model "validity" and therefore an
unreliable guide to future forecasting performance.
However, model validity cannot be compared without taking
account of differences in exogenous variables across
models.  It was argued above that no satisfactory procedure
has been found for assessing differences in exogenous
variables in different models.  If that argument is correct,
ex ante evidence should be considered as one, albeit
imperfect, indicator of relative model validity.  Ex ante
evidence is, of course, subjective in the sense that it is
not mechanically replicable.  On the other hand, econometric
models have typically had very short lives, most undergoing
frequent, if not continual, respecification.  Until
econometric models reach final versions that remain
unchanged for long periods of time, as a practical matter it

is not clear that models can be regarded as more stable than
the procedures by which forecasters estimate the future
values of exogenous variables.

Historical ex ante evidence is not, however, sufficient to
judge future forecast reliability or model "validity." For
these purposes, ex ante evidence must be combined with some
sort of assumption that future performance will resemble
that of the past. The relevance of historical ex ante
evidence for model validity and future forecasting
performance rests ultimately on the assumption that more
valid models can be used to generate more accurate
forecasts. Although this assumption seems impossible to
verify, those who reject it must either replace it with a
superior alternative or abandon their quest for "the true
model."


A FRAMEWORK FOR COLLECTING AND INTERPRETING EX ANTE EVIDENCE

Estimating future values of exogenous variables is only the
first step in constructing an ex ante forecast with a
macroeconometric model. The remaining steps are often
lumped together under the rubric of subjective adjustments,
or, somewhat more affectionately, "tender loving care." In
practice, subjective adjustments are undertaken for at least
three conceptually distinct types of reasons:

(1) Adjustments for systematic patterns in the single
equation residuals. These may be either mechanical (e.g.,
incorporated into the estimation technique) or subjective.

(2) Adjustments for external (or "noneconomic") factors.
These may be separated into events known to have occurred
before the forecast is issued (e.g., a strike in progress)
and events expected to occur during the forecast period
(e.g., imposition or relaxation of controls).

(3) Adjustments for "unreasonable" outcomes in preliminary
forecast runs (including failure of the model to converge to
a solution). "Unreasonable" results may be those outside
the range of historical experience, those that would not be
tolerated by the government or private agents, or those that
simply conflict with the forecaster's subjective judgment of
what he or his clients would find credible.

It is apparently not uncommon for econometrically oriented
forecasters to conduct 10 to 15 trial solutions, readjusting
on the basis of the information in each run, before arriving
at their final "control" forecast (Young, 1978, p. 34).
This process is depicted in Table 2. The first row
represents exogenous variable selection. The remaining rows
depict the various types of motivations for subjective
adjustments. The first column represents the choices made
prior to the initial model run--presumably, no adjustments

TABLE 2

AN ILLUSTRATIVE FRAMEWORK OF FORECASTING PROCEDURES

| | Prior to Initial Solution | Solution number | | | |
|---|---|---|---|---|---|
| | | 1 | 2 | ... | n |
| 1) Estimates of Future Values of Exogenous Variables | | | | | |
| 2) Adjustments for Systematic Patterns in Residuals<br><br>A. Mechanical<br>B. Subjective | | | | | |
| 3) Adjustments for External Factors<br><br>A. Prior to Forecast Release<br>B. Anticipated Future Impacts | | | | | |
| 4) Adjustments for "Reasonableness" | | | | | "Control" Forecast Released |

for "unreasonable" results are necessary at this stage. The second column represents the changes made on the basis of the first trial solution, and includes the first adjustment for "unreasonable" full model outcomes. This procedure is assumed to terminate on the nth trial when the forecaster is either exhausted or satisfied with the results.

Most forecasters retain and most forecast users see only the results from the nth solution.[6] The nth solution clearly reflects substantial interaction between the model and the forecaster. This forecast is only remotely related to the original, "pure model" forecast even though this final stage is frequently imprecisely called an econometric model forecast.

In an interesting experiment, Fair issued a series of ex ante forecasts based on his forecasting model (Fair, 1971) which contained minimal amounts of subjective adjustments: exogenous variables were selected by relatively mechanical procedures prior to running the model, serial correlation adjustments were built into the estimation procedure, and the only external information included was the adjustment of historical data to reflect the subjectively estimated impact of strikes. No adjustments were made for expected or actual events outside the model such as the imposition or relaxation of wage and price controls. The performance of the Fair "pure model" forecasts has been described in detail elsewhere (McNees, 1975, pp. 25-26). For the present purpose, it is sufficient to note that the predictive record was generally inferior to forecasts that were adjusted more thoroughly. At least in the current state of the art, judgment is a necessary ingredient to the most accurate ex ante forecasts. On the other hand, the experience with the Fair model forecast shows that, from mid-1970 through mid-1975, respectable forecasts of some variables (business fixed investment, net exports, and consumption of nondurables and services) could be generated mechanically, although forecasts of real GNP, inflation, and residential investment, while not absurd, were distinctly inferior to others.[7]

Unfortunately, Fair's experiment with his forecasting model was discontinued.[8] Some further light could be shed on the role of econometric models in forecasting, or the "art vs. science" question, if econometrically inclined forecasters would replicate the Fair experiment, by doing a little additional record keeping (incurring only small additional disc storage costs). Econometric forecasters should be encouraged to store a "first pass" solution, or perhaps several preliminary solutions, along with their final "control" solution to be used for later comparison. Although each solution reflects both "art" and "science," the two sets of forecasts would represent the relative extremes along the "pure model" and "heavily judgmental" continuum.

This type of information--two or more forecast sets from each forecaster--would be more informative than Fair's experiment in which his "pure model" forecast could only be compared with the subjectively adjusted forecasts of other forecasters using very different econometric models. It may also be more interesting if the "first pass" or "pure model" runs reflect forecasters' best judgment about future external events likely to affect the outcome (e.g., the imposition and relaxation of wage and price controls) as Fair's did not. The important point is that several forecasters/model proprietors must agree in advance on a common set of permissible adjustments.

The only experiment of this type is that with the quarterly model of the Bureau of Economic Analysis (BEA) (Hirsch, Grimm, and Narasimham, 1976). The authors collected five sets of forecasts, two ex post and three ex ante, with varying amounts of "judgmental intrusion." On the basis of the eight variables presented, judgmental adjustments generally make a positive contribution to forecast accuracy (Table 3, Panels A and B). Ex ante forecasts reflecting adjustments for "preliminary model outputs," "partial information pertaining to the first quarter of the forecast," and "reasonableness and consistency," as well as largely mechanical adjustments, were more accurate than those reflecting only mechanical adjustments for past residuals.[9] Similarly, fully adjusted ex post forecasts were generally more accurate than mechanically adjusted ones. There were, however, exceptions in which the additional judgmental adjustments produced less accurate forecasts: the four- through six-quarter-ahead ex ante forecasts of real nonresidential fixed investment were substantially inferior after adjustments; the one- through four-quarter-ahead ex ante forecasts of the implicit GNP price deflator (IPD) were marginally inferior; the ex post forecasts of real personal consumption expenditures were dominated by the mechanically adjusted versions (with the margin of superiority declining as the forecast horizon was extended); and the ex post IPD forecasts beyond a one-quarter horizon were dominated, sometimes substantially, by the mechanical versions. This evidence illustrates that judgmental adjustments can and have at times detracted from forecast accuracy. Thorough study of when judgmental intrusions add to and detract from forecast accuracy is a largely unexplored, potentially fruitful topic for future research.

The authors of the BEA experiment point out several reasons their five sets of data are not strictly comparable (see, in particular, their footnotes 15, 16, and 17) so that "the conclusions to be drawn are at best tentative." (p. 240) The minor differences that seem inevitably to arise in experiments with large models are a potentially more serious problem when the experiment is implemented with different models. The major limitation of their study, however, is

TABLE 3

EFFECT OF JUDGMENTAL ADJUSTMENT AND EXOGENOUS
VARIABLE CERTAINTY ON FORECAST ERRORS

A. Ratio of RMSEs of ex post outside sample forecasts with judgmental adjustments
to RMSEs of ex post outside sample forecasts with mechanical adjustments only,
BEA Quarterly Model, 1970:3-1973:2.

| Variable | forecast horizon | | | | | |
|---|---|---|---|---|---|---|
| | 1 | 2 | 3 | 4 | 5 | 6 |
| GNP | .74 | .70 | 1.12 | 1.30 | .83 | .68 |
| Real GNP | .68 | .78 | 1.09 | 1.29 | .86 | .55 |
| Real Personal Consumption Expenditure | 1.52 | 1.40 | 1.47 | 1.38 | 1.24 | 1.03 |
| Real Nonresidential Fixed Investment | .77 | .65 | .47 | .52 | .46 | .38 |
| Real Change in Business Inventories | .51 | .66 | .63 | .77 | .76 | .61 |
| Corporate Profits | 1.14 | 1.20 | .62 | .79 | .56 | .45 |
| GNP Deflator | .85 | 1.57 | 2.32 | 2.22 | 1.64 | 1.40 |
| Unemployment Rate | 1.35 | 1.10 | .91 | .84 | .48 | .33 |

B. Ratio of RMSEs of ex ante forecasts with judgmental adjustments to RMSEs of
ex ante forecasts with mechanical adjustments only, BEA Quarterly Model,
1970:3-1973:2.

| | 1 | 2 | 3 | 4 | 5 | 6 |
|---|---|---|---|---|---|---|
| GNP | .58 | .70 | .60 | .72 | .82 | .53 |
| Real GNP | .59 | .94 | .76 | .83 | .73 | .44 |
| Real Personal Consumption Expenditure | .99 | .93 | 1.12 | .97 | 1.03 | .86 |
| Real Nonresidential Fixed Investment | .78 | .94 | 1.26 | 1.38 | 1.43 | 1.58 |
| Real Change in Business Inventories | .57 | .69 | .65 | .71 | .67 | .83 |
| Corporate Profits | .92 | .86 | .84 | .91 | .95 | .91 |
| GNP Deflator | 1.07 | 1.20 | 1.13 | 1.09 | .98 | .78 |
| Unemployment Rate | .47 | .65 | .70 | .93 | .94 | .94 |

Table 3 (continued)

C.  Ratio of RMSEs of ex post forecasts with mechanical adjustments only to RMSEs of ex ante forecasts with mechanical adjustments only, BEA Quarterly Model, 1970:3-1973:2.

| Variable | \multicolumn{6}{c}{forecast horizon} |
|---|---|

| Variable | 1 | 2 | 3 | 4 | 5 | 6 |
|---|---|---|---|---|---|---|
| GNP | 1.57 | 1.28 | .90 | .70 | .83 | .69 |
| Real GNP | 1.85 | 2.13 | 1.60 | 1.15 | 1.16 | 1.03 |
| Real Personal Consumption Expenditure | 1.01 | .94 | 1.01 | .92 | .96 | 1.02 |
| Real Nonresidential Fixed Investment | 1.22 | 1.44 | 1.82 | 2.13 | 2.34 | 3.57 |
| Real Change in Business Inventories | 1.29 | 1.30 | 1.38 | 1.23 | 1.21 | 1.90 |
| Corporate Profits | 1.37 | 1.28 | 1.45 | 1.84 | 2.72 | 2.71 |
| GNP Deflator | 1.31 | .87 | .46 | .40 | .59 | 1.03 |
| Unemployment Rate | 1.79 | 1.83 | 1.96 | 1.76 | 1.88 | 2.30 |

SOURCE:  Albert A. Hirsch, Bruce T. Grimm and Gorti V.L. Narasimham, "Some Multiplier and Error Characteristics of the BEA Quarterly Model," in Econometric Model Performance, Lawrence R. Klein and Edwin Burmeister, eds., University of Pennsylvania Press, 1976, pp. 243-245.

not inherent in this approach--it is simply that there are
very few observations, a problem common to most post-sample
studies. Unfortunately, this experiment has not been
continued.

All ex ante experiments of this type entail some interaction
between the model and the model proprietor's judgment. Even
the most heavily adjusted forecasts by model proprietors
undoubtedly reflect insights gained from the preliminary
simulations of the model. Given the prominence of
econometrically oriented forecasters and the widespread
publicity their forecasts receive, it is undoubtedly true
that all forecasts, even those issued by forecasters who do
not maintain formal econometric models, reflect information
derived from model simulations. At the other extreme, even
"pure model" ex ante forecasts reflect the judgmental choice
of exogenous variable values.

In theory, ex ante predictions might be expected to be less
accurate than ex post simulations based on actual values of
exogenous variables. In practice, many studies have found
ex ante forecasts more accurate than ex post ones. When ex
ante forecasts employ judgmental adjustments this result is
interpreted as showing that the judgmental adjustments
contribute more to accuracy than uncertainty with respect to
future values of exogenous variables detracts. This same
result appears, however, in forecasts generated mechanically
with the BEA model. As shown in Panel C of Table 3, the
mechanically generated ex post simulations are typically
less accurate than the mechanically generated ex ante
simulations. This shows that a forecaster may, without
using subjective adjustments, be able to select the future
values of exogenous variables in such a way as to offset the
errors his model would make with the actual values of the
exogenous variables. The disadvantage of not knowing the
actual values of the exogenous variables is apparently
outweighed by the forecaster's familiarity with the probable
errors his model would make. If this result held for larger
samples and other models, it would imply that estimates of
the predictive accuracy of models overestimate the accuracy
that can be achieved in ex ante forecasting with econometric
models.

Interaction between model and model user seems inevitable
because political, social, and institutional "noneconomic"
events outside the scope of the model influence the future
course of economic activity. Unless these factors can be
successfully modeled, it is unreasonable to expect
econometric models will ever be used without judgmental
intrusion. The ideal model will be one in which a portion
of the economy can be represented by a "stable" (i.e.,
invariant with respect to the more common changes in
exogenous variables) system of equations, freeing the model
user's time (and perhaps sharpening his insights) to
investigate the effects of external "noneconomic" events.

Thus, because of their interaction, it may be impossible to
resolve definitively the relative contributions of model and
modeler. Nevertheless, the potential benefits of keeping
two (or more) sets of forecasts reflecting differing degrees
of judgmental adjustments seem well worth the costs, which
appear very low. The widespread use of adjustments for a
variety of different purposes, combined with current
record-keeping procedures, does not permit an informed
opinion on the value of econometric models in forecasting.
Given this state of affairs, it comes as little surprise
that knowledgeable people maintain diametrically opposed
views on this issue, but it is incomprehensible that those
opinions are apparently held with high degrees of confidence
(Armstrong, 1978 and McNees, 1978a).

SUMMARY AND CONCLUSIONS

Wildly extravagant claims both for and against econometric
models are commonplace both in the press and, increasingly,
in the professional literature. These contradictory claims
reflect the limitations of model testing procedures that
have been proposed and the way these tests have been
implemented and interpreted. A major problem in designing,
implementing, and interpreting tests of econometric models
is what has here been called "the dilemma of model
comparisons"--the strict view that ex post tests are the
only valid test of a model qua model conflicts with the fact
that, when models contain significantly different sets of
exogenous variables, ex post comparisons are not strictly
valid. This paper reviews three possible responses to this
dilemma: comparisons with time series equations, formal
procedures to allow for exogenous variable uncertainty, and
ex ante forecasting performance.

Comparisons of time series equations with structural
econometric models avoid rather than solve the problem of
how to compare models. Although time series equations can
be useful for diagnostic and some forecasting purposes, they
provide little useful information for evaluating econometric
models when tests of the two approaches are properly
conducted and interpreted. Past comparisons confined to
one-period-ahead performance ignore error accumulation or
offsetting, an important feature of any attempt to model the
dynamics of the economy. Ex post model simulations benefit
greatly from information excluded from time series
estimates. Because any linear structural model whose
exogenous variables can be assumed to be generated by
covariance stationary processes can be transformed into time
series equations, comparisons may shed some light on the
importance of nonlinearities common to most large-scale
macroeconometric models. To assume that exogenous variables
are generated by covariance stationary processes may,
however, introduce superfluous errors into a model
solution. Basically, the immense differences, in both

concept and construction, between time series equations and
structural econometric models render comparisons between the
two less informative for validation purposes than direct
comparisons between alternative structural models.

Definitive, direct comparisons of structural models,
however, are difficult if not impossible because of the
strong assumptions required. Fair has recently proposed an
innovative technique for estimating the uncertainty of a
forecast from an econometric model that vividly illustrates
the difficulties of the problem. All such comparisons
require some "constancy assumption." Yet a constancy
assumption which holds reasonably well for one model would
be likely to be violated for different, alternative models.
In addition, there is no obvious assumption regarding
exogenous variable uncertainty that would capture the
interaction among exogenous variables and between exogenous
and endogenous variables that would be encountered in
practical applications of the models such as forecasting.
Unless a common set of assumptions for implementing the Fair
method can be agreed upon, there appears to be no analytical
basis for comparing the validity of different models.

Ex ante forecasting is one way of standardizing for
differences in exogeneity among models. In contrast to ex
post simulations, forecasters' estimates of future values of
exogenous variables are based solely on information
available at the start of the forecast period but, in
contrast to mechanical methods, do reflect both the
historical patterns of interaction among exogenous variables
and between exogenous and endogenous variables as well as
expected deviations from those patterns. While the accuracy
of ex ante forecasts is used for evaluating model/forecaster
combinations, it has traditionally been regarded as
irrelevant to model validity. Comparisons of model
validity, however, require some means of accounting for
differences in exogenous variables among models. If, as was
argued here, there is no definitive method of accounting for
differences in exogenous variables among models, ex ante
evidence should be regarded as one, albeit still imperfect,
indicator of relative model validity. Using historical ex
ante evidence to compare model validity or to assess future
forecast performance rests ultimately on an assumption that
more valid models can be used to generate more accurate
forecasts.

I am indebted to my colleague Richard W. Kopcke for numerous
discussions of every aspect of this paper. Geoffrey Woglom
and Neil Berkman provided valuable comments on the section
on time series comparisons and Ray Fair on the section
concerning his method. Neither they, the Federal Reserve
Bank of Boston, nor the Federal Reserve System necessarily
agree with any of the opinions expressed in the paper.

## FOOTNOTES

[1]Howrey, Klein, and McCarthy (1976) have analyzed in-sample, one-period comparisons between SEM and TSM. Their analysis isolates two factors that affect such comparisons: (1) The current and lagged values of the exogenous variables (and other lagged endogenous variables) in the SEM are likely to be highly correlated in the sample with the lagged values of the endogenous variable of interest. This makes the additional information about the structure appear small. (2) Estimation procedures for large SEM do not generally minimize the in-sample squared error as effectively as a least-squares estimate of a TSM. These are persuasive reasons for discounting in-sample comparisons (but are both reasons to expect superior post-sample performance from an SEM).

[2]Practically, the set of TSE estimated without restrictions from the sample period data may not be those that incorporate the appropriate restrictions of the corresponding SEM. This problem, however, plagues the estimation of both TSE and SEM. The practical problems of estimating TSE and SEM are discussed further below. For present purposes it is sufficient to note that, under the Zellner-Palm assumptions, the appropriate set of TSE could be derived analytically.

[3]A hybrid simulation using actual values of policy variables was suggested to me by Franco Modigliani in a private conversation.

[4]For present purposes, this evidence is taken at face value. The same conclusion emerged from two separate tests. The nature of the tests and the quality of the evidence are discussed elsewhere.

[5]This observation is based on a comparison of Tables 5 and 6 in Fair (1978b). One might expect Fair's estimate to exceed ex post RMSEs since the former measure acknowledges exogenous variable error and the latter does not.

[6]Alternative forecasts are frequently presented but these are also the final results of another iterative process, not the intermediate solutions represented by columns 1 through n-1 in Table 2.

[7]The moderate forecasting success of the Fair model has been attributed to the practice of reestimating the model quarterly. For isolating "pure model" forecasting ability, reestimation (as opposed to respecification) is irrelevant, however, as it requires no subjective judgment.

[8]Fair has resumed his experiment with his econometric model. The experience so far has been too limited to permit an evaluation of the results with the new model.

[9]Similar results for eleven variables over a substantially longer forecast period were reached in McNees (1975), pp. 28-29.

[10]The "pure model" ex ante forecasts of the Fair forecasting model are a partial exception to this generalization. (Fair, 1976, Table 3)  Ex post forecasts of nominal GNP and many of its components were substantially more accurate than the ex ante forecasts.  Ex ante forecasts of a few variables, particularly real GNP, the labor force, and the unemployment rate, were substantially more accurate than the ex post predictions.


## REFERENCES

[1]   Armstrong, J. Scott, Forecasting with Econometric Methods:  Folklore versus Fact, J. Bus. 51 (1978) 549-564.

[2]   Cooper, J. Phillip and Charles R. Nelson, The Ex Ante Prediction Performance of the St. Louis and FRB-MIT-PENN Econometric Models and Some Results on Composite Predictors, J. Money, Credit, and Banking 7 (1975) 1-32.

[3]   Cooper, Ronald L., The Predictive Performance of Quarterly Econometric Models of the United States, in: Hickman, B.G. (ed.), Econometric Models of Cyclical Behavior, Studies of Income and Wealth, 36, Vol. 2, National Bureau of Economic Research, 1972, 813-925.

[4]   Dhrymes, Phoebus J., et al., Criteria for Evaluation of Econometric Models, Ann. Econ. Soc. Measure. 1 (1972) 291-324.

[5]   Fair, Ray, A Short-Run Forecasting Model of the United States Economy, (Lexington, Mass., Heath Lexington Books, 1971).

[6]   _____, Estimating the Expected Predictive Accuracy of Econometric Models, Cowles Foundation Discussion Paper No. 480, (January 17, 1978, revised October 1978a).

[7]   _____, An Analysis of the Accuracy of Four Macroeconometric Models, Cowles Foundation Discussion Paper No. 492, (August 11, 1978b).

[8]   _____, An Evaluation of a Short-Run Forecasting Model, in:  Klein, L.R. and Burmeister, E. (eds.), Econometric Model Performance (Philadelphia, University of Pennsylvania Press, 1976), 27-45.

[9]   Hirsch, Albert A., Bruce T. Grimm and Gorti V.L.
      Narasimham, Some Multiplier and Error Characteristics
      of the BEA Quarterly Model, in:  Klein, L.R. and
      Burmeister, E. (eds.), Econometric Model Performance
      (Philadelphia, University of Pennsylvania Press, 1976),
      108-125.

[10]  Howrey, E. Philip, Lawrence R. Klein and Michael D.
      McCarthy, Notes on Testing the Predictive Performance
      of Econometric Models, in:  Klein, L.R. and Burmeister,
      E. (eds.), Econometric Model Performance (Philadelphia,
      University of Pennsylvania Press, 1976), 108-125.

[11]  Ibrahim, I.B., and T. Otsuki, Forecasting GNP
      Components Using the Method of Box and Jenkins,
      Southern Econ. J. 42 (1976) 461-470.

[12]  McNees, Stephen K., Are Econometricians Useful?:
      Folklore versus Fact, J. Bus. 51 (1978a) 573-577.

[13]  _____, An Empirical Assessment of "New
      Theories" of Inflation and Unemployment, in:  After the
      Phillips Curve:  Persistence of High Inflation and High
      Unemployment, Conference Series No. 19, Federal Reserve
      Bank of Boston (June 1978b), 29-46.

[14]  _____, An Evaluation of Economic
      Forecasts, New Eng. Econ. Rev. (November/December 1975)
      3-39.

[15]  Nelson, Charles R., The Prediction Performance of the
      FRB-MIT-PENN Model of the U.S. Economy, Am. Econ. R. 62
      (1972) 902-917.

[16]  Young, Richard M., Forecasting the U.S. Economy with an
      Econometric Model, presented at the London Business
      School Economic Modelling Conference, July 1978, to be
      published by Heinemann Press.

[17]  Zellner, Arnold and Franz Palm, Time Series Analysis
      and Simultaneous Equation Econometric Models, J.
      Econometrics 2 (1974) 17-54.

LARGE-SCALE MACRO-ECONOMETRIC MODELS
J. Kmenta, J.B. Ramsey (editors)
© North-Holland Publishing Company, 1981

EVALUATION OF ECONOMETRIC MODELS BY
DECOMPOSITION AND AGGREGATION

Gregory C. Chow

Econometric Research Program
Princeton University
Princeton, New Jersey
U.S.A.

## 1.  INTRODUCTION

Is an econometric model too large, or not large enough?  This is
the question which we hope to answer in this paper.  This question
is concerned with the choice of alternative models differing in
size.  An answer could conceivably come from a priori reasoning
or theorizing, but the one suggested here is based purely on
statistical inference using the information contained in a finite
sample of n observations.  We shall develop in Section 2 a statistical criterion for model selection, and derive in Section 3
explicit expressions based on this criterion for the selection
of simultaneous-equation models of different sizes.

We will define the "size" of an econometric model designed to explain a given set of dependent variables by the number of functionally independent parameters in the model.  By this definition
the size of a macroeconomic model consisting of a system of simultaneous stochastic equations will depend on whether it can be
decomposed or aggregated.  Given the same set of dependent variables to be explained, if a model is decomposable into submodels
each capable of explaining a subset of dependent variables, then
the number of parameters required to explain any subset would be
smaller than in the case of a fully integrated system of simultaneous equations.  If the model is not decomposable but block
recursive, the matrix of the Jacobian for transforming the random
residuals into the dependent variables will be block triangular
and the covariance matrix of the residuals will be block diagonal,
both leading to a smaller number of parameters than in a completely interdependent system.  By aggregating across equations,

one is also likely to reduce the number of parameters required
to explain any subset of dependent variables, thus reducing the
size of the model for each subset.  In Section 4, the statistical selection criterion will be applied to decide whether a
model should be made block triangular and whether certain dependent variables should be aggregated.  Section 5 contains concluding remarks.

The basic viewpoint taken is that the better of two models is
the one which, by the method of its construction, will on the
average predict future observations better.  Here better predictions could be defined by a smaller expected sum of squared
deviations from the future observations.  However, we will define better predictions by a smaller expected sum of the log-
likelihood ratios of the true density of the future observations
to the density specified by the model.  Specifically, let $g(\cdot)$
be the true density of each of n independent future observations
$(\tilde{y}_1,\ldots,\tilde{y}_n)=\tilde{Y}$, and let $f(\cdot|\theta)$ be the density specified by a pos-
sible model.  Better predictions by $f(\cdot|\theta)$ will be defined by a
smaller expectation

$$(1.1) \quad I_n[g;f(\cdot|\theta)] = E \sum_{i=1}^{n} [\log g(\tilde{y}_i) - \log f(\tilde{y}_i|\theta)] \geq 0$$

where the expectation is evaluated by the true density $g(\cdot)$.
The mean log-likelihood ratio $I[g;f(\cdot|\theta)]=E\log[g(y)/f(y|\theta)]$ is
also called the mean information for discrimination between $g(y)$
and $f(y|\theta)$, as discussed in Kullback and Leibler (1951), Savage
(1954, p. 50), and Kullback (1959, p. 5).

To illustrate the use of the mean log likelihood $E(\log f(y|\theta))$
as a measure of how well f approximates g, consider a univariate
y having a normal distribution with mean $\mu$ and variance v.  If
the approximate distribution is normal with mean $\theta_1$ and variance
$\theta_2$, its mean log likelihood is

$$(1.2) \quad E[\log f(y|\theta)] = E\{-\frac{1}{2}\log 2\pi - \frac{1}{2}\log\theta_2 - \frac{1}{2}(y-\theta_1)^2/\theta_2\}$$

$$= -\frac{1}{2}\log 2\pi - \frac{1}{2}\log\theta_2 - \frac{1}{2}[v+(\theta_1-\mu)^2]/\theta_2.$$

For any given $\theta_2$, the value of $\theta_1$ which maximizes the mean log

likelihood (1.2) is the true mean $\mu$ itself. If $\theta_1=\mu$, the value
of $\theta_2$ which maximizes (1.2) is the true $v$ itself. This measure
is better than the mean squared prediction error for judging
the goodness of fit for f. If we let $\theta_1=\mu$ but $\theta_2=5v$, the mean
squared prediction error would be $E(y-\theta_1)^2=v$, the smallest at-
tainable. However, the model f may be a very poor approximation
of g because $\theta_2$ is very different from the true $v$.

Having adopted better predictions, defined by the information
measure (1.1), as the criterion for selecting alternative models,
we would like to stress that the correct model, even if it is
known, is not necessarily the one to be selected because it may
contain too many unknown parameters. For example, let the true
regression model be linear in $X_1$ and $X_2$ with coefficient vectors
$\beta_1$ and $\beta_2$. If $\beta_2$ is fairly small, and if only a finite sample
of n observations is available, the model linear in $X_1$ alone as
estimated by the method of least squares may yield better predictions than the model linear in both $X_1$ and $X_2$. The reason
is that the larger model, though correctly specified, may be
more poorly estimated because of the larger number of parame-
ters. Larger sampling errors in the estimates $\hat{\beta}_1$ and $\hat{\beta}_2$ may
lead to larger prediction errors for future observations. Thus
if two different models $f_1(\cdot|\theta_1)$ and $f_2(\cdot|\theta_2)$ are proposed for
the prediction of the same dependent variable, one should not
merely ask how well $f_1$ and $f_2$ would do when $\theta_1$ and $\theta_2$ can be
consistently estimated by an infinite sample, but how well the
estimated $f_1(\cdot|\hat{\theta}_1)$ and $f_2(\cdot|\hat{\theta}_2)$ based on a finite sample would
do, on the average, allowing for the sampling distributions of
$\hat{\theta}_1$ and $\hat{\theta}_2$. To predict n future observations $(\tilde{y}_1,\ldots,\tilde{y}_n)=\tilde{Y}$, the
model selection criterion is

$$(1.3)\quad E_{\hat{\theta}}I_n(g;f(\cdot|\hat{\theta})) \equiv E_{\hat{\theta}}\{E_{\tilde{Y}}\sum_{i=1}^{n}[\log g(\tilde{y}_i) - \log f(\tilde{y}_i|\hat{\theta})] .$$

Akaike (1973; 1974) adopted the mean log-likelihood ratio (or
information) of a future observation for model selection and
proposed an estimate of the mean of $E_{\tilde{y}}[\log f(\tilde{y}|\theta)]$ over the
sampling distribution of the maximum likelihood estimator $\hat{\theta}$.
We will modify Akaike's derivation and correct an error in his

estimate of $E_{\hat{\theta}}E_{\tilde{y}}[\log f(\tilde{y}|\hat{\theta})]$, thus proposing an alternative in-formation criterion for model selection. We will also apply this criterion to the selection of simultaneous-equations models.


2.  DERIVATION OF AN INFORMATION CRITERION


We assume that the true density $g(\cdot)$ equals $f(\cdot|\theta°)$ and that an approximate model results from imposing a set of r linear res-trictions $H'\theta=-b$ on the parameters. The purpose of this section is to provide an estimate of $E_{\hat{\theta}}I_n[g;f(\cdot|\hat{\theta})]$ where $\hat{\theta}$ is the max-imum likelihood estimator of $\theta$ subject to the restrictions $H'\theta=-b$ imposed by the approximate model.

When $\theta$ is given, the mean information for discriminating between $g(\cdot)$ and $f(\cdot|\theta)$ using n future observations $(\tilde{y}_1,\ldots,\tilde{y}_n)=\tilde{Y}$ is

(2.1)     $I_n[g;f(\cdot|\theta)] = E_{\tilde{Y}} \sum_{i=1}^{n} [\log g(\tilde{y}_i) - \log f(\tilde{y}_i|\theta)]$

$$= E_{\tilde{Y}}[\log L(\tilde{Y};\theta°) - \log L(\tilde{Y};\theta)]$$

where $L(\tilde{Y};\theta)$ denotes the likelihood function and where the ex-pectation is evaluated by the true density $f(\cdot|\theta°)$. As $\theta$ is un-known, we assume that n observations $(y_1,\ldots,y_n)=Y$ are available to provide a maximum likelihood estimate $\hat{\theta}$ of $\theta$ subject to the required restrictions. The estimated model $f(\cdot|\hat{\theta})$ is to be judged by the expected information

(2.2)     $E_{\hat{\theta}}I_n[\theta°;\hat{\theta}] = E_{\hat{\theta}}[E_{\tilde{Y}}\log L(\tilde{Y};\theta°) - E_{\tilde{Y}}\log L(\tilde{Y};\hat{\theta})]$.

Akaike (1973; 1974) has provided an estimate of $E_{\hat{\theta}}[E_{\tilde{Y}}\log L(\tilde{Y};\hat{\theta})]$ for model selection, since the term $E_{\tilde{Y}}\log L(\tilde{Y};\theta°)$, though un-known, is the same for all approximate models. This section proposes an alternative estimate, under the assumption that $\theta$ is subject to the known linear restriction $H'\theta+b=0$. The result will be shown to apply to the case of nonlinear restrictions $h(\theta)=0$ by utilizing the work of Silvey (1959).


To estimate $E_{\hat{\theta}}E_{\tilde{Y}}\log L(\tilde{Y};\theta)$, we first define $\theta*$ as the parameter of the best approximate model which satisfies the restriction

H'θ*+b=0.  Being "best" here means having maximum information, i.e.

$$E_{\tilde{Y}} \log L(\tilde{Y}; \theta^*) \geq E_{\tilde{Y}} \log L(\tilde{Y}; \theta).$$

To find θ* we differentiate the Lagrangian expression

$$L = E_{\tilde{Y}} \log L(\tilde{Y}; \theta) - \lambda'(H'\theta + b)$$

assuming differentiation and the expectation operation can be interchanged, yielding

(2.3) $$n^{-1} E_{\tilde{Y}} \left[ \frac{\partial \log L(\tilde{Y}; \theta^*)}{\partial \theta} \right] - H\lambda = 0$$

(2.3) and H'θ*+b=0 can be solved for θ* and λ*.  In the language of Sawa (1978), θ* is the pseudo-true parameter of the pseudo-true model f(·|θ*).

Having defined θ*, we expand logL(Ỹ;θ̂)* about θ*,

(2.4) $$\log L(\tilde{Y}; \hat{\theta}^*) = \log L(\tilde{Y}; \theta^*) + \frac{\partial \log L(\tilde{Y}; \theta^*)}{\partial \theta}(\hat{\theta}^* - \theta^*)$$

$$+ \frac{1}{2}(\hat{\theta}^* - \theta^*)'\frac{\partial^2 \log L(\tilde{Y}; \theta^*)}{\partial \theta \partial \theta'}(\hat{\theta}^* - \theta^*)$$

with θ̂=θ̂* denoting the maximum likelihood estimates of θ*, or of θ subject to the imposed restriction.  The expectations of the three terms on the right-hand side of (2.4) will be estimated in turn.

(2.5) $$E_{\hat{\theta}^*} E_{\tilde{Y}} \log L(\tilde{Y}; \theta^*) = E_{\tilde{Y}} \log L(\tilde{Y}; \theta^*) \simeq \log L(Y; \theta^*)$$

$$= \log L(Y; \hat{\theta}^*) + \frac{\partial \log L(Y; \hat{\theta}^*)'}{\partial \theta}(\theta^* - \hat{\theta}^*)$$

$$+ \frac{1}{2}(\hat{\theta}^* - \theta^*)'\frac{\partial^2 \log L(Y; \theta^*)}{\partial \theta \partial \theta'}(\hat{\theta}^* - \theta^*)$$

$$= \log L(Y; \hat{\theta}^*) + \frac{1}{2} \operatorname{tr}\{\frac{\partial^2 \log L(Y; \theta^*)}{\partial \theta \partial \theta'}(\hat{\theta}^* - \theta^*)(\hat{\theta}^* - \theta^*)'\}.$$

The first step of (2.5) amounts to estimating the expectation $E_{\tilde{Y}} \log L(\tilde{Y}; \theta^*)$ by the sample analogue logL(Y;θ*).  The second line involves expanding logL(Y;θ*) about θ̂*, with the second term vanishing because θ̂* is obtained by maximizing logL(Y;θ) subject to H'θ̂*+b=0 and thus satisfies

(2.6) $$n^{-1} \frac{\partial \log L(Y;\hat{\theta}*)}{\partial \theta} - H\hat{\lambda} = 0.$$

The expectation $E_{\tilde{Y}}$ of the second term on the right-hand side of (2.4) vanishes because of (2.3). For the third term, we have

(2.7) $$E_{\hat{\theta}*} E_{\tilde{Y}} \{ \frac{1}{2}(\hat{\theta}*-\theta*)' \frac{\partial^2 \log L(\tilde{Y};\theta*)}{\partial\theta\partial\theta} (\hat{\theta}*-\theta*) \}$$

$$= \frac{1}{2} tr\{ E_{\tilde{Y}} \frac{\partial^2 \log L(Y;\theta*)}{\partial\theta\partial\theta'} E_{\hat{\theta}*}(\hat{\theta}*-\theta*)(\hat{\theta}*-\theta*)' \}.$$

Defining

(2.8) $$J(\theta*,\theta°) \equiv -E_{\tilde{Y}} \frac{\partial^2 \log L(\tilde{Y};\theta*)}{\partial\theta\partial\theta'}$$

where the parameter $\theta°$ is used to define the distribution of $\tilde{Y}$, we substitute (2.5) and (2.7) for the first and third terms on the right-hand side of (2.4) to obtain

(2.9) $$E_{\hat{\theta}*} E_{\tilde{Y}} \log L(\tilde{Y};\hat{\theta}*) \simeq \log L(Y;\hat{\theta}*) - tr\{J(\theta*,\theta°)E(\hat{\theta}*-\theta*)(\hat{\theta}*-\theta*)'\}.$$

In (2.5) the two matrices inside the curly brackets have been replaced by their expected values.

The formula (2.9) remains valid for nonlinear restrictions $h(\theta)=0$ on $\theta$. The only changes in the above derivations are to replace $H'\theta+b$ by $h(\theta)$ and to interpret $H$ as the matrix of partial derivatives of $h(\theta)$, evaluated at $\theta=\theta*$ for (2.3) and at $\theta=\hat{\theta}*$ for the computation of $\hat{\theta}*$ in (2.5). The models will be ranked by (2.9), the one having the highest value to be selected. The remaining problem is to provide estimates of $J(\theta*,\theta°)$ and $E(\hat{\theta}*-\theta*)(\hat{\theta}*-\theta*)$.

To find the distribution of the maximum likelihood estimate $\hat{\theta}*$ subject to the restrictions $H'\theta*=-b$, we follow the work of Silvey (1959). Expanding $\partial \log L(Y;\hat{\theta}*)/\partial\theta$ in (2.6) about $\theta*$, we get

(2.10) $$n^{-1} \frac{\partial \log L(Y;\theta*)}{\partial\theta} + \left[ n^{-1} \frac{\partial^2 \log L(Y;\theta*)}{\partial\theta\partial\theta'} + o(1) \right] [\hat{\theta}*-\theta*]$$

$$+ H\hat{\lambda} = 0.$$

Since $\theta*$ is obtained by minimizing $n^{-1}I_n[g;f(\cdot|\theta)]$ as we did in (2.3), or alternatively by maximizing $n^{-1}E\log L(Y;\theta)$, subject to

H'θ+b=0, we have

(2.11)
$$n^{-1} \frac{\partial E\log L(Y;\theta^*)}{\partial \theta} + H\lambda^* = 0.$$

Subtraction of (2.11) from (2.10) yields

(2.12)
$$\begin{bmatrix} -n^{-1} \dfrac{\partial^2 \log L(Y;\theta^*)}{\partial\theta\partial\theta'} + o(1) & -H \\ -H & 0 \end{bmatrix} \begin{bmatrix} \hat{\theta}^* - \theta^* \\ \hat{\lambda} - \lambda^* \end{bmatrix}$$

$$= \begin{bmatrix} n^{-1} \dfrac{\partial \log L(Y;\theta^*)}{\partial\theta} - n^{-1} \dfrac{\partial E\log L(Y;\theta^*)}{\partial\theta} \\ 0 \end{bmatrix}.$$

Abbreviating $L(Y;\theta^*)$ by $L^*$, we observe that the asymptotic distribution of $n^{-1}[\partial\log L^*/\partial\theta - \partial E\log L^*/\partial\theta]$ is normal by the central limit theorem and its mean is zero by the law of large numbers. The covariance matrix of $n^{-\frac{1}{2}}[\partial\log L^*/\partial\theta - \partial E\log L^*/\partial\theta]$ is

(2.13)
$$V_{\theta^*} = n^{-1}\left[ E\, \frac{\partial\log L^*}{\partial\theta} \cdot \frac{\partial\log L^*}{\partial\theta'} - \frac{\partial E\log L^*}{\partial\theta} \cdot \frac{\partial E\log L^*}{\partial\theta'} \right].$$

As n increases, the sample mean $-n^{-1}\partial^2\log L^*/\partial\theta\partial\theta'$ approaches its expectation $n^{-1}J(\theta^*,0°)$. Therefore, the solution of (2.12) yields an asymptotic distribution for $n^{\frac{1}{2}}(\hat{\theta}^*-\theta^*)$ and $n^{\frac{1}{2}}(\hat{\lambda}-\lambda^*)$ which is normal with mean 0 and covariance matrix

(2.14)
$$\begin{bmatrix} P_{0^*} V_{\theta^*} P_{\theta^*} & P_{\theta^*} V_{\theta^*} Q_{\theta^*} \\ Q'_{\theta^*} V_{\theta^*} P_{\theta^*} & Q'_{\theta^*} V_{\theta^*} Q_{\theta^*} \end{bmatrix}$$

where

(2.15)
$$\begin{bmatrix} P_{\theta^*} & Q_{\theta^*} \\ Q'_{\theta^*} & R_{\theta^*} \end{bmatrix} = \begin{bmatrix} n^{-1}J(\theta^*,\theta\ ) & -H \\ -H' & 0 \end{bmatrix}^{-1}$$

$$= \begin{bmatrix} nJ^{-1}-nJ^{-1}H(H'J^{-1}H)^{-1}H'J^{-1} & -J^{-1}H(H'J^{-1}H)^{-1} \\ -(H'J^{-1}H)^{-1}H'J^{-1} & -n^{-1}(H'J^{-1}H)^{-1} \end{bmatrix}.$$

This result was given by Silvey (1959, Lemma 1, p. 394).

In the important special case when the restrictions consist
entirely of zero restrictions on a subset of parameters, we
arite $\theta^*=(\theta_1^*\quad 0)$, $H'=[0\quad I]$, and

$$(2.16)\qquad J(\theta^*,\theta^0) = \begin{bmatrix} J_{11}(\theta^*,\theta^0) & J_{12}(\theta^*,\theta^0) \\ J_{21}(\theta^*,\theta^0) & J_{22}(\theta^*,\theta^0) \end{bmatrix}$$

The matrix $P_{\theta^*}$ from (2.15) becomes

$$(2.17)\qquad P_{\theta^*} = \begin{bmatrix} nJ_{11}^{-1}(\theta^*,\theta^0) & 0 \\ 0 & 0 \end{bmatrix}$$

and the covariance matrix of $(\hat{\theta}_1^*-\theta_1^*)$ from (2.14) becomes

$$(2.18)\qquad J_{11}^{-1}(\theta^*,\theta^0)\left[E\,\frac{\partial logL^*}{\partial\theta_1}\cdot\frac{\partial logL^*}{\partial\theta_1'}\right]J_{11}^{-1}(\theta^*,\theta^0)$$

since $ElogL^*/\partial\theta_1=0$ as $\theta_1^*$ is obtained by maximizing (differentiating) $ElogL(Y;\theta_1,0)$ with respect to $\theta_1$.  Combining (2.18)
with (2.9), we have the following model selection criterion in
this case:

$$(2.19)\qquad logL(Y;\hat{\theta}^*) - tr\{E\left[\frac{\partial logL^*}{\partial\theta_1}\cdot\frac{\partial logL^*}{\partial\theta_1'}\right]J_{11}^{-1}(\theta^*,\theta^0)\}.$$

Akaike (1973) was incorrect in claiming that $J_{11}^{-1}(\theta^*,\theta^0)$ is the
asymptotic covariance matrix of $\hat{\theta}_1^*$, as we have shown in (2.18).
If this claim were valid, the trace term in (2.19) would become
k, the number of unknown parameters in $\theta_1$, and (2.19) would become Akaike's information criterion which selects the model
having the largest value for the maximum log likelihood minus
the number of parameters to be estimated.  The claim is incorrect because only when the model is correctly specified, i.e.,
when $\theta^*=\theta^0$, do we have $J_{11}^{-1}(\theta^*,\theta^*)$ as the asymptotic covariance
matrix of $\hat{\theta}^*$.  In order to apply our criterion (2.19) to simultaneous-equation models, we have to estimate $J(\theta^*,\theta^0)$ and
$E(\theta^*-\theta^0)(\theta^*-\theta^*)'$ as given by (2.14), or by (2.18) in the special
case of zero restrictions on $\theta^*$.  This is our task in the next
section.

3. ESTIMATION OF THE INFORMATION CRITERION FOR SIMULTANEOUS-
   EQUATIONS MODELS

In this section, we will provide an estimate of the information
criterion for the selection of linear simultaneous-equations
models, while leaving a discussion of its econometric applications to the following section. Let the true model be

$$(3.1) \qquad Y\Gamma^\circ + XB^\circ = U \qquad\qquad EU'U = n\Sigma^\circ \equiv nR^{\circ-1}$$

where Y is an nxg matrix of endogenous variables, X is an nxk
matrix of exogenous variables, and selected elements of $\Gamma^\circ$ and
$B^\circ$ are zero because of the identification restrictions. Let
the approximate model be

$$(3.2) \qquad Y\Gamma^* + XB^* = U^* \qquad\qquad EU^{*'}U^* = n\Sigma^* \equiv nR^{*-1}$$

where the elements of $\Gamma^*$, $B^*$ and $\Sigma^*$ are subject to additional
linear restrictions. The elements of these "pseudo-true" parameters are obtained by a constrained maximization of

$$(3.3) \quad E\log L(Y;\Gamma,B,R) = -\frac{ng}{2}\log(2\pi) + \frac{n}{2}\log|R| + n\log|\Gamma|$$
$$- \frac{1}{2}\mathrm{tr}\{R \cdot E(Y\Gamma+XB)'(Y\Gamma+XB)\}$$

where the expectation E is evaluated by assuming that Y is generated by the true model.

To evaluate the matrix $V_{\theta^*}$ of (2.13), we need the derivatives
of $\log L(Y;\Gamma,B,R)$ evaluated at $\Gamma^*$, $B^*$ and $\Sigma^*$ minus their expectations. The derivatives are, with $U^*=Y\Gamma^*+XB^*=(u_1^*\ldots u_g^*)$,

$$(3.4) \qquad \frac{\partial \log L^*}{\partial B} = -X'U^*R^*$$

$$(3.5) \qquad \frac{\partial \log L^*}{\partial \Gamma} = -Y'U^*R^* + n(\Gamma^{*'})^{-1}$$

$$(3.6a) \qquad \frac{\partial \log L^*}{\partial r_{ij}} = n\sigma_{ij}^* - u_i^{*'}u_j^*$$

$$(3.6b) \qquad \frac{\partial \log L^*}{\partial r_{ii}} = \frac{1}{2}(n\sigma_{ii}^* - u_i^{*'}u_i^*).$$

Defining the true reduced-form to be

(3.7)    $Y = -XB^\circ\Gamma^{\circ-1} + U\Gamma^{\circ-1} \equiv X\Pi^\circ + V$

$$EV'V = n\Omega^\circ \equiv n\Gamma^{\circ'-1}\Sigma^\circ\Gamma^{\circ-1}$$

we can write

(3.8)    $U^* = Y\Gamma^* + XB^* = X(\Pi^\circ\Gamma^*+B^*) + V\Gamma^* = D + V\Gamma^*$

where

(3.9)                          $D = EU^* = X(\Pi^\circ\Gamma^*+B^*).$

Therefore, the derivatives given by (3.4) and (3.5) minus their expectations are

(3.10)              $\dfrac{\partial \log L^*}{\partial B} - E\dfrac{\partial \log L^*}{\partial B} = X'V\Gamma^*R^*$

(3.11)   $\dfrac{\partial \log L^*}{\partial \Gamma} - E\dfrac{\partial \log L^*}{\partial \Gamma} =$

$$= -\Pi^\circ'X'V\Gamma^*R^* - V'DR^* - V'V\Gamma^*R^* + n\Omega^\circ\Gamma^*R^*.$$

The expectations of (3.6a) and (3.6b) are zero.

Since only the unknown elements of $B^*$ and $\Gamma^*$ are of concern, we denote by $\beta_i$ and $\gamma_i$ respectively the column vectors consisting of only the unknown elements in the $i^{th}$ columns of $B^*$ and $\Gamma^*$. Similarly, $X_i$ and $Y_i$ denote the matrices composed of those columns of $X$ and $Y$ which are associated respectively with the unknown coefficients in $\beta_i$ and $\gamma_i$. Also, we will denote $X\Pi^\circ$ by $\tilde{Y}^\circ$, $X\Pi^* \equiv -XB^*\Gamma^{*-1}$ by $\tilde{Y}^*$, and $\Gamma^{*'}\Omega\,\Gamma^*$ by $W$ for convenience. Using these notations together with (3.10) and (3.11), we derive the required components of $nV_{\theta*}$ as

(3.12)                     $\text{Cov}\left[\dfrac{\partial \log L^*}{\partial \beta_i} \quad \dfrac{\partial \log L^*}{\partial \beta_j'}\right] = X_i'X_j(r_i^{*'}Wr_j^*)$

(3.13)     $\text{Cov}\left[\dfrac{\partial \log L^*}{\partial \gamma_i} \quad \dfrac{\partial \log L^*}{\partial \gamma_j'}\right] = \tilde{Y}_i^{o\,\prime}\tilde{Y}_j^o (r_i^*\,'Wr_j^*) + \Omega_i^{o\,\prime}\Gamma^* r_j^* r_i^*\,'D'\tilde{Y}_j^o$

$$+ \ \tilde{Y}_i^{o\,\prime}Dr_j^* r_i^*\,'\Gamma^*\Omega_j^o + n\Omega_{ij}^o r_{ij}^* + n\Omega_i^{o\,\prime}\Gamma^* r_j^* r_i^*\,'\Gamma^*\,'\Omega_j^o$$

(3.14)     $\text{Cov}\left[\dfrac{\partial \log L^*}{\partial \gamma_i} \quad \dfrac{\partial \log L^*}{\partial \beta_j'}\right] = \tilde{Y}_i^{o\,\prime}X_j (r_i^*\,'Wr_j) + \Omega_i^{o\,\prime}\Gamma^* r_j^* r_i^*\,'D'X_j$

where $\Omega_i^o$ denotes a matrix composed of only those columns of $\Omega^o = (\omega_{ij}^o)$ which are associated with the unknown elements of $\gamma_i^*$, and $\Omega_{ij}^o$ denotes a matrix extracted from $\Omega^o$ whose rows correspond to the unknown elements of $\gamma_i^*$ and whose columns correspond to the unknown elements of $\gamma_j^*$. The proof of (3.13) has utilized the relation, for $V = (v_1 \ldots v_g)$,

$$E(v_1'v_2)(v_3'v_4) = n^2\omega_{12}^o\omega_{34}^o + n\omega_{13}^o\omega_{24}^o + n\omega_{14}^o\omega_{23}^o$$

which implies

$$EV'V\Gamma^* r_i^* r_j^*\,'\Gamma^*\,'V'V = n^2\Omega^{o}\Gamma^* r_i^* r_j^*\,'\Gamma^*\,'\Omega^o + n\Omega^{o}\Gamma^* r_j^* r_i^*\,'\Gamma^*\Omega^o$$

$$+ \ n\Omega_{ij}^o (r_i^*\,'\Gamma^*\,'\Omega^o\Gamma^* r_j^*).$$

By contrast, the elements of $J(\theta^*, \theta^o)$ as derived from differentiating (3.4) and (3.5) are

(3.15)     $-E\ \dfrac{\partial \log L^*}{\partial \beta_i \partial \beta_j'} = X_i'X_j r_{ij}^*$

(3.16)     $-E\ \dfrac{\partial \log L^*}{\partial \gamma_i \partial \gamma_j'} = \tilde{Y}_i^{o\,\prime}\tilde{Y}_j^o r_{ij}^* + n\Omega_{ij}^o r_{ij}^* + n\gamma^{j(i)}\gamma^{i(j)\,\prime}$

(3.17)     $-E\ \dfrac{\partial \log L^*}{\partial \gamma_i \partial \beta_j'} = \tilde{Y}_i^{o\,\prime}X_j r_{ij}^*$

where $\gamma^{i(j)}$ denotes a column vector consisting of those elements of the $i$th row of $(\Gamma^*)^{-1}$ which correspond to the unknown elements of $\gamma_j^*$. Note that when $(\Gamma^*, B^*, R^*) = (\Gamma^o, B^o, R^o)$, i.e., when the approximate model coincides with the true model, (3.12), (3.13) and (3.14) will reduce to (3.15), (3.16) and (3.17) respectively, as $r_i^*\,'Wr_j^* = r_i^{o\,\prime}\Sigma^o r_j^o$ will become $r_{ij}^o = r_{ij}^*$ and $D = 0$.

We next derive the expectations involving the derivatives of

logL with respect to $r_{ij}$. Using (3.6) we obtain by straightforward manipulations, with $\Gamma^{*\prime}\Omega^{O}\Gamma^{*}=W=(w_{ij})$,

(3.18a)    $$E\left[\frac{\partial \log L^{*}}{\partial r_{ij}} \cdot \frac{\partial \log L^{*}}{\partial r_{k\ell}}\right] = n[\sigma^{*}_{ik}w_{j\ell} + \sigma^{*}_{jk}w_{i\ell}$$

$$+ (\sigma^{*}_{i\ell}-w_{i\ell})w_{jk} + (\sigma^{*}_{j\ell}-w_{j\ell})w_{ik}]$$

(3.18b)    $$E\left[\frac{\partial \log L^{*}}{\partial r_{ii}} \cdot \frac{\partial \log L^{*}}{\partial r_{k\ell}}\right] = n[\sigma^{*}_{ik}w_{i\ell} + (\sigma^{*}_{i\ell}-w_{i\ell})w_{ik}]$$

(3.18c)    $$E\left[\frac{\partial \log L^{*}}{\partial r_{ii}} \cdot \frac{\partial \log L^{*}}{\partial r_{kk}}\right] = \frac{n}{2}[\sigma^{*}_{ik}w_{ik} + (\sigma^{*}_{ik}-w_{ik})w_{ik}]$$

and the corresponding expressions

(3.19a)    $$-E\left[\frac{\partial^{2} \log L^{*}}{\partial r_{ij}\partial r_{k}}\right] = n[\sigma^{*}_{ik}\sigma^{*}_{j\ell} + \sigma^{*}_{jk}\sigma^{*}_{i\ell}]$$

(3.19b)    $$-E\left[\frac{\partial^{2} \log L^{*}}{\partial r_{ii}\partial r_{k}}\right] = n\sigma^{*}_{ik}\sigma^{*}_{i\ell}$$

(3.19c)    $$-E\left[\frac{\partial^{2} \log L^{*}}{\partial r_{ii}\partial r_{kk}}\right] = \frac{n}{2}\,\sigma^{*2}_{ik}.$$

Again, when the approximate model coincides with the true model,
we have $W=\Sigma^{O}=\Sigma^{*}=(\sigma^{*}_{ij})$, and (3.18) will be identical with (3.19).

As can be seen by differentiating (3.4) and (3.5), the expecta-
tions of $\partial^{2}\log L^{*}/\partial\beta_{i}\partial r_{k\ell}$ and $\partial^{2}\log L^{*}/\partial\gamma_{i}\partial r_{k\ell}$ are zero.  Therefore, letting $\alpha$ denote a column vector composed of the unknown
elements of $\beta_{1},\ldots,\beta_{g},\ \gamma_{1},\ldots,\gamma_{g},\ r$ denote a column vector consisting of $r_{11},\ldots,r_{1g},\ r_{22},\ldots,r_{2g},\ r_{33},\ldots,r_{gg}$  and $\theta'$ denote
$(\alpha'\ \ r')$, we can write

(3.20)
$$nV_{\theta^{*}} = \text{Cov}\left[\frac{\partial \log L^{*}}{\partial \theta}\right] \equiv \begin{bmatrix} \text{Cov}\left(\dfrac{\partial \log L^{*}}{\partial \alpha}\right) & 0 \\ 0 & \text{Cov}\left(\dfrac{\partial \log L^{*}}{r}\right) \end{bmatrix}$$

where the elements of $\text{Cov}(\partial\log L^{*}/\partial\alpha)$ and $\text{Cov}(\partial\log L^{*}/\partial r)$ are
given by (3.12) - (3.14) and (3.18) respectively.  These ma-

trices, together with the elements of $J(\theta^*,\theta^\circ)$ given by (3.15) - (3.17) and (3.19), provide an explicit expression for the asymptotic covariance matrix of $\hat{\theta}^*$ through (2.14) and also for the adjustment factor $\mathrm{tr}\{J(\theta^*,\theta^\circ)\mathrm{Cov}(\hat{\theta}^*)\}$ used in our model selection criterion (2.9). In actual applications, the parameters of the models (3.1) and (3.2) required to evaluate $J(\theta^*,\theta^\circ)$ and $\mathrm{Cov}(\hat{\theta}^*)$ are unknown, but can be estimated by the method of maximum likelihood.

In the important special case when $B^*$, $\Gamma^*$ and $\Sigma^*$ are obtained by additional zero restrictions on the parameters of the model (3.1), $\Sigma^*$ being block diagonal, our model selection criterion becomes (2.19) with an adjustment factor equal to

(3.21)
$$\mathrm{tr}\{\mathrm{Cov}\left[\frac{\partial\log L^*}{\partial\theta_1}\right]J_{11}^{-1}(\theta^*,\theta^\circ)\}$$
$$= \mathrm{tr}\{\mathrm{Cov}\left[\frac{\partial\log L^*}{\partial\alpha}\right]\left[-E\,\frac{\partial^2\log L^*}{\partial\alpha\partial\alpha'}\right]^{-1}\}$$
$$+ \mathrm{tr}\{\mathrm{Cov}\left[\frac{\partial\log L^*}{\partial r}\right]\left[-E\,\frac{\partial^2\log L^*}{\partial r\partial r'}\right]^{-1}\}$$

where the four matrices on the right-hand side are given by (3.12) - (3.19).

To appreciate the result (3.21), consider the special case $\Gamma^\circ = \Gamma^*=I$ and $X_i=X$ for (i=1,...,g), which is a model of g linear regressions. If the approximate model has $k_1$ explanatory variables, (3.21) is reduced to

(3.22)
$$k_1\sum_{i=1}^{g}(r_i^*{}'\Sigma^\circ r_i^*)/r_{ii}^* + \mathrm{tr}\{\mathrm{Cov}\left[\frac{\partial\log L^*}{\partial r}\right]\left[-E\,\frac{\partial^2\log L^*}{\partial r\partial r'}\right]^{-1}\}.$$

For the case of a multiple regression model, with g=1, (3.22) is further reduced to

(3.23)
$$k_1\,\frac{\sigma_{11}^\circ}{\sigma_{11}^*} + \frac{\sigma_{11}^\circ}{\sigma_{11}^*}\left(2-\frac{\sigma_{11}^\circ}{\sigma_{11}^*}\right)$$

which is identical with the result of Sawa (1978, Theorem 3.2, p. 1280). When the approximate regression model coincides with the true model, $\sigma^O_{11}=\sigma^*_{11}$; the adjustment constant (3.23) becomes $k_1+1$ or the number of parameters, as in Akaike's formula. In general, $\sigma^*_{11}>\sigma^O_{11}$ when the approximate model differs from the true model, and the adjustment factor will be smaller than the number of parameters. For example, let the true model have 8 parameters (7 coefficients plus $\sigma^O$) and the approximate model have only 6 coefficients, and let $\sigma^O_{11}=.9\sigma^*_{11}$. The adjustment constant for the approximate model is 5.4+.99=6.39, smaller than 7 or the number of parameters. The difference between the two trace terms to be subtracted from the respective maximum likelihood functions is 8-6.39=1.61, as compared with 8-7=1 by Akaike's formula. Thus the rule (3.23) favors the small model more than Akaike's rule does. This example suggests that, when the model already contains many parameters, our information criterion is quite strict in allowing the addition of one more parameter. As Sawa (1978, p. 1283) has shown, the information criterion based on (3.23) is equivalent to a t test for an additional coefficient using a critical value which can be larger than 2 when $k_1$ is large and n is small.

## 4.   SHOULD A MACROMODEL BE DECOMPOSED OR AGGREGATED?

If one accepts the view that the "true" economic world is a very large and interdependent system of simultaneous stochastic equations, as many economists tend to accept, one is faced with the almost insurmountable problem of estimating very large systems of simultaneous equations. After making significant contributions to the identification and estimation of simultaneous equations, T. C. Koopmans (1950) asked, "When is an equation system complete for statistical purposes?" He gave very strict statistical conditions which would permit one to specify certain variables as exogenous and/or predetermined for the purpose of explaining the remaining endogenous variables, thus reducing the size of the model for the latter variables. One wonders when, if ever, these strict conditions stated by Koopmans will be met. T. C. Liu (1955, 1960), being convinced that the "true" world is a completely interdependent system of simultaneous

equations, questioned how one could ever estimate the true
parameters even if the sample were infinite; the necessary conditions for identification would not be met since each equation
contains too many variables. Franklin Fisher (1961), coming to
the rescue, argued that if the coefficients of the dependent
variables in each structural equation, though numerous, are
mostly very small, then treating them as zero in order to satisfy the identification condition will only lead to very small
inconsistencies in the estimation of the remaining parameters.
On the other extreme, Herman Wold (1953) argued that the world
is recursive anyway and there is no great statistical difficulty
in estimating its parameters.

While we grant that the true economic model might very well be
a very large and completely interdependent system of simultaneous equations, an econometrician might wish to estimate not
the true model but only an approximate model because the sample
is finite. One realizes that the conditions stated by Koopmans
for defining the exogenous and/or predetermined variables are
never met, that the coefficients of many endogenous and exogenous variables in a structural equation are not zero as Liu has
pointed out, and that the true model for quarterly economic
time series is not strictly recursive in the sense of Wold.
However, one might not wish to raise the question of F. M.
Fisher, whether by making certain assumptions necessary for
identification, the remaining parameters in a true model can be
almost consistently estimated. One is seldom in a position to
estimate the parameters of the true model because the number of
available observations is often smaller than the number of its
parameters. One is mainly interested in the parameters $\theta^{\Lambda}$ of
the approximate models because they are the models relevant for
practical purposes. To illustrate, let the true model be

$$- y_{1t} + \theta_1 y_{2t} + \theta_2 x_{1t} + \theta_3 x_{2t} + \cdots + \theta_{100} x_{99,t} = u_{1t}$$

$$\theta_{101} y_{1t} - y_{2t} - \theta_{102} x_{1t} + \theta_{103} x_{2t} + \cdots + \theta_{200} x_{99,t} = u_{2t}$$

where all parameters are small except $\theta_1$, $\theta_2$, $\theta_{101}$ and $\theta_{103}$.

This model is unidentifiable. Fisher points out that if $\theta_3$ and $\theta_{102}$ are extremely small, the remaining parameters can be estimated almost consistently. Our viewpoint is that the approximate model f with $\theta_1$, $\theta_2$, $\theta_{101}$ and $\theta_{103}$ as the only non-zero coefficients to be estimated might be the best approximation according to the information criterion when say 50 observations are available. Although the maximum likelihood estimators of $\theta_1^*$, $\theta_2^*$, $\theta_{101}^*$ and $\theta_{103}^*$ will not consistently estimate the true $\theta_1$, $\theta_2$, $\theta_{101}$ and $\theta_{103}$, the model f can still be the best approximation for prediction purposes.

Furthermore, Fisher (1961) is concerned with the "cost of approximate specification in simultaneous equation estimation," implying that something is lost by using an approximate model because of the inconsistencies in the estimation of the true parameters. We wish to emphasize the "benefits" of an approximate specification because specification errors are not necessarily bad. On the right-hand side of equation (2.9), the second term tends to increase as sampling errors in estimating $\theta^*$ by $\hat{\theta}^*$ increase. The first term $\log L(\tilde{Y}; \hat{\theta}^*)$ tends to decrease as specification errors in using $f(y|\theta^*)$ to approximate $g(y)$ increase. Large specification errors from assigning zeros to coefficients will reduce the first term but may reduce the second even more, thus producing a better model for prediction. We are less concerned, than Fisher was, about whether an extremely small specification error would obtain if the sample were infinite. Rather, we are more concerned with the total error, due to both specification and sampling, in using an estimated model for forecasting, realizing that the specification error will almost always be present. Even when one knows that a large model is more nearly correctly specified than a small model, the latter can still be selected by the information criterion. It is possible for the true world to be completely interdependent, but for a block-recursive model, estimated from a finite sample, to be a better approximation than an estimated simultaneous model. We will apply the selection criterion of Section 3 to decide which of the two models to use, one being simultaneous and the other block recursive, or one being disaggregated and the other aggregated.

First, consider the choice between a simultaneous model

$$(4.1) \qquad [Y_1 \quad Y_2] \begin{bmatrix} \Gamma_{11} & \Gamma_{12} \\ \Gamma_{21} & \Gamma_{22} \end{bmatrix} + X[B_1 \quad B_2] = [U_1 \quad U_2]$$

and a block-recursive model obtained by the restrictions $\Gamma_{21}=0$ and $\Sigma_{12}=\frac{1}{n}\,EU_1'U_2=0$. The information criterion (2.19) - (3.21) can be applied to choose between them if they are both estimated by the method of (full-information) maximum likelihood. A statistical criterion is thus provided to decide whether a system of simultaneous econometric equations should be decomposed into two recursive blocks. Equivalently, it can be used to decide whether a general equilibrium or a partial equilibrium model should be selected. The latter model is represented by a block-recursive system which treats $y_1$ as exogenous in the explanation of $y_2$.

The second issue is whether one should aggregate across equations. For example, real consumption expenditures $y_{1t}$ and $y_{2t}$ for two commodity groups may satisfy

$$(4.2) \qquad y_{1t} = \theta_1 y_{3t} + \theta_2 , y_{1,t-1} + \theta_3 x_{1t} + u_{1t}$$

$$y_{2t} = \theta_4 y_{3t} + \theta_5 , y_{2,t-1} + \theta_6 x_{2t} + u_{2t}$$

where $y_{3t}$ may be disposable income and $x_{1t}$ and $x_{2t}$ relative prices. The sum of these equations is

$$(4.3) \qquad y_{1t} + y_{2t} = (\theta_1+\theta_4)y_{3t} + \theta_2 , y_{1,t-1} + \theta_5 , y_{2,t-1}$$

$$+ \theta_3 x_{1t} + \theta_6 x_{2t} + (u_{1t}+u_{2t}).$$

Let $y_{4t}=y_{1t}+y_{2t}$ be aggregate consumption and let $x_{4t}=w_1 x_{1t}+w_2 x_{2t}$ be an aggregate price index with constant weights. An aggregate equation for $y_{4t}$ can be written as

$$(4.4) \qquad y_{4t} = \theta_7 y_{3t} + \theta_2 y_{4,t-1} + (\theta_3/w_1) x_{4t} + u_{4t}$$

provided that

(4.5)                                $\theta_5 = \theta_2$ and $\theta_6 = \theta_3(w_2/w_1)$.

This example illustrates that aggregation across equations can
be expressed as linear restrictions on the parameters of the
disaggregate model. The choice between a disaggregate model
and an aggregate one can be made by the information criterion.
Three cases will be distinguished depending on the common subset of endogenous variables which both models are supposed to
explain or predict.

In the first case, one is interested in predicting the individual components $y_{1t}$ and $y_{2t}$ as well as all other endogenous variables in the disaggregate model. One should retain equations
(4.2) for the true model, and apply the information criterion
to decide whether the restrictions (4.5) will yield a better
approximate model. This is done by estimating the model using
the method of maximum likelihood with and without these restrictions. The information criterion for the large model equals
the maximum value of its log likelihood minus the number of parameters. For the restricted model, it equals the maximum value
of the log likelihood minus an adjustment factor equal to
$\text{tr}\{J(\theta^*,\theta^0)(\text{Cov}\hat{\theta}^*)\}$. Explicit expressions for $J(\theta^*,\theta^0)$ and
$\text{Cov}\hat{\theta}^*$ were given in Section 3.

In the second case, one is interested in predicting the aggregate $y_{4t}=y_{1t}+y_{2t}$ and all other endogenous variables in the model.
One should then retain equation (4.3) instead of (4.2) for the
true model, treating $(\theta_1+\theta_4)$ as one parameter. The approximate
model imposes the restrictions (4.5) on the parameters of this
equation.

In the third case, one is interested in predicting the aggregate $y_{4t}$ and a (possibly small) subset of other endogenous variables, including the inflation rate and the unemployment rate,
for example. The true model and the approximate model are as
defined in the last paragraph. This case differs from the first
two cases since only a subset of endogenous variables are of

concern. We will have to consider the reduced-form equations
for the subset in question. Two solutions to this model selection problem can be given.

For the first solution, the reduced-form equations for each
model are estimated by the method of least squares, or maximum
likelihood without allowing for the overidentifying restrictions from the structure. Here the two models explaining the
common subset of endogenous variables are treated simply as two
linear systems of regression equations. If the true model is
written to include $y_{4,t-1}$, $y_{2,t-1}$, $x_{4,t}$ and $x_{2,t}$ as its predetermined variables, the approximate model excludes $y_{2,t-1}$ and
$x_{2,t}$. To estimate the expected information for the approximate
model, one can subtract the adjustment constant given by (3.22)
from the maximum likelihood of the reduced form explaining the
subset of endogenous variables of interest.

For the second solution, the estimates of the reduced-form parameters are derived from the full-information maximum-likelihood estimates of the parameters of the corresponding structures. The expected information for the approximate model can
be estimated by evaluating the two terms given in (2.9). The
first term $\log L(Y;\hat{\theta}^*)$ is the log likelihood of the reduced form
for the selected endogenous variables evaluated at $\hat{\theta}^*$, which
here denotes the above derived estimates of the reduced-form
parameters. The second term equals the trace of the product of
$J(\theta^*,\theta^0)$ and $\text{Cov}(\hat{\theta}^*)$. $-J(\theta^*,\theta^0)$ is the expectation of the matrix of the second partials of the above log likelihood with
respect to the elements of $\theta^*$. Explicit formulas for its
elements are given by (3.15) and (3.19). The remaining task is
the estimation of $\text{Cov}(\hat{\theta}^*)$. The covariance matrix of the estimates $\hat{\alpha}^*$ and $\hat{r}_{ij}^*$ of the structural parameters, from which the
reduced-form parameters $\hat{\theta}^*$ are derived, can be obtained by
using the formulas given in Section 3. Given this covariance
matrix, the covariance matrix $\text{Cov}(\hat{\theta}^*)$ of the estimates of the
corresponding reduced-form parameters can be estimated by the
formula given in Dhrymes (1973, p. 122). This solution is
applicable to the choice between any two linear simultaneous-

equation models for the purpose of explaining a common subset
of endogenous variables, provided that one can write down a
general model as the true model and express both models by
suitable linear restrictions on the parameters of the true model.
One of the two models might serve as the true model if they are
nested, as in our discussion of aggregation.


## 5.   CONCLUDING REMARKS

It is not difficult, at least in principle, to extend our result
to the selection of nonlinear simultaneous equations and of
equations estimated by methods other than full-information
maximum-likelihood.  No matter whether the model is linear or
not, provided that the estimate $\hat{\theta}*$ of $\theta*$ is consistent and
satisfies the restriction $H'\hat{\theta}*=-b$ and $(\theta*-\hat{\theta}*)'[\partial logL(Y;\hat{\theta}*)/\partial\theta]$
is approximately zero, our information criterion (2.9) remains
valid as it can be seen by reviewing (2.4) and (2.5) used in its
derivation.  To estimate (2.9), one can easily evaluate
$logL(Y;\hat{\theta}*)$ and approximate $J(\theta*,\theta^{o})$ by taking analytical or
numerical derivatives of $-\partial^2 logL(Y;\hat{\theta}*)/\partial\theta\partial\theta'$.  The more difficult problem is to estimate the covariance matrix of $\hat{\theta}*$ when
the approximate model is incorrect, i.e., when $\theta^{o}\neq\theta*$.  If computational expenses are not an issue, one can always apply
Monte Carlo to find the covariance matrix of $\hat{\theta}*$ under the assumption that the true parameter vector equals its estimate $\hat{\theta}^{o}$
which is obtained by the same method as $\hat{\theta}*$.  It remains a problem to find a computationally less expensive way to estimate
the covariance matrix of $\hat{\theta}*$.

An alternative approach to model selection is to rank a model
by the Jeffreys-Bayes posterior probability for it to be true
after the data Y are observed.  If $L(Y;\theta)$ is the likelihood
function specified by the model M, the posterior probability
$P(M|Y)$ for the model to be true equals the prior probability
$P(M)$ for the model times

$$\int L(Y;\theta)p(\theta|M)d\theta = E_{\theta}L(Y;\theta)$$

where $p(\theta|M)$ is the prior density of the parameter of the model M. If $P(M)$ are equal for all models, the posterior probability criterion selects the model having the highest $\log E_{\theta}L(Y;\theta)$ where the expectation $E_{\theta}$ is evaluated by the prior density of $\theta$. By contrast, the information criterion selects the model having the highest $E_{\hat{\theta}}E_{\tilde{Y}}\log L(\tilde{Y};\hat{\theta})$ where $\tilde{Y}$ denotes future observations and the expectation $E_{\hat{\theta}}$ is evaluated by the sampling distribution of $\hat{\theta}$ based on the data Y. The former criterion uses the data Y to judge a model specified by $L(\cdot;\theta)$ <u>and</u> by the prior density $p(\theta|M)$. The latter criterion uses future observations $\tilde{Y}$ to judge a model specified by $L(\cdot;\hat{\theta})$ where $\hat{\theta}$ has been estimated by the sample data Y. Insofar as the econometric models to be selected refer to models which have been estimated by the sample data for future prediction, and not models which had been specified before the sample period together with some prior density function $p(\theta|M)$ of its parameter vector, the information criterion appears to be more relevant.

FOOTNOTE

I would like to thank an anonymous reviewer for his helpful comments and acknowledge support from the National Science Foundation under grant No. SOC77-07677.

REFERENCES

[1] Akaike, H., Information theory and an extension of the maximum likelihood principle, in: Petrov, B. N. and Csáki, F. (eds.), Proceedings of the Second International Symposium on Information Theory (Academiai Kiadó, Budapest, 1973).

[2] Akaike, H., A new look at the statistical model identification, IEEE Transactions on Automatic Control AC-19 (1974) 716-723.

[3]  Dhrymes, P. J., Restricted and unrestricted reduced forms:
     Asymptotic distribution and relative efficiency, Econome-
     trica 41 (1973) 119-134.

[4]  Fisher, F. M., On the cost of approximate specification in
     simultaneous equation estimation, Econometrica 29 (1961)
     139-170.

[5]  Koopmans, T.C., When is an equation system complete for
     statistical purposes?, in Koopmans, T. C. (ed.), Statis-
     tical Inference in Dynamic Economic Models (John Wiley &
     Sons, New York, 1950).

[6]  Kullback, S., Information Theory and Statistics (John
     Wiley & Sons, New York, 1950).

[7]  Kullback, S. and Leibler, R. A., On information and
     sufficiency, Annals of Mathematical Statistics 22 (1951)
     79-86.

[8]  Liu, T. C., A Simple Forecasting Model for the U.S. Economy,
     Staff Papers, International Monetary Fund (1955) 434-436.

[9]  Liu, T. C., Underidentification, structural estimation, and
     forecasting, Econometrica 28 (1960) 855-865.

[10] Sawa, T., Information criteria for discriminating among
     alternative regression models, Econometrica 46 (1978)
     1273-1292.

[11] Silvey, S. D., The Lagrangian multiplier test, Annals of
     Mathematical Statistics 30 (1959) 389-407.

[12] Wold, H. in association with Juréen, L., Demand Analysis
     (John Wiley & Sons, New York, 1953).

LARGE-SCALE MACRO-ECONOMETRIC MODELS
J. Kmenta, J.B. Ramsey (editors)
© North-Holland Publishing Company, 1981

DISCUSSION

Zvi Griliches

Much of the objection to large models is motivated by a lack of
understanding of the internal mechanisms of large models and
thus much of the debate of large versus small models is misleading.  Appropriateness of a model should be the issue.

As to the incorporation of economic theory in such models, it
has traditionally been a one-way street.  Econometric models
attempt to incorporate economic theory as well as they can, but
they produce relatively little feedback to the theoreticians.
They produce, instead, "sellable" economics which can be profit-
ably sold to outsiders.  They provide the link to the real world
but only in one direction.  In this context one may view McNees
as a "one-man consumers union."

The procedures proposed by Chow are to be welcomed.  They provide an intellectual defense for comparing the likelihoods of
different  models, making an appropriate adjustment for differences in their size.  They way a penalty for size is introduced
is to consider the possibility that error is added also by the
variances of the estimated coefficients, which could be reduced
at the cost of some increase in bias, by dropping some of the
variables or equations from the model.  In a sense, this procedure belongs to the class of pre-test estimators and provides
an argument why one might use an F-ratio larger than one for
accepting the null hypothesis that some of the parameters are
zero.

My problem with the suggested procedure is not statistical but
conceptual.  In a sense Chow's suggestion does not go far

enough.  Asymptotically his adjustment does not matter.  It says
pick the model that has the higher adjusted  $R^2$  (the adjustment
is a bit more than the usual one but the difference disappears
in largish samples.  It is on the order of  $\frac{K}{2} (\frac{\log n}{n} - \frac{2\pi}{n})$
which goes to zero reasonably rapidly as  n  increases).  But
I would not pick the more complex model in large samples unless
it changed the  $\bar{R}^2$  or the coefficients by an economically
significant amount.

I am also bothered by the generalized variance metric for comparing models.  It suggests that we sacrifice bias in some of
the coefficients for a reduction in the variance of others.
The procedure changes all the parameters but summarizes the results with one number.  There is an index number problem here
and I am not sure that the implicit utility function represents
my preferences.  I may care about some of the coefficients much
more than others and may not wish to trade off the precision of
some of the parameters for others according to the metric implied by the precision matrix.  Similarly, Chow considers an
approximation to the correct model without discussing the
definition of approximation.  One may get reasonably good estimates of some or most coefficients but rather imprecise estimates of the implied roots of the model.  Without a more explicit loss function and more informative priors I doubt whether
such mechanical simplification rules are really wise.  Here, as
elsewhere, you do not get much for putting in very little.

# VI.  CONCLUSION

LARGE-SCALE MACRO-ECONOMETRIC MODELS
J. Kmenta, J.B. Ramsey (editors)
© North-Holland Publishing Company, 1981

# SUMMARY OF THE GENERAL DISCUSSION

Jan Kmenta
Department of Economics
University of Michigan
Ann Arbor, Michigan

James B. Ramsey
Department of Economics
New York University
New York, New York

Each of the four sessions at the conference consisted of
a brief presentation of the scheduled papers, a set of
comments by formal discussants, and general discussion from
the floor. In what follows we present a summary of the major
points raised in the general discussion recorded during the
conference. As might be expected, the contents of the discussion do not lend themselves to a presentation in the form
of neat and succinct conclusions. Instead, our aim is to capture the spirit of the exchange of views and to indicate some
of the various positions taken by the participants.

## Forecasting Economic Variables
The major themes of the discussion on forecasting
economic variables were the practice of subjective adjustment
of estimated coefficients (often the constant terms) called
"add-factoring", the problem of model validation, and the
preferred method of estimation. The question of the proper

specification and the proper size of a macro-model were also
raised.

The common practice of changing the values of coefficients when the forecast values are considered inappropriate
was defended by a number of model producers.  McCarthy contended that it is possible to be too prissy in insisting upon
complete scientific respectability when dealing with a problem
that is inherently not solvable.  The use of add-factoring
may involve utilizing information not incorporated in the
model (such as the high probability of a UAW strike every
third year), although some add-factoring may be capricious.
A similar view was put forward by Eckstein, who emphasized
that add-factoring is a procedure by which external information is brought to bear on the forecasting process, and by
which one can deal with a structural change in a practical way.
According to Eckstein, the structure of the economy is really
not stable, even though many of our statistical procedures are
based on the pretense that it is.  Add-factoring reflects a
reaction to learning from past errors.

A critical view of the subjective adjustment of models
was voiced by Fair, who maintained that at least some of the
external information can be taken into account in a mechanical
way.  Data revisions, for instance, can be handled by re-
estimating the model each quarter; the "drift" in equations
can be minimized by accounting for serial correlation; and so
on.  In Fair's experience, treating a model in a mechanical
way seems to lead to forecasts that are not too bad compared
to subjectively adjusted forecasts.  Fair suggested that model
producers should issue two forecasts, one mechanical and one
subjective, and let the future judge whether the subjective
adjustments improve the forecasts or not.  In this context
Griliches pointed out that if it is necessary for the model
producers to keep changing their models, then it means that

our understanding of how the world really works is not very
good. What good is a model, asked Griliches, if it does not
stay long enough in one place to be looked at?

Concerning the question of model validation, Brunner
asserted that the demand for accuracy of forecasts has received too much emphasis at the expense of a proper incorporation of economic theory into the models. According to Brunner,
accurate forecasting performance need not represent a confirmation of any cognitive claim advanced in the model. Eckstein
agreed that _ex_ _ante_ forecasts offer no proof of any cognitive
claims embodied in the model, and stated that a good model is
a good representation of the economy if it can reproduce
history. Christ, on the other hand, warned that emphasis on
reproducing history may cause the modeller to fit the
accidental aspects of data to the detriment of explaining the
underlying regularities. The way to protect ourselves against
that, suggested Christ, is to test for stability of parameters. Finally, Laidler offered an example of the usefulness
of model validation by noting the recent substantial revisions
of the London Business School model. It appears that these
revisions were motivated by the model's poor performance in
forecasting unemployment and inflation in the early 1970's
compared to the "back-of-envelope" forecasts of other economists.

A point of considerable interest and a focus of a lively
debate was the issue of single _versus_ system methods of
estimation. Howrey claimed that the big pay-off comes from
getting the dynamics in each equation right and that this may
lead to a single equation approach to estimation. Fair agreed
that accounting for serial correlation is important but contended that one does gain something by going from limited
information to full information methods. Zellner noted that
the ordinary least squares (OLS) method may be superior in
small samples under very specific circumstances but that con-

sistent, efficient estimators are preferable in large samples.
Some current optimal finite sample estimators are apparently
averages of the OLS and particular consistent estimators,
with the weight of the former going to zero as the sample size
increases. Darby pointed out that in a number of existing
models there are so many predetermined variables relative to
the number of available observations that 2SLS are identical
to OLS. Modigliani declared his preference for OLS with
autoregressive transformations, on the grounds that OLS are
"objective" since they do not call for a choice of exogenous
variables as is the case in two- or three-stage least squares
estimation. Kuhn was somewhat more cautious in advocating
the use of an instrumental variables procedure only when OLS
seem to give highly implausible results.

Concerning the issue of the appropriate size and specification of a model, Goldfeld thought that the issue of size
receives too much attention, and that the real issue is one of
correctness of the model. Consideration should be given to
the common situation that an error in one single equation can
upset the entire system. Ando countered by asserting that a
large model may contain only a small number of core equations
surrounded by a large number of auxiliary equations. The
extent of the repercussions of an error in a single equation
would then depend upon whether it was a core equation or an
auxiliary one. Zellner drew attention to the fact that
"size" is not simply a question of the number of variables
and equations but also of complexity, and referred to the
contributions of Jeffreys and Rothenberg in the literature.
Many conference participants agreed with Dutta that the
relevance of the size of a model is an unsettled issue.

### Advancement of Economic Knowledge and
### the Size of Macro-econometric Models

The discussion under the above heading centered on the
issues of parameter stability and policy analysis, of model
revision, and of model size.  Also raised was the issue of
using mean square error as a criterion of accuracy in estimation and forecasting.  The question of parameter stability was
largely motivated by the contention of Lucas[1] that the parameters of macro-econometric models reflect expectations of
agents, and that these expectations change in response to
policy decisions, thus making the parameters of the existing
models inherently unstable.  Accordingly, there would also be
no kind of policy analysis that would be worth doing except
for analysis of changes in rules.  Sims disagreed with the
latter conclusion and suggested that a distinction ought to be
made between changes in policy rules and an application of
unchanged rules under different conditions.  Macro-econometric
models are useful tools for projection of policy under the condition that the policy rule and the reaction function are unchanged.  Eckstein pointed out that model builders view policy
changes, and especially changes in policy regimes, simply as
a form of a structural change, and he considered this to be
quite justifiable.

The matter of parameter stability was given practical
content by a change noted in the estimated multiplier of the
DRI model whose value fell substantially between 1974 and
1978.  Eckstein explained this change by pointing out that,
because of the inadequate forecasting performance of macro-
econometric models in this period, the DRI model was rebuilt.
The new model included the flow of funds and the balance
sheets, and incorporated a better way of dealing with supply,
with the price implications of high utilization rates and of
delivery delays, and so on. The underlying consumption theory
was also changed to reflect the impact of uncertainty and
inflation.

Eckstein's remarks opened the subject of model revision
which, according to him, most practical model builders see as
a way of keeping up with a changing world.  In this view
add-factoring is seen, to a larger extent, as a temporary
measure applied between major model revisions to reflect
structural change, data revisions, and new policy parameters.
Eckstein recognized that these procedures turn the model
builders into moving targets for critique by theoreticians,
but he maintained that if accurate forecasting is to be one of
the purposes of model building, econometric models have to be
constantly adopted.

The use of objective and subjective external information
was also advocated by Sims, who saw two ways of making use of
such information--through formal Bayesian methods or informally through what was earlier coined by Rasche as "postnatal
tender loving care."  According to Sims, these add-ons and
adjustments and "tender loving care" represent reasonable and
practical procedures for moving towards acceptable estimates.
However, model builders have an obligation to distinguish
clearly between restrictions imposed a priori on grounds of
economic theory, and restrictions imposed for forecasting
purposes.  The latter should be made explicit and form a
part of the model's documentation.  Tobin commented that there
is a big difference between re-estimating a model with known,
unchanged specification and changing the specification of a
model by adding new dummy variables and making ad hoc correc-
tions for forecasting purposes.  Following earlier remarks by
Brunner, Tobin maintained that re-estimation with unchanged
specification, unlike subjective adjustments of a model is
a replicable procedure, and a distinction should be made between the two procedures.  Ando pointed out that usually only
the crucial equations of a model need to be re-estimated.
Klein noted that each revision of a model should be regarded
as a model in its own right but thought that the "add-ons"
do not really alter a model, but simply realign it for fore-

casting purposes.

The issue of parameter stability appeared also to have implications concerning the appropriate size of a model. According to Klein, the Lucas proposition that parameters are a function of policy decisions cannot be analyzed in small models because policy changes are complex. As an example, Klein cited the recent tax changes which involved a large number of variables and coefficients, and he expressed doubt that such a policy change could be adequately embodied in a small model. Taylor agreed with Klein but maintained that there is also a range of interesting questions, such as the inflation - unemployment trade-off, which can be adequately treated in a small model. Jonson thought that "coverage" was an important criterion of model size. A large model would then be one which covers a large section of the economy and leaves few variables to be treated as exogenous. Kmenta commented that a highly relevant aspect for model size is the degree of complexity of a model. If a seemingly large model can be broken up into a number of independent blocks, then the model size is effectively reduced.[2] This leads to the issue of representing the economy as a general equilibrium model or as a set of partial equilibrium models, an issue which apparently receives far too little attention in methodological discussions of this sort.

Concerning the choice of estimation techniques, Zellner thought that the apparent increase in emphasis on maximum likelihood estimation (MLE) is too extreme. He referred to Stein's analytical results, which show that there exist estimators that uniformly dominate ML estimators in finite samples for regression and other problems. Furthermore, ML estimators pose problems in that they often do not possess finite moments, and in these cases their mean square error is infinite. Anderson believed, though, that mean square error may not be an appropriate criterion. To illustrate his point he compared a normal distribution, characterized by a large variance but a

finite mean square error, with a Cauchy distribution, characterized by a small scale parameter but an infinite mean square
error.  In reference to those estimators that do not possess
higher-order moments, Christ suggested the use of a truncated
loss function.  To this end Krasker pointed out that any
reasonable cut-off points will serve the purpose of constructing a usable loss function if the sample is large.

### Construction of Macro-econometric Models

The discussion evolved around the economic content of
macro-econometric models and around the associated issues of
forecasting and the size of a model.  The question of the use
of varying parameter models was also raised.

The perceived failure to emphasize both the economic content and the scientific validation of macro-econometric models
was sharply criticized by Meltzer in a series of pointed
questions.  Econometric forecasting flourishes because it sells
well, but what do we learn from the forecasting models about
economics?  Ando, for instance, stated that there is a claim
that the demand-for-money equations in many econometric forecasting models went wrong, but how do we know?  Is it something that we can agree on?  Is there a scientific test that
would enable us to reach that conclusion?  Modigliani claimed
that from macro-econometric models we learn about the properties of the economy, but how do we learn?  And do we all learn
the same thing?  Eckstein asserted that with macro-econometric
models we reproduce the past as best as we can, but what good
does that do?  The fact is, claimed Meltzer, that the most
important issue, namely that of scientific validation of
models, has not been addressed!

The issue of the economic content of macro-econometric
models also emerged in the exchange between Fair and Sims.
Fair criticized Sims' six-variable vector autoregressive model
on the grounds of the lack of adequate theoretical content and
an inferior forecasting capability.  Sims countered by stating
that, in building a model to test competing economic hypotheses, he avoided making the kind of restrictions one has to

impose in order to get a good mean square error in forecasting. After all, we know that the mean square error of forecasts may be improved by imposing even _false_ hypotheses. Further, Sims said, the vector autoregressive models cannot be all that different from standard simultaneous equation models, since most of the latter imply vector autoregressive stationarity if the exogenous variables are stationary. Finally, Sims claimed that Fair's methods of disaggregating forecast errors into the main sources of uncertainty are useful for comparing models with different economic content but inappropriate for a model with no economic content. But the method might be reasonably used in comparing a version of the vector autoregressive model in which constraints have been imposed with a standard macro-econometric model.

Another difficulty with the Sims' representation of the form

$$y_t = \sum_i \alpha_i y_{t-i} + \sum_i \beta_i u_{t-i},$$

where $y_t$ is a vector of variables and $u_t$ a vector of disturbances, was claimed by Granger to be that the u's include omitted variables. The interpretation of these disturbances is thus ambiguous, and it would seem desirable to distinguish between small and large "shocks".

On the subject of forecasting, Granger noted that the attempts to rank models on the basis of their forecasting performance faces the difficulty of establishing a basis of comparison since one model may be better at forecasting, say, GNP while another model leads to a better forecast of, say, consumption. This suggests that it might be possible to combine the forecasts from, say, a large model and one from a small model in such a way that the combined forecast would beat both of them consistently. The point of this is that if we can find a method that forecasts better than the current models, it means that the current models can be improved in operational ways.

The matter of forecast accuracy in relation to model size was emphasized by Klein. One can presumably construct a small model that would, on average over many periods, forecast GNP as well as any large model. Where the large models are considerably better than the small ones, though, is at a critical point when something really important happens. For instance, since 1970 three main events affecting the U.S. economy have been the energy crisis, the breakdown of the Bretton Woods system leading to fluctuating exchange rates, and the importance of agricultural prices as a result of the Soviet grain purchases in 1975. A model that does not have an entry point for such events, argued Klein, is going to give misleading results. Further, one cannot segregate these events by considering a separate agricultural sector or a separate energy sector. For instance, a frequent response to the oil embargo was that oil imports are only a very small fraction of GNP and thus cannot have a great effect on the economy. This argument, however, ignored the full impact of the use of fuel in the economy as indicated by an input-output analysis. Since we do not know where and when the next major event will occur, Klein maintained that we need a big, detailed system which incorporates these effects. Besides, clients using econometric forecasts demand details.

Concerning the issue of ex ante versus ex post forecasting, Klein expressed a firm belief that ex ante forecasting is the only one that really matters. Ex post forecasting requires that one knows something that is very hard to know, and it can make one look very good in retrospect. According to Klein, the only way to make a sensible judgement of a forecasting performance is by repeated checking of ex ante forecasts over time. One cannot be repeatedly successful unless one has a pretty good system.

Finally, a question was raised by Meltzer concerning the neglect of the Cooley-Prescott varying parameter approach by model builders. A random walk for a constant term may pro-

vide a way of handling the problem of add-factoring in a
scientifically satisfactory and reproducible manner. Klein
responded by claiming that while such an approach may perform
well in constructed experiments, it is inadequate when dealing
with realities such as an anticipated strike or a turning
point.

## Evaluation of Macro-econometric Models

The major themes discussed in the last session of the
conference were the apparent conflicts between the scientist
and the practicioner, the econometrician and the time series
analyst, and the large and the small model proponents.

According to Fischer, econometric models are evaluated
by different loss functions by commercial and government users
than by theoreticians. The former are concerned about the
accuracy of forecasts whereas the latter worry about correct
specification. Consequently, the profession may never be able
to come up with a single statistic which allows the ranking
of models. All consumer unions, even though they name the
"best" product, still publish a number of other comparative
statistics so that the user can choose other products according to his personal loss function.

The criticism of the current practice of econometric model
builders by the "prissy" theorist was brought sharply into
focus by Ramsey, who noted that theorists do not object to the
attempts to incorporate unanticipated information into a model.
What the theorists object to is massaging the data and manip-
ulating the coefficients in order to bring the model into
accord with the modeller's prior conceptions. The modelling
process then merely becomes a method for creating a contraction
mapping from the data to the researcher's prior notions about
parameter and forecast values. In such a case the model is
of no great use, and the methodology of statistical inference
becomes completely irrelevant. What the theorists want is an
experimental model that can be tested, pulled apart, rebuilt,
and retested, until we find out how the world really works.

Such a model is of no use to anyone but the experimental
scientists and the commercial modellers cannot afford such a
luxury.

Further elaboration of this point was offered by Christ,
who pointed out that scientists need to know whether a proposed theory represents anything that could be called "an
invariant law" or not. For this purpose they need ex post
forecasting performance because the ex ante performance is not
exclusively based on a scientific theory. In Christ's view it
is important that the data that are used to check the model's
performance include some data that were observed after the
model was specified, because otherwise one might have constructed an extremely good fit by judicious data mining, which is
not going to work in the future.

On the question of size of a model, Ramsey feared that,
in our era of larger and larger models, the number of parameters to be estimated grows at a faster pace than the number
of available observations. The possibility that one could
estimate parameters with greater precision as time goes on is
thus remote.

An interesting resolution of the conflict between large
and small econometric models was offered by Powell, who
suggested that one can have both types of models at the same-
time. The condition is that one has to believe that the
economy naturally separates into a macro-economy characterized
by a small number of relations (say, 22 to 25), and a micro-
economy, the dimensionality of which is limited only by the
available data base and by one's imagination. In addition, one
has to believe that the endogenous variables of the macro-
economy play a role distinct from that of the micro-endogenous
variables. In this paradigm, the macro-economy encompasses
aggregate consumption, investment, and government expenditure,
and all the fiscal and financial markets in the economy, while
the micro-economy is represented by the neo-classical optimiz-
ing models. The choice of exogenous variables depends on the

intended use of the model.

The time series versus simultaneous equations debate was considered by Hymans to be empty. One should feel neither disturbed nor overjoyed by the fact that under certain circumstances time series models outperform simultaneous equation models. At least, following the work by Zellner-Palm, one should realize that time series models may predict well, but this does not make them valid competitors for the simultaneous equation models since there is no economic knowledge to be gained from them. Even in their purported strong field, namely forecasting, they are of little use because they furnish no explanation to go with their forecasts. For almost all interesting questions in economics one needs the answers provided by a structural model; and if one tries to determine which structural model gives better answers, a comparison with time series models is of little use.

The remarks of Hymans provoked some disagreement. Granger maintained that if time series models can outperform simultaneous equation models, then the latter must be misspecified. Howrey reported on some experiments suggesting that univariate ARIMA forecasts have a three- to four-times larger prediction error than their multivariate counterparts. Consequently, econometric forecasts that are no better than univariate ARIMA forecasts perform very poorly relative to multivariate ARIMA forecasts. Finally, Zellner mentioned that many researchers including himself, have recently emphasized the fruitfulness of combining the traditional structural econometric models with modern time series approaches in building, analyzing, and using models.

In his closing remarks Kmenta noted that the gap between the practical and the academic econometrics of macro-econometric models has been, if not narrowed, at least honestly recognized during the conference. This is important since frequently all wear both hats, and since we all have a common goal, namely the understanding of the working of the economic system. The fact that this system may be a moving target

should not be an insurmountable obstacle; the universe is
also forever in motion and yet we have a good deal of understanding of its mechanism.  It is hoped that, as a result of
this conference, the practicioners will be more concerned
about the need for explicit statements of hypotheses, and that
the theoreticians will devote some effort to the solution of
the problem posed by the use of ad hoc adjustment procedures.


## Footnotes

[1] See R. Lucas, "Econometric Policy Evaluation: A Critique,"
    in K. Brunner and A. Meltzer (eds.), The Phillips Curve
    and Labor Markets (Amsterdam: North-Holland, 1976),
[2] See H. A. Simon, "Causal Ordering and Indentifiability," in
    W. C. Hood and T. C. Koopmans (eds.), Studies in
    Econometric Method (New York: Wiley, 1953).